GUARDIAN JOE

GUARDIAN JOE

HOW LESS FORCE HELPS THE WARRIOR

ILLUSTRATED

H. JOHN POOLE
FOREWORD BY
GEN. ANTHONY C. ZINNI USMC (RET.)

POSTERITY
PRESS

Cataloging-in-Publication Data
Poole, H. John, 1943-
Guardian Joe
    Includes bibliography and index.
    1. Infantry drill and tactics.
    2. Military art and science.
    3. Military history.
I. Title.   ISBN: 978-0-981865973   2018   355'.42
Library of Congress Control Number: 2017953577

Cover art composition © 2017 by Posterity Press
Edited by Dr. Mary Beth Poole

First printing, United States of America, March 2018

For all those U.S. security personnel who wish to make a difference.

GIVE ME, O LORD MY GOD, WHAT IS LEFT THEE, THAT WHICH NO ONE ASKS OF THEE. I DO NOT ASK THEE FOR REST OR TRANQUILITY, EITHER OF SOUL OR BODY. I DO NOT ASK THEE FOR RICHES, FOR SUCCESS, OR FOR HEALTH.

SO MANY ASK THEE FOR THESE, MY GOD, THAT NONE MUCH BE LEFT THEE. GIVE ME, LORD, WHAT IS LEFT THEE. GIVE ME WHAT THE OTHERS REFUSE. I WANT RISK AND ANGUISH; I WANT FIGHT AND PAIN. GIVE ME THESE, MY GOD, ONCE AND FOR ALL. GIVE ME THE CERTAINTY THAT THESE WILL ALWAYS BE MY PORTION, FOR I WILL NOT ALWAYS HAVE THE COURAGE TO ASK FOR THEM OF THEE. GIVE ME, O LORD, WHAT IS LEFT THEE. GIVE ME WHAT OTHERS DO NOT WANT. BUT ALSO GIVE ME COURAGE, STRENGTH, AND FAITH. AMEN.

> — PRAYER FOUND IN THE POCKET OF A 19-YEAR-OLD FRENCH PARATROOPER KILLED IN ACTION AT THE BATTLE OF DIEN BIEN PHU [VIETNAM] IN 1954

(Source: Courtesy of American Society for Defense of Tradition, Family, and Property, from "Do You Want to Be a Catholic Hero," Crusade Magazine, Sept./Oct. 2015)

Contents

Part Five: Fully Embracing a Higher Form of Combat

Part Six: Advantages of This Less Lethal Approach

Part Seven: Historical Examples of Not Killing

Part Eight: Enough Skill to Make Less Force Possible

Part Nine: Increasing the GI's Situational Awareness

Part Ten: Contact Avoidance

Part Eleven: Idiosyncrasies of 21st Century Conflict

ILLUSTRATIONS

Maps:

TABLES

FOREWORD

I recently read Ron Chernow's excellent book, *Grant*. I was impressed with learning that Confederate generals were pall bearers for Grant's and Sherman's funerals and that veterans from Confederate units, as well as sons of Robert E. Lee, marched in Grant's funeral procession. Despite the horrific conflict they lived through, there was a degree of mutual respect and moral conduct they tried to adhere to. The civility and compassion at Appomattox was remembered and respected by the combatants. War, as all of us who have experienced it know, is a dehumanizing experience. Young men, and now women, who live through the horrors of the battlefield have all their sense of values and morality challenged. The after effects of this are clearly evident in the number of our service members who struggle with PTSD [post-traumatic stress disorder] and other post-combat issues. Enemies we face today bring no respect for conventions, codes, or morality, and the temptation to be reduced to their level of ruthlessness and brutality is ever present. Even our political masters have made compromises that challenge our moral standards in authorizations regarding prisoner of war treatment, waver of rights, and interment of citizens.

John Poole knows the face of war well. He quotes the words of John Boyd, a brilliant theorist on war, that there are three parts to war: the physical, the mental, and the moral. Poole raises a timely and important question regarding the moral aspect. Have we become so focused on the physical and mental parts and neglected the moral part? In this book he makes the compelling case that the moral part may be far more [of] a contributor to victory than the physical and mental. It is not a matter of being just the right thing to do, it can be the most important factor in succeeding in a conflict.

We invest a great deal of resources and time in training and educating our warriors in how to apply an ever more lethal and technologically advanced panoply of physical materiel. We also make an equal investment in the mental aspect, learning how to out-think and out-maneuver the enemy. How much, however, do we invest in the moral aspect? Every time there is an atrocity committed by one of our service members or units, we have to ask ourselves where did the leadership, training, and education fail in the moral component of the trilogy.

This is a critically important book that provides deep insights into the issues of morality in the way we conduct military operations in the 21st Century. It is a must read for our political and military leaders as well as for every member of our Armed Forces.

GEN. ANTHONY C. ZINNI USMC (RET.)
FORMER HEAD OF CENTCOM

PREFACE

From the World War II (WWII) cover, some may assume this book is about issues with which the United States (U.S.) military has already dealt. It isn't. It addresses perfectly valid "combat lessons learned" of various eras that the Pentagon's doctrinal bureaucracy has yet to incorporate into its schools and manuals. Yet, *Guardian Joe* will probably not be read by most of America's ground combat officers. That's because it focuses on the lowest ranks that many think elementary, and less force than most deem necessary. All realize that technology has had an effect on small-unit maneuver. That should mean that U.S. infantry and special-operation teams—with all of their latest equipment—are now operating near the current state of the tactical art. But what if the lethality of the World War I (WWI) machinegun was never fully embraced (like with enough crawling)? Then, the whole foundation of U.S. wartime methodology would still be a little shaky. And America's modern-day "finest" would continue to find themselves in untenable situations.

U.S. squads should have long since demanded any needed adjustment to their tactical procedures. But, if too little maneuver has occurred below platoon level or tiny teams been micromanaged, such recommendations may never have surfaced long enough to be institutionalized. It is, after all, counter-intuitive to think that a military unit within which every member does precisely as told would have trouble handling one with looser lowest-echelon control. So, no small-unit tactics of America's former foes would have been copied. Nor will U.S. hierarchical strictness ever diminish, no matter how many studies are done to highlight its side effects. Yet, there is still the Pride of Poughkeepsie to consider. He or she might welcome a few suggestions on how best to survive such "less-than-optimal" circumstances.

That filthy, sweaty, dirt-encrusted, foot-sore, camouflage-

painted, ripped-trousered, tired, sleepy, beautiful little son
of a b— who has keep the wolf away from the door for over
two hundred years.[1]
  — *Green Side Out,* by Duncan

Needless to say, the average American rifleman might do quite
well with a more productive combat role. In truth, his is the most
complicated of all military fields. So, only required would be for
his unit to better acknowledge the extra warrior potential. That
potential goes far beyond marksmanship, endurance, and following orders.

That's why *Guardian Joe* will be of help to every U.S. service
member wishing to make a difference. Sadly, the most elite among
them already believe themselves capable of any enemy challenge.
That's the unfortunate by-product of too much headquarters'
hype.

Of course, this book's ultimate objective is to make all Pentagon infantrymen and special operators so proficient at ground
combat that America easily fulfills its providential duty of saving
the world. Contrary to popular opinion, real combat proficiency
has more to do with compassion and initiative, than savagery and
obedience. Those who would claim otherwise may have become
overly enamored with top-echelon power or defense contract money. There is more to be gained on future battlefields from decen-
tralizing control over infantry training and operations than from
all the latest surveillance, targeting, and remote-killing devices
put together.

Most U.S. military books are written by high-ranking retired
officers. From a loyalty-demanding and strategy-oriented background, they routinely draw upon "conventional wisdom" to show
how better to conduct a war from the top down. Such an endeavor
takes no illustrations, small-unit vignettes, or footnotes. For the
recent inductee trying to learn more about his or her military specialty, it proves too philosophical to be of much use (or interest). To
further jeopardize their quest, some well-intended editor has also
removed most of the "how-to" detail.

Guardian Joe is not like that. It has been written by someone
with 30 years as a squad tactics instructor, after 20 as a commissioned infantryman. An 11-year "reversion to enlisted status" gave
this retired Marine some unique insights into why the Pentagon
has had so much trouble winning wars of late. So, after briefly

discussing the U.S. infantry commander's wartime perspective, he shows which skills his enlisted subordinates must have to follow the full modern-day intent of their instructions. For company grade officers responsible for their troops' success/survival in war, it offers a rare glimpse into irregular warfare. For those troops themselves, it is the "first ever" manual on how to maximize both pride and longevity in combat.

Largely responsible for the U.S. Marines' victory over the tactically superior Japanese in WWII was the edge a survival-oriented combatant has over one wishing a glorious death. The same "mindset differential" has recently helped modern-day Government Issues (GIs) to persevere over the minions of radical Islam. But, for most American service personnel, just surviving a long time is not enough. Their ultimate objective is to make some meaningful contribution along the way.

It has often been said that war is the most obscene of man's various inventions. Because the foe invariably resorts to "evil," those with a limited religious background logically assume that GIs must be allowed some fairly base forms of behavior just to counteract it. Further to assist in this righteous quest, they first teach the young Americans to hate the foe, then how totally to destroy him. But, that much wartime killing does not easily mesh with how most people are created. What happens to the Pride of Poughkeepsie after such a trial of conscience? If he or she has had to violate any of God's laws in the performance of their combat duties, how then will it affect the rest of their lives? Is that destructive a battlefield orientation really necessary? Or might the young Yanks have done just as well on the field of honor with a more Christian way of fighting?

All U.S. citizens have been endowed by their Creator with the same subliminal need to rise above their human condition—to somehow transcend the material "here and now" to achieve something of lasting significance. Most clerics describe this natural instinct as shedding one's earthy bonds to more easily reach his or her spiritual threshold. A quick look at Americans' favorite movies of all time best delineates this syndrome. Among the top six are "Gone with the Wind" (1939), "Casablanca" (1942), and "Schindler's List" (1993).[2] The first explores the life of a woman who sacrifices almost everything to restore some semblance of Southern gentility to her war-ravaged plantation. The second is the story of a man who abandons a thriving business and his love for a freedom fighter's wife to more fully oppose the Nazis. The last is the true account of a rich Nazi playboy who saves the lives of over 1200 Jews and then weeps uncontrollably at the thought of not saving one more. Along the cinematic wayside have fallen tens of thousands of tributes to sex and violence. Their impact has proven just as fleeting as the evening sun for a reason. They didn't appeal to most moviegoer's "divine spark"—their latent desire to save a child from drowning, help their community after a tornado, or otherwise display their innate courage.

This "guardian" impulse should in no way be suppressed in America's military boot camps, for winning any future war may depend on it. Gone are the days of trying to destroy all possible resistance. Now, conflicts are more successfully concluded through at least some humanitarian effort by tiny, semi-autonomous teams. Until this change to warfighting is more widely accepted, everyone in the U.S. Armed Forces (including recent joinees) must openly push for the most moral strategies and maneuvers. So doing can have earthly consequences, but its absence can prove mentally debilitating. While sometimes hard for all commissioned and noncommissioned officers to see, fledgling GIs could usefully obey their own collective conscience. That's because it most likely comes from the Holy Spirit. While some organizational mottoes may differ, military professionals generally follow the same descending order of allegiance: (1) first to God; (2) next to country; (3) and only then to one's military outfit.

Such advice equally applies to America's law enforcement community. If not military veterans themselves, most American policemen follow some semblance of Pentagon procedure. While many now operate in virtual war zones, they are still the guardians of local society. As with America's corps of overseas liberators, their training must fully reflect this underlying responsibility. And they must come to see mercy as an appropriate response to the additional dangers involved.

"We do not rise to the level of our expectations, but fall to the level of our training."[3]
— Archilochus, professional Greek soldier, 650 B.C.

Lt.Col. H. John Poole USMC (Ret.)
former Fleet Marine Force Gy.Sgt. &
Illinois Bureau of Investigation agent

ACKNOWLEDGMENTS

American society has been gradually deteriorating through a minority faction's effort to eliminate any reference to "Our Creator" from all aspects of U.S. life. Those who would do so to save the American government from divine influence have made an egregious mistake. They have forgotten what complete havoc a State without enough moral direction can produce. Ethics are complicated. They can never be totally achieved through a sectarian set of rules. Under stressful circumstances, the average human will need some outside advice to make even the most logical decision.

One of the most reliable ways to excel at life's many challenges is to live by God's most humanistic guidelines. Even in mortal combat, they can pay huge dividends. Thanks be to God for all things productive.

PART ONE

THE CURRENT U.S. FOCUS

"WHAT DIFFERENCE DOES IT MAKE TO THE DEAD, THE ORPHANS AND THE HOMELESS, WHETHER THE MAD DESTRUCTION IS WROUGHT UNDER THE NAME OF TOTALITARIANISM OR THE HOLY NAME OF LIBERTY OR DEMOCRACY?"
— MAHATMA GANDHI

(Source: Mahatma Gandhi, "Non-Violence in Peace and War.")

1 THE DICHOTOMY OF U.S. INTENTIONS

- Has America always championed human rights?
- How well does its preferred way of war follow this aim?

Somebody's mother got hurt in this "precision" bombardment.

(Source: "St. Lo Patrol," by Olin Dows, U.S. Army Center of Military History, from this url: http://www.history.army.mil/art/dows/4_229_46.JPG.)

A Painful Reality

President Eisenhower's warning about "the acquisition of unwarranted influence . . . by the military industrial complex" has made little difference since 1961.[1] There is still so much money to be made from firepower-related technology that such gadgets have now come to define the American way of war.

U.S. tacticians have for many years known that firepower and surprise are virtually interchangeable (equally powerful) in battle. Yet, the benefits of more maneuver at the small-unit level have so far escaped most Pentagon planners. Nor does the U.S. public take sufficient exception to the fact that this country hasn't decisively won a ground conflict since WWII. As a result, guns—and the maximum damage they are able to inflict—seem currently to dominate the American psyche.

However, within some of the more progressive U.S. police departments, the role of "fringe-element disciplinarian" is now being replaced by "community guardian." For such departments, additional equipment hadn't helped them to maintain good order and discipline. So, they returned to the old "two friendly cops on a beat" approach. That's when the weapon of choice was a night stick. People occasionally got whacked alongside the head for too little reason, but they didn't end up dead. In the role of public protector, law enforcement personnel feel less under personal attack. As such, they are much less likely to overreact to confrontation. Role perceptions have a significant influence over every American soldier as well.

Just as most police department heads agree that lethal force should only be the last resort, so do most military strategists realize that most wars aren't won through killing. They are more greatly affected by which side runs short of strategic materiel. Yet, for whatever reason, the U.S. military still practices a "high-tech" version of 2nd Generation Warfare (2GW)—killing as many enemy combatants as possible. This continued focus on attrition has created a number of "unintentional" excesses: (1) too many civilian casualties; (2) too much "short-round" fratricide; and (3) too many enemy soldiers shot while trying to surrender.

Out of consideration for those who have had to follow a 2GW approach to battle, the moral implications of such excesses are seldom discussed in America. Those fine young GIs were simply doing their job. But, taking too much liberty with God's laws while under governmental orders may still have a psychological effect on them. In fact, it can be just as hard on unit cohesion, as on individual morale. To have the best chance at winning a modern conflict, the U.S. military must now shift to the more advanced 3rd or 4th Generation of Warfare (3GW or 4GW). While the former bypasses the enemy's strongpoints to more easily reach his wartime wherewithal, the latter is simultaneously waged in the political, economic, psychological/religious, and martial arenas. With less death being inflicted comes less vengeance, and more probability of a lasting peace.

Colonel John [R.] Boyd, the greatest American military theorist of the 20th Century, observed that war is waged at three levels: the physical, the mental, and the moral. The physical level—killing people and blowing things up—is the least powerful level. The mental level, where maneuver warfare is largely waged—getting inside the other guy's head—is more powerful than the physical. But the moral level is the most powerful level of all.[2]
— William S. Lind
tactical advisor to 29th Marine Commandant

Why the Pentagon Oversight?

America has clearly been suffering from dichotomy of intentions. While Washington continues to champion human rights around the world, its preferred way of war is still through "overwhelming firepower." That much firepower has not only killed large numbers of opposition soldiers, but also noncombatants and GIs who got too close.

According to Pope John Paul II, one must try to kill as few opposition soldiers as possible during a "just war" to be on firm moral footing.[3] While the enemy casualty statistics from America's most recent wars are disturbing, those for noncombatant and accidental U.S. deaths are even more so. A full third of Okinawa's 450,000 civilian occupants perished in the Allied invasion of that tiny island during WWII, with another third being wounded.[4] A few of Okinawa's residents had willingly fought alongside the Japanese, but most had been involuntarily "impressed" as laborers.[5] Then, a staggering 15 to 20 percent of all U.S. casualties in Vietnam were from friendly fire (mostly errant bombs and shells).[6] As the Pentagon's various munitions became better guided, the number of civilians and GIs accidentally hit has fallen, but not nearly enough. Unnecessary death remains a tragic part of the U.S. military experience.

Law Enforcement Ramifications

As most American police departments are largely composed of military veterans, their procedures are still largely based on U.S.

5

tactical doctrine. Among the basic axioms of that doctrine is "fire superiority." Fire superiority leads to death, and death to some risky rationalizations. While some soldiers conclude that defenders not killed during one assault may be encountered on the next, certain cops worry that murderers not killed during their apprehension may be freed on some legal technicality. Both segments of U.S. society consider a wounded adversary to be just as dangerous as a healthy one, so neither sees much benefit from capturing instead of firing "center mass" into armed opposition. In fact, over the years, only the law enforcement community has made much of an effort to take captives at all. But the initial predisposition toward too much force is definitely shared. That's because U.S. ground troops and policeman are—in varying degrees—both being prepared—for 2GW (Attrition Warfare). That's means their target is human.

While mortal force is sometimes the only option in both lines of work, it is seldom the best way to achieve a lasting resolution to any disagreement. Just as police departments are not allowed much collateral damage on U.S. streets, neither should Pentagon units while liberating a foreign nation. Wounding is preferable to killing, and unharmed surrender is by far the best option. It has often been said the American security establishment lacks enough "human intelligence" to do its job. By that is meant enough input from frontline observers. The interviewing of more battlefield prisoners would go a long way toward solving that particular problem.

Less Shooting Takes More Maneuver

America has been blessed with some of the best "big-picture thinkers" on the planet. But what if the answer to this long-term dilemma were to involve something so basic, as easily to be assumed already corrected? If the "high achievers" in charge had spent more time in their introductory assignments, they might better remember how much "nonrate" potential went completely untapped.

With something called Maneuver Warfare (MW), the U.S. Marine Corps attempted to advance from 2GW to 3GW in the late 1980's. Still, with a few impromptu exceptions, the Corps hasn't been able to conduct MW at the squad level since Evans Carlson managed that prodigious feat on his Long Patrol at Guadalcanal early in WWII. He was able to do so through an understanding of Maoist Mobile Warfare—a style based on many of the same MW parameters developed by the Germans during the latter stages of World War I (WWI). Fully to understand how Carlson's Raiders were so exceptionally trained, one has only to look within the first few chapters of *Gung Ho*.

"So what," might venture the contemporary—more digitally oriented—Marine leader. Here's the problem with not extending that same maneuver orientation down to the tiniest part of every unit. Without more self-sufficient squads, the entire U.S. Marine Corps can never fully practice its new doctrine. In the *Maneuver Warfare Handbook,* William S. Lind makes quite clear that "excellence in techniques is vitally important to [MW]."[7] Only squads, fire teams, buddy teams, and individuals (because of their size) are able to operate through prerehearsed (yet still somewhat flexible) "techniques"; and only a squad or smaller can totally surprise an accomplished adversary.

No Pentagon Reform Necessary

Luckily, there's an easy way to create world class, semi-autonomous squads that has yet to be tried *en masse* by any of America's infantry or commando organizations. It may seem too simplistic to be of value. But, again, not enough emphasis on the basics is the only way something this strategically vital could have been overlooked by so many highly dedicated Army, Navy, and Marine Corps leaders.

Just as in football, each squad must continually practice a company-wide portfolio of squad, fire team, buddy team, and individual tactical techniques. At least three of each will be required for every expected type of enemy encounter Then, during an enemy contact, the squad leader has only to choose the most situationally appropriate squad maneuver and then let all subordinate elements adapt their own techniques to unforeseen circumstances. What results is the "holy grail" of close combat—a good chance of momentum through considerably less predictability. No part of that squad will ever exactly mimic its public-domain manual, or past behavior.

Within an appendix to *Global Warrior* is how such a portfolio of advanced infantry techniques can be initially developed and then continually adjusted to contingency needs. Only intended as a supplement to the standardized small-unit training, this method has already been field tested and refined at 41 separate battalions. As in 3GW, each American squad then seeks only enough direct enemy contact to get its new job accomplished—destroying materiel and gathering intelligence (often through captives). Throughout this new mission, its members are now fully capable of taking on many times their number of enemy combatants in direct mortal combat.

While only operating alone on patrols, most modern-day U.S. squads are considered no more than part of an air-and-artillery-backed platoon. Platoons are too big to have techniques. That's because 40 or so people cannot adapt a rehearsed maneuver to changing conditions without continual "in-house" guidance. That guidance often comes in the form of "frag orders" from their platoon leader. But why allow such a time-consuming series of interruptions, when a single well-trained squad on "autopilot" can often do the same job as a platoon immediately. That's why every effort must now be made to produce more tactically adept U.S. infantry squads. Their self-sufficiency will not come from better use of all available firepower, but largely through the avoidance of unnecessary enemy contact.

The Now Possible Paradigm Shift

If most wars are not won through killing, then why should American servicemen and women continue to be trained as life takers. Though sometimes unavoidable in combat, killing does not come easily to the average American teenager. It is not among his or her natural predispositions. In fact, young children must be taught to hate.

Now that the nonmartial arenas of 4GW are being so heavily exercised around the world, there is even less reason for the "shooting center mass" mentality to be instilled into U.S. troops. *Guardian Joe* will show how to accomplish standard military missions with less force. In some cases, less force will facilitate intelligence gathering; in others, just more 3GW depletion of enemy supplies and equipment. At present, most of America's infantry and commando units lack enough small-unit skill to fully conduct either form of advanced warfare. While some within the U.S. special-operations community may now come close to complying with this requirement, it's not as a result of any headquarters mandate. Plus, most of their members have yet to qualify as light-infantry assault and defense experts—warriors with little need for advanced electronics or supporting arms. After all, fancy gear does get shot and wet in combat, while planes and artillery are not always available.

How U.S. Police Could Benefit

With no push for standardization from a national headquarters, many U.S. police departments have developed quite good Special-Weapon Assault Team (SWAT) techniques—particularly for the urban environment. While their shift to more daring and initiative from the overly cautious response at Columbine is to be applauded, the overreaction by some officers to less serious events needs work. That's why the U.S. law enforcement community should also welcome a study on what less force might ultimately accomplish.

For all U.S. Armed Forces and law enforcement personnel in search of more productivity in mortal combat, the following discussion should prove quite rewarding.

2 ___ 2GW FIXATION BUT NO CULTURE OF DEATH

- By whom has U.S. society been called a culture of death?
- Is that allegation in any way justified?

Death has never been the aim in America, only an all too frequent result.

(Source: Correl Gallery Clipart with image designator "31F001.tif.")

Noncombatants Haven't Been Intentionally Slain

Many Church leaders worry that America may now have a "culture of death." While considerable lethality has resulted from various Washington policies (both foreign and domestic), American citizens would never knowingly participate in such a culture. To view an actual culture of death, one has only to visit Communist China. During that country's "Cultural Revolution" from 1966 to 1975, up to nine million Chinese citizens are known to have expired from inhumane governmental edicts.[1] America's excesses have been far less profound.

The number of indigenous civilians slain during the U.S. military's many pre-invasion bombardments and subsequent "meat-grinder-like" operations has not been officially quantified. But, one should not be too quick to judge such a blood letting. Those in charge at the time could see no other way to get the better of their tactically superior Japanese, German, or Communist adversaries. It is now only through 20-20 hindsight and more understanding of squad tactics that other options become available.

Yet, what has transpired on foreign battlefields pales to what still goes on at home. Since the "Roe vs. Wade" Supreme Court decision of 1973, nearly 59 million unborn American children have been thrown away.[2] That's more innocent civilian life than Hitler and Stalin managed to destroy in tandem.[3] This nation's holocaust equivalent just hasn't drawn as much attention. That's because most abortion rights activists don't see themselves as promoting harm to anyone. Their definition of when life begins differs from that of the Catholic Church. Even after the "fetus" has become fully viable outside the womb, they see it as an inanimate extension of the female body. Thankfully, for those activists and all expectant mothers, mortal sin requires full realization of another human life being taken.

Respect for All Life Remains Big Part of U.S. Policy

While the Chinese and Iranians now consider revolution to be a prerequisite of every nation's growth, America has steadfastly pursued peace around the world. Human rights may be low on the list of priorities for Beijing and Tehran, but they remain the driving force behind most of Washington's diplomatic efforts overseas. Though the American dream may have been somewhat altered over the years, there are few other places on earth where the average citizen enjoys as much hope for the future. Thus, one must look beyond America's culture for why she seems irreconcilably associated with much collateral damage, abortion, or other forms of societal aggrievement.

Might such excesses ever be the product of organizational structure? Tall, top-down organizations—those most common within the U.S. government—routinely suffer a communications gap between their highest and lowest echelons. Often, their leaders are largely insulated from what gets learned where "the rubber meets the road." This factor alone could result in inhumane policies. Is it possible that Pentagon leaders have yet to realize that piecemeal ground occupation would more greatly restrict a foreign criminal element than aerial bombardment?

Other U.S. government agencies suffer from a different kind of "top-heaviness." The tiny Judicial Branch has been paying little, if any, attention to God's laws or natural law. How can it hope to be properly attentive to those truths that lie beyond the scope of science?

While attempting to clarify Congressional legislation, the Supreme Court will sometimes create the equivalent of new legislation. Yet, the Preamble to the Constitution clearly states: "All legislative Powers herein granted shall be vested in a Congress of the United States, which shall consist of a Senate and House of Representatives." Using a lack of medical, philosophical, and religious consensus as the excuse during "Roe vs. Wade," the Supreme Court made no attempt to resolve the issue of when life begins. "There is no medical or scientific proof that life is present from conception," wrote the Court. Then, by failing to accept arguments that the fetus was a person, it effectively ignored the Due Process Clause of the 14th Amendment. That Clause clearly stipulates that no state shall "deprive any person of life, liberty, or property, without due process of law." And thus came to pass one of the most destructive verdicts in the annals of jurisprudence. Even the original complainant would change sides. Before becoming the principal party in the "Roe vs. Wade" law suit in 1973, Norma McCorvey (Jane Roe) had been forced to deal with a lot of adversity in her life without the benefit of baptism. Once baptized in 1995, she immediately switched to the "prolife" camp.[4]

Neither in 1856 did that same highly revered Supreme Court acknowledge—in the Dred Scott case—that African slaves were actually human beings.[5] So, the immensely powerful third cog of the U.S. government is certainly capable of a few mistakes with regard to the most ethical treatment for somewhat alien segments of society. With both "Dred Scott vs. Sanford" and "Roe vs. Wade," the Supreme Court had used the constitutional privacy rules as its reason for not adequately responding to a life-or-death issue. On both occasions, the result has since proven disastrous. Thus, it would be unfair to accuse U.S. society of ever intentionally suppressing the human spirit. Organizational inertia seems to have played a much bigger role in these and other societal excesses. Still, in a democracy, the overall public must share in the responsibility.

What Happens Now

While America's favorite warfighting style and abortion laws may both entail the loss of innocent life, neither has become so embedded in U.S. culture as never to change. Unfortunately, this book can only demonstrate how easily to amend the battlefield methods.

Still, much is to be gained by all U.S. military professionals now becoming aware of another way to reduce the number of noncombatant casualties. These same new ways would also lower their own losses. This won't become obvious without first reviewing the cost of some past battles.

PART TWO

NOW NEEDED FOR FUTURE CONFLICTS

"THE BEST FORM OF 'WELFARE' FOR THE TROOPS IS FIRST-CLASS [MORE COMPREHENSIVE] TRAINING, FOR THIS SAVES UNNECESSARY CASUALTIES."
— ROMMEL

(Source: *The Rommel Papers,* © 1953 by B.H. Liddell Hart, p. 226)

3 A CLOSER LOOK AT AMERICA'S WAR RECORD

- ● Have U.S. forces really won almost all of their battles?
- ● Is a constant flow of future victories to be expected?

The Vietnam War was largely fought from behind barbed wire.

(Source: http://search.usa.gov public-domain image from this url: http://www.quartermaster.army.mil/oqmg/Professional_Bulletin/Units/images/C_225th_Fwd_Spt_Bn.jpg.)

The Victor's Version of What Happened

Most big-battle history has been written by the side that ends up winning the war. Perhaps that's why U.S. combat chronicles mention so little strategic or tactical error by American units. Even the best of armies will occasionally make both varieties of mistake.

During WWI, the U.S. Marines were among the first Americans to fight. While they eventually won the Battle of Belleau Wood, it was only after taking terrible losses on their way into that forest.[1] (See Map 3.1 and Figure 3.1.)

Gen. Charles C. Krulak said he took his first walk a year ago, starting near the town of Lucy-le-Bocage, where the WWI marines launched their attack June 6.

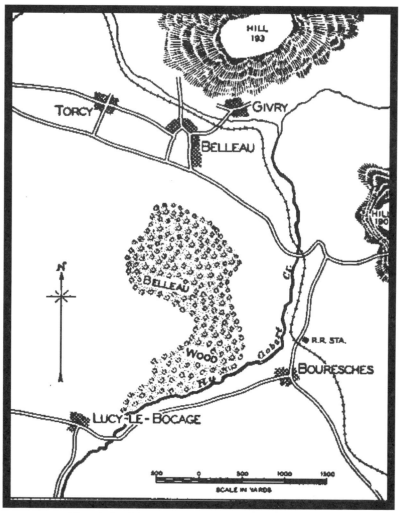

Map 3.1: A Wheat Field Had to Be Crossed
(Source: FMFRP 12-2, "Infantry in Battle," p. 31.)

Figure 3.1: Unhappy U.S. Survivors Finally Enter the Wood
(Source: Public-domain painting by Georges Scott [1873-1943] illustration for French magazine from https://commons.wikimedia.org/wiki/File:Scott_Belleau_Wood.jpg.)

"I walked toward the tree line through waist-high wheat, just as they did 80 years ago," the Commandant said. "History books describe that 800-yard advance, but I never fully appreciated it until I walked it myself. The Germans had every square inch of that field covered by machinegun and artillery fire. The Marines paid dearly with every step they took."[2]

— *Leatherneck Magazine*, August 1998

Then, during the Germans' Spring Offensives of 1918, any Doughboy line could be easily penetrated by a lone Stormtrooper squad employing a special "surprise-oriented" assault technique.[3] Thus, while the addition of U.S. forces had definitely turned the tide of the overall war, those forces still suffered from a few defensive deficiencies.

Figure 3.2: Massed Firepower Was the Preferred Way of War
(Source: FM 22-100 [1983], p. 30.)

During WWII, the only widely recognized setbacks for American forces were at Bataan in the Philippines, Kasserine Pass in Tunisia, Anzio in Italy, and the Hürtgen Forest in Germany. Even the Battle of the Bulge (where German tanks got 30 miles behind U.S. lines [4]) came—through subsequent aerial bombardment—to look like a resounding victory (more on that shortly).

Then, during the Korean War, other examples of this "overly optimistic" assessment of battlefield proficiency again appeared. While all U.S. Army occupiers were initially pushed back over a hundred miles into the Pusan Perimeter, the only other incident even vaguely to resemble a reversal was the Chosin Reservoir pullout. Yet, when the fully formed U.S. phalanx attempted to penetrate North Korea for a second time in 1953, it was unable to do so. That's because the new Communist defense line was an underground strongpoint matrix, complete with "localized" supply depots. (See Table 3.1 for the U.S. losses in such battles.)

KEY U.S. BATTLE CASUALTIES

Battle of Belleau Wood: 1087 Marine casualties on the first day, 5199 Marine losses for entire battle, over 10,000 dead, wounded, and missing of all U.S. troops involved [5]

Battle of Bataan: Out of about 31,000 U,S troops around Manila at time of the Japanese invasion, up to 22,000 captured and interned at Bataan, most others may have perished [6]

Battle of Kasserine Pass: 6500 casualties [7]

Battle of Anzio: 23,173 casualties (5,538 killed, 15,558 wounded, and 2,947 captured or missing, no nonbattle losses counted) [8]

Battle of Hürtgen Forest: 33,000 casualties (24,000 killed, wounded, or missing, and another 9000 victims of disease or battle fatigue) [9]

Battle of the Bulge: 108,347 casualties (19,246 killed, 62,489 wounded, 26,612 missing, no nonbattle losses counted) [10]

Battle of Pusan Perimeter: 19759 casualties (4,599 killed, 12,058 wounded, 2,701 missing, 401 captured, no nonbattle losses counted) [11]

Battle of Chosin Reservoir: 17,843 casualties (1,029 killed, 4,894 missing, 4,582 wounded, 7,338 nonbattle losses) [12]

Table 3.1: U.S. Losses in Key WWI, WWII, and Korean Battles

NOW NEEDED FOR FUTURE CONFLICTS ─────────────────────────

During that time [just preceding the 1953 Korean hill battles], anyone who happened to enter the mountainous area of our positions could hear the sound of earthwork. . . . Gradually, a defense system took shape. It was backed up by supporting [strong] points with tunnel fortifications as main structures. . . . Here one could find all kinds of facilities . . . as well as defended fortifications, communications entrenchments, and crisscrossing main tunnels and branch lines. . . . Even though the enemy continued dropping thousands of bombs that exploded on top of the mountains, our commanders were able to sit down and peacefully read books and newspapers or play cards and chess.[13]
— *Mao's Generals Remember Korea*

By the time the Vietnam War rolled around, this predisposition toward "always looking good" had reached its zenith. Much of the rank and file came to believe that Congress, the *New York Times,* or Jane Fonda had lost the war.

More About the Battle of the Bulge

Not only did U.S. forces pay a higher price in casualties at the Bulge (108,347 from Table 3.1) than the highest official estimate at the time (89,000 [14]), but the German losses may have been unnaturally inflated.

Hitler attacked through the Ardennes in mid-December 1944 with Panzer tanks plus hastily assembled and poorly supported *Volksgrenadier* (people's infantry) divisions. Luckily, the 82nd and 101st airborne divisions were nearby recuperating from Operation Market-Garden, and General Patton's 3rd Army was able to turn north on a moment's notice.

The ensuing battle officially ended on 28 January 1945. One researcher claims overall German casualties to be 120,000 and American 100,000,[15] whereas another has German losses of 100,000 and American of 80,987.[16] Better substantiated estimates tell a different story.

On 8 January 1945, Hitler authorized the pullback of all German forces from the tip of the Bulge.[17] From the time they attacked out of the Ardennes until the 1st and 3rd U.S. Armies closed their pincers on a mostly empty salient at Houffalize on 16 January 1945,[18] the Germans suffered 44,420 casualties and the Americans 50,805.[19] If rear security for the retreating German column was only 13 miles from Hitler's Westwall at the time, how many aircraft-inflicted losses that column took for the next 12 days is mostly speculation. Uniformed personnel are difficult to identity from an altitude of 20,000 feet, and an accurate count of actual combatants injured is scarcely possible from aerial photographs.

One author hypothesizes the newly inducted and quickly trained German soldiers did well at the Bulge because of better German leadership. Better small-unit infantry tactics probably had more to do with it.[20] The Americans, on the other hand, had mostly relied on their firepower.

> [T]he majority of American divisions needed overwhelming artillery . . . and close air support to best their German opponents.[21]
> —*For the Common Defense,* Millett and Maslowski

The Underlying Problem

Which side suffered the most casualties at the Battle of the Bulge is clearly not the same as who won it. The victory belongs to the side that ended up holding the ground. But, the apparent attempt to make U.S. forces look statistically more lethal than their foe is still troubling. Tactical withdrawal has long been a legitimate maneuver. That's what the U.S. Marines like to think happened at the Chosin Reservoir.

It's easy to assign some negative rationale—like "lying," "cover-ups," or "denial"—to the widely held belief that U.S. forces almost never lose a fight. Its source may be quite different, however. While the "team loyalty requirement" for all U.S. service personnel almost certainly plays a role, the changing definition of "winning an enemy contact" may be ultimately at fault. Traditionally, it meant controlling the ground on which the skirmish occurred. But, if the foe were to move below ground, or the skirmish victor too quickly continue on with his sweep of the region, even that meaning would be in question.

There's often a thin line between winning and losing in war. Sometimes, a martial defeat can serve as a psychological victory.

But, there is a universally recognized requirement for the side wishing to consistently do well. It must learn from its mistakes. While it may be painful to admit to losing a single engagement, that's the only sure way to improve between them. As integrity challenged as Asian Communist negotiators may be, their soldiers still follow a very productive tradition from their pre-Communist days. They see great dishonor in claiming to have won a battle they didn't. Often outgunned by a Western opponent, they thus tend to get more and more tactically proficient during any prolonged conflict.

U.S. forces, on the other hand, seem only to change in the type and duration of firepower applied. While they also attempt to tell the truth after every engagement, they come under more bureaucratic pressure. There are several things that might detract from a purely objective after-action report: (1) it must often be done with the unit still engaged; (2) it is written by a career-oriented commander who can't adequately poll all subordinates; (3) both unit and commander are under extreme pressure "never to lose"; and (4) victory is regularly assessed through an Attrition Warfare formula. With regard to the last, the size of the opposing force and its losses sometimes stay in play long after the actual clash has concluded. That creates too much of an opportunity for unintentional padding of the numbers. In Vietnam, one infantry commander would go around and ask his men after each firefight how many dead enemy soldiers they had seen. He made little attempt to determine how many opposition bodies had been viewed by more than one subordinate.[22]

On a few occasions (like General MacArthur on New Guinea), U.S. commanders have intentionally claimed victory before the battle was even over.[23] "Spinning" the facts a little must have been thought to facilitate the next phase of the offensive. Yet, as any churchgoer knows, any modification to the truth—however minor—can be risky. Not only does it set a bad example for subordinates, but it can lead to more serious fabrications.

Overwhelming Firepower Has Its Limitations

To evict U.S. forces from Vietnam, the North Vietnamese Army (NVA) needed no air strikes, only a handful of light amphibious tanks, and occasional artillery fire from the Demilitarized Zone (DMZ). None were used on a regular basis, because the enemy's tactics were so surprise oriented that they did not require any preliminary bombardment. That was just as well for them, because heavily vegetated terrain does not facilitate any supporting arm for either combatant. (See Figure 3.3.)

Very few U.S. tanks got anywhere near a heavy firefight in Vietnam. They invariably blew off a tread *en route.*[24] Ever since the Japanese refined the technique in WWII, all Asian Communist troops have been good at disabling tanks from hidden spider holes. Initial minesweeping does no good. The spider hole occupant simply attaches a piece of communications wire to a carefully camouflaged above-ground tank mine, and then drags it under the tank after its protective infantry has passed.[25]

By the end of the Vietnam War, over seven million tons of

Figure 3.3: Tanks Will Always Have Difficulty in Close Terrain
(Source: FM 17-1 [1966], p. 179.)

bombs had been dropped on Vietnam, Laos, and Cambodia—more than twice the amount used by the Allies throughout Europe and Asia during WWII.[26] All those bombs, along with ten times that many artillery shells, would all go for naught. So, one wonders which American asset might have wielded enough power to actually win the war.

4 THE GRADUAL DEMISE OF DARING AND INITIATIVE

● How large were most U.S. landings in the 19th Century?

● Why were so few U.S. service personnel involved?

How many early Americans did it take to enter an enemy camp?

(Source: MCRP 3-02H [1999], fig. I-2.)

Overwhelming Numbers Not Once Necessary

Back in the 18th and 19th Centuries, America did not need a huge landing force and onshore logistic and supporting-arms bases to accomplish most overseas missions. (See Table 4.1.) A single squad was often enough, and it didn't have to be comprised of infantrymen. A few U.S. sailors could just as easily get the job done, as in the movie "Sand Pebbles."[1] When U.S. Army or Marine Corps personnel were involved, all business ashore was mostly by tiny detachment.

The Marines, in particular, have a long history of doing things

1843 China: Sailors and Marines from the St. Louis landed after clash with locals at the trading post in Canton.

1854 China: U.S. ships landed forces to protect American interests in and near Shanghai during Chinese civil strife.

1855 China: U.S. forces protected American interests in Shanghai and fought pirates near Hong Kong.

1856 China: U.S. forces landed to protect U.S. interests at Canton and to avenge an assault upon an unarmed U.S. boat.

1859 China: Naval force landed to protect U.S. assets in Shanghai.

1866 China: U.S. forces punished an assault on the American consul at Newchwang.

1894-95 China: Marines stationed at Tientsin and penetrated to Peking to protect U.S. assets during Sino-Japanese War.

1894-95 China: A naval vessel was beached and used as a fort at Newchwang for protection of American nationals.

1898-99 China: U.S. forces provided a guard for the legation at Peking and the consulate at Tientsin during contest between the Dowager Empress and her son.

1900 China: U.S. troops protect foreign lives during the Boxer Uprising, particularly at Peking. Then, permanent legation guard maintained in Peking, and periodically strengthened.

1911 China: As Nationalist Revolution approached, a small naval party unsuccessfully tried to enter Wuchang to rescue missionaries, and a small landing force guarded U.S. property and consulate at Hankow. Marines deployed to guard the cable stations at Shanghai; landing forces sent for protection to Nanking, Chinkiang, Taku and elsewhere.

1912 China: On Kentucky Island and at Camp Nicholson, U.S. forces protected Americans and U.S. interests during revolutionary activity.

Table 4.1: Tiny U.S. Military Landings in China Alone
(Source: "Instances of Use of United States Armed Forces Abroad, 1798-2010," by Richard F. Grimmett, CRS #R41677, 10 March 2011.)

1912-41 China: The dynasty overthrow during the Kuomintang Rebellion in 1912, and the invasion of China by Japan, led to many local demonstrations and protective U.S. landings from 1912 on to 1941.

1916 China: American forces landed to quell a riot taking place on American property in Nanking.

1917 China: American troops were landed at Chungking to protect American lives during a political crisis.

1920 China: A landing force was sent ashore for a few hours to protect lives during a disturbance at Kiukiang.

1922-23 China: Marines were landed five times to protect Americans during periods of unrest.

1924 China: Marines were landed to protect Americans and other foreigners in Shanghai during Chinese factional hostilities.

1925 China: Riots and demonstrations in Shanghai brought the landing of American forces to protect lives and property in the International Settlement.

1926 China: Nationalist attack on Hankow brought the landing of American naval forces to protect American citizens. A small guard was maintained at consulate general when the rest of the forces were withdrawn. Likewise, when Nationalist forces captured Kiukiang, naval forces were landed for the protection of foreigners.

1927 China: Fighting at Shanghai caused American naval forces and Marines to be increased. A naval guard was stationed at the U.S. consulate at Nanking after Nationalist forces captured the city. American destroyers later used shell fire to protect Americans and other foreigners.

1932 China: American forces were landed to protect American interests during the Japanese occupation of Shanghai.

1934 China: Marines landed at Foochow to protect U.S. Consulate.

Table 4.1: Tiny U.S. Military Landings in China Alone (cont.)
(Source: "Instances of Use of United States Armed Forces Abroad, 1798-2010," by Richard F. Grimmett, CRS #R41677, 10 March 2011.)

Figure 4.1: Eight U.S. Marines Led Attack on Pirate Stronghold
(Source: Public-domain image of "Lieutenant Presley O'Bannon at Derna" from https://commons.wikimedia.org/wiki/File:Attack_on_Derna_by_Charles_Waterhouse_01.jpg.)

with the least number of people. To defeat the Barbary pirates of Libya at Derna in 1805, they needed only an eight-man shipboard detachment of Marines at the head of 400 or so local mercenaries. (See Figure 4.1.) While this impromptu attack force was supported by the guns of two U.S. ships, it was also up against 10 times its number of enemy defenders.[2]

Then, in 1836 during Mexican-American War, some "Texas Marines" kept up the same tradition of daring and initiative. This time, there was no advance warning of their attack through ultimatums or bombardment.

On 2 June, Maj. Isaac Burton, with twenty mounted riflemen, was patroling *[sic]* the shores of Capano Bay looking for straggling units of the Mexican army, when he spied a Mexican schooner standing into the bay from the Gulf. Burton hastily concealed his horses and men. "Thinking big," he then boldly walked down to the beach and signaled the ship, which immediately put a boat over the side with five men aboard. When the boat reached the beach, Maj. Burton had a delegation awaiting the occupants. The five occupants admitted the ship was bringing in supplies to the Mexican army and was hoping to meet elements of the army at the bay.

Burton quickly placed sixteen troopers in the boat, rowed out to the schooner, and captured it without a fight. The Texas officer ordered the Mexican captain to set sail for the Texas port of Velasco, farther up the coast. Unfortunately, the wind had died and the ship was becalmed in the bay. Two weeks passed, and still no favorable wind came up. On 17 June, two more Mexican schooners appeared at the mouth of the bay. Still "thinking big," Burton held a pistol at the captain's head and forced him to hail the other two skippers to invite them on board. As the two Mexican officials stepped on board the captured schooner, Maj. Burton confronted them and demanded the complete surrender of both vessels. The astonished Mexicans immediately complied.

A favorable wind finally came up and Burton, with all his horses on board, triumphantly brought the three schooners into Velasco with much pomp and ceremony. From that time on, Maj. Burton and his twenty Rangers were known throughout the country as the Texas Horse Marines.[3]

— Marine Corps Gazette, August 1978

The Modern-Day Sequel

On 15 May 1975, during the much-publicized "Mayaguez Incident," a reinforced platoon from Delta Company, 1st Battalion, 4th Marines (D/1/4), was tasked with retrieving the American ship from Cambodian pirates. Those 48 Yanks had little trouble doing so, after all shipboard personnel had been incapacitated by gas.

At 0710, a division of USAF A-7's laid riot control agents on Mayaguez. Holt [a U.S. destroyer] then proceeded alongside and the Marines under Maj. Porter's command, in an action reminiscent of the 18th Century, boarded Mayaguez at 0725.[4]

— *Marine Corps Gazette,* October 1977

Believing some of the ship's original crew to be already ashore at nearby Koh Tang island, a command group, 81 mortar platoon, and two rifle companies from Battalion Landing Team (BLT) 2/9 concurrently assaulted that tiny terrain feature. Its 20 or so estimated inhabitants turned out to be considerably more well-armed and battle-ready Khmer Rouge. While the invading Marines were to acquit themselves quite well over the next 24 hours, many of their transport helicopters would be either damaged or (in a few cases) completely destroyed. No amount of U.S. firepower from either sea and air could have altered that outcome. By the morning of 16 May, the landing force had been extracted. Previously spotted on a commandeered Thai fishing boat *en route* to Kompong Som, the Mayaguez crew had already been rescued.[5]

In retrospect, one sixth as many Marines had been needed for a much more challenging mission in 1805, and one third as many for almost the same task in 1836. Such a trend has two explanations from a headquarters standpoint. Either Marine safety had been of greater concern in 1975, or what fewer people can accomplish less well appreciated. U.S. lives have always been highly valued, but their loss may have had more political repercussions at the end of the Vietnam War. In fact, that may be when too much emphasis on "Force Protection" first started to undermine America's foreign interventions. But, in terms of actual personnel endangered, the earlier incidents did much better. Whereas 48 were risked in 1975 (not counting the partial BLT], only 16 were put at jeopardy in 1836, and just eight in 1805. So, the leaders in 1975 must have thought a single squad too weak to seize a larger ship, though likely manned by fewer crewmen. That a lone squad could have more surreptitiously boarded her played no apparent role in their decision.

Fewer Attackers Need More Surprise

As just implied, the U.S. military may now attribute less value to the element of surprise than it did early in the 19th Century. That it has since enjoyed a firepower advantage over most adversaries would certainly explain the mistake. If one expects to "steam-roll" his opponent, than any number of people can be involved without ever trying to sneak up on or outmaneuver the foe. But then, to add insult to injury, that august military establishment has indirectly "institutionalized" this disregard for surprise. Its 2GW doctrine has for quite some time "recommended" that assault elements outnumber all defenders by at least three to one.[6] Yet, nothing bigger than a U.S. squad has any chance of totally surprising even a seasoned woodsman. Luckily, that doctrinal guidance was not in effect during the first part of the 19th Century. Otherwise, neither one of those magnificent U.S. victories would have been possible.

"Small-Unit" Daring Had Begun to Wane

Something else had come into play in all three of the above-mentioned examples—the proximity of higher headquarters. More daring and initiative had been possible where those in ultimate charge were not as easily contacted. Better 20th Century communications would make more standoff control possible. Where the situation continually changes, too much "direction from above" could easily limit the prerequisite initiative. It's not quite clear whether it did so during the Mayaguez Incident. The gas attack made perfect sense from a hostage rescue standpoint, but it also forfeited any chance of total surprise. In the early 1800's, a couple of U.S. sailors might have snuck aboard the enemy ship before its seizure, hidden near the hostages, and then protected them during the assault. *Ninjutsu*-trained Asian military and police personnel still have such capabilities, but in the West such activity is generally thought to be too risky.

Suffice it to say that lack of U.S. courage is not now, nor ever has been, the problem. Tens of thousands of U.S. service men and women have freely made the ultimate sacrifice, after doing something instrumental for overall victory. While such a claim cannot be verified through either battle chronicle or medal citation, most former field commanders know it to be true.

Over the years, less and less trust has simply been placed in tiny U.S. units. If anyone or anything is to blame, it is most probably too much "top-down" pressure. In 1917, in a vain attempt to salvage WWI, the Germans turned over two monumental responsibilities to lone infantry squads led by noncommissioned officers (NCOs): (1) the spearpoint of most attacks, however large; and (2) authority to abandon their building block of every soft strongpoint matrix.[7] While America's adversaries in the Pacific and Vietnam are known to have followed suit, the Pentagon never did. It remains committed to infantry squads that exist only as an integral part of their parent company. As a result, U.S. commanders haven't had the option of totally surprising an opponent on the battlefield—that which only a "world-class" semi-autonomous squad can make possible. Such a profound limitation carries with it an unnecessary increase in casualties.

[A] small unit, a squad or even a fire team, that is properly trained in modern, post-machinegun techniques can be just as effective as a much larger unit, while offering the enemy fewer targets. The German Army, which excelled in drawing lessons from its combat experiences, found as early as World War I that the only difference between a squad attacking a machinegun position and a company doing so was in the number of casualties suffered. Not surprisingly, by 1918 the *Stosstrupp,* a squad-sized unit, was the basic German tactical building block. In contrast, in most Marine infantry units today, the squad is regarded as merely a subset of the platoon, seldom trained for independent action. The result, in combat, is likely to be a lot of dead Marines, Marines whose deaths could have been avoided if tasks were assigned to smaller units.[8]
>   — William S. Lind,
>   tactical advisor to 29th Marine commandant

How Important Are America's Special Operators?

While it is true that U.S. Army Special Forces, Navy "Sea Air and Land" (SEAL), and Marine Raider teams have been allowed more autonomy on the battlefield of late, very few are expert at light-infantry assault, defense, or Escape and Evasion (E&E) tactics.[9] As a result, most make no attempt to attack fully prepared enemy defenses (those with concentric rings of barbed wire, hidden claymores, and interlocking bands of grazing machinegun fire). All those modern electronics give them more targets to shoot at, but in no way obscure their own presence. In fact, a near naked hunter could more easily sneak up on an experienced defender than the average U.S. special operator. His estimated 125,000 North Korean and 400,000 Chinese counterparts do not suffer from this doctrinal blind spot.

Traditionally, America's commandos have been special-forces soldiers who conducted raids behind enemy lines. They were occasionally forced to perform short-range infiltration of a strongpoint protected by barbed wire, mines, and grazing fire. But normally, they enjoyed some way of sidestepping the unpleasantries of an infantry counterpart. As a result, those infantrymen more often became "worst-case-scenario" surprise-assault experts (like how to take a bunker for which all approaches are fully covered by those behind it). Thus, while now allowed more initiative than most U.S. infantry squad members, America's current crop of special operators will still need their "more-microterrain-oriented" brethren to handle a major Asian army. Just to stay alive, those "raggedy" brethren must be far more skilled than most people realize.

5 HIDDEN GI RISKS WITHIN THE ___ U.S. OPERATING STYLE

- Do U.S. assaults routinely expose GIs to enemy MG fire?
- Might more subunit leeway better utilize the microterrain?

"High diddle diddle right up the middle" has its drawbacks.

(Source: FM 100-5 [1994], p. 56.)

Execution Problems Where the Rubber Meets the Road

There are many circumstances—besides enemy action—that can bring grief to a U.S. rifleman. Some have to do with his now thinking that electronics make him less detectable by the opposition. Others involve too little procedural leeway at the lower echelons of his unit. Here are just a few of the ensuing pitfalls for the Pride of Topeka: (1) taking part in a parent-unit mission without any recourse to the most appropriate squad, fire team, buddy team, and individual methods; (2) expecting to exactly follow some tactical technique as practiced; (3) unnecessarily rushing into a dangerous situation; (4)

walking point without enough experience; (5) getting separated from his unit; (6) being unintentionally targeted by friendly fire; (7) becoming wounded; and (8) not remaining cool headed through unexpected forms of adversity. American infantry training has currently become so tightly controlled that even seasoned instructors have trouble passing along "combat lessons learned." To properly appreciate the following "in-depth" discussion, each reader must try to imagine recently joining a deployed unit as a junior rifleman.

Not Using All Available Techniques

For an infantry squad, a tactical technique is like an offensive or defensive football "play." Fire teams, buddy teams, and individuals also have techniques. Those of a lone rifleman might be compared to a halfback's "reverse" or lineman's "stunt." Most football teams enjoy a full portfolio of plays, each with its own composite moves for subordinate elements. It's small wonder then, that any infantry squad that too closely follows the few procedures in its manual will

Figure 5.1: A Risky Upright Assault Is Not Always Required
(Sources: FM 23-30 [1988], p. 5-3; FM 7-8 [1984], p. 3-28.)

have trouble performing a difficult mission. Without more than one maneuver/formation to choose from, no tiny infantry element could regularly move down the field or hold the line. That's because no offensive or defensive action is good enough to keep on working after the enemy has already seen it.

When most U.S. infantry commanders issue a tactical order, they assume that their people already know how best to execute that order. This is a very dangerous assumption that no Asian Communist counterpart would make. He would instead learn which squad, fire team, buddy team, and individual techniques his people had been regularly practicing, and then to which mission they might apply.[1]

The official U.S. manuals mostly contain a single tactical solution for each general category of enemy contact under ideal conditions. That's all that the average GI is required to know. If there is any rehearsal going on inside his unit, it is for these few stratagems — exactly as published and along a fairly unobstructed surface. In essence, the Pentagon has now so associated standardization of effort with additional firepower, that it readily accepts the resulting predictability. Such is the U.S. way of war.

Within such a "hamstrung environment," infantry units tend to fight exactly how they have trained, despite differing circumstances. For example, if the orders are given to storm an enemy position, everyone automatically assumes that it has to be done at once. What if sundown is only four hours away, and no other unit will be affected by waiting a few hours? The difference might be ten fewer casualties. (Figures 5.1 and 5.2 should adequately emphasize this point.)

Instant obedience may still be expected of recently inducted riflemen, but it is not always implied nor appropriate for the tiny elements to which they belong. Those elements must often be allowed to switch over to the most situationally consistent technique for accomplishing their mission.

Expecting All to Go as Rehearsed

To be of much use, all techniques must be continually re-enacted by the assigned element. At that point, they become like muscle memory. Unfortunately, squad movements are seldom rehearsed in all types of terrain. When one is then run over unfamiliar ground

Figure 5.2: Nighttime Crawlers Are Harder to Target
(Sources: FMFM 1-3B [1981], p. 4-19; FM 90-10-1 [1982], p. B-4.)

in a war zone, major problems can arise. Anything in the way—like rocks, bushes, deadfall, or wall—can cause the entire maneuver to bog down or break apart, particularly if its members are not permitted enough initiative. Fortunately, most techniques provide a certain amount of terrain versatility. Even in dense underbrush, some semblance of linear alignment can still be maintained by everyone just "guiding to right or left" (staying up with the man on that side).

A really massive obstruction creates more of a problem. If an "on-line" squad suddenly encounters heavily cluttered woods, it may be tempted to move forward in column. Subsequently following the path of least resistance could encourage ambush. (See Figure 5.3.) But, when one or more members of a linear array run into a big bramble bush or jumbled tree fall, their best course of action is either to go around or through that obstruction (single file) to quickly resume their place in the original line. To try to deal with such a blockage any other way would be to forfeit not only momentum, but also morale. The exception, of course, is where there is evidence of a current enemy presence—like fresh dirt. Then, the appropriate action would be for a total pause to all proceedings.

Moving Too Fast for Existing Circumstances

The extent of one's forward motion plays an important role in how surprised the enemy will be, but it need not be rapid or upright.

Figure 5.3: Staying Almost on Line Takes Only Exercise
(Source: Courtesy of A.E. Taras, from "Podgotovka Razveghika: Sistema Spetsnaza GRU," © 1998 by A.E. Taras and F.D. Zaruz, pp. 144, 145, or 152.)

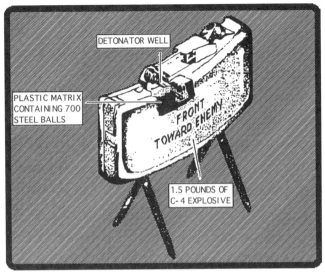

Figure 5.4: Barrier Item Most Ignored by Assault Procedures
(Source: FM 7-11B1/2 [1978], p. 2-IV-B-1.2.)

Figure 5.5: It Takes Time to Surprise a Proficient Defender
(Source: FM 7-11B1/2 [1978], p. 2-II-A-5.2.)

Crossing a tiny grassy area in a few quick bounds may work well for some daylight assaults, but so too would crawling very slowly across the same area after dark. Only required to surprise one's quarry is to move more rapidly than he deems feasible. If a squad clears one side of a contested street faster than the next-block defenders think possible, those defenders may not be quite ready when that squad enters their area. An interesting example of this syndrome occurred on Operation Maui Peak in Vietnam. There, on an almost bald hilltop during a full moon, several NVA soldiers still managed to sneak within grenade range of Marine defenders. To do so, they had only to dress up like bushes and crawl in more slowly than the naked eye can discern under low-light conditions.[2] They simply closed the gap faster than any defender could imagine.

While this slower application of the speed principle takes more patience, it also permits continually readjusting to unforeseen circumstances. Its alternative—outright "charging" somebody—can prove very unhealthy. A woods-wise defender can often detect an inbound attack force at quite a distance through old-fashioned means. Then, if that force has the assumed need for a stand-up assault, other problems quickly ensue: (1) missed cues as to the enemy's defensive barrier plan (like where the claymores are); (2) rushing the cadence on a "by-the-numbers" assault technique (like failing to exit a bunker buster's backblast area); or (3) unnecessarily drawing the defenders' attention (like through some distinct motion signature). Of course, any movement whatsoever while fully visible to an already alerted enemy can so telegraph one's intentions as to prove virtually suicidal.

So much as one boobytrap or hidden piece of barbed wire in the way of an assault formation can be a real "deal breaker." Encountering either on the way in to an objective will usually forfeit any chance of totally surprising its defenders. Prelocating such likely components to their barrier plan takes time. (See Figures 5.4 and 5.5.) That's why it's so important to run every assault against a prepared enemy position in a fairly deliberate manner (after at least some reconnaissance and rehearsal.)

Assuming March Security Role Without Special Training

During the Vietnam War, it was widely reported that U.S. "new guys" were often put on point. (See Figure 5.6.) Whether that was

Figure 5.6: "New-Guy" Security Team
(Sources: MCOP1550.14D [1983], p. 10-8; FM 22-100 [1983], p. 164.)

to rapidly provide them with "on-the-job" training must be left up to the reader. For whatever reason, people who had been mostly trained in following orders and operating weapons were suddenly thrust up against the world's best light infantry. While the Vietnam era private was far from the Appalachian ridge runner of 1942, he still had some knowledge of the out-of-doors. As such, he soon discovered a few survival axioms: (1) any security role is a two-man job; (2) the pair walk in a staggered column; (3) lead man looks nearby for tripwires, footprints, etc.; (4) rear man looks farther ahead; (5)

the two never lose sight of the main element; (6) both carry their rifles (with slings over their shoulders) ready to fire; and (7) as point element, they stay far enough ahead of the main body to keep it out of any extended open area. The only difference with a flank- or rear-security mission is that flankers stay up with the unit leader, whereas rear security stalks the main element.

What normally gets a new patrol security man into trouble is his tendency to report everything he sees back to the unit leader, though some might require immediate personal action. Should he encounter an enemy counterpart, he who is too slow to shoot often loses.

Getting Separated from the Unit

One time during the Vietnam War, a young Marine came huffing and puffing into the headquarters element of a G/2/5 sweep just north of An Hoa. (See Figure 5.7.) He claimed to have fallen asleep at the last rest stop and then been left behind. He was winded because the enemy had been chasing him around the currently occupied rise for the last half hour. As improbable as this story sounds, no one doubted it at the time. In the U.S. infantry, grunts are lucky to get two hours of sound sleep per night. Then during the day, they take "power naps" whenever possible. In retrospect, that Marine's assigned buddy or fire team leader should have been held responsible for the near tragedy.[3]

A U.S. listening post (LP) is also a very dangerous place to be in wartime. Even when those manning it are smart enough to sneak into it after dark, their footprints or crawl marks are still clearly visible to any trained tracker. Right before the big Japanese attack on Guadalcanal's Henderson Field perimeter, Marine legend Chesty Puller had been forced to use a 46-man listening post.[4]

Along with any march security role also comes the chance of not enough parent-unit assistance in times of trouble. There are any number of ways the participant may temporarily drop out of sight, or get too far away to be rescued. But, the real danger lies in his parent unit calling for indirect-fire support while he is still deployed. This most often happens to a point element that has just crossed a big danger area to find an enemy ambush on the far side. A seasoned scout would have crawled the last few yards into the treeline, and

Figure 5.7: Being Completely Alone Can Prove Dangerous
(Source: FM 90-5 [1982], p. 2-12; FM 100-5 [1994], p. 37.)

then had a shallow depression along which to return to his unit if the bullets started to fly. Otherwise, he might easily be assumed to be dead right before a U.S. artillery barrage was summoned.

Yet, the chances of suddenly disappearing increase exponentially when one is fighting an Asian opponent who is fond of tunneling. Some GI got pulled out the bottom of a shell hole he was defending on Iwo Jima in the historical drama "Flags of Our Fathers."[5] Such a thing would be certainly possible after any U.S. assault on a barely discernible enemy strongpoint. On the night of 20-21 May 1945 at the Horseshoe segment of the Sugar Loaf Complex on Okinawa's Shuri Line, 3/4 was massively counterattacked from holes in the ground just outside the part they held.[6] This danger from below did not end with WWII. Had U.S. troops not abandoned Khe Sanh when they did in 1968, they might have encountered hundreds of opposition commandos pouring out of the ground inside their perimeter. Recently acquired enemy maps show the place to have been closely ringed by subsurface emplacements.[7] A Khe Sanh defender, Marine Corporal Bob O'Bday, later reported the following: (1) no sightings of trenches on his many security patrols; (2) no rumors of trenchlines that close to the perimeter; (3) shell holes with false bottoms that may have been used as mortar positions; (4) rectangular patches of subsurface dirt that had been made to look like tilled fields; and (6) digging sounds that were audible from the bottom of his perimeter position.[8]

According to a Reuters [news service] report dated March 18th, 1968, the siege of Khe Sanh was a three-level encirclement: in the air, on the ground, and under the ground.[9]
— *The 30-Year War*
The Gioi Publishers, Hanoi

Friendly Fire Problems

The U.S. military still practices a "high-tech" version of 2GW — killing as many enemy soldiers as possible. As a result, it regularly expends a great deal of firepower at the least provocation. (See Figure 5.8.) Frequently, the U.S. rifleman finds himself too close to that firepower. For example, he takes part in a patrol that spends too long exiting a friendly perimeter after dark. A reinforced Marine squad tried to different exit to the Dong Ha perimeter one night in the Autumn of 1966 to keep from being followed. Unfortunately, the perimeter watch was subsequently changed, and that squad found itself under grenade attack from a replacement watchstander.[10] Nor does the young American want to participate in any patrol that does not go to its assigned ambush site. To keep the artillery ammunition fresh, U.S. forces conduct H&I (Harassing and Interdiction) fires every night. Their targets are only checked against the planned destinations of all friendly patrols.

Then, there is the inexperienced artillery observer or occasional short round. When some "propellant increments" on a mortar round fail to burn, a short round results. Artillery batteries will also "shoot out" of the assigned target area for a number of reasons.

There are ways for the Pride of Topeka to limit the risk, but by far the best is his willingness to dive for cover at the least hint of an incoming round.

Figure 5.8: Friendly Fire Results in Many U.S. Casualties
<small>(Source: FM 7-8 [1984]; p. 4-25; MCO P1500.44B, p. 15-26; MCI 7311B, p. 115.)</small>

Getting Wounded

As previously suggested, it's not all that hard for a U.S. rifleman to become a casualty. (See Figure 5.9.) This syndrome is generally attributed to his not always doing as told or trained, but one could make just as good a case for his doing it under inappropriate circumstances. His most challenging time is during an attack on a prepared enemy position. If a stand-up assault has been ordered, he must remain upright and moving forward until told otherwise. He cannot stop even to help a fallen buddy. And only after his leader has authorized crawling or "fire and movement" (leapfrogging) can he do either. While such an assault is quite risky in the daytime, it is still his duty to perform over and over. Yet, there are a few things he can do to lessen the risk: (1) crouch down so as to make a smaller target; (2) sprint as best he can between masking objects (while still maintaining the same place in formation); and (3) accurately shoot any defender in his lane.

Only when badly wounded, should he personally desist from that assault. If possible, he seeks cover. Only if he is ahead of everyone else, should he toss a grenade at the enemy. When a Marine lieutenant found himself in that position during the Vietnam War, he chose not to throw that grenade after the closest of five "Chicoms" landed at the lip of his shell hole.[11] Any other decision might have been his last.

Yet, the annals of U.S. heroism are full of examples of servicemen who continued to fight after being wounded, some at the cost of their lives. They had decided the reward was worth the risk. Where the lives of one's pals are at stake or the mission, more daring is likely.

Depending Too Heavily on Rage and Adrenalin

Civilian street fights are often precipitated by rage. To the extent that either combatant can maintain that same level of rage for several minutes, he may do quite well. But, none of the martial arts

Figure 5.9: One May Have to Fight After Being Wounded
(Source: FM 22-100 [1983], p. 217.)

experts incorporate rage into their tournament or movie protocols. There, they remain quite calm and deliberate in the their actions. Battlefield action is like that too. While an increase in adrenalin may be of some help, much anger is not. Some claim a little fear also sharpens one's focus. (See Figure 5.10.) Not much close combat occurs anymore in war because of the proliferation of small arms. One's physical prowess only comes into play while trying to outmaneuver one's opponent during a prolonged firefight. In fact, the more muscular of the two may be at a disadvantage. During WWII, the smallest Marine in the outfit was often chosen to carry the formidable BAR (Browning Automatic Rifle) because he made less of a target.[12] But, even a small target must think well on his feet to survive for long in heavy action. As with David versus Goliath, the average Joe who can keep his wits about him has the edge over a more powerful foe.

Most U.S. Troops Prepared for a Different War

The U.S. rifleman has become most proficient at 2GW matters because that's how the Pentagon still operates. Meanwhile, his most likely foes have switched to 3GW and 4GW. 3GW and the U.S. Marines' new doctrine of MW are largely synonymous. In MW, one avoids an adversary's manpower concentrations (battlefield bastions) to more easily get at his strategic assets (logistic and control apparatus). Among its main precepts are: (1) surfaces and gaps; (2) focus of main effort; (3) centers of gravity; (4) speed and surprise; and (5) commander's intent.[14] Needless to say, both styles of advanced warfare require all frontline warriors to exercise a certain degree of initiative. As such, some initiative is also required to counter them.

Neither 3GW nor 4GW is strictly a Western invention. Many Asian nations have practiced something nearly identical since WWI, and quite similar for eons (thanks to Sun Tzu).[15] Both styles of more advanced warfare are highly dependent on small-unit action. That may be why the Pentagon has tried so hard to avoid them. To make a greater contribution, the individual rifle squad wood need enough proficiency to operate completely alone without any fire support. Such a thing would not make the weapons manufacturers very happy. Nor would it please those military leaders who prefer a fully unified whole.

Figure 5.10: A Warrior Thinks More Clearly When Calm
(Source: FM 7-11B1/2 [1978], p. 1-I-A-9.)

Some Initiative Possible While Still Following Orders

From the standpoint of both commander and his lowest-ranking subordinate, the key issue is how much self-sufficiency the squad, fire team, buddy team, and individual rifleman can be permitted. It should be fairly apparent to both segments of U.S. society that too little initiative from any composite infantry element, however small, can have dire consequences. It will almost certainly result in too many casualties, and some compromise of the parent unit's mission.

In the past, the U.S. commander's 2GW orientation led him to believe that his best chances of winning any enemy contact was for all subordinates to do exactly as told. Having since come to understand both 3GW and 4GW, he now sees the inconsistencies in that way of thinking. No Asian counterpart aware of the ancient Chinese strategies of the "false face" and "art of delay" can be beaten that way.[16] When first encountered, his unit will appear to be using a standard U.S. formation. Then, it will wait for the American outfit to make the first move. The Asian unit's initial array was in reality a feint. So, the first U.S. move produces little, and the original quarry ends up striking its tormentor from an unsuspected direction.[17] Should the foremost American fighters not quickly enough react to this unforeseen attack (the Asian's main effort) by reinterpreting their orders, their parent unit could suffer serious consequences. It may either fail at its mission altogether, or take so many casualties readjusting to actual circumstances as to make its final victory bitter-sweet.

Of utmost importance as any infantry element attempts to practice 3GW or 4GW is the "commander's intent." For often, only the spirit of his orders can be followed.[18] Short-range combat happens quickly. It's easier to ask for forgiveness than permission. Where seconds count, frontline fighters must often kill someone. But, all the while, they must realize that lethal force—by itself—wins few wars.

6 WHAT EVENTUALLY WINS MOST WARS

● If the kill ratio doesn't decide most conflicts, what does?

● Does the better equipped/supplied side always win?

Small-unit initiative can greatly diminish a foe's wherewithal.

(Source: FM 7-93 [1987], cover.)

The General Rule

Each war is different, and some have been won by highly un-likely means. Still, over time, the path to victory appears to follow a definite pattern. The side to lose a prolonged conflict is generally the one that runs short of wartime materiel. It happened to the Germans in WWI and the Japanese in WWII, though both armies enjoyed semi-autonomous squads with which to spearhead attacks and anchor defense matrices.

Might that also be why 3GW tries so often to bypass the foe's frontline troops—to more easily get at his resupply convoys and depots? Any damage to such "centers of gravity," in turn, restricts the amount of firepower he can bring to bear. With the advent of heavily disguised and sometimes below-ground ordnance production and distribution sites, a U.S. ground presence became the only way to win. The same thing holds true for both conventional or unconventional (guerrilla) warfare. In effect, there can be no consolidation without wide-spread occupation.

There are a few ramifications to this logistical reality for the best supplied infantry forces in the world. Among them are how their lowest echelons—those regularly to make enemy contact—can best contribute to the war effort. To do so, all American nonrates must first safeguard their own supplies/equipment, and then try to confiscate or destroy those of the opposition. So doing can be dangerous.

For example, after failing to retrieve a forward-deployed claymore in February 1967, a squad from A/1/4 was told to go back alone several miles to retrieve it. That it would have to follow the southern edge of the DMZ was not considered. Rumor had it that the Viet Cong (VC) had seized enough claymores from a South Vietnamese convoy early in the war to last them the remainder. With each mine spewing a lethal swath of steel balls, one more in enemy hands was too many.[1]

The Change Due to Asymmetric Warfare (AS)

Most armed conflicts are now being fought in an asymmetrical fashion—i.e., by opposing groups or nations with unequal military resources. "The weaker opponent uses unconventional weapons and tactics . . . to exploit the vulnerabilities of its enemy."[2] Unfortunately, the weaker side has been winning more often of late. That does not come as particularly good news to the self-described "strongest military" in the world. Its job is not to be strong *per se,* but to be victorious.

> Since Thucydides, the root principle of international relations theory has been that power implies victory in war. Thus, in asymmetric conflicts, the strong actor should almost always win. . . . Yet if one divides the roughly 200-year period covered in the Correlates of War data set, two related

puzzles emerge. First, weak actors were victorious in nearly 30 percent of all asymmetric wars. . . . Second, weak actors have won with increasing frequency over time.[3]
— *How the Weak Win Wars,* by Arreguin-Toft

Here, Toft attributes the term "strong" to the side with more "material power."[4] While the weak side may enjoy more resolve, he thinks an incorrect strong-side strategy more often creates the problem.[5] Unless that strategy can somehow circumvent all internal "vulnerabilities," a shortfall occurs when the two adversaries meet. In other words, the strong side pays the price for using the wrong tactics and equipment to counter the unconventional methods of its weaker opponent.

What asymmetric warfare *aficionados* often fail to mention is that the side with the most wartime materiel is often Western in orientation. Besides enjoying more than enough battlefield wherewithal, it does most things from the "top-down." Its opponent, on the other hand, is from an Eastern culture or extremely poor. Either background leads to a "bottom-up" approach to combat. Thus, if the Pentagon wants better to handle asymmetric warfare in the future, it must first field the most agile and self-sufficient small units possible.

The U.S. Marine Corps has had MW (essentially 3GW) as its official doctrine since the early 1990's. Among the axioms of this new way fighting is that firepower and surprise are virtually interchangeable on the battlefield. The more that Marines sneak up on their quarry, the less shooting they must do to finally suppress him. Because the weaker side has had little firepower from the outset, it has necessarily come to depend upon sophisticated small-unit maneuvers.

More Now Depends upon Tiny-Element Initiative

Most of America's adversaries—Communists, Islamists, and criminals—now operate from the bottom up. While far too freewheeling for a control-bent Western army, this alternative way of fighting can be quite effective. It depends more upon clever opportunism than brute force. For example, a series of successful attacks against enemy weak points are strung together to establish momentum.

Whereas, in the West, momentum is only attempted through a big knockout blow. One way tends incrementally to build up the confidence and proficiency of the individual fighter and his tiny infantry element. The other tends to give both an inflated opinion of their abilities. Through it all, the enlisted U.S. infantryman must remain constantly alert. His is a world of intermittent boredom and danger. He can be easily undermined by any number of things, not all of which are enemy generated.

The "Overly Applauded" Parent-Unit Umbrella

The apparent consensus in America is that each U.S. rifleman is so well trained and protected by his parent unit, that he will experience much less danger than his Eastern counterpart. But wouldn't the side that most often succeeds at tiny encounters have the best chance of overall victory? Most battles are just a series of engagements anyway, and each engagement made up of encounters. Without that overall victory, any U.S. casualties at all would be too many. So, how the opposing sides prefer to operate makes a tremendous difference. While tiny U.S. infantry elements come to depend almost entirely on their unit's edge in firepower, their less-well-equipped enemy counterparts develop surprise-oriented maneuver.

What happens to a heavily armed U.S. grunt who encounters a more agile and devious foe? Those wonderful young GIs can't shoot what they don't detect. Among the best ways of surprising someone is first to hide. On Iwo Jima, during one of the fiercest battles of all time, the average Marine rifleman seldom saw an enemy soldier.[6] Luckily, there's a nebulous factor that has helped GIs to overcome this handicap (but not without extra losses). Even seasoned veterans don't fully understand it. "Uncommon valor was a common virtue," is how Admiral Chester Nimitz described this intangible variable on Iwo Jima. What allowed those hastily trained Marines to still take a virtually impregnable island more probably lay somewhere between self-confidence and unit cohesion. The Leathernecks of that era would do anything for a fellow member of their own outfit. For up to 25 hellish days, they kept on fighting for each other until death finally granted far too many a reprieve.

Certainly, enough U.S. perseverance at the lowest echelons is just as powerful as enemy "resolve." As in sports, every battlefield combatant who keeps on fighting despite constant adversity still has a chance. That's why all U.S. riflemen should never stop trying. Many of their opponents are far too eager to die a glorious death. Still, a more tactical orientation might do those painfully mortal GIs a lot of good while operating near the edge of their parent-unit umbrella.

Shouldn't common sense play a role in all combat? Where orders allow it, a temporary withdrawal can be far more helpful to the overall war effort than a series of unsuccessful attacks. One leaves the individual fighter intact to fight another day, whereas the other doesn't. While individual fighters are generally easier to replace than supplies or equipment, an experienced one is invaluable. Of course, continuing to "try" requires staying alive. The authority for enlisted personnel occasionally to move backwards is not new to warfare. It was granted to lone German squads in 1917.[7] That's how the longtime defensive "state of the art"—a soft, strongpoint matrix—first came into existence.

Why this much squad agility scares most American leaders is hard to say. They have continually claimed that the U.S. fighting man is as smart, well disciplined, and brave as any enemy counterpart. If this be true, then the Pride of Ypsilanti and his pals could certainly be trusted to develop enough small-unit proficiency to win a low-intensity war. Only required, after all, would be enough leeway to move in any direction.

Or perhaps, it's the fear of atrocity that prevents those U.S. leaders from delegating enough authority to the infantry squads. Moral error in combat is a legitimate concern, particularly for any bottom-echelon grunt being directed to use more force than is really necessary to accomplish his mission.

PART THREE

THE NEW WAY'S NECESSARY PARAMETERS

"HONOR IS EVERYTHING. . . . YOU FOLLOW THE RULES OF WAR FOR YOU—
NOT FOR YOUR ENEMY. YOU FIGHT BY THE RULES TO KEEP YOUR
[OWN] HUMANITY." — WWI AERIAL-TACTICS INSTRUCTOR

(Source: As told to Franz Stigler by commanding officer Gustav Roedel during pilot training, from "Individual Honor," Jacksonville Daily News (NC), 3 February 2013, p. 27)

7 PROTECTING EACH U.S. COMBATANT'S HUMANITY

- Does the Pentagon worry about each GI's mental health?
- How well does the traditional way of fighting safeguard it?

All killing, however well justified, tends to erode one's humanity.

(Source: "Strong Men Weep," by David Lax, U.S.Army Ctr.of Mil.Hist., posted Oct.'01, from url: http://www.history.army.mil/images/artphoto/artchives/2001/avop10-01_2.jpg)

Virtue Need Not Come from Headquarters Alone

Everyone doing precisely as told in combat produces the most honorable result as long as the unit leader realizes all of his tactical options and then has all instructions fully disseminated. Unfortunately, one or the other may fail to occur. That's why U.S. ground force commanders have been given so much moral leeway over the years. If each continually does the best he can, the end result is thought to justify the means. Still, extra insurance on so important an issue would be nice. What if all subordinate elements were also to guard against ethical excess?

61

All GIs Must Avoid Moral Error While Doing as Told

Implicit in every U.S. military order is for the recipient to additionally comply with the Law of War. Should some unexpected moral quandary arise in its execution (like a pregnant woman in the way), the recipient is expected to resolve that dilemma.

The Armed Forces of the United States shall comply with the Law of War.[1]
— DoD Directive 5100.77

The Law of War basically spells out each service member's responsibilities under the Hague and Geneva Conventions.[2] For all U.S. Marines, the following restrictions apply:

(1) Fight only enemy combatants
(2) Do not harm enemies that surrender
(3) Do not kill or torture prisoners
(4) Collect and care for all wounded, whether friend or foe
(5) Do not attack medical personnel, facilities, equipment
(6) Destroy no more than the mission requires
(7) Treat all civilians humanely
(8) Do not steal or disrespect private property/possessions
(9) Prevent/report all violations of the Law of War.[3]
— MCO 3300.2

Battlefield Scenarios Are Seldom Static

All U.S. commanders further realize that local circumstances may change after their order has been issued, thereby requiring a few minor "on-the-spot" modifications. Where full compliance was not possible, few unit leaders would take exception to only the spirit of their original order being followed.

The idea of an instruction not being precisely obeyed might worry a high-ranking officer trying to build enough cooperation between varied units for a joint operation. But, it doesn't really concern a rifle company commander already in heavy contact with the enemy. One understandably focuses on a team effort, while the other cares mostly about defeating an opportunistic foe. The difference between winning and losing against such a foe can be so tenuous as to make a "lapse" in discipline a blessing in disguise. At such times, victory has more to do with reacting to a recently spotted enemy ruse than sticking with the original plan. Thus, it is only reasonable for all infantry commanders to offer some "wiggle room" to every subordinate element. The average Asian, Islamic, or criminal opponent likes to operate from the bottom up—namely, through "death by a thousand (seemingly inconsequential) razor cuts." In other words, the bottom-most U.S. echelon will first spot any change to the foe's agenda. That's why even the lowest-ranking fighter must be allowed some degree of initiative. It would minimally entail two things: (1) the chance to immediately report any unusual sighting; and (2) limited authority to do something on his own about that sighting.

A good example might be a shallow, yet perfectly square, indentation in the earth that a U.S. private spots while walking flank guard for his squad's patrol. That patrol is late getting home, and his immediate superior thinks all "new guys" stupid. The indentation is too big and square to connote a mine, so the private correctly surmises the opening to a below-ground chamber. If—without specific orders but in compliance with security responsibilities—that U.S. rifleman were to do a little quick digging, he might discover something of immense strategic importance. Were that something to be a big ammunition cache, it might go otherwise undetected and end up costing America the war. A grenade from that private might have made all the difference.

Such acts of lowest-echelon initiative will not normally come back to haunt the unit commander, providing all of his nonrates have been properly schooled on when and how to exercise it.

The Role of Humanity in Combat

As John Boyd was shown to believe in Chapter One: "The moral level [of warfare] is the most powerful."[4] That implies the edge goes to the side with the most moral objectives and ways of achieving them.

Longtime proponents of 2GW dwell much more on the indiscretions of opposition forces than their own. Their goal, after all, is to kill as many enemy soldiers as possible. Within that much expected lethality of result lies more chance for ethical excess. In America's most recent examples of urban combat, suspected enemy strongpoints were sometimes set alight. Unfortunately, the Geneva Convention Protocol of 1980 specifically discourages the use of an incendiary device where civilians might be present.[5] (See Figure 7.1.) The point here is not to read so much into the Protocol as to

Figure 7.1: GIs Cannot Cause Flames Where Civilians May Be
(Source: search.usa.gov public-domain image from this url: http://www.nps.gov/history/history/online_books/npswapa/extContent/usmc/pcn-190-003140-01/images/fig10.jpg)

discourage small-unit initiative, but rather to point out how the decreased lethality of 3GW might have precluded the decision. One following 3GW precepts would have bypassed the enemy's personnel to more easily get at his centers of gravity (supplies, command center, etc.). So doing can be a lot less risky. And it is incumbent upon every U.S. fighter to remain fully functional as long as possible.

PLAYING THE
LONG GAME

- Is it the Service member's job to look good, or be good?
- Does being good always help a military career?

Just reaching the battlefield can be excessively tiring.

(Source: http://search.usa.gov public-domain image from url: www.nps.gov/history/history/online_books/npswapa/extContent/usmc/pcn-190-003120-00/images/fig1.jpg.)

The Overall Strategy Must Be to Win the Conflict

To wage war, Western military organizations rely mostly on long-established bureaucratic procedure. Every headquarters learns of the situation from its intelligence branch and then tells each subordinate-unit commander what to do. After that commander issues his orders, all subunits use standard ways to perform their portion of the mission. But, whether each composite method has been actually effective is seldom questioned. That is automatically assumed to be the case. In essence, the reputation of the organization has taken precedence over the welfare of the nation. If things then go so

67

badly wrong in battle that no amount of casualty count manipulation can obscure them, the commander is relieved. But, any underlying procedural shortfalls within his unit are seldom addressed because they are—in all likelihood—Service wide. That's the downside of the standardization of procedures with which top-down military bureaucracies so doggedly pursue unity of effort. Then, they can continue to fight wars the same way for years without ever making previously noted adjustments. Meanwhile, their own members and the voting public continue to believe that the Pentagon is doing the best it can under the circumstances.

Squad Combat Is Not That Complicated

What fails to meet expectations inside an infantry or special operations squad is not as easy to sweep under the rug. People end up dead when outdated procedure is used under the wrong circumstances. Whether enemy soldiers can be more easily detected through thermal imaging or other "technological marvels" makes little difference to a wily opponent. With all the electronic paraphernalia that modern-day GIs must wear, he has little trouble detecting their approach.

Just as procedural adjustments are made by football teams at halftime, so must they be regularly determined and applied for infantry or special-operations squads in the heat of combat.

What's the Long Game Tactically?

The preferred role for each young infantryman would be to outmaneuver any direct opposition well enough to win the engagement. So doing would entail extra risk, and possibly having to fight on after being wounded. The first part would be logical (if not fully practiced) operating procedure for most U.S. grunts; the second born out of necessity or courage.

The U.S. Medal of Honor (MoH) has been won by all kinds of people for any number of reasons. Some of those people have come running up from their unit's rear as if providentially summoned to take charge of someone else's problem. Others, without hesitation, have made one risky move too many to save their buddies from almost certain death. But, the annals of history also contain episodes in which the recipient just keeps doing whatever it is that will finally allow him to complete his assignment. In effect, he continues to play the long game though every natural instinct says he can't. Such was case in one example from the Chosin Reservoir in Korea and another from Tam Ky in Vietnam. The exploits of these two MoH winners were chosen, because both have just recently been called to their final reward.

For conspicuous gallantry and intrepidity at the risk of his life above and beyond the call of duty while serving as a rifleman with Company F, in action against enemy aggressor forces. When all the other members of his fire team became casualties, creating a gap in the lines, during the initial phase of a vicious attack launched by a fanatical enemy of regimental strength against his company's hill position, Pvt. Cafferata waged a lone battle with grenades and rifle fire as the attack gained momentum and the enemy threatened penetration through the gap and endangered the integrity of the entire defensive perimeter. Making a target of himself under the devastating fire from automatic weapons, rifles, grenades, and mortars, he maneuvered up and down the line and delivered accurate and effective fire against the onrushing force, killing 15, wounding many more, and forcing the others to withdraw so that reinforcements could move up and consolidate the position. Again fighting desperately against a renewed onslaught later that same morning when a hostile grenade landed in a shallow entrenchment occupied by wounded marines, Pvt. Cafferata rushed into the gully under heavy fire, seized the deadly missile in his right hand and hurled it free of his comrades before it detonated, severing part of 1 finger and seriously wounding him in the right hand and arm. Courageously ignoring the intense pain, he staunchly fought on until he was struck by a sniper's bullet and forced to submit to evacuation for medical treatment Stouthearted and indomitable, Pvt. Cafferata, by his fortitude, great personal valor, and dauntless perseverance in the face of almost certain death, saved the lives of several of his fellow marines and contributed essentially to the success achieved by his company in maintaining its defensive position against tremendous odds. His extraordinary heroism

throughout was in keeping with the highest traditions of the U.S. Naval Service.[1]
— MoH Citation for Pvt. Hector A. Cafferata Jr.

Whereas Private Cafferata was just an ordinary rifleman, the next story is about the radio operator of an Army infantry platoon. While not technically grunts, such radio operators still perform a vital function by helping their commanders to coordinate the action.

Specialist Four Santiago J. Erevia distinguished himself by acts of gallantry and intrepidity above and beyond the call of duty while serving as a radio telephone operator in Company C, 1st Battalion (Airmobile), 501st Infantry, 101st Airborne Division (Airmobile) during search and clear mission near Tam Ky, Republic of Vietnam on May 21, 1969. After breaching an insurgent perimeter, Specialist Four Erevia was designated by his platoon leader to render first aid to several casualties, and the rest of the platoon moved forward. As he was doing so, he came under intense hostile fire from four bunkers to his left front. Although he could have taken cover with the rest of the element, he chose a retaliatory course of action. With heavy enemy fire directed at him, he moved in full view of the hostile gunners as he proceeded to crawl from one wounded man to another, gathering ammunition. Armed with two M-16 rifles and several hand grenades, he charged toward the enemy positions behind the suppressive fire of the two rifles. Under very intense fire, he continued to advance on the insurgents until he was near the first bunker. Disregarding the enemy fire, he pulled the pin from a hand grenade and advanced on the bunker, leveling suppressive fire until he could drop the grenade into the bunker, mortally wounding the insurgent and destroying the fortification. Without hesitation, he employed identical tactics as he proceeded to eliminate the next two enemy positions. With the destruction of the third bunker, Specialist Four Erevia had exhausted his supply of hand grenades. Still under intense fire from the fourth position, he courageously charged forward behind the fire emitted by his M-16 rifles. Arriving at the very edge of the bunker, he silenced the occupant within the fortification at point blank range. Through his heroic actions the lives of the wounded were saved and the members of the Company Command Post were relieved from a very precarious situation. His exemplary performance in the face of overwhelming danger was an inspiration to his entire company and contributed immeasurably to the success of the mission. Specialist Four Erevia's conspicuous gallantry, extraordinary heroism, and intrepidity at the risk of his own life, above and beyond the call of duty, were in keeping with the highest traditions of military service and reflect great credit upon himself, his unit, and the United States Army.[2]

— MoH Citation for Spec. Four Santiago J. Erevia

Longevity with Regard to the U.S. Rifleman

If American "snuffies" get any medal at all for their combat exploits, it's often the little purple one with black edges (signifying they have been killed in action). It makes no difference how fierce that fighting was, the lack of formal recognition for any heroics is almost always the same. That fighting happened quickly; it normally involved a lot of other people; and their commanding officer had little, if any, time between missions to research the details. In effect, that snuffy is like an indentured gladiator in a world where only his handlers get much credit. But, snuffies also have the broadest shoulders of all U.S. service personnel. The only reward they wanted was just to earn the respect of fathers and grandfathers. Theirs is the pride of an actual combatant, the one on whom winning or losing ultimately depends. Below is the story of a young Marine who found himself in a world of hurt, yet continued to play the long game in what would turn out to be one of the most crucial battles of the Vietnam War.

Upon the Hill of Angels

Missionaries may have called this place "Hill of Angels," because of how many people died there. In which war and for what cause, no one can remember. But, in May 1967, the men of 1st Battalion, 4th Marines (1/4) were about to find out how strategically important it was to the NVA. Con Thien Combat Base was on a 158-meter-high

71

rise some 10 miles northwest of the major U.S. installation at Dong Ha. Each could be just barely seen from the other. Only two miles below Vietnam's DMZ, Con Thien sat within a small indentation to that invisible boundary. (See Map 8.1.) It was surrounded by elephant grass and three types of trees that grew in clumps no taller than 12 feet. The highest part of the camp looked like a squat pile of red mud. This was to be the key bastion along the McNamara Line—a bulldozed firebreak that had been intended to limit enemy infiltration. As of May 1967, that firebreak was 200 meters wide and 10,600 meters long. It ran from Con Thien eastward to Gio Linh on Route 1.[3]

Unbeknownst to many of Con Thien's current occupants, 8 May was the anniversary of the fall of Dien Bien Phu to the Viet Minh in 1954.[4] That might help to explain some of the NVA precedents in ordnance that night (flame throwers). Yet, through the actions of three understrength Marine squads with a 1st Raider Battalion heritage, there would be no repeat of that debacle. After the outer defenses of Con Thien had been penetrated by the enemy, a tiny mechanized force carrying two of those three U.S. squads would deploy from its inner perimeter to try to plug the breach.

At 0245H on 8 May, Companies A and D with the Alpha [more likely Bravo] Command Group at Con Thien came under an intensive 82mm mortar attack, followed by a ground attack from the east in Company D sector. Sapper units breached the wire under cover of a mortar barrage with bangalore torpedoes and moved small units inside the wire. These small elements were heavily armed with satchel charges and TNT charges and used them to blow bunkers and trench lines. At approximately 0400H, two battalions of NVA attacked the perimeter through the breach made by the sapper units armed with flamethrowers, RPG [rocket-propelled grenade] . . . launcher and various assortments of small arms, explosives, etc. . . . Company A was directed to send a platoon reaction force to assist Company D as well as escort two LVTs [Landing Vehicles Tracked] and two M-42's [Army self-propelled 40mm anti-aircraft guns] with ammo resupply. *En route* to Company D's right flank, the right rear sprocket of the leading LVT became enmeshed in barbed wire, freezing and stopping the vehicle. The vehicle came under fire and the M-42's and one LVTH [probably just a plain LVT without the howitzer] were struck by RPG rockets and set afire trapping personnel inside. The other LVTH was set afire with a satchel charge. The penetration was limited and the breach in the perimeter was closed just prior to daylight.[5]

— 1/4's After-Action Report for 8 May 1967

John L. Coy was a member of the A Company squad riding the lead "Amtrac" of the rapid-reaction force. Here's how he then played the long game—not only to survive personally, but also to help his buddies defeat their nemesis.

I was in the [first] Trac that got hung up. . . . I . . . [had] traded with Perry and grabbed the gun [M-60] with three assault packs [portable ammo belts] when we loaded on [the Amtrac]. I was . . . going to be the first one to open fire. [T]hen we got hit. [A]n RPG came in the left side "if facing out[ward]," went threw *[sic]* the driver's abdominal area, and I had just stood up from a squat position. My right leg

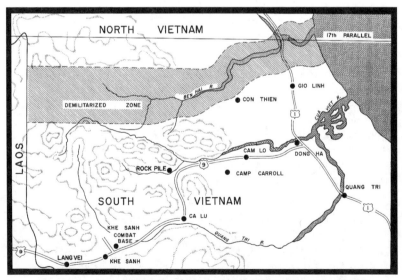

Map 8.1: Con Thien Was Only Two Miles from the DMZ
(Source: Map based on illustration designator "amtrac.org - bullalo03.jpg," from official website for 1st Amtrac Battalion.)

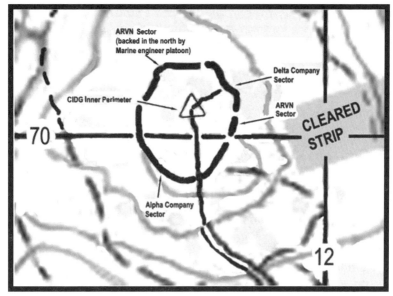

ARVN Sector
(backed in the north by
Marine engineer platoon)

Delta Company
Sector

CIDG Inner Perimeter

ARVN
Sector

CLEARED
STRIP

70

12

Alpha Company
Sector

Map 8.2: How Security Sectors May Have Been Assigned
(Source: Map based on "1:50,000 USGS, Viet.Series L7014, Map Sheet 6342-1"; McDonnell's article, Guthrie's e-mails; foxco-2ndbn-9thmarines.com/ConThienFSB.gif.)

was forward when the round passed threw my inner thigh
4 inches above my knee and filleted [my leg] from knee to
groin, also cauterized it, then made its way through a couple
more Marines and [finally] exploded. [I] lost consciousness
for a moment and when I came to, I was yelling to drop the
ramp. I emptied the assault pack [shot the M-60] and fell
on my knees to reload. Fire was everywhere. When the
Trac got hit again I was thrown forward. I saw the M-60 on
the "duster" [M-42] and jumped on the tread. Then, it got
hit and blew me off. When I looked up I saw some [people]
inside the Trac burning and remember Amos and Huckleberry with their backs to the Amtrac as the diesel fuel ran
on them and them screaming as they died. [I] made my way
back to the [last] bunker and got hung up in [barbed] wire.
I yelled [to] this Marine to pull me out as I reached up with

my left hand, and he yanked. [A] gook shot and killed him and shot me through [the] left elbow. Funny, I just this moment realized I had an AK-47 because I [then] shot the gook. [I] must have gotten it in between [the] Trac and wire. [I] did not know who pulled me. I crawled in[to] the bunker and another Marine was inside. I took my belt off and put it around my leg and cinched it off. [I] had a hole about the size of a nickle through my left elbow so I ripped off some of my t-shirt and plugged the hole. Then something bounced off my left ankle, and it was a grenade. So I kicked it, and it went off, putting shrapnel in [the] left side of [my] leg and hip. [It] took both legs [of the other Marine] off below the knees. I was knocked out for a moment, then tied off the Marine's legs. He was out. Then, [I] pulled sandbags over to hide him. I got out of the bunker and started moving [back] to my lines, and then I was in the air [for what] seemed like 5 or 6 minutes. So when I landed, it was in a small crater maybe smothered and I blacked out. When I came to, the sun was rising, and I am lying on my back looking between my feet. I still have this AK-47 across my chest and 3 gooks are running at me. Must have lost a lot of blood because I could not raise the weapon off my chest. But, low and behold, they were ARVN [Army of the Republic of Vietnam] and dragged [me] to where Martin was. They took me to [a] medivac site [that] gave me water and morphine. [I] was told to guard a couple [of] prisoners. Next thing I remember was [being] above Con Thien in [a] chopper and seeing all the dead bodies and the flames. We were all shooting the shit earlier that [previous] day—Amos, Huckleberry, Perry, Labega, Kreh, Sanders, and Findlay. Then they were gone. Anyway, when I saw my name misspelled in the book, I had to laugh. My hometown paper had me as John L. Cole because Mom was married to a Cole at that time. [He is also misrepresented as John McCoy in *Gung Ho*].[6]

— former PFC John L. Coy USMC, 22 May 2016

As the quote reflects, John had sought no additional acknowledgment for his actions that night, only to correct the record. Yet, what he went through simply to survive should be of great help to future infantry enlistees. The members of another Alpha Company squad had been on the second Amtrac and almost totally incinerated by a flame thrower as they tried to exit. Suffice it to say that they and John's pals would have also "played the long game," had they made it through the first few horrific minutes. They would have hung in there out of a sense of duty to God, country, Corps, and each other. That their leaders had been spared another Dien Bien Phu was a direct result of that enlisted dedication. The Corps' lowest-ranking infantrymen are—through their very mission—always ready "to close with the foe."

9 NEVER SUCCUMBING TO A DEFENSIVE MINDSET

- Will a static defense always stop a proficient attacker?
- Might elasticity and counterattack instead work?

Most wars are won by attacking; bayonets permit total surprise.

(Source: *OPNAV P34-03* [1960], p. 406.)

The Constant Temptation

It's been said that the defense in football earns championships. One also hears that the Japanese were beaten in the Pacific by waiting for their Banzai charge, and that modern-day "Force Protection" is vital to any foreign intervention.

Many armies that have insisted on continuous offensive action have been badly hurt: (1) the French and British in WWI by German machineguns; (2) the Japanese in WWII by trying to sneak too many follow-on troops through a squad breach in the U.S. barbed wire at Guadalcanal; and (3) the NVA in Vietnam by "Puff the Magic

Dragon" gunships. Still, a widely accepted axiom of war is that every good defense must necessarily include a number of offensive aspects.[1]

A Difficult Study to Do

Promoting a proactive defense is one thing, but showing how to do one with minimal force is another. One of the best Western examples may be the Finns' use of "*Motti* Warfare" against the massive Soviet incursion of late 1939. While this defense did result in considerable loss of Russian life, it would rely more on weather and terrain than bomb and bullet. The Finnish example thus demonstrates how tiny infantry elements without any help from tanks, planes, or heavy artillery can effectively stymie a huge and fully supported invasion force. To do so, those elements need only a limited supply of small-arms ammunition, demolitions, and antitank mines. The "lesser degree of force" then comes through their use of smaller caliber weaponry, with its reduced potential for fratricide, collateral damage, and momentum-limiting procedure.

The Historical Backdrop for *Motti* Warfare

"*Motti*" is Finnish military slang for a totally encircled enemy unit, or center of resistance.[2] It has been borrowed from the Swedish word for "measure," as it was applied to cubic-meter stacks of firewood that had been left to be collected later. The reference to *mottis* in military tactics then came to mean the formation of "bite-sized" enemy units.[3]

Associated with *Motti* Warfare was a multifaceted maneuver for destroying a more powerful enemy invader piecemeal. Used extensively by the Finns in their Winter (Russo-Finnish) War of 1939-40, it was especially effective against a motorized enemy force moving up a forest road. Once committed to such a confining avenue, all participants could at some point be trapped. Where water features or heavy woods precluded any interference from enemy tanks, a good-sized Finnish light-infantry unit would intercept the column to stop and isolate it. Then, through a combination of mines, ambush, and trees across the road, the Finns would sever the stalled procession of vehicles at several susceptible places. Light-infantry detachments could then move through those cuts to double-envelop and harass all resulting segments. As those segments or *mottis* became sufficiently weakened, a special assault unit from the Finnish reserve would be brought to bear against them, one at a time. If any *motti* proved too strong to be safely annihilated, it was simply left to run out of food, fuel, and ammunition. After being resupplied by air, some of the larger Red Army *mottis* did hold out until the end of the Russo-Finnish War. Still, they had become unavailable for any other operations.[4] Every such column reduction rewarded the Finns with enough good news and wherewithal to continue waging the lopsided war.

The largest *motti* battles of the Winter War occurred at the Battle of Suomussalmi (in the Kainuu region half way up Finland's eastern side). There, three Finnish regiments enveloped and destroyed two Soviet divisions and a tank brigade that had tried to move up a narrow conduit through the forest.[5] Along the Raate-Suomussalmi road, Finnish forces subsequently captured 43 tanks, 71 field guns, 260 trucks, 1170 horses, 29 antitank guns, and other badly needed ordnance and supplies.[6]

Motti Strategy Was Profound

The degree of offensive insight behind a *"motti* style" of defense was considerable. The beleaguered Finns had discovered that an invading force of any size and strength—in close terrain—eventually follows a route that makes it destructible through a relatively safe plan of attack.

The basic tactical doctrine assumes that the enemy will follow avenues of approach which will make him vulnerable to encirclement, after which his forces are to be destroyed piecemeal. This is accomplished by forcing the enemy to follow routes outlined by either natural or artificial obstacles until he reaches the terrain selected for his annihilation.[7]
— *Combat Forces Journal,* January 1950

Of course, the Finns had also realized that they did not have enough wartime materiel to defeat the Russian bear. Their only hope was to steal some of his, while delaying the invasion long enough to secure a favorable peace accord. So, within the overall Finnish strategy behind *Motti* tactics lay the ultimate reason of its success. That success depended more upon Russian enclave occupants losing heart than getting shot. It had thus ventured into one of the scarcely appreciated nonmartial arenas of 4GW—the effect of weather, terrain, and mobility on enemy psychology. In the process, some of the Finns' infantry maneuvers had become so initiative driven as still to be considered unorthodox in Western military tradition. Evidence of that will be presented shortly.

The closest modern-day facsimile to *Motti* Tactics may be the "Swarm Tactics" that Chechen rebels used on the Soviet mechanized column that tried to enter Grozny on 31 December 1994.[8] Like the autonomous squads that had made the narrow enclave along the Volga River at Stalingrad impervious to German attack in late 1942,[9] those Chechen "swarmers" had no headquarters control. And, it was through this same lack of Westernized "organization" that such a resounding victory may have been possible. That Soviet armored brigade at Grozny was to lose 4800 of 6000 personnel, 20 of 26 tanks, and 102 of 120 armored personnel carriers in 72 hours.[10]

Combining Warfare with Natural Circumstances

These pre-WWII Finns had been faced with having their tiny country finally gobbled up by a huge and expansionistic neighbor. What they did in response would allow a modern-day (and well-equipped) American expeditionary force to more widely distribute its military might.

Two factors contributed to the Finnish army's improbable holding action of 1939-40. Both had to do with the traditionally Oriental concept of cooperating with, as opposed to resisting, the various forces of nature.[11] That harnessing of the environment would stretch beyond cold weather and inhospitable terrain to the inherent strengths and weaknesses of "human nature." In the West, recent inductees are considered not only a danger to established procedure, but also to themselves. In Finland, they were more wisely thought an asset—at least to the extent that they followed their collective instincts. This willingness to depend upon the individual Finnish fighting man and his tiny group, is what made the strategy of freezing, starving, and demoralizing a very tough Soviet opponent actually feasible. If that Finnish optimism had been misplaced, many more friendly casualties would have resulted from all the short-range infiltration of *Motti* Tactics.

The later Grozny facsimile would, of course, involve urban terrain. The rural terrain of 1939 Finland had been much less restrictive. There, a light-infantry unit had moved to one side of the approaching Red Army column. Mostly motorized or mechanized in heavy woods, such a cavalcade became essentially road-bound. So, after halting the string of vehicles, the Finns attacked at its rear to block any retreat, resupply, or reinforcement. After reconnoitering and pestering the stalled procession for a while, they attacked through several natural gaps. Then, Finnish detachments widened those gaps and moved through to double-envelop all column segments or *mottis*. Next, tiny patrols from each detachment "hugged" and continued to wear down their respective enclave. (See Figure 9.1.) While this gradual reduction process usually took the form of limited, pinpoint probes, it was occasionally supplanted by a larger assault against a particularly lucrative target. The combined effect of all this Finnish offensive activity would then prove both demoralizing and unhealthy to many of the besieged Soviet troops in subzero temperatures.

Of note, no drones or other advanced electronics had been used by the Finns, nor would they have helped them any. When it comes to closely harassing enemy defensive positions, no amount of "heat signature" or other electronic surveillance will make sneaking around two-man (sometimes roving) listening posts or between individual fighting holes any easier. Thus, as hard as it may be for contemporary Pentagon buyers to reconcile, no amount of modern defense industry gadgetry will allow U.S. forces to now do what the Finns were able in 1939. The scale at which it occurred is simply too small to be mastered by anything other than the individual soldier's God-given potential.

Those Finns Exposed to Evolutionary Doctrine

Most Finnish troops were familiar with German tactical principles and had German training manuals in their possession. They were thus fully "familiar with the ideology of the post-WWI German soldier."[12] Because *motti* meant "encircled enemy center of resistance" in the local dialect,[13] the Finns may have also recognized it as a "center of gravity." This is a Clausewitzian term that became an integral part of the MW doctrine developed by the WWI Germans and then adopted by the U.S. Marine Corps in 1991.

> Center of gravity is those characteristics, capabilities, or localities from which a military force derives its freedom of action, physical strength, or will to fight.[14]
> — *Ground Combat Operations,* MCWP3-1

Within the 3GW methodology of MW, centers of gravity were among the most lucrative physical targets of the "main effort." It was through this main effort that overall victory could finally be achieved.

Figure 9.1: Unknown Soldier Drawing from the Winter War
(Source: After asking permission of pinterest.com, from image designator "b0a98fccc5628b9163cedb39ff43e0cc.jpg," © pinterest)

[The] main effort . . . is designed to successfully attack an enemy . . . critical vulnerability, or center of gravity.[15]
— *Ground Combat Operations,* MCWP3-1

. . . To win, we must focus [most of our] combat power toward a decisive aim. There are two . . . concepts that help us to think about this: centers of gravity and critical vulnerabilities. . . .

Thus, we direct our main effort against a center of gravity through a critical enemy vulnerability, exercising strict economy elsewhere.[16]
— *Warfighting,* MCWP1

Most Western armies operate mostly from the top down and strictly rely on their "command and control" structures and communications networks. As such, both characteristics become vulnerabilities associated with a center of gravity. Besides campfires and field kitchens, the Finnish troops had also been targeting Soviet headquarters elements and communication lines.[17]

The Genius Was in the Details

First, the approaching procession of Soviet vehicles was reconnoitered by small Finnish patrols. Then, at an appropriate place where the road-bound invader would not want to be ambushed (like while crossing a water feature), he was. After the front of the column was pinned down, the remainder was cut off at its very rear from any outside support. Other road-crossing attacks simultaneously divided the entire force into sections.[18] The double-envelopment of each section created a *motti*. And that *motti* could be methodically weakened by tiny Finnish teams. Many of the most important particulars have luckily been preserved by history.

A long break in the enemy column offers an ideal place to cut the column. . . .

When all supporting [light-infantry] weapons are in position . . . , the breakthrough detachment rushes to execute the cut. Then, the cut is widened to 500 to 700 yards. A strong road block is established at the flank of the break. The engineers lay mines and establish obstacles [often an abatis of trees] which deny this stretch of road to enemy use. . . . All enemy communication lines are cut and the task of isolating the assigned sections *(mottis)* . . . begins. . . . A previously designated element of the attacking unit crosses the road to begin the envelopment of the enemy column from the opposite side of the road. One element remains on the near side . . . and begins the envelopment of the enemy column [there]. . . .

In general, the operations of all cutting points are executed simultaneously, day or night. This creates maximum confusion of the enemy and prevents strong counterattacks.[19]

— *Combat Forces Journal,* January 1950

Extent of Squad Involvement in *Motti* Tactics

A "quarry-hugging" harassment mission is most logically the job of a squad-sized element. Only something that small can sneak through the protective array of opposition outposts. After finding a soft spot in the enemy's main body, it then conducts a limited, pinpoint attack of some kind. That attack can range anywhere from a lethal spray of automatic weapons fire to a well-placed thermite grenade or "molotov cocktail." Because no ground-gaining assault had actually taken place, the attackers can then easily withdraw to do more damage elsewhere.

In military usage, *motti* refers to an enemy group surrounded by Finnish patrols each of from eight to twelve men armed with automatic arms.[20]

— *Combat Forces Journal,* January 1950

The strength of patrols varies from a squad to a platoon. Their missions demand speed and surprise; consequently, they are lightly equipped and travel on skis. . . . They are armed with light automatic weapons and hand grenades, and carry light demolitions. . . .

Following the initial reconnaissance, they attack the enemy from all directions. This creates the illusion that the attacking force is everywhere, and the enemy never knows where to expect the next attack. . . . Enemy security posts are

avoided. Patrols hold fire until within close combat range of the main enemy force. . . . Favorable objectives are marching troops, bivouacked units, motor columns, and supply dumps. Guerrilla patrols . . . [sometimes] plant mines . . . in the rear of the enemy. . . . Each patrol carries out more than one mission; after attacking at one point, it moves rapidly by ski and attacks a different part of the column.[21]
— *Combat Forces Journal*, January 1950

Especially targeted by those mostly squad-sized Finnish patrols had been Red Army campfires and field kitchens—usually through the use of standoff small-arms fire. That tended to weaken the resistance of any "nonlocal" to the sub-Arctic winter (as cold as minus 40° Fahrenheit at night).[22] Without enough warmth and sustenance, many of the Soviet troops—from the more temperate Ukraine region—began to suffer the affects of frostbite, hypothermia, undernutrition, and poor morale. To what extent such factors contributed to the final casualty count has not been quantified. Of particular note here, however, none were the direct result of much military force.

Impromptu Attacks Take "On-the-Spot" Decisions

Repeatedly to probe those heavily defended Soviet *mottis* without getting injured, the Finnish squads would utilize *Sissi* tactics. Only together would those two concepts "permit small, battle-hardened units to fight on even terms against numerically superior forces."[23]

Sissi combat denotes small unit actions which have the objective of hitting the enemy at one point. Each participant is briefed on the objective, and [then] the method of execution is left up to the group.[24]
— DA Pamphlet 20-291
Effects of Climate on Combat in Russia

Only very rarely in British, French, and American military operations is the final plan of attack left up to each tiny maneuver element. All three of the West's most experienced armies would have more probably required their squads closely to follow some standardized procedure. Might that be what all three now need to change to finally acquire "state-of-the-tactical-art" offenses and defenses. NCO group decisions do, however, constitute an integral part of the fully tested and refined "bottom-up" squad training supplement in the appendix to *Global Warrior*.[25]

The Occasional Big-Unit Assault

To further demoralize the beleaguered Red Army column, Finnish units of company size or larger would conduct fully reconnoitered and rehearsed assaults against particularly vulnerable objectives. This so worried the Russians that they would increase the size of their security outposts (further weakening the actual *mottis)*. Some historians have falsely concluded that such assaults were conducted in "human-wave" fashion. More probably, they were done through first stalking the quarry as in U.S. "fire and movement" without actually shooting (perfectly silent leapfrog advances), and then a short combined rush at the very end. Under cover of darkness, such troops in hooded white cloaks and moving in noiselessly through the trees would have been hard to detect.

The enemy is approached on skis in small, well-separated groups echeloned in depth. The crouching skiers, camouflaged in snow shirts, rapidly approach the enemy in short bounds. Just before the final rush, they kick off their skis.[26]
— DA Pamphlet 20-292, *Warfare in the Far North*

There is evidence of at least three different kinds of Finnish assaults against Russian positions. First was that from a fake *motti* after its hidden direct-firing cannon had blasted the dugouts and tanks of a nearby Russian neighbor.[27]

Then, there was that of a surprise assault unit within each Finnish regiment. The Finnish Army had already incorporated German Stormtrooper assault technique from WWI,[28] but would not have shown it to every rifleman. This type of noisy assault generates its surprise from wire-breaching explosives and bunker-aimed grenades simulating a mortar barrage.

Finally, three dozen Finnish soldiers on line could have simply followed through on their sentry-stalking routine to secretly enter a Russian *motti* (through short-range infiltration). Such a thing would have been silently accomplished without supporting arms, and more easily by trained commandos. That may be why the first attack outside the village of Suomussalmi had lacked any preparatory indirect fire to give the enemy warning.[29] It has been said that no artillery was available on that particular occasion, but not having to call or adjust fire would have allowed a special commando unit to more quickly move on to another objective.

A small detachment of fifty men, consisting of . . . skiers and wilderness hunters was sent to the battlefield. This raid force constantly roaming through the woods, undertook operations, striking here and there, time and again, killing . . . enemies, knocking out a tank, supply trucks or other vehicles. Before long, the narrow road was blocked by motionless steel giants.[30]
— *A New Era of Warfare,* by Duncker

The Finnish troops who raided the Russian-held Murmansk Railway during the Continuation War (part of WWII) are known to have received commando training.[31]

Motti Warfare Also Works in Warm Weather

At the Battle of Ilomansti in August 1944 during this same Continuation War, the Finns again used *Motti* Warfare against two much bigger and better-armed Red Army contingents.[32] That battlefield was also heavily forested and crisscrossed by connecting rows of rivers, lakes, and swamps. As a result, few roads ran through it.

A Very Interesting Antitank Procedure

These Finns had a slightly different, but equally unorthodox, solution for immobilizing enemy tanks. Something like it would be used by the Japanese in the Pacific,[33] and then very probably by the NVA/VC in Vietnam.

Men are placed in pairs, one on each side of the road over a distance of 75 to 100 yards. Each man digs a shelter for himself and thoroughly camouflages it. Tanks, which generally drive along the road in platoons of 5 vehicles each, are allowed to advance to a point where the first tank is abreast of the last pair of men. Here, it is destroyed by a mine drawn across the road in its path. This is usually a signal for the other pairs of men to take advantage of the resultant confusion and simultaneously destroy the other tanks. To accomplish the destruction of such a tank group, terrain is selected where it is difficult for the tanks to leave the road, as in dense woods or on stony ground.

A mine drawn across the road is constructed of four ordinary tank mines coupled together with wire, the distance between each mine being about 1 inch. A wire about 25 yards long is attached to each end of the series of mines, and by means of this wire they are drawn across the road. The parts of the wire lying on the road are camouflaged. Since the bottom of the mine is indented and does not slide easily, a plank or strip of tin must be placed underneath. As the tank approaches, the mines are drawn onto the road in front of it.

Stopping of the first tank in the column is the signal for a general attack. An antitank mine is thrown in front of the track of each tank and combustible bottles are thrown simultaneously. Immediately after the detonation of the antitank mine and the immobilization of the tank, a grenade thrower jumps or climbs onto the tank and throws a hand grenade through the roof shutter of the turret.[34]

— U.S. Intel. Report on Finnish Tactics in WWII

More Modern Terminology

For the U.S. military theorists of today, *Motti* Warfare would simply be considered a 4GW variant of "distributed operations." While somewhat new to contemporary American strategists and tacticians, this way of beating a larger and better armed opponent would have made perfect sense to the Minutemen who embarrassed the British at Concord.

Not surprisingly, several of America's less-well-equipped foes have also over the years come to rely on a close facsimile to the *motti* decimation procedure. For example, the NVA appear to have used it on a largely road-bound contingent of U.S. Marines who attempted to approach the DMZ on "Operation Buffalo" in 1967 during the Vietnam War. At least, that's what the civilian chronicle of this operation would indicate.[35] Not only was that column segmented and then attacked piecemeal, but the Finnish trick of dragging a mine across the path of a tank may have also been applied to the relief force.

The Undeniable Strength of *Motti* Warfare

Through incredible daring and enough delegation of decision-making authority to small light-infantry contingents, the Finnish Army had done nearly the impossible in 1939-40. This was no small Red Army attack.

Soviet troops totaling about one million men attacked Finland on several fronts [late in 1939]. The heavily outnumbered [and poorly equipped] Finns put up a skillful and effective defense that winter, and the Red Army made little progress.[36]
— *Encyclopedia Britannica*

Not only had the massive Soviet invasion been temporarily halted, but the Finns took surprisingly few casualties in the process. In the Battle of Suomussalmi, the fully supported Red Army contingent suffered 10-times-more casualties than the under-equipped and outnumbered defenders. Of note, those Finnish defenders needed no tanks, planes, or heavy artillery to get the job done.

In this battle a Finnish provisional division with a strength of 11,750 attacked two [reinforced] Red Army divisions with an aggregate strength of 38,000. Finnish casualties were 900 killed, 1,770 wounded, and 30 prisoners of war, [for a] total of 2700. Red Army casualties were 27,500 killed and 1500 captured, [for] a total of 29,000.[37]
— *Combat Forces Journal*, January 1950

Map 9.1: Finnish Areas Conceded in 1940
(Source: Wikipedia Encyclopedia, s.v. "Winter War," under provisions of GNU Free Doc. Lic., designator "Finnish_areas_ceded_in_1940.png," © n.d.)

At no point had the hard-pressed Finnish forces resorted to the strictly defensive mindset that would have ultimately spelled their doom. In January of 1940, the massive invading army finally breached the Mannerheim line through an overwhelming application of supporting arms. Still, Finland would remain mostly intact after conceding the Karelian Isthmus, some land north of Lake Ladoga, and a little more in the more northern Salla region to the Soviets as part of the Moscow Peace Treaty of March 1940. (See Map 9.1.)

Offensive Spirit Tempered by "Real-Time" Reason?

Throughout that long ordeal of whittling down a strong enemy column, the Finns were cautious. To ensure the tactical logic behind most attacks, they let each set of participants decide how best to conduct them at the last moment. What those participants had just learned from close range of that target's current circumstances then virtually guaranteed success ("recon pull" in MW terms). In some cases, that collective decision may have been to bypass the target altogether. Most of the offensive debacles of history have come from too doggedly following a remotely envisioned attack plan. That plan's lack of situational detail was then never corrected, and headquarters slow to realize the maneuver's futility.

Would *Sissi* Tactics Work for GIs

It's unfortunate that *sissi* sounds so much like "sissy," because those tiny teams of Finnish soldiers who used *Sissi* Tactics against heavily defended *mottis* were in no way lacking in virility. In fact, most modern-day American counterparts would jump at the same chance to personally damage the foe. Recent U.S. inductees are at first as independently minded as the 1939 Finns, so the same degree of initiative is at least possible. But, GIs are not as comfortable out-of-doors. So, minimally, they would need more wilderness survival instruction.

The relative deficiency within American infantry squads may date back to their first written manuals around WWII. It has been reputably reported that all tactical procedures were made intentionally simplistic to encourage subsequent modification for each scenario. Unfortunately, such rationale fails to mesh with what regularly transpires at the lowest echelon of a "top-down" military organization. There, recent enlistees are thought to be so lacking

NECESSARY PARAMETERS FOR THE NEW WAY ───────────────

in discipline as to have to follow every published maneuver exactly. Most soon deduce that any initiative—however well intended—may be punished, and that deviating from what the manuals show may be treated as a violation of orders. Still, specially indoctrinated U.S. infantry squads and commando teams could still avail themselves of the advanced *sissi* methodology. A last-second group decision will almost always work better than a pre-arranged plan of attack, because it takes into account the latest situational nuances. But beware, collective decision making only works for a dozen or fewer personnel. To conduct even a limited attack, those personnel will still need a full array of prerehearsed squad, fire team, buddy team, and individual techniques. Only then, will they have enough "muscle memory" to execute whatever they together decide to do. Each element would additionally require the authority to "transcend technique" during the actual attack to compensate for any still-unforeseen circumstance. What makes so much tactical potential possible is something that Western "big-picture thinkers" too often under-respect—what being small in combat can get accomplished.

Luckily, most American police departments do not suffer from this same under-use of small units. However, their frontline personnel are shown how to handle 4GW problems.

PART FOUR

WARFARE CONVERGING WITH LAW ENFORCEMENT

"A MAN IS NOT [FULLY] JUSTIFIED BY OBSERVANCE OF THE LAW, BUT ONLY
THROUGH FAITH IN JESUS CHRIST [OR HIS TEACHINGS]."
— GALATIANS 2:16

(Source: Attributed to the Christian Bible.)

10 U.S. GRUNTS NOW NEED POLICING SKILLS

- How might law enforcement abilities help the rifleman?
- Why is he deemed too preoccupied to need them?

It takes a police investigation to reveal actual enemy agents.

(Source: "Vietnam Suspects," by Ronald A. Wilson, U.S. Army Center of Military History, posted October 2006, from this url: http://www.history.army.mil/art/A&I/1006-4.jpg.)

All Armed Conflict Subject to Some Rules of Law

The current Law of Land Warfare is actually an amalgamation of any number of declarations, conventions, treaties, and judgments since before the U.S. Civil War.[1] Most famous among them are the Hague and Geneva Conventions. All such limitations are well beyond the scope of this book. Suffice it to say that no combat element of any size can: (1) torture a prisoner; (2) shoot one trying to surrender; or (3) fight by overly painful or perverted means. Normally that latter provision has to do with germ-coated arrows or spikes, poison gas, etc. But, to the extent that it applies to flame must be further examined. Most 21st Century hostilities are projected to occur in urban areas—i.e., those inhabited by civilians. That's because of changing demographics and the lower intensity of 4GW combat. As a direct result, all deployed U.S. soldiers and Marines must now be careful not to set anything on fire. One of the biggest temptations of urban combat is to burn down an enemy strongpoint to keep from having to assault it. If so much as one civilian is hiding in its basement, or that fire spreads to another occupied building, the GI who lit the match will now be in violation of international law.

Old-fashioned flamethrowers have not been part of the U.S. arsenal since 1978, when the Department of Defense (DoD) unilaterally stopped using them. They were of questionable effectiveness in modern combat and a public relations hazard due to the horrific death they inflicted. However, their wartime employment has only actually been banned against military targets within a concentration of civilians.[1] In effect, most army use of flamethrowers was stopped by the Convention on Certain Conventional Weapons (concluded at Geneva on 10 October 1980 and entered into force in December 1983. Washington subsequently ratified the Prohibitions or Restrictions on the Use of Incendiary Weapons (Protocol III), on 23 December 2008.[2]

Still, there are other ways of dispensing flame. Besides thermite and white phosphorous (screening) grenades, there is now the M202A1 Flame Assault Shoulder Weapon—a launcher of incendiary rockets. This weapon had mostly been relegated to military storage by the mid-1980's, but it has since been spotted on the weapons inventory of some American units deployed to Afghanistan.[3]

Because of these new limitations, the modern-day American "snuffy" must be much more careful about what he does in battle than his predecessors. If he can be punished for violating the new parameters, then why not show him how most successfully to operate within them? The full spectrum of minimal force comes to mind, along with how the U.S. rifleman might legally respond to a foe infraction.

The Elephant in the Room

Of course, every U.S. military command—from the Pentagon

on down—firmly believes that it adequately prevents combat excesses. For each conflict, its lawyers come up with specially tailored "Rules of Engagement." But, such Rules normally cover broad issues, like "Don't damage religious structures" or "Don't respond to village-originated sniper fire with artillery." Such warnings are most helpful to company commanders and above. While they may filter down to the troops, they seldom address the most common dilemmas faced by each individual fighter.

As a member of a 2GW-oriented military, the average U.S. soldier must only do as told to escape alleged improprieties. That's assuming he fully heard and then understood his instructions. Unfortunately, he must still watch out for "particularly inhumane missions." Illegal orders need not be obeyed, and so doing could get him punished. In other words, the average GI has been placed—by well-meaning superiors—between a rock and a hard place. To make his rather fragile existence even more tenuous, the headquarters that has ordered a questionable act is often so far removed from its consequences, as never to suspect wrongdoing. That burden—along with any residual feelings of guilt—falls squarely upon the shoulders of the frontline skirmisher (or person of lowest rank).

Some Moral-Decision Training Thus Necessary

Only once in U.S. Marine Corps history is there any record of something like moral guidance being formally attempted. All of Carlson's WWII Raiders received an "Ethical Indoctrination." Unfortunately, it only "ensured that each man knew what he was fighting for and why."[4] There is no evidence of it containing any advice on the moral pitfalls of infantry combat. The individual Raider's job likely stayed the same as every other infantry or special operations snuffy to this day—"to close with and destroy the enemy."

Dedicated proponents of America's traditional way of war (2GW) would argue that the individual rifleman cannot be bothered with the moral ramifications of all actions. The order he is about to obey has already been screened for its ethical correctness. To do the right thing, he has only to execute it. Unfortunately, most warfare now takes on more of a 4GW nature in which inhab-

Figure 10.1: Civilians Must Be More Carefully Handled in 4GW
(Source: Courtesy of Sorman Information and Media, from "Soldf: Soldaten i falt," p. 144, © 2001 by Forsvärsmakten and Wolfgang Bartsch.)

itant sensibilities make a big difference. In effect, all combatants must—like good policemen—always safeguard the local population.

Policing Skills Long Sought for Infantry

Ever since President Truman referred to America's response to North Korea's invasion of South Korea as a "police action" under U.N. (United Nation) auspices, Unconventional Warfare (UW) experts have stressed the correlation. No war since Korea or Vietnam has been as heavily contested on the battlefield, but all obey the same underlying principle—the "hearts and minds" of the people matter. Civilian populations tend to be more gently treated by peace-loving policemen than by combat-oriented soldiers. That's how the two roles have started to converge. Why hasn't the U.S.

military so far adapted to this new reality? The answer is quite simple. The Pentagon has become so fixated with more firepower and control over those who wield it, that it has trouble fielding a 4GW-qualified unit.

> [Aggressor] 4GW forces thrive on [the] devastation and insecurity of the people; . . . [I]ncreasing the devastation and insecurity, as . . . with most [Western] military approaches, is counterproductive in that they do nothing more than create greenhouses for terror. . . . [Instead] needed . . . are small near[ly] autonomous units of truly light infantry that can play the role of police . . . rather than occupiers in the greenhouses of terror. . . . [Such a deployment] requires a military paradigm shift away from centralized control and micro-management, much as the late Col. John Boyd often argued.[5]
>
> — *Unconventional Warfare Review*, January 2007

Martial 4GW Too Spread Out for Normal Combat

What happens in the martial arena of 4GW is of lower intensity and farther apart than the enemy initiatives of traditional warfare. In a worldwide War on Terror, each Improvised Explosive Device (IED) explosion, suicide bombing, or assassination is most productively treated as a local crime. As would neighborhood police, the nearest U.S. contingent first collects all evidence of each incident. Then, within its own intelligence gathering apparatus lies a good chance of identifying both perpetrator and motive. For example, it learns through local contacts whether any strangers have entered the area (or residents left). That then constitutes a good start on the list of suspects.

How to conduct a full investigation is just as straight forward. One way is to gradually eliminate suspects by determining which have valid *alibis*. To do so, the U.S. unit first seals off the location of the incident to pedestrian and vehicular traffic with yellow crime scene tape or its equivalent. After interviewing onlookers and sweeping this enclosure for clues, it determines whether what happened was an attack on the Coalition or otherwise motivated. As any beleaguered nation becomes more volatile, there will be more organized crime and acts of civil disobedience. Either one can

trigger a shooting or explosion. While every execution-style killing might seem like an attack against a government sympathizer,
it may instead be the result of a drug deal, gang feud, extortion
scheme, or marital infidelity. Both the Communists and Islamists
will try to exacerbate the chaos. Inherent in their style of warfare
is encouraging so many incidents that Coalition forces can't react
to them all. In that way, they uncover (remove Coalition protection
from) various strategic targets.

So, instead of dispatching an armored column to each occurrence, Coalition headquarters should allow local outposts to initially
respond. When all incidents are first referred to the nearest U.S.
contingent, more of the Coalition's manpower will be available for
the protection of dams, electricity grids, fuel depots, and other public
service projects. All will be crucial to some semblance of order on
the streets.

How much the members of that American contingent know
about police work will largely determine whether it can assume
this new role. Of particular importance will be their knowledge of
basic criminal investigative aids and practices. The whole idea is
to solve as many crimes as possible at the local level, so that nation
as a whole does not descend into anarchy. For the full spectrum of
"infantry-appropriate" police procedure, see Chapters 9 through 12
of *Dragon Days.*[6]

Of course, a law-enforcement-focused infantry squad could no
long use all of its traditional firepower. Now, maneuver would be
at a premium.

11 SWATs Can't Use All U.S. Infantry Tactics

● Why aren't all military maneuvers helpful to policemen?
● Which ones would prove counterproductive?

SWATs can't heavily bombard anyone, so they rely more on surprise.

(Source: public-domain material, from U.S. Army's "War on Terror Images," at this url: http://www.history.army.mil/books/wot_artwork/images/19b.jpg.)

Police Mission Now More Like That of the Military

Countering an overseas criminal faction should be like fighting insurgents, but there has been a distinct difference over the years for Americans. For deployed U.S. security personnel, the first foe has enjoyed more legal protection than the second. Inside the U.S., the Miranda Warning displays some of the more subtle rights of a suspected law breaker: (1) to remain silent; (2) to consult with an attorney; (3) to have the attorney present during questioning; and (4) to have a free court-appointed attorney. Elsewhere, criminal suspects would not likely receive as much courtesy.

However, Washington has yet to deem any foreign insurgent worthy of protection under the Geneva Conventions (having not yet ratified the 1977 Protocols).[1] If non-uniformed separatists don't qualify for Geneva Convention protection either, then America's Armed Forces might occasionally help a brutal dictator to further subjugate his population.

Such a "policy paradox" would make it difficult for U.S. service personnel to comply with all internationally recognized Laws of War. Among the Geneva Convention combatant rights are the following: (1) to be allowed to surrender after raising one's hands; (2) not then to be tortured for information; and (3) not finally to be summarily executed. In 1980, the U.N. Convention on Certain Conventional Weapons added a provision to "prohibit the use of weapons that are indiscriminate or of a nature to cause superfluous injury or unnecessary suffering."[2] Whether Washington plans to pass this new benefit along to foreign insurgents is not yet clear.

But Police Cannot Use Same Degree of Force

America's military regularly expends more ordnance than all of its police departments put together. That's because lethal force is less often authorized in law enforcement than in warfighting. A suspect must be putting someone else's life in immediate danger to be normally shot by police. Even then, innocent bystanders are carefully avoided. That means the traditional U.S. military *mantra* of "firepower superiority" has limited application to American police work. If there is the remotest possibility of a single civilian in the same building with someone to be arrested, then nothing must be done during that apprehension to risk a structural fire. If, on the other hand, armed perpetrators have entered a school, then the first responders must go immediately in after those gunmen without waiting for instructions, backup, SWATs, or anything else. In fact, any police assault (forceful entry) in urban terrain tends to be much more intensely executed than its military counterpart. That's why its lead element needs bullet-proof shields.

In essence, America's policemen are more aggressively performing certain types of missions than its infantrymen or special operators. Certainly, one faces more public scrutiny than the other. However, both segments of society are equally brave, so the reason for the police increase in speed and danger must have to do with the expectation of more surprise. With the advent of helicopter drop-offs, heavy boots, and unwieldy electronics, U.S. grunts and commandos have all but forgotten what it's like to completely surprise a defender. Even if they could sneak up undetected to within rushing distance of those manning a prepared enemy position, their assault procedures have been standardized for so long that an appropriate response might be ready.

Meanwhile every municipality's police department has been developing its own ways of operating, so that no prospective criminal can precisely predict what he will face for the first time from local authorities. That gives all U.S. SWAT team members more of a chance at surprise and momentum than the average GI. Undoubtedly at fault is the inertia endemic in any big bureaucracy. During a raid, most U.S. commandos are so closely linked by radio with their headquarters that much personal initiative is virtually impossible. What all too often takes its place is slow, methodical, and fully predictable behavior.

Some U.S. Infantry Maneuvers of No Use to Policemen

Most active policing gets transacted through one- or two-man patrols, "backup" swarms, and squad-sized SWAT attacks. So, almost all military patrolling procedures are applicable, except for ambushing. During any surprise confrontation in law enforcement, the suspected criminal must be verbally apprised of a police presence and then given the chance to surrender. Only an escaped felon can be legitimately shot while trying to run away (such rules may vary between States). U.S. military ambushes are not traditionally like that. Maximum firepower gets first applied to the "kill zone," and then bodies are searched.

Some military assaults are also applicable to law enforcement. Yet, the customary "base of fire" would not usually be possible because of the chance of stray bullets striking civilians. More appropriate to police work would be a completely quiet form of entry more common in Asian militaries—i.e., a short-range-infiltration attack. Sneaking into an upper story or bottom center of a contested building, for example, could greatly facilitate the building's eventual seizure. Such a maneuver also has a better chance of retrieving hostages alive. See *Homeland Siege* for the latest research on that subject.

Of course, policemen also continually defend things. It can be a whole community, or just key witnesses before a trial. But again, that defense must be accomplished with little, if any, firepower option. While a state-of-the-art "soft strongpoint matrix" might have some utility in law enforcement, a makeshift perimeter of roving outposts would more easily provide the protection. One makes little provision for collateral damage, while the other at least tries to spare noncombatants. Nor would "close defensive fires" have any police utility.

Which GI Moves Do Have a Cop Application?

A few useful police variants to standard U.S. military tactics come immediately to mind: (1) chance encounters while patrolling; (2) street crossing; (3) building entrance; (4) room take-downs; and (5) cordon operations. But, almost always, less firepower must be applied by law enforcement personnel. That generally means only well-aimed shots. Because there are never enough snipers, every officer must be so trained.

The military masters of less shooting do so out of limited stores of ammunition. For encirclements and double envelopments (neither of which are authorized by U.S. military doctrine), they make sure their quarry is above or below all attackers (elevation-wise). For example, in the woods, the quarry is either on a tiny hillock, or all attackers up in trees. If everyone in the encircling force is then careful to stay behind cover while they shoot, they can easily avoid fratricide. By the same token, the average police seizure of an urban floor or room would work much better if all participants (wherever they are on its periphery) stay in the prone position and then only crawl forward. That way, any legitimate opposition can be eliminated by shooting upwards.

The military chance-contact maneuver of "fire and movement" also has a slightly different police application. Both involve closing with an enemy contingent of undetermined size up imaginary lanes. When properly executed, no friendly moves until there is a diversion elsewhere. Nor does any friendly stay upright long enough for an adversary to "draw a bead" on him. Through requiring constant rehearsal, this form of hasty attack will work on any uneven ground that is devoid of barbed wire. The military version can be easily converted to a "cover-and-stalk" police version. In other words, there would be no firing at all unless some of the stalkers are spotted. After such a maneuver to within 20 yards of a quarry, that quarry would be so surprised and intimidated as probably to throw up his hands in surrender. The silent assault by white-clad Finnish skiers through snowy nighttime woods in Chapter 9 would have been quite similar. But, in the "cover-and-stalk" model, all attackers take turns moving from tree to tree. Within lightly forested terrain, defenders will have trouble detecting a motion signature this randomly piecemeal, even in the daytime.[3]

Might This Help to Refine America's Way of War?

While more firepower would contribute very little to future law enforcement, U.S. infantrymen could better perform 3GW and 4GW with some policing skills.

That's because a cop gladly sidesteps any local trouble makers to get at his suspect (as in 3GW), and a cop tries never to hurt innocent bystanders (as in 4GW).

PART FIVE

FULLY EMBRACING A HIGHER FORM OF COMBAT

"[AN] EPOCHAL SHIFT [IN HOW WARS ARE FOUGHT] HAD OCCURRED . . . IN THE SMALL VILLAGE OF BINT JBIEL . . . AND . . . DEFILE OF WADI SALUKI [IN 2006], WHERE HEZBOLLAH FIGHTERS AMBUSHED AND DESTROYED A BATTALION'S WORTH OF ISRAEL'S BLITZKRIEG HEAVY TANKS. . . . [IN THE FUTURE,] SKILLED INFANTRYMEN WILL MAKE MECHANIZED WARFARE A RELIC OF THE MACHINE AGE."
— MAJ.GEN. R.H. SCALES U.S. ARMY (RET.)

(Source: Maj.Gen. Robert H. Scales, U.S. Army (Ret.), "Infantry and National Priorities," *Armed Forces Journal*, December 2007, pp. 14-17)

12 3GW CONDITIONING AND TACTICS

- Are drone-fired missiles enough against ISIS?
- Which ground maneuvers need to be added?

Personally attacking a foe by surprise causes no collateral damage.

(Source: MCRP 3-02H [1999], fig. 1-2.)

Everyone's Forgone Conclusion

While Washington sincerely wants its 21st Century wars to be less gory, it still plans to fight them through technological advances in firepower. Any suggestion of more maneuver along the ground has been met with the argument that light infantry (however tactically adept) won't be able to stand up to enemy armor. But such "heart-felt protectors of U.S. life" may be unaware of the latest battlefield developments. As pointed out by Maj.Gen. Scales in the Part Five quote, light infantry can now be combined with nearly invisible and remotely controlled anti-armor devices.

A More Comprehensive Style of War Is Thus Possible

So far, no 21st Century conflict has involved any grandiose land battle. Nor has its occasions of extreme violence been constant. Yet, almost all of America's attempts to adapt to this new environment with a less risky and more humane way of fighting have revolved around new technologies. While major steps in the evolution of small-unit tactics occurred during WWI (in response to the machinegun),[1] the Pentagon has yet to institutionalize them. In essence, it still practices a "higher-tech" version of 2GW—killing as many enemy soldiers as possible through more carefully targeted munitions. Unfortunately, the only war to have been recently won that way was the one against tiny Serbia in 1999. A similar bombardment of Mummar Gadhafi's Libya in 2011 merely resulted in another failed state.

Thus, while definitely helpful to the U.S. economy, the Pentagon's way of adapting to this new reality has enjoyed only limited success on the battlefield. It would seem that the hearts and minds of a foreign population are every bit as important to defeating terrorism as they were to counterinsurgency. Through shortfalls in intelligence, too much collateral damage still occurs no matter how "smart" the missiles and bombs become. William S. Lind, the U.S. father of 4GW and Marine Corps MW (a 3GW variant) may have finally put his finger on the difficulty. According to him, "[A] Second Generation military has no chance of victory in a Fourth Generation war."[2] Like the opposition in Vietnam, ISIS [Islamic State of Iraq and Syria] has been conducting 4GW—albeit a particularly warped version.

ISIS remains an anomaly to most Western strategists—a bottom-up Islamist entity with the combined attributes of a criminal enterprise and rebel army. In the martial arena, it has become a force to be reckoned with. To complement a natural propensity for loosely controlled swarm tactics, ISIS needs only the captured supplies and equipment of already vanquished foes. Yet, it still dabbles in all three of the nonmartial arenas of 4GW. Politically, as a self-proclaimed caliphate, it discourages all foreign opposition—through the mass executions of any group that opposes its territorial ambitions. Economically, it draws enough operating funds from oil wells captured, drug flow facilitation, and hostage ransoming. In the religious/psychological arena, it claims to be the only valid Salafist movement. Then, through misinterpretation of the *hadiths*, it tries to justify the horrific beheadings of Western journalists or aid workers and burning of at least one Allied pilot.[3] While the religious appeal of such brutal executions may be limited, their psychological impact has been considerable. When combined with sophisticated social-media outreach, it produces both fear and (in certain misguided circles) admiration. What then results is an endless stream of new recruits. Such activities bear all the earmarks of 4GW.

Yet, to beat ISIS (as cold blooded as it is), Allied forces must accidentally injure very few civilians, irrespective of their political or religious affiliations. That means state-of-the-art ground maneuvers, instead of the all too convenient bludgeoning with supporting arms.

> In most Fourth Generation situations, it is more important *not to kill* the wrong people than it is to kill [the] armed opponents. . . . Any time an innocent person is wounded or killed . . . , his family and clan members may be required by local culture to take revenge. Whenever that happens, Fourth Generation opponents are likely to get a new stream of recruits.[4]
> — William S. Lind, U.S. father of MW and 4GW

Mr. Lind's implication is painfully clear—to best impede ISIS recruiting, the Allies must use less force. Instead of continuing to bomb areas in which noncombatants work or live, it must only go after ISIS fighters who have somehow been lured out into the open. To occupy their Syrian capital of Raqqa with minimal civilian casualties, something like the unexpectedly fast NVA attack on Saigon would have worked better than the indeterminately long Allied assault on Mosul.

The Communist Lesson

To avoid the casualties of openly assaulting a city, the Red Asian military leader secretly infiltrates it. First, some of his best troops covertly occupy its middle and blend in with the local populace.[5] Then, once key buildings have been captured, those troops attack outwards toward the city's edge.[6] While NVA armored columns did strike toward the center of Saigon in 1973 to reinforce already present commandos, they didn't really have to. The North Vietnamese call this type of urban maneuver a "blooming lotus." It effectively outflanks a Western-style exterior perimeter.

This methodology was developed in 1952 in an assault on Phat Diem. Its key characteristic was to avoid enemy positions on the perimeter of the town [3GW]. The main striking columns move[d] directly against the center of the town seeking out command and control centers. Only then were forces directed outward to systematically destroy the now leaderless units around the town. . . .

This approach contrasts sharply with Western doctrine, which traditionally would isolate the town, gain a foothold, and systematically drive inward to clear the town [2GW]. This sets up a series of attrition-based battles that historically make combat in built-up areas such a costly undertaking [for residents as well].[7]

— "'Urban Warrior'—A View from North Vietnam"
Marine Corps Gazette, April 1999

4GW Requires a Full 3GW Capacity

3GW is not the only successor to attrition (2GW) warfare. 4GW came next, though the interim method was never fully mastered by the West. Bypassing a foe's strongpoints to more easily get at his strategic assets has gone by a number of different names over the years, among them Maoist Mobile Warfare (from the 1930's).[8] Because this way fighting seeks to destroy enemy materiel, it tends to avoid not only manpower concentrations, but also enemy contact in general. That's why it depends so heavily on advanced small-unit maneuver. For a "bottom-up" Eastern society, tactical improvements at the lowest echelons of a military organization come far more easily than for a "top-down" Western society.

These [modern] challenges can be met only by demanding that our national-level-policy and planning staffs look at war from the ground up rather than the top down.[9]

— Maj.Gen.Robert H.Scales,U.S.Army (Ret.), 2010

3GW and the U.S. Marines' new doctrine of MW are largely synonymous. In MW, one avoids an adversary's battlefield bastions to more easily get at his logistic and control apparatus. To do so, it watches for: (1) surfaces and gaps; and (2) centers of gravity. Then it applies: (1) focus of main effort; (2) speed and surprise; (3) "recon pull"; (4) mission-type orders; and (5) commander's intent.[10] If 2GW were as helpful to modern warfare as 3GW, the Marine Corps would not have switched its doctrine to MW in 1990. Unfortunately for the Corps, a full 3GW capacity has proven unexpectedly elusive. In a country that demands full compliance with the civilian leader's directives, it has failed to decentralize control over its own lowest echelons enough to achieve that capacity.

The "4GW-Important" Side-Benefit of 3GW

By avoiding violent contact wherever possible, 3GW limits injury not only to innocent civilians, but also to enemy combatants. The latter is one of the least-acknowledged prerequisites of the more moral way of fighting envisioned by America's premier military strategist—Col. John R. Boyd."[11]

In order to be legitimate, the "defense" must be carried out in a way that causes the least damage and, if possible, saves the life of the aggressor.[12]
— Pope John Paul II

The Transition from 2GW to a Higher Form of War

The elevated degree of headquarters' control that is endemic to 2GW can be difficult to eliminate. This is best illustrated through two examples from history.

At the Battle of Sedan in 1940, the lower echelon initiative inherent in 3GW allowed the German Panzers to prevail. Over and over at decisive moments, elements of the 3GW Wehrmacht (mostly its NCOs) took action while their French counterparts waited for orders. What the French did was tactically sound, but often too late.[13]

In *Fighting Power,* Martin van Creveld illustrates why Third Generation MW doctrine cannot be fully embraced by a Second

Figure 12.1: The Marine Raiders of WWII
(Source: Official recruiting poster, image designator "post_usmc_168th-birthday_ww2.jpg," retrieved from U.S. Nat. Archives and Records Admin. by www.bluejacket.com.)

Generation, inward-focused, process-ridden, centralized institution.[14] 3GW minimally calls for the decentralization of control over small-unit training and operations.

GIs Still Too Ill-Prepared and Hamstrung for 3GW

As per Martin van Creveld's painful but accurate conclusion, U.S. units may never become very good at MW or 3GW without supplementary conditioning and tactics. Yet, U.S. infantry forces need not scrap all their time-honored 2GW methods, only add a few of the 3GW variety. Sadly, the Asian Communist Armies seem to have already discovered this foolproof way of limiting resistance to change. The People's Liberation Army (PLA) of Mainland China requires that every infantry element down to the squad level be able to quickly switch between static attrition, mobile maneuver, and guerrilla warfare.[15] The guerrilla part of this requirement is what instills enough initiative and confidence in their troops for small groups to operate semi-autonomously (perform the Chinese version of 3GW).

U.S. precedents for this type of 3GW training are few. U.S. infantrymen have been mostly trained in following orders and firing their weapons. While guerrilla warfare and E&E are two aspects of UW that apply to infantrymen,[16] only the Marine Raiders of WWII have had this kind of preparation before facing a more numerous foe. (See Figure 12.1.)

In fact, the Raiders may have been the first U.S. troops to be formally trained in any kind of UW (as all U.S. special operators now should be). Former Raiders remember speed marches, nighttime stealth, hand-to-hand combat, obstacle crossing, etc. They also recall most of their instruction being conducted by their own squad leaders and platoon sergeants. The extent to which composite element techniques were addressed during these individualized sessions is important. Enjoying a better learning dynamic than standardized training, such sessions among frontline personnel would have resulted in more surprise-oriented technique. One former 3rd Battalion Raider remembers "recon-pull-type" attack missions (approaching Japanese base camps with the help of local citizens), and point men not being allowed to fire their weapons to preserve the element of surprise.[17]

The Corps' official Marine Raider Training Center became operational at Camp Pendleton, California, in early February 1943. Under the leadership of Lt.Col. James Roosevelt, Carlson's vision initially influenced the curriculum—with guerrilla warfare classes supplementing those on more conventional individual skills.[18] Freewheeling aggressor duty also took the place of "canned" exercise participation. But, giving more autonomy to the rifleman and his fire team conflicted with the U.S. rank system and was therefore on borrowed time.

Within the unit training at Carlson's 2nd Battalion, individual Raiders were then encouraged during "one-on-one" self-defense exercises to come up with their own way of initially deceiving an onrushing assailant. This harkens back to the ancient Chinese concepts of "false face" and the "art of delay."[19] That same mindset would certainly influence how those Raiders executed their small-unit maneuvers.

A Modern-Day Sequel to Such 3GW Training

Any contemporary U.S. outfit attempting to move between enemy strongpoints on an active battlefield would first risk plunging fire from both flanks. Then, it might face encirclement and annihilation. Initially required for such a dangerous maneuver would be long-range infiltration (that accomplished obscurely by squad-sized units). Each group of fighters would then have to be ready to tackle an enemy force many times their number. That might take defending against a human-wave assault or breaking out of an enemy cordon — all without any supporting arms. These are far more sophisticated endeavors than any U.S. manual presently explains. All American squad leaders will further need more tactical-decision making experience, battlefield authority, and ways to augment their limited portfolio of techniques.

After some of that same self-defense orientation experienced by the WWII Raiders (except this time against several assailants in a row or at once), contemporary GI's could take full advantage of a "bottom-up" training program. Through such a program — without any previous knowledge of the evolution of squad tactics — they could quickly develop state-of-the-art technique for whatever circumstances they expected to encounter. The only requirement would be that their collective opinions be field tested against simulated casualty assessment or some indicator of surprise (speed, stealth, or deception). The "bottom-up" training progression in the first appendix to *Global Warrior* accomplishes that.[20] Then, to perform 4GW, they would need only less lethal force.

13   4GW CONDITIONING
_____ AND TACTICS

● Why is 4GW so difficult for the Pentagon to perform?

● How might GIs de-escalate the violence in a foreign war?

It takes talking with local residents to make allies out of them.

(Source: FMFM 2-1 [1967], p. 115.)

No Easy Task

The U.S. father of 4GW has gone so far as to say that any Pentagon attempt to intervene in the internal 4GW of another country will almost certainly fail. He claims there are too many strategic factors working against such an effort. To the peoples of other nations, U.S. troops represent a foreign state, a different culture, and often another religion. Their very presence thus undermines the power of the government being assisted.[1] Because most GIs are not yet fully qualified for 3GW, William S. Lind sees no way that they can wage the next higher form of warfare anywhere but at home.[2] Luckily, he does admit to gangs and other criminal elements often creating an environment overseas in which a 4GW attack can more easily happen.[3] So, while not sophisticated enough culturally, ideologically, or politically, to help other countries to wage their own 4GW, GIs could still help them to remove its precursors. However, those young Americans would have to conform to Mr. Lind's preferred way of a host country resisting 4GW attack—the "de-escalation" of violence.[4]

As noted in the last chapter, the two expansionary entities currently behind most of the world's problems (the Communists and Islamists) are both waging 4GW. So, only required of most U.S. foreign-assistance contingents would be some policing know-how, no in-country footprint, and minimal force. Nor could any participating U.S. service member be a party to anything corrupt, high handed, or otherwise unbecoming of the state being supported. While certainly a tall order, that would make some sort of 4GW-related U.S. military assistance still possible. That's extremely fortunate for the Free World, because China, Iran, and now Russia are secretly behind much of that expansion.

Something Like 4GW Has Been Around a Long Time

The extension of armed conflict into nonmilitary activity is not new. Some 500 years before the birth of Christ, Sun Tzu was talking about all the ways a war might be won without any actual fighting. More recently, the American public watched on television as GIs met political, economic, and religious/psychological resistance in Vietnam, Iraq, and Afghanistan. Now, 4GW's martial arena is said to have hosted several advanced warfare variants—to include Guerrilla (GW), Unconventional (UW), Irregular (IW), and Hybrid (HW). Because successfully waging this more comprehensive "kind of strife" (4GW) does not require the foe to be mastered militarily, it can be quite difficult to counter. Its mostly Eastern *aficionados* will sometimes allow a martial-arena loss, just to gain some advantage on one of the nonmartial objectives.

It is true that Asian "bottom-up" cultures more easily develop enough initiative-driven, light-infantry expertise to wage 4GW.[5] But, it would be unfair to say that no Western nation could add enough bottom-up input to its mostly top-down methodology to match the feat. The Germans did it while trying to win WWI,[6] and the Finns did it again while trying to counter the massive Soviet invasion of 1939-40.[7]

On 26 January 1918, *Attack in Position Warfare* was published for the [German] commanders of units larger than battalion size. It talked of a battle mission type of orders that told subordinates what to do, but not how to do it. The work pointed out that "each attack offers opportunities for self-designated activity and mission-oriented action *[initiative]*, even down to the level of the individual soldier."[8]
     — *Stormtrooper Tactics,* by Gudmundsson

The most important command principle [for the Finnish army of 1939] was the German system of decentralized command. . . . With these mission-type orders, small-unit leaders (and even soldiers) were delegated powers to exhibit their initiative and independent action. The use of common sense and flexibility were encouraged, as were "bottom-up" improvisations.[9]
     —"New Approaches to . . . Warfare,"by Tuunainen

America's Biggest 4GW Handicap

Certainly the Pentagon's apparent relegation to "only those things which are military" has made it hard for deployed U.S. commanders to insure enough of the nonmartial accompaniments to any modern mission. When asked about how things were going in Afghanistan, Secretary of Defense Rumsfeld and other military officials would often say, "We don't do drugs."[10] Neither did the Central Intelligence Agency (CIA).[11] But, that's just from too little coordination between governmental departments, not from an endemic weakness of all Western republics. Might America have never been very good at 4GW because of too strict a delineation of responsibilities between bureaus? If that were true, there would be a simple solution. First, the President directs a more holistic approach to all overseas intervention. Then, the Pentagon starts holding weekly briefings at which all other agencies are told how they could help with the war effort. Long-term 4GW need not be totally choreographed as long as all participants measure the success of their efforts, and then refine or replace those not working. While admittedly difficult within a Western bureaucracy, such a thing is still possible

Possible 4GW Conditioning for the Troops

To make no footprint at all in a foreign country, U.S. military contingents would have to do the following: (1) be very small and widely separated; (2) require no U.S. supporting-arms or logistical in-country support; (3) be only loosely controlled by their own headquarters; (4) wear local garb; and (5) have some mission other than military intervention. Further to participate in the preferred "de-escalation model,"[12] all participating U.S. personnel would have to learn—like most police do—how to resolve local confrontations without having to kill someone.[13]

World-class light infantry easily follows the first four of the above parameters.[14] To minimally qualify, U.S. grunts would only need further instruction in two UW capabilities: (1) how to hide when about to be overrun; and (2) how—with no supporting-arms assistance—to break out of an enemy encirclement. To comply with the fifth parameter, those U.S. grunts could serve in beleaguered nations as specialty law enforcement trainers. Then, just as long-time policemen do, they would soon become quite adept at minimal force.

Foreign Police Outpost Augment

To maintain order in especially dangerous parts of the world, local police outposts require paramilitary training. U.S. infantry squads could provide that training while being temporarily stationed there. Some regional indoctrination might be necessary, but it would not have to be much more extensive than what U.S. Marine embassy guards regularly receive. Such "temporarily reinforced" outposts could then help host-country governments at a number of different locations: (1) near contested polling stations; (2) astride drug conduits; (3) where it is too risky for local and U.S. businesses to compete with Chinese counterparts; (4) within gang-infested areas; and (5) along trade routes through restive regions.

U.S. Peace-Keeping Squads Reduced the Graft in Vietnam

According to *Life Magazine* in 1967, American squad-sized components of Combined Action Platoons (CAPs) worked against local "graft" in South Vietnamese villages—with its inevitable links to Saigon.[15] Only really necessary was a way those squads could quickly report any "regime-emissary" excess up their own chain of command. In that way, all U.S. service personnel were able to maintain their own moral integrity, though Vietnamese police, army, or militia members occasionally stooped to theft, rape, torture, or summary execution.

American Marine Generals Lewis W. Walt and Victor H. Krulak had been the brilliant "godfathers" of this CAP Program. Still considered—by most counterinsurgency experts—to be the only way through which the Vietnam War could have been decisively won, it effectively turned the Maoist method in upon itself. One of its unexpected side benefits was the indirect production of the first truly light infantrymen the Pentagon had seen since Carlson's Raiders.[16]

In 1967, a 2nd Battalion, 4th Marine Regiment inspector described the early CAP role in this way. "Their mission was to protect the village against Viet Cong infiltrators and to assist in the general pacification programs." The latter included everything from medical and construction aid to protection against enemy confiscation of food and conscripts. The CAPs around the Phu Bai Marine Base had too little preplanned artillery to keep from being overrun,[17] so a 360° buffer zone was instead established—of tiny roving ambushes. This would almost completely eliminate the possibility of collateral damage.

Somewhat later, 1st CAG headquarters published the following CAP objectives: (1) to find and destroy local VC and VC infrastructure; (2) to protect assigned villages and friendly infrastructure; and (3) to attack the conditions supporting the insurgency through civil action, psychological operations, and population and resources control. They were undoubtedly to complement Gen. Walt's previous guidance: (1) to protect Vietnamese authorities; (2) to provide military training to the PFs (Popular Force militiamen); and (3) to collect intelligence. But, something of great future significance also happened. By 1970, III MAF Headquarters was calling the CAPs an "aid to local law enforcement."[18]

Too Risky a Mission for Present-Day GIs?

With the CAP program, might the precedent for modern Pentagon 4GW assistance to foreign nations have been already established, tested, and refined? A friendly compound in a rural village would pose the same defensive challenges as a police outpost within an urban neighborhood. The CAP program may have resulted in a few U.S. casualties, but its degree of success more than made up for them. He who is not willing to risk any lives at all in war will have a very hard time winning one. That is the unfortunate price of participation.

The official casualty statistics seem to indicate that less than 7% of all the CAP compounds were ever overrun.[19] Of the 14 men in each U.S. contingent, no more than a third would have been inside their compound on any given night.[20] So, where fewer than four Marines died, the compound defenses can be assumed to have held.

The CAP program was born in August 1965. By August 1967, there were 75 CAPs and another 39 authorized. Between January and August 1967, 15 all-out attacks were made on those platoons, with four suffering "heavy casualties," according to *Life Magazine*.[21] However, the official casualty statistics for that period show only one or two being overrun (having suffered four or more killed in action (KIA).[22] This *Life* article goes on to claim that Echo-2 in the village of Hoa Hiep some 12 miles north of Da Nang had been "overrun" in November 1966.[23] But, there may be a considerable problem with semantics here. Of the six Marines in that village at the time of the attack, only one had been killed and four wounded. That sounds more like the VC had penetrated the CAP compound and then exited without bothering to consolidate their gains. If this were the definition of overrunning an Allied position, then every American base and permanent outpost in Vietnam was about to be overrun repeatedly.[24]

Only one or two fully compromised units out of 75 is a very respectable record. Those same casualty statistics show only 11 more compound defense collapses over the next four years.[25] By 1969, the number of CAP platoons had reached 102.[26] At the time of the program's demise in 1971, as many as 2,200 U.S. service personnel may have been involved.[27] Even Gen. Westmoreland (proponent of the subsequently adopted "search-and-destroy-sweep" strategy) later admitted in his memoirs that the Combined Action Program had been one of the more "ingenious innovations developed in South Vietnam."[28] Yet, it would be the former Marine Raider who best envisioned its potential.

Of all our innovations in Vietnam, none was as successful, as lasting in effect, or as useful for the *future* as the Combined Action Program [italics added].[29]
— Maj.Gen. Lewis William Walt USMC

Those 20th Century CAP Marines hadn't received any instruction on how to hide while being overrun or single-handedly break out of an encirclement. Future "foreign-police-outpost" reinforcements will.

The CAP Defense Method Involved Less Force Than Usual

A foreign village friendly to the U.S. is normally protected by a barrier of barbed wire and the overwhelming bombardment of any attacker. Through the 3GW defense preference of ambushes in series, those Vietnam era Marines better safeguarded their villagers' livelihood, mobility, and tranquility.

PART SIX

ADVANTAGES OF THIS LESS LETHAL APPROACH

"WE HAVE PERFECTED OUR WEAPONS; OUR CONSCIENCE HAS
FALLEN ASLEEP; AND WE HAVE SHARPENED OUR IDEAS TO JUSTIFY
OURSELVES. . . . AS IF IT WERE NORMAL, WE CONTINUE TO SOW
DESTRUCTION, PAIN, [AND] DEATH." — POPE FRANCIS

(Source: BRAINY QUOTE AT THE FOLLOWING URL: HTTPS://WWW.BRAINYQUOTE.COM/TOPICS/WEAPONS)

14 FEWER WARS THAT ___ GO ON FOREVER

- Why—since 1953—has America's wars taken so long?
- How much does its normal way of fighting affect this?

After six years of trying, the Pentagon has yet to capture Joseph Kony.

(Source: FM 100-20 [1981], p. 198.)

Too Much Killing Is Known to Be Counterproductive

Most military professionals readily agree that open warfare should only be pursued as a last resort. That's much of the reason behind political and diplomatic processes. But Pope John Paul II is not the first world leader to have said that as few enemy soldiers should be killed as possible once active fighting breaks out. Sun Tzu did so too—long before the time of Christ.

> Only when the enemy could not be overcome by these [political] means was there recourse to armed force, which was

applied so the victory was gained: (a) in the shortest possible time; (b) at the least possible cost in lives and effort; (c)
with infliction on the enemy of the fewest possible casualties
[italics added].[1]
— Sun Tzu, *The Art of War*

Intensive Bombing Makes Little Difference to Certain Foes

Most Vietnam War veterans now realize that their conflict
did not turn out well. The fault was not theirs, however, but that
of Washington—in its poor choice of overall strategies. One need
not dig too deeply to find its source. Hadn't Gen. Westmoreland's
"search-and-destroy-sweep" proposal fully complied with the
Pentagon's longtime preference for overwhelming firepower? Unfortunately, fully orchestrated "sweeps" will little disturb an elusive
enemy. After dropping more bombs during the Vietnam War than
in all of WWII, America and its allies then still managed to lose the
conflict.[2]

The total tonnage of bombs dropped over North Vietnam,
South Vietnam, Cambodia, and Laos came to about 8 million
(. . . [over twice] the tonnage used in all of World War II).[3]
— *Vietnam War Almanac*

While such a comparison still raises the "hackles" of many who
gave it their all in Vietnam, it is not without precedent. In December 1945 the *U.S. Strategic Bombing Survey* reliably reported that
German industrial production had actually increased during the
Allied bombing campaign.[4]

None of the [later] bombing did any good. German industry
went underground and spread out.[5]
— member of Strategic Bombing Survey team
Last Days of World War II on History Channel

The same unfortunate result then happened again when some
600,000 tons of bombs were deposited on North Korean soil in the
early 1950's.[6]

The terrible irony of the bombing of North Korea was that

it didn't affect the war effort. . . . We never found a way to stop their supply lines for example. These little guys with A-frames on their backs carrying several hundred pounds of supplies could not be hit by bombing. The reason for this is very simple. It goes back to the bombing survey done of WWII. . . . Bombing is not an effective strategy for ending a war or stopping supply.[7]

— Bruce Cumings, renown historian of East Asia
PBS Special, *Korea — The Unknown War*

What Has So Far Been Too Painful to Admit

Not only will a badly outgunned opponent spread out and "harden" his resupply effort, but—especially within Asia—he may also disperse all personnel and move how he fights below ground. Didn't one perform all such adjustments in the Western Pacific during the latter stages of WWII, at Korea's 38th Parallel in 1953, and then again throughout the Vietnam War?

By some accounts, all 20,000 defenders of Iwo Jima had—through the subterranean shift—become nearly impervious to American bombardment and return fire.[8] Luckily for the U.S. Marines, most WWII examples of this particular strategy occurred on miniscule islands. While enough excavation protected the enemy occupiers from heavy U.S. ordnance, subsequent hole plugging was to limit their above-ground forays.

Pentagon Error Due to More Than Digging and Dispersal

But, the enemy's subsurface "disposition" was not the only reason that heavy U.S. bombardment failed to subdue him in Vietnam. An innovative and "relatively unconventional" warfare style had emerged that was quite large in influence, yet still small in composition—just as legendary Marine general Chesty Puller had predicted after Korea.

I'm afraid we haven't recognized the most important lesson from Korea. The Communists have developed a totally new kind of warfare. . . . This is total warfare, yet small in scope, and designed to neutralize our big . . . weapons. Look at

Vietnam. The French outnumbered the Communists [by]
two to one, yet they [the French] were still massacred.[9]
— Lt.Gen. Lewis B. "Chesty" Puller

In this new way of fighting, one requires no aircraft, tanks, artillery, or many kinds of resupply. In fact, any modern-day proponent
might do quite well with only what he could steal from an oversupplied Western proxy (just as ISIS has in Iraq). This well-tested
alternative to the Pentagon's standard approach to war is of much
lower intensity. That it also causes less collateral damage greatly
appeals to local populations. It is the perfect "martial" fit for the
multidimensional 4GW that makes most of its headway through
the civilian-heavy political, economic, and religious/psychological
arenas.

More Recent History

Since the interdiction-oriented conflict in South Vietnam, "smart"
bombs and missiles have come to define the Pentagon's normative
approach to any overseas confrontation. These are munitions that
more often hit what they are aimed at. That can be very effective
where the parent organization's target-identifying apparatus (now
virtually devoid of any "human intelligence") has correctly surmised
the grid coordinates. Further assumed, of course, is that there will
be no innocent bystanders around for the explosion—something
that is very hard to establish from satellite photos and telephone
intercepts.
So, to determine how much "smart" ordnance has actually
changed warfare, one has only to look at its track record. Unfortunately, a heavy U.S. bombing campaign has only attained its
intended result once of late—in Serbia during 1999. In Iraq, Afghanistan, Libya, and a few other places, it has generally failed to
achieve its desired effect.
To be effective in a modern 4GW conflict, aerial bombardment
(however "smart") must remove something the enemy badly needs
without harming (or scaring) any civilians. That means leveling one
of ISIS' recently captured and revenue-producing oil facilities after
its civilian work force has been lured elsewhere. Normally, such
a feat can only be accomplished by a tiny team of ground-deployed
saboteurs.

The Prerequisites to Rapid Victory

Open warfare is fairly simplistic. Either the enemy commander must be quickly convinced to sign a peace accord, or his various forces will have to be defeated piecemeal. For no recent opponent has the Pentagon's initial "shock and awe" bombardment produced such an accord.

To beat a more maneuver-oriented adversary piecemeal takes some real doing. Most of America's traditional foes operate from the bottom up. That means they like to string together tiny victories at the local level, instead of constantly pushing (like most Western armies) for a regional sweep. Successfully combatting this style of warfare takes blanketing the entire locale with lone (but more tactically adept) squad-sized units. No amount of U.S. firepower can protect that many separate detachments at once. Each must be able to avert annihilation on its own.

Such a scenario is no longer a "nice-to-have" for future wars, but an absolute necessity. It takes "boots on the ground" whose owners are good enough at maneuver to survive as tiny well-dispersed elements without any assistance from American artillery or warplanes.

Just as the NVA so painfully demonstrated in Vietnam, it is possible for any national army to fight this way. American forces would only need more "truly light" infantry ability. How to obtain it with a tiny supplement to each company's training curriculum has already been outlined in an appendix to a previous publication.[10] Failing to use it will only perpetuate a less-than-satisfactory success rate at small conflicts. Since Korea, America's foes haven't needed as much preparatory fire and technology, nor have they caused as much collateral damage. Despite the irreconcilable hanging of a few local mayors, this has given them enough public support to successfully conduct 4GW.

> The North Koreans were like ghosts. They passed over the countryside and left no mark on it in many ways. But when you use the rock crusher techniques of an American army, you hurt your friends. And that was true in Vietnam as well as in Korea.[11]
> — Brig.Gen. Edwin Simmons USMC (Ret.)
> former head of Hist. and Museums Div., HQMC

Why the Pentagon Has Been Slow to Accept This Solution

Light infantry units can only defeat a more powerful aggressor by operating through tiny elusive contingents that largely rely on the initiative of each member. Most Western armies prefer everyone (particularly the lower ranks) to do precisely as told. Nor have their standardized small-unit tactics led to the complete surprise of many battlefield opponents over the years. As a direct result of such factors, no semi-autonomous U.S. infantry squad will be possible until control over training and operations has finally been decentralized.

Properly preparing America's youth for modern combat requires two new steps at the company or school level: (1) monitoring how they collectively feel about their role in parent-unit maneuvers; and (2) tactical experimenting (against simulated casualty assessment) with all recommended additions to their technique portfolio. Without such additions, there will continue to be no *bona fide* learning dynamic at the squad and below, only more of the same highly predictable (and potentially fatal) instructions for frontline fighters. All that electronic paraphernalia will make them no less easily detected by the foe.

While any generalization is risky, so too is not keeping up with the worldwide evolution of squad tactics. Since the Vietnam War, it has become increasingly clear that America's defense establishment cannot defeat any "bottom-up-operating" (criminal-or-Asian-oriented) foe without first allowing more initiative from its own lowest echelons. This problem is not new. In 1942, Lt.Col. Evans Carlson went so far as to develop a special training program to try to correct this same shortfall in his Marine Raiders. While his methods have yet to be officially deemed necessary, they are fully documented in Chapters 3, 4, and 7 of *Gung Ho.*[12]

Root Problem of U.S. Military Assistance Overseas

A U.S. expeditionary force cannot successfully consolidate the region it has just liberated without fully occupying it. For a sizeable region, such an occupation requires a myriad of tiny outposts from U.S. or local forces. Such an outpost takes American infantrymen who are skilled enough to survive while badly outnumbered and devoid of any outside support. Or, they must know enough to show indigenous personnel how to do it. That's because no amount of standoff firepower is enough to handle that many separate units in trouble at the same time. Nor will local troops enjoy such a crutch after taking over the entire mission. Without widespread security, there will be no end to the insurgency nor a properly operating democracy. The bottom-up methodology of the aforementioned squad training supplement makes it perfect for the training of troops with a different cultural background.[13]

That each company using this supplement would end up with slightly different squad techniques has a hidden (if not major) benefit—less predictability in combat. With less predictability comes more mission accomplishment and fewer casualties. When all friendly units do precisely the same thing, the enemy is usually ready for it.

15 LESS TELEGRAPHING OF INTENTIONS

- How bad can it get when a quarry knows what to expect?
- Why isn't DoD more worried about small-unit predictability?

Impromptu opportunism can be much safer than a master plan.

(Source: FM 7-11B/11C/CM [1979], cover.)

Repetitive Actions Have Consequences in War

Most U.S. tactics manuals make little provision for the adversary's response to their maneuvers. For example, nowhere in the published assault methods is there mention of an enemy claymore. Within those closely obeyed depositories of organizational wisdom, two things have been assumed: (1) headquarters always knows what it's doing; and (2) following its standardized procedures will routinely produce a happy result. Even if the foe fails to read what the Pentagon has made easily accessible on the world market, he's not going to just sit there and take it. To have the best chance of survival, U.S. troops can no longer do what is fully predictable without some expectation of an enemy countermeasure. Just for starters, all GIs must be forewarned of claymore mines and how most quickly to disarm one. Like all else, the ways of war continue to evolve. To keep up with the latest "refinements," all tall top-down Western military organizations must first overcome their bureaucratic aversion to change. In modern combat, no more than one infantry company generally takes part in any given engagement. The days of regimental clashes are long gone. That means each separate U.S. company can now be allowed to have a few of its own tactical techniques. The cost of ignoring this opportunity for its squads and below will be unnecessary loss of life.

Firepower and Surprise Are Interchangeable in Combat

Military units with "abundant" firepower will seldom take the time to outmaneuver any opponent. Just as in U.S. Operations Killer and Ripper in Korea, they will just bowl over whatever gets in their way.

> When in Korea, the U.S. 8th Army counterattacked [in the fourth battle for Seoul] during February of 1951, it did so by leveling everything in its path.[1]
> — "Entirely New War," *Korea — The Unknown War*

Unfortunately, there is a price to be paid for taking this "path of least resistance" too often in wartime. Individual units within this powerful U.S. phalanx grow unfamiliar with how most effectively to maneuver, to include all the ways their tiniest elements might still dodge return fire.

> Because the American infantry units did not match up well in tactical ability with their Communist counterparts, they had little choice but to let supporting arms do their work for them. History records what happened as another meat grinder.[2]
> — "Entirely New War," *Korea — The Unknown War*

Just as in any natural disaster, there will always be local

residents who—for whatever reason—fail to leave during such an attack. Where cities are involved (like Seoul), their numbers can be substantial. While departing occupiers are often blamed for the carnage, one still wonders if some might have been due to Allied collateral damage.

> The advance [on Seoul] of the seven American divisions now in the line was the twentieth-century successor to the Roman "tortoise": instead of long columns, exposed to surprise attack, Ridgway's units now deployed at every stage for all-around defense in depth, securing themselves against infiltration while they waited for the massed artillery and air strikes to do their work upon the Chinese positions [and all else].[3]
>
> — *The Korean War,* by Hastings

So concentrated a barrage has no way of distinguishing between soldier and civilian. Operation Ripper had been preceded by the largest artillery bombardment of the Korean War. In the middle, the U.S. 25th Infantry Division then quickly established a bridgehead across the Han River. To the east, U.S. IX Corps reached its first phase line on 11 March. During the night of March 14–15, elements of the South Korean 1st Infantry Division and the U.S. 3rd Infantry Division then liberated Seoul. This marked the fourth and last time the capital would change hands since June 1950. The Communist forces had been compelled to abandon the city when the U.N. approach from the east threatened to encircle them.[4]

> On March 7, [Operation] Killer was succeeded by [Operation] Ripper. . . . The envelopment of Seoul by the success of Ripper made the Communist evacuation of the capital inevitable. On March 14 the victors recovered a devastated city, a metropolis of ruins and corrugated iron in which, of the principal buildings, only the Capitol and the railway station survived.[5]
>
> — *The Korean War,* by Hastings

Leadership by Example

After the overall commander has authorized such a devastating approach, it becomes far more difficult to keep every member of any actual assault in check. Participating in this final liberation of Seoul would be ROK (Republic of South Korea) troops. Ever since the uprising on Cheju Island, many ROK units had considered anyone who allowed themselves to be overrun by the Communists to be sympathizers.[6] At Inchon (while still on the way to Seoul), South Korean troops again exercised too little fire discipline.

> Inchon was just a sea of rubble. . . . Now don't forget that all of these civilians are being liberated by the South Koreans. I think the South Korean soldiers were mad because they shot at everything that moved. And all these kids and old ladies are walking along with their hands up because they are terrified of these South Korean soldiers.[7]
> — Bert Hardy
> *Picture Post* Photographer
> PBS Special *Korea — the Unknown War*

The Possible Disconnect in Western Tactical Thought

Like the British at Bunker Hill, the Pentagon may still believe that foreign irregulars will cut and run from a deliberate attack by a professional army. Were this same assumption then applied to physically small and heavy besieged enemy regulars, it might have some very unpleasant consequences. If every assault quarry were eventually expected to "skedaddle," then there would be no need to overcome any countermeasures.

So, the ordnance-fixated Pentagon continues to go "high diddle diddle right up the middle" with all guns blazing. Yet, all too often, their target turns out to be a partially manned feint that looks from a distance like a Western formation. As a result, the U.S. attack develops so much momentum that the few actual defenders have only to move below ground to escape its wrath. Meanwhile, the majority of enemy firepower has remained hidden on the flanks of a U.S. phalanx that seems consistently "to win." But, what has it really won—more pride in its own invincibility, a few more enemy casualties, more strategically worthless ground that will never be occupied? All that does not somehow lead to a peace accord has been done in vain.

However, the cost of such a irrepressible way of operating may have been only a few GIs sniped, or occasionally injured by their own equipment, so the U.S. public doesn't complain. What difference did a little collateral damage make to the war's ultimate outcome? Who cares if a few civilians dumb enough to get in the way subsequently switch allegiance? Why won't the enemy come out and fight? Such is the tragedy of placing more emphasis on traditional procedure than on final outcome.

Why the Change Has Been So Hard

Attacking a competent defender by complete surprise usually takes moving undetected to where he can be quickly rushed (a few yards away). That's because he will seldom expose himself to well-aimed shots. But, either offensive feat takes a highly proficient ground troops—those who can fend for themselves deep within enemy territory.

Of course, only partial surprise of that defender would be much easier to accomplish. It can take as many forms as there are good ideas. But, unless some digression from established procedure can be routinely authorized, that assault force will still take unnecessary casualties. This is no less true with the advent of advanced surveillance and targeting technologies. All that gear is loud, and much of it emits an electronic signature.

Such an assessment can be very difficult for modern-day American warriors to accept. Advances in U.S. ordnance have been so frequent that there seems no real need to dodge enemy counterfire. Yet, recent history begs to differ. While fighting heavy Israeli armor in southern Lebanon in the summer of 2006, *Hezbollah* convincingly demonstrated how most effectively to counter a highly sophisticated "Western-style" incursion. The lesson involved the "remote-control killing of modern tanks" from a belt of below-ground strongpoints. Because there were no human operators anywhere near the target acquisition or destruction devices, there would be no heat signatures for aerial reconnaissance to locate.

[There were] bunkers housing . . . advanced eavesdropping and surveillance equipment and monitoring cameras.[8]
— *The Times* (UK), 10 August 2006

Next, through a combination of video camera and computerized missile, *Hezbollah* managed to destroy over 50 of the latest tanks (by the Israelis' own count).[9]

In one hidden bunker, Israeli soldiers discovered night vision camera equipment connected to computers that fed coordinates of targets to the Sagger 2 missile.[10]
— *The Washington Post,* 14 August 2006

What the Israelis Lacked

Like the Pentagon, the Israelis had no "light" infantrymen. The truly light grunt is self-sufficient under most circumstances (as was every member of Roger's Rangers in the French and Indian Wars or Carlson's Raiders during WWII). After easily reading the ground around him, he knows how best to deal with any number of hidden adversaries. To stay alive, he constantly looks for new ways to surprise them.

There are several ways well-prepared defenders might be sufficiently bewildered to make them less risky to attack: (1) sneak a few people in the back after preparing to attack from the front; (2) crawl in at night beneath a man-high base of fire; (3) emerge in small numbers from a short-grass-covered field during a noon meal or watch relief; or (4) move in at night against a backdrop of distant flares. When the enemy's command structure or indirect-fire capability is disrupted through the first ruse, his defense plan will be affected. With the second deception, he will expect the assault force from a different direction. Through the third trick, he should be caught completely off guard by a few well-camouflaged crawlers. The fourth stratagem will make useless all but the most sophisticated night vision devices.

The common thread seems clear. The size of the attack must remain somewhat small at first. It is far easier to reinforce a tiny "bridgehead," than it is to initially strike a fully prepared enemy position with a three-to-one manpower advantage (as required by U.S. doctrine [11]). There tend also to be more healthy hostages from whom to retrieve valuable intelligence.

140

16 — CAPTIVES HAVE INTELLIGENCE VALUE

- Why doesn't the Pentagon use more human intelligence?
- How might captured enemy riflemen be of use?

Nonrate POW's could reveal hard-to-unravel squad assault technique.

(Source: FM 7-8 [Aug. 1984], pp. F-1, I-9.)

Every Style of War Has Limitations

The whole purpose of Attrition Warfare is to inflict more death and destruction upon the enemy than he can muster in return. Whether or not all that killing of opposition soldiers helps to conclude the conflict, it remains the primary mission. Sadly, frontline personnel are among the easiest wartime assets to replace. History records about the same number of casualties for both winner and loser in many big battles. Sgt. Alvin C. York's exploits during WWI should have opened America's eyes to another—more productive—way of operating. Lethal force was definitely involved, but it no longer constituted an all-encompassing end in itself. Instead, it was only the precursor to a much more strategically significant occurrence.

Upon being drafted, the highly religious York became a "conscientious objector." He then managed to overcome his inner conflict over Jesus's advice to "love your enemies" by discovering another Biblical passage: "Render . . . unto Caesar the things that are Caesar's." During the Meuse-Argonne Offensive of 1918, he and two subordinates proceeded to kill over 20 German soldiers and capture 100 more to save their own patrol from annihilation. When asked why he did that much deadly shooting, the former hunter from rural Tennessee said: "To save lives."[1] Needless to say, 100 more "knowledge-laden" captives could have done more to promote the Allied war effort than the same number of additional corpses. Because a brutal foe will often consider any raising of hands to be suicidal, wholesale surrender seldom occurs in battle without some evidence to the contrary. Thus, Sgt. York's heroic actions may have not only generated vital intelligence, but also helped to precipitate more sizable capitulations later in the war.

The WWII Experience

U.S. troops experienced at least two prisoner-related problems during WWII. First, they were forced to operate in both theaters against an enemy that was more tactically adept at the squad level. Then, through the code of *Bushido,* one of those adversaries had come to disdain all capitulation (whether personal or otherwise). Neither factor did much to raise the number of captives taken by American forces in any theatre. Nor did they decrease the amount of U.S. bombardment.

All of this was to prove quite problematic for the Americans. For example, there had been quite a few Asian laborers forced to build fortifications throughout the Japanese occupied islands: (1) thousands of local residents impressed for that purpose on Okinawa;[2] (2) Korean "hostages" sent to New Guinea, Tarawa, Kwajalein, Roi-Namur, Guam, Saipan, and Tinian[3]; and (3) workers of both nationalities present at Peleliu.[4] Yet, when those islands were finally taken by U.S. forces, most casualty counts did not fully distinguish the fate of forced laborers from Japanese defenders. In all fairness to the U.S. commanders on the ground during those landings, some Okinawans and Koreans had also been impressed into the Japanese army.[5]

Yet, the U.S. Marine Corps must have finally realized that too much emphasis had been placed on "killing" during the early stages of the Pacific War. That's why the 1950 movie "The Halls of Montezuma" made such a big deal out of showing that all frontline Leathernecks were eventually told to take more prisoners.[6] This same docudrama appears to reveal how Japanese captives helped U.S. forces locate a hidden railway gun on Saipan. That huge gun had been coming out of a hillside tunnel above Magicienne Bay on the narrow-gauge railroad tracks of a sugarcane plantation to heavily bombard both the U.S. headquarters and its various maneuver elements.[7]

The New Vision Grows in Scope

Since WWII, the U.S. Dept. of Defense has had less luck winning extended conflicts. After bringing its full arsenal to bear, it obtained only an armistice (formal cease fire agreement) in Korea and funding cutoff in Vietnam. That's when the underlying problem became apparent. The Asian Communists had become good at 4GW, while the Pentagon hadn't. Part of the fault lay in the strict separation of responsibilities between U.S. government agencies, but the rest had to do with the Pentagon's continuing quest for more destructive (albeit "smarter") ordnance.

While the resulting "higher-tech" version of Attrition Warfare (2GW) still worked during certain wartime scenarios, it could no longer be relied upon to achieve an overall cessation of hostilities. Initially destroying all things to more easily rebuild them later may have had its place in the bloody past. But, winning a lower-intensity modern conflict takes more attention to the nonmartial arenas. And what concurrently happens in the way of violent action must be carefully gauged so as not to alienate the general population. Overflying homes with missile spewing drones would be hard-pressed to qualify.

So, the U.S. war machine's traditional emphasis on destroying every vestige of resistance became implicitly replaced with making friends out of enemies. This paradoxical wartime strategy became more obvious during America's expeditionary adventures to Iraq and Afghanistan, where tribal loyalties were soon discovered to be the key to victory. If tribal elders could somehow be swayed to the U.S. point of view, their respective militias quickly turned from adversary into ally. Of considerable note, money had more to do with that auspicious end than threatening or killing elders.

The Communist Record on Hostage Taking

Suffice it to say that Mao had much less regard for human life than most Western leaders. Yet, he would often spare battlefield prisoners as a psychological ploy. His Communist successors then proceeded to make a veritable art form out of "reeducating former enemy soldiers and sympathizers." While this process was mentally debilitating, it certainly contributed more to a durable occupation than the starvation and brutalization that came to define Axis prisoner of war camps.

America's Parallel History

Of course, U.S. forces have also captured many opposition soldiers over the years. Largely because of the Pentagon's continuing emphasis on overwhelming force, such hostage taking has more often occurred where many try to surrender at once. But, most who have succeeded were well treated. During the Vietnam War, apparent defectors were even given the opportunity to become Kit Carson Scouts.[8] In a conflict that would later be remembered as a 4GW masterpiece for the opposition, this new program proved very helpful to the Allies. Not only did the supposed defectors know of the enemy's advanced tactical methods, but also where he was locally hiding.

Ordinary enemy captives could also reveal such interesting things if they wanted to. And the art of interrogation has now advanced to the point where no torture would be necessary to find it out. Just as the Chinese Communists like to do during any intelligence gathering operation, one has only to collect enough pertinent details from different sources and then correctly piece them together. Unfortunately, most U.S. intelligence analysts have failed to keep up with the evolution of squad tactics worldwide, so they couldn't identify state-of-the-art technique. Nor would they look below ground for how the enemy regularly manages to escape. But, if an American expert in worldwide squad tactics were carefully to question 20 to 30 enemy riflemen, he could soon piece together most of the enemy's lowest-echelon assault and defense procedures. From them, he might surmise the current strategy of the opponent from a "bottom-up" culture.

Other Western Nations Have Done Even More with POWs

The Selous Scouts of Rhodesia went so far as to turn many battlefield captives into fully vetted members.[9] How they did so will be later covered. But, such a profound reversal of fortunes also deserves mention here. As Sun Tzu has intimated on many occasions, the ultimate objective of war is a durable peace. Of immense help in that regard would be avoiding the long-term animosities that can ensue from open combat.

> The greatest victory is that which requires no battle.[10]
> — Sun Tzu

This same perfectly logical approach to one's own "personal struggles" appears throughout Christian literature. That should give it adequate credibility as a wartime strategy.

> Through his holy prophets he [God] promised of old
>   that he would save us from our enemies,
>   from the hands of all who hate us. . . .
> In the tender compassion of our God
>   the dawn from on high shall break upon us,
>   to shine on those who dwell in darkness and
>   the shadow of death,
>   and guide our feet into the way of peace.[11]
> — Canticle of Zecharia, Luke 1:68-79

Obviously, the two sides wouldn't be fighting if they liked each other, but—as in wedlock—not always being in agreement need not lead to divorce. Striving to treat a battlefield adversary with respect and wary compassion is not much different from what happens in peace talks at the highest level. Often just wounding him better helps the war effort.

17 WOUNDING MORE IMPAIRS FOE INFRASTRUCTURE

- Can slightly injuring an enemy work to one's advantage?
- On which occasions might this be possible?

Patrolling enemy soldiers can be easily shot in the legs.

(Source: MCO P1550.14D [1983], pp. 1-3, 10-8.)

The Very Nature of Battle

To win a lengthy armed conflict, one side must hammer away at whatever is strategically vital to the other (like headquarters elements, supply chains, or particularly vital pieces of ground). Easily to close with such targets, it must limit the number of enemy soldiers in the way. This can be done by simply bypassing those soldiers. Or, as in high-tech 2GW (America's preferred wartime format), applying overwhelming force to effect a breakthrough. Then, a high enemy kill rate is thought to be almost as beneficial to the overall war effort as the removal/occupation of the original objective. Yet, there is an inherent problem with such an approach to all manner of resistance. The first is that extended wars are not won through killing, because people are generally the easiest of all wartime assets to replace. The second is the loss of the "moral high ground" in the prosecution of what is in reality a 4GW evolution. According to the Pope John Paul II, killing as many enemy soldiers as possible is not the most ethical way of fighting.[1]

Other Ways of Taking Opposition Soldiers out of Action

In light of the above-mentioned drawbacks, one wonders how else those opposition soldiers (to include close-in defenders) might be kept from interfering with the drive against the foe's strategic assets. Most obvious would be the surrender of those soldiers. Another, might be their retreat. A third, though seldom considered in wartime, would be just wounding or otherwise incapacitating them. The Khmer Rouge crew of the Mayaguez was sprayed with a debilitating gas right before the ship was retaken by U.S. Marines in 1975.[2]

Under the following conditions, a wounded or disoriented man might more easily cooperate: (1) if he knew he was not going to be summarily shot; (2) if U.S. medical care were available; and (3) if eventual repatriation were likely.

It has also been said that a wounded man poses a much greater strain on the support apparatus of his parent organization than a dead one. Many dollars and man-hours must be dedicated to his evacuation, treatment, and recuperation; not to mention what may be limited medical supplies. Thus, wounding him starts to looks more and more advantageous, if he cannot be made to surrender. Sounds a lot like the most humane way of apprehending a dangerous criminal, doesn't it?

Which Circumstances Might Permit a Wounding

Many police recruits are now being told that failing to shoot a threatening individual center mass might make him even madder. Society's increased abuse of narcotics may be partially to blame. But, enemy soldiers are seldom encountered in a "hopped up" condition, though they may be carrying heroin syringes. And while an increase in aggression has been known to follow a battlefield injury, the more likely result is "complete resignation." Only for the occasional superman does "any more interest in fighting" generally ensue. So, unless one's battlefield opponent is known to be taking Phencyclidine (PCP), alpha-Pyrrolidinopentiophenone (a-PVP), or a few other mind bending drugs, this law enforcement concern has no wartime application. In other words, the combat quarry's wounding should sufficiently limit his ability to resist. As with main battle tanks, any lessening of mobility is the next best thing to complete destruction. The wounded man might keep trying to shoot his rifle, but he will only do so while considerably impaired and from the original location. He will not be encountered during any subsequent friendly offensives or defensives, as is the common excuse for excess lethality in open combat.

Thus, the intentional wounding of enemy soldiers becomes a viable way of furthering most war efforts. How might that non-life-threatening injury be inflicted? A leg shot on any upright human being seems perfectly feasible for the world's best marksmen. For every other opposition soldier, blinding or concussion munitions could temporarily incapacitate them long enough for GIs to safely approach. Once their weapons had been confiscated, how much more fighting could they reasonably manage?

America's WWII adversaries in the Pacific were, of course, the exception to this far more humane way of operating. Their Code of *Bushido* made all Japanese captives extremely dangerous until fully searched and constantly watched. Any ostensible sign of surrender might be closely followed by a grenade. But, here again, initial impressions might have made a difference. If surrender were thought to be shameful, then wouldn't respectful behavior toward the first prisoners taken help to counter that falsehood? And couldn't enough compassion toward those who give up help to dissuade others from continuing to resist? Sun Tzu warns against trying to tackle an adversary who feels cornered. That's because unnecessary violence generally ensues.

When you surround an army, leave an outlet free. Do not press a desperate foe too hard.[3]
— Sun Tzu

Accepting medical treatment after fighting hard enough to be

injured should be nearly as honorable as making the ultimate sacrifice. Adversaries with irrational beliefs must be made to realize
this.

Build your opponent a golden bridge to retreat across.[4]
— Sun Tzu

While a WWII devotee of *Bushido* or present-day minion of ISIS
might have difficulty relating to such an argument, the sane member
of most military entities won't. In effect, the ultimate reward for
following Pope John Paul II's advice (about less killing of enemy
soldiers) might be twofold: (1) fewer friendly losses; and (2) the first
U.S. ground conflict decisively won since WWII.

The Enemy's Overall Needs Were Few in Vietnam

The opponent in Vietnam needed no tanks, planes, or artillery to
hold his own in battle. Nor did he need many kinds of ammunition.
Down his mortar tubes, he could drop stolen U.S. 60mm and 81mm
rounds. Through his .51 caliber heavy machineguns, he could fire
captured U.S. .50 caliber bullets. If he had wanted to, he could have
reloaded the expended 7.62-39mm shell casings from his rifles and
light machineguns with the primers, powder, and slugs of captured
North Atlantic Treaty Organization (NATO) 7.62x51mm cartridges.
He could have also found enough food on South Vietnam's Coastal
Plain to sustain most of his operations. However, it was much easier
for his main force units to be resupplied with some of these neces-
sities via the Ho Chi Minh Trail. What he most needed from the
North was medical assistance. Much of the equipment for a field
surgery center could not have been easily transported by bicycle.
Medivacking wounded soldiers home would have been equally difficult. So, every time an opposition soldier got wounded (instead
of killed), it put a great deal of strain on his already hard-pressed
support system.

Problems are compounded for the North Vietnamese Army/
Viet Cong . . . by the constant threat of medical supply
shortages, primitive supply and evacuation procedures, and
substandard sanitary conditions and practices.[5]
— CIA Report on NVA/VC Medical Capabilities

The structure and depth of this medial support establishment inside the invaded nation was considerable. Whatever part of the enemy's army had to be dedicated to such things was no longer available for fighting.

NVA/Viet Cong units in South Vietnam place considerable emphasis on evacuation of their personnel wounded in battle. . . .

. . . A hierarchy of battalion, regimental, and divisional level aid stations and hospitals has been established to evacuate and treat sick and wounded troops. The organization of each medical unit is dependent upon the military unit to which it is assisted. . .

The VC have a well-organized, coordinated medical supply system. . . . This system has been maintained on a priority basis, often at the expense of the population in North Vietnam.[6]

— CIA Report on NVA/VC Medical Capabilities

The ratio of enemy killed to wounded in Vietnam was 1.0 to 1.5.[7] Because of the difficulty in taking care of the wounded, the North Vietnamese had to rely heavily on other countries (particularly China) for enough medical supplies.

Medical supply depots were created in South Vietnam [starting about 1964], and at this time, the VC began to receive increasing medical support from Communist Bloc countries, mostly in the form of medical supplies.[8]

— CIA Report on NVA/VC Medical Capabilities

The enemy in Vietnam was using surprise-oriented tactical techniques that were far more advanced than those of the U.S. infantry. To keep such techniques (and any other sensitive military intelligence) from being discovered, they carefully avoided the capture of any wounded member. To do so, they often had to quit fighting.

The Viet Cong make great effort to recover their dead and wounded. . . . [T]he wounded and dead constitute an important source of intelligence to the enemy. When the Viet

Cong is hit, his two adjacent comrades quit the fight and assist him to the rear.[9]
— CIA Report on NVA/VC Medical Capabilities

Then, the quite tedious movement of wounded personnel to the rear would commence. All the while, evacuation personnel had mostly to be provided by the next higher unit in the chain of command.

The wounded that are not ambulatory are carried back [to the battalion medical station 400 to 2500 meters back] by members of their [infantry] platoon assigned by their platoon leader. . . After treatment, all wounded . . . are evacuated to a regimental dispensary that is located from one to four kilometers behind the battalion. . . .

Further evacuation of wounded to regional, provincial, and divisional hospitals is also accomplished by civilian or military units.[10]
— CIA Report on NVA/VC Medical Capabilities

The All Too Frequent Alternative

By the way U.S. units fight, they encourage all opposition to flee as they approach. Unless every hill and trail junction then has strategic value, such an enemy withdrawal does nothing for the Allied war effort.

18 THE QUARRY NEED NOT BE ALLOWED TO ESCAPE

- Why do U.S. attacks regularly permit defenders to leave?
- Have the exit route bombardments been effective?

Hard-to-assault foe bastions can be just surveilled and bypassed.

(Sources: FM 7-11B1/2 [1978], p. 2-II-C-4.2; FM 7-8 [1984], p. 3-28.)

A Few Double Envelopments Might Have Helped

Through assumed doctrine, small U.S. infantry units will only singly envelop (attack from a lone flank) any fortified or urban objective. Along level and unaltered ground, the Army's "Bounding Overwatch" maneuver also involves moving up just one side of the next opposition. While the reason for no double-envelopments makes some sense (lessening the possibility of fratricide), the end result doesn't. There is now a much better chance that many defenders will get away. To achieve a truly decisive victory, more encirclement would be necessary.

Given the chance, America's traditional foes will—in large part—pull back from a concentrated U.S. attack. While a devotee of overwhelming firepower might see this as a sign of weakness, it really is not. Those who withdraw become instantly available for other missions. Of course, the U.S. military would much prefer to confront each opposition member just once. But, for safety's sake, that meeting cannot entail a final U.S. ground assault against trapped enemy fighters.

The Generally Missed Opportunity

Almost every U.S. ground attack since the start of WWII has involved the rearward movement of enemy defenders. That's because America's most likely adversaries have learned that a "soft" defense in depth is one of the best ways to contest a powerful advance. Among those who have become adept at this reverse way of operating are the Germans,[1] Japanese,[2] Russians,[3] North Koreans,[4] Chinese,[5] and North Vietnamese.[6] While almost never considered an option by a prideful Western commander, tactical withdrawal is a perfectly legitimate way of fighting. It has made those mostly Eastern foes much harder to beat in the long run. The same enemy soldiers keep popping up, after an overly optimistic U.S. casualty assessment declares them destroyed.

Only through a greater degree of encirclement might more success be possible. But in the West, such a thing only happens at the grandest of scales because of the doctrinal presumption. Through a pincers movement at the Bulge, two U.S. armies tried to capture large numbers of German troops during WWII. Most of those troops had already departed the salient by the time those pincers closed at Houffalize on 16 January 1945.[7] Then, many a GI would have to face a Bulge veteran later in the war.

Such is the tragedy of more emphasis on firepower than maneuver during offensive combat. For the desired effect, direct fire must rain down on the quarry from more than just his front and one side. A tiny part of the attacking force must also sneak around back to impede his rearward exodus. With a few exceptions (like Lt.Col. Hackworth in Vietnam [8]), most U.S. commanders deem such a further deployment of their personnel to be either unnecessary or suicidal. They would rather continue to "roll over" the foe, than to risk a serious set-piece confrontation. The interdiction of retreating defenders then becomes the job of indirect fire or aerial bombardment. Unfortunately, even with overhead surveillance and smart ordnance, such a plan creates more noise than actual damage. Through more tactical leeway, most departing defenders will have either "gone to ground" or so widely dispersed as to become relatively invulnerable to such a U.S. response.

How Surrounded Strongpoint Occupants Fare

During a WWII enemy offensive, both German and Russian commanders expected a few of their often squad-sized strongpoints in every defense matrix to get cut off and surrounded. Unless specifically told to wait for a friendly counterattack, the occupants of those tiny bastions then had the authority to fight their way out. As a somewhat safer alternative, the Soviets permitted exfiltration by composite elements.[9]

To shift to a fallback position from a squad strongpoint on Peleliu, Iwo Jima,[10] or Okinawa, Japanese troops usually had their own private tunnel. By 1953, the occupants of several such forward positions within the Chinese defense belt at Korea's 38th Parallel would share the same below-ground exit.[11] But, by the time Vietnam rolled around, the art of operating below ground to escape U.S. fire had fully evolved. The extensive Cu Chi tunnel network just northwest of Saigon may have been much more than a way for bunker occupants to reach their supply storage rooms. From the 124 miles of Cu Chi district excavations,[12] the VC could secretly enter the night encampment site of almost any U.S. maneuver force in the region.[13] One NVA soldier remembers how easily his comrades moved considerable distances below ground.

> [In 1965] the Americans were carrying out military operation in Cu Chi. We were moving almost a thousand men from village to village through underground tunnels.[14]
> — Col. Huong Van Ba, NVA artillery officer

The Cu Chi tunnel complex seemed thus to service a soft, underground strongpoint defense matrix. Here's what a former VC recalls about it.

[About 1965] we took a bus to Cu Chi, where I was led into an ordinary village house and found myself being conducted through a maze of tunnels that started from the covered hole in the house's bunker. The main tunnel in this system was called Tong Nhut Road. It connected village to village and in some places had entrances from almost every house. In those places, if there was an enemy attack, an entire hamlet might disappear.

. . . The Cu Chi tunnels served as a defense, a trap for Americans or ARVN troops, a supply area, and a stop for new recruits coming out from Saigon into the jungle.[15]
— Trinh Duc, VC village chieftain

East Asians also like to slip piecemeal through Western lines after their unit gets cornered. Or they just hide below ground until their omnipotent attacker moves on to his next surface victory. One way or the other, they manage to stay in the fight. Where large numbers of escapees are involved, the U.S. war effort takes a hit. That's why U.S. war planners worry about how many NVA and VC may have actually evaded an Allied cordon around Hue City in 1968.[16] (See Map 18.1.)

The Hue City Masterpiece

Of course, reoccupying Hue would also involve retaking the Citadel. Just to enter it, the U.S. Marines had to go by boat to the Navy's LCU (Landing Craft Utility) ramp on the Perfume River just above the northeast corner of that ancient fortress. While South Vietnamese troops then attempted to clear the Citadel's interior west of the culturally protected Imperial Palace, the Marines drove toward its southeastern corner. (See Map 18.2.) En route, they had to deal not only with machinegun fire from the Palace, but also a "rearward-moving" defense matrix. Enemy troops would fight doggedly for one street and then fall back unseen to previously prepared positions on another. In essence, every other street in Zone D contained heavily fortified blocks between which roving teams of snipers appeared to operate to keep them from being too easily identified as partially open.[17]

How lengthy and painful that fight was for the Leathernecks is now a matter of public record. But what happened next was to raise

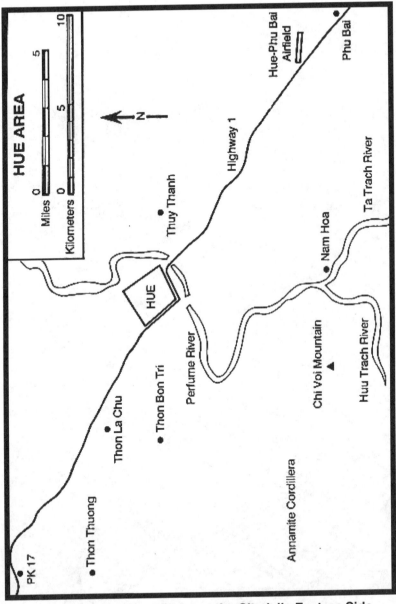

Map 18.1: Exit Possibilities at the Citadel's Eastern Side
(Source: Courtesy of Pacifica Military History, from "Fire in the Streets: The Battle for Hue, Tet 1968," © 1991 by Eric Hammel.)

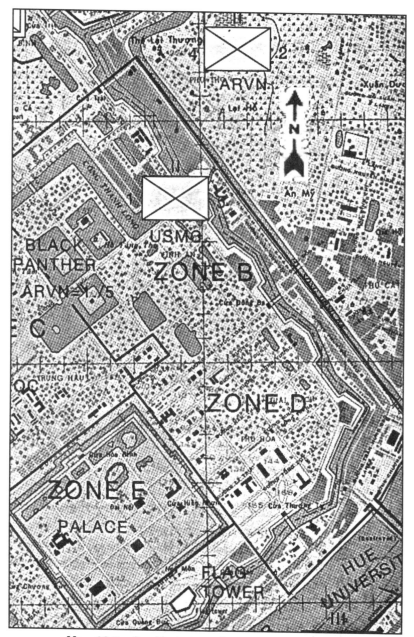

Map 18.2: Southeastern Corner of the Citadel
(Source: "U.S. Marines in Vietnam: The Defining Year 1968," Hist. & Museums Div., HQMC, p. 165.)

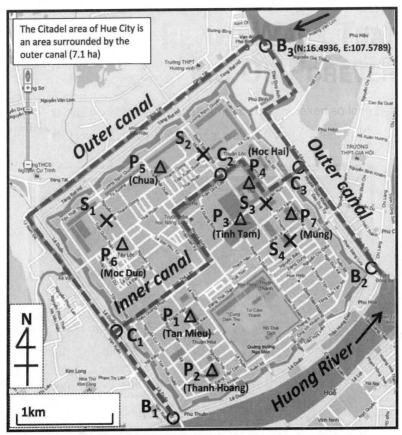

The Citadel area of Hue City is an area surrounded by the outer canal (7.1 ha)

B_3 (N:16.4936, E:107.5789)

Map 18.3: Water Features in and Around the Citadel

(Source: Courtesy of researchgate.net and iwapublishing.com for use of the map in "Characterization of Water Pollution in Drainage Networks ... in the Citadel area of Hue City," by Y. Nagano, T. Teraguchi, P. K. Lieu, and H. Furumai, from "Water Science & Technology," 70(4): 612-619, August 2014, ©)

still unanswered questions about the ultimate fate of those retreating defenders. Upon reaching the southeastern wall of the Citadel on 23 February 1968, the Marines of 1st Battalion, 5th Regiment (1/5) noticed that their last objective had been NVA-held bunkers and passages in that wall itself.[18] Yet, from the scarcity of enemy bodies, they could only deduce that their opposition had somehow withdrawn into the Imperial Palace.[19] Unfortunately, when the 1st ARVN Division's elite Black Panther Company stormed the Palace the very next day, they found it empty.[20]

A good place to start the search for those missing defenders is the environment itself. The whole area was covered with water features. Hue City lies squarely in the path of the northeast monsoons that can last until April. Yearly, it receives up to 120 inches of rainfall.[21] So, at some point, all excess water flows into the Perfume River. After the NVA had blown the An Cuu bridge across the Phu Cam Canal, U.S. forces had to come up the Perfume to assault the Citadel from the back. After all that river traffic, U.S. authorities must have assumed the entire watercourse to be too well patrolled for enemy use.

As one can more easily see from Map 18.3, the Citadel had been originally ringed by water-filled trenches. Even its royal compound sported a moat. And across the Citadel floor ran the "Royal River" or Ngu Ha Canal that was at the center of its early drainage and sewage disposal system. Most of the partially covered ditches along both sides of the Citadel's main streets are now known to have emptied into this interior canal.

Further limiting the number of souls who could be seized at this ancient fortress were some completely hidden and dry "movement routes." Its dirt-filled walls were riddled with Japanese passageways from WWII, and a royal palace of this vintage would have had its own secret tunnel to beyond the fortress walls. So secretly to exit Hue, the NVA had only to combine all of these wet and dry conduits near the fort with any leading away from it that were still under VC control. Then, some probably went east and others south. (See Maps 18.4.) That's because the NVA seldom departed an attack objective the same way they had come in. In this case, it had been mostly from the west and northwest.

One Hanoi publication was later to document who escaped, during which period, and where they were headed.

> From 23-25 February [1968], the main forces, the commandos, the local troops, the militia, and the wounded gradually and secretly withdrew [from the Citadel] to the liberated areas and the zonal bases in the Tri Thien mountain ranges.[22]
>
> — *Tet Mau Than 1968 Event in South Vietnam*
> The Gioi Publishers, Hanoi

There had been a Bình Tri Thiên province added to that of Thua Thiên–Hue around 1990. So, the most likely place for the Tri Thien mountains is where the foothills of the Annamite Range most closely approached the ocean southwest of Hue. (Look again at Map 18.1.)

In the Hue City region at the time of the attack are known to have been 10 full Communist battalions (four from two separate NVA regiments and six more from the VC's main force).[23] While further details of the escape already fill five chapters of *Phantom Soldier* and *The Tiger's Way,* enough have been inserted below to confirm its occurrence. Either Saigon or Washington would have found what became of those missing defenders embarrassing, so Allied history instead focuses on how many Hue residents may have been executed by the Communists.

The Eastward Evacuation

After the battle for Hue was over (around 4 March), 2nd Battalion, 5th Marines (2/5) was to make a very interesting discovery to the east of the city.

Leaving the southern sector to the 1st Brigade, 101st Airborne on the 29th, the two Marine battalions [2/5 and 1/5] entered their new area of operations to cut off any NVA forces trying to make their way from Hue to the coast. Although encountering few enemy forces, the two battalions uncovered "fresh trench work along the route of advance, 3000 meters long with 600 fighting holes." Captain Michael Downs, the Company F Commander, remembered a trench complex that "traveled in excess of five miles" with overhead cover every 15 meters. As Downs remarked, "that had to be a way to get significant reinforcements into the city." The search for significant North Vietnamese forces proved fruitless.[24]

> —*U.S.Marines in Vietnam:The Defining Year,1968*
> History and Museums Division, HQMC

Such a route could have also been used for the evacuation of wounded defenders. What if the underground passageway from the Imperial Palace had led right beneath "Phase Line Green" (Mai Thuc

Map 18.4: The Enemy-Controlled Corridor South of the Citadel
(Source: "U.S. Marines in Vietnam: Fighting the North Vietnamese in 1967," Hist. & Museums Div., HQMC, p. 212.)

Loan street) to just outside the Dong Ba Gate? (See Map 18.5.) That would explain why the enemy fought so hard for that gate. After the Marines had crossed over Mai Thuc Loan to attack its counterparts to the southeast, they would have assumed all parts of it under Allied control. The final entry to a captured NVA document further confirms this hypothesis.

> Feb. 23, . . . , [we] destroy one assault boat, two other boats, kill 23 Americans in Thuong Tu Gate, [and] Dong Ba Gate.[25]
> — "Twenty-Five Days and Nights of Continuous Fighting and the Wonderful Victory"

Such a thing is also possible without the royal exit. The Citadel walls were laced with Japanese-built tunnels. Who's to say that a secret passageway did not run the length of that wall between the Nha Do and Thuong Tu Gates, and then between the Thuong Tu and Dong Ba Gates? There was also a major diversion to the west on the night of the 23rd.

> [O]n the night of the 23rd, . . . [there was] another NVA attempt to break through South Vietnamese defenses in the western sector of the Citadel.[26]
> — U.S. Marines in Vietnam: Defining Year, 1968
> History and Museums Division, HQMC

After those stretchers had been however hauled to the Dong Ba Gate, their occupants would have had a much better chance of escaping if that gate had faced a part of the river bank that was not yet in Allied hands. Then, the wounded could have been moved across a northern loop of the Perfume River by the local VC infrastructure. With a bamboo bridge just below the water's surface (by then a well-known VC trick),[27] there would have been no need for boats.

It so happens that on the night of 23 February the enemy still controlled the area between the eastern side of the Citadel and the Perfume River. And throughout the period 21-26 February, the region east of the Perfume also remained free of Allied interference. The two ARVN battalions initially operating in this area had been evicted by a large enemy force during the first few days of February.[28] That enemy force may have had as its mission to build and

163

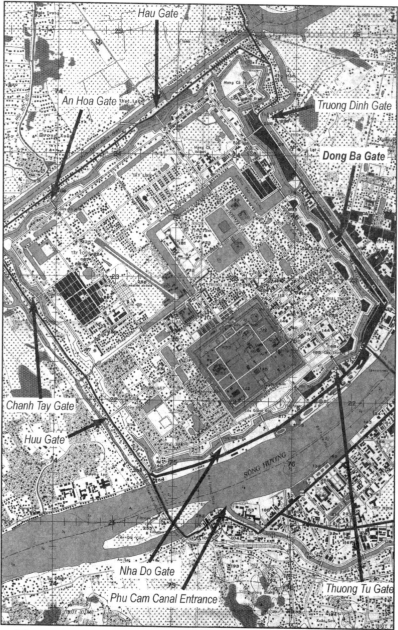

Map 18.5: Key Terrain Features at (or near) the Citadel Wall
(Source: Courtesy of Univ. of Texas at Austin, Castanada Map designator "txu-oclc-21740104-hue-1968.jpg"; gate locations from "Fire in the Streets," by Hammel, p. xvii.)

protect an evacuation route. The two ARVN Ranger battalions assigned to later clear the whole zone did not arrive in Hue City until 22 February,[29] and would not occupy the built-up area between the northeast wall and the river until 25 February.[30]

The Much Bigger Southward Exodus

Within Central Vietnam, the heaviest part of the rainy season had just drawn to a close at the end of January 1968.[31] The Perfume (Huong) River had its headwaters in the Annamite Mountain Range that extended well into Laos.[32] That big a watershed takes a while to empty. So, throughout the month of February, that river would have been full of runoff water and erosion debris—now moving a little more slowly. In this tropical part of the world, that means everything from coconuts to tree limbs continuously floating downstream. At night, in such a jumbled riverscape, motionless swimmers would have been extremely difficult to distinguish from flotsam. They could have ducked their heads whenever an illumination flare popped, or just continued to drift along with all the little bits of torn foliage.

All natural and enhanced night vision capabilities of the Allies would have been negated by the recurring flares. There were no heat-sensing devices in those days. Even a modern-day version would have had trouble spotting a water-cooled swimmer. Neither was Allied visibility helped by the limited extent of ambient light. From 23 February to 26 February 1968, there was only a "waning crescent" moon above the usual cloud cover. Then, the next four nights may have been completely dark.[33] All factors had combined to provide a wonderful exit opportunity for the large number of enemy troops still inside the Citadel. Whether or not it was fully used, there also existed a fairly safe route to the southern outskirts of town.

Exposing Asian Intrigue Takes Western Imagination

Here's how thousands of relatively healthy opposition soldiers could have escaped the Allied cordon. Starting on 23 December (the date of the eastern evacuation), those NVA and VC fighters had only to exfiltrate Allied lines piecemeal on three consecutive

165

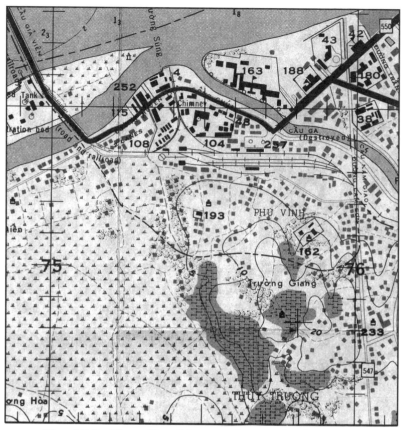

Map 18.6: Close-Up of Approaches to the Ridgeline
(Source: Courtesy of Univ. of Texas at Austin, Castanada Map designator "txu-oclc-21740104-hue-1968.jpg.")

nights. Such a feat is much easier to accomplish where no ARVN
or GI is willing to sit—namely, at the very edge of a watercourse or
upon otherwise wet ground. As such, squad-sized groups of ten men
each could have taken turns swimming the east-west portion of the
Perfume below the Citadel to where the Phu Cam Canal entered it.
(Look again at Map 18.4.) Their motion would have been scarcely
noticeable among the illumination induced shadows from riverbank

structures. Then, by following drainage ditches, those enemy troops could have reached a southward-running ridgeline that was still in VC hands.[34] (See Map 18.4.) On 26 February, elements of 2/5 tried unsuccessfully to take portions of a 2000-yard ridge running due south from the confluence of the Phu Cam Canal and Perfume River (at the southern corner of the Citadel). Not until the next day was that task finally accomplished by the full battalion.

On the morning of the 27th, Marine air and artillery bombarded the enemy defenses. After the last fires had lifted, all three companies of the 2nd Battalion rushed forward. Reaching the crest of the hill without encountering opposition, the Marines discovered that the enemy had departed during the night. Strewn around the hillscape were 14 enemy bodies.[35]

— *U.S.Marines in Vietnam:The Defining Year,1968*
History and Museums Division, HQMC

During the fight for this ridge, the Marines of 2/5 took fire from a Buddhist pagoda to their south.[36] Three kilometers below the Citadel (with a good view of the Perfume) lay the seven-story-high Thien Mu Pagoda.[37] That would have been roughly south of the proposed "VC Ridgeline" on Map 18.4,[38] whereas the squat Temple of Heaven ("Obj. 3") lay to the southeast.[39] A little farther south of that pagoda at the very edge of the Annamite foothills were more Nguyen Dynasty tombs and the famous Dong Thien Tri caves. That makes the Thien Mu Pagoda the mostly likely forward observation/command post for the NVA force that had invaded Hue. After all, the enemy's Tri-Thien-Hue Military Region headquarters was later determined to be atop Chi Voi Mountain—about nine more kilometers to the south-southwest of the Citadel.[40]

The Other Possible Route to the Ridgeline

While the Imperial Palace (with its escape tunnel entrance) and Huu Gate were captured on the 24th of February, the extreme southern corner of the Citadel did not fall until early on the 25th.[41] That's where the Nha Do Gate was located just east of the bridge across the Perfume. (Look back at Map 18.5.) Besides swimming up the Phu Cam Canal to where some drainage ditch led to the top of the VC-controlled ridge, the departing NVA could have taken a more direct route that was almost as wet. Clearly shown on the now declassified map of the area in 1968 are the contour lines of a finger at the end of that ridgeline. From the Perfume River on down, there was marsh all along the western edge of this finger. (See Map 18.6.) Thus, after swimming between Perfume bridge pylons, the exfiltrators could have slipped in shadow across the midstream islet and then 1000 meters farther south along the rim of that swamp. At this point, there would have been no more Allied forces between them and the high ground.

This Was No Small Vanishing Act

By the U.S. Marines' own estimate, about 5000 enemy soldiers had entered Hue City in February of 1968.[42] At least that many did so because one military history site shows 8000 in the area at the time.[43] NVA units were not as big as their U.S. counterparts. Thus, it soon became apparent that more than an NVA regiment had tried to hold—for as long as possible—the national capital of Vietnam (both north and south) from 1802 to 1945. In fact, it had been a full makeshift division.

> Lieutenant Colonel Pham Van Khoa, the South Vietnamese Thua Thien Province chief, remained in hiding until rescued by [the] American Marines . . . [and] overheard a conversation among some enemy officers. According to Khoa, the North Vietnamese mentioned a division taking part in the battle and the division headquarters was "in an unknown location south of the city of Hue inside a pagoda."[44]
> —*U.S.Marines in Vietnam:The Defining Year,1968*
> History and Museums Division, HQMC

That a division-sized force had actually attacked Hue is clearly visible on Map 18.7 from the U.S. Army Center for Military History. In fact, it shows two full regiments (one NVA and one VC) entering the Citadel itself. Of the Communist units that initially fought for the southern part of the city, it can be assumed that many then withdrew into the ancient fortress to help maintain the legitimate seat of an alternative government for as long as possible. The exact number of enemy soldiers who subsequently survived this "last stand" is now difficult to ascertain. What is conclusively known is that only slightly over 1000 would die in all fighting throughout the entire city.

According to the South Vietnamese, captured Communist documents admitted to 1,042 killed and an undisclosed number of wounded (TF X-Ray AAR Hue City; 1st InfDiv, Adv Tm

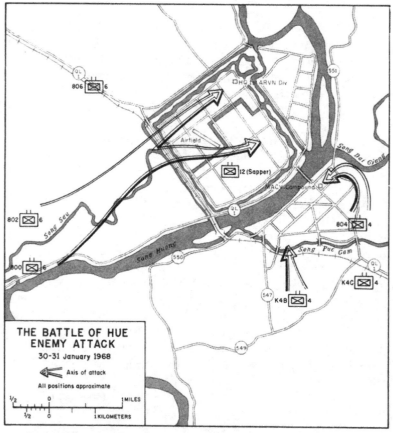

Map 18.7: Enemy Forces Involved in the Attack on Hue

(Source: With iimage designator "Map_Battle_of_Hue-Army_MHC.gif," this map is obviously from the U.S. Army Center for Military History; it was retrieved in April 2017 from the following url: http://www.tom.pilsch.com/AirOps/hue-battle.html.)

3, CAAR, Hue; Budd, AAR; 14th MHD, "The Battle of Hue,"
March 68; Pham Van Son, *The Tet Offensive*, p. 271).[45]
—*U.S.Marines in Vietnam:The Defining Year,1968*
History and Museums Division, HQMC

With far less refined evacuation procedures than those of the
Allies, the NVA often reported equal numbers of killed and wounded.
If 5000 soldiers had been engaged, 1000 killed, and 1000 wounded,
then up to 3000 uninjured must have gotten away with their casualties in tow. The most obvious exit route would have been the
Perfume River itself. Over the course of three very dark nights,
that many people—in tiny groups, each holding on to a buoyant
tree limb—could have easily drifted down river until a vacant bank
had been reached. While such an undisciplined "skedaddle" would
never be considered by the leader of a Western "pocket," it makes
perfect sense to the Eastern mind. Something nearly as unlikely had
occurred beneath the streets of Warsaw in August of 1944. That's
when one encircled Jewish enclave secretly joined another by its
many members noiselessly wending their way single-file through
the sewers.[46]

While the U.S. Marines would later acknowledge that only 1042
NVA soldiers had been killed at Hue, they apparently believed that
the other 4000 had been somehow "handled" by the ARVN.[47] Yet,
nowhere is there any evidence of their final disposition. News photos
of the period reveal only a few wounded VC in custody.

There is always the possibility that large numbers of
enemy soldiers simply hid in well-provisioned rooms beneath the streets of Hue until all U.S. occupiers had left.
As far back as 200 B.C., Hue had been the seat of Chinese military
authority in the kingdom of Nam Viet.[48] Any urban area that old is
bound to have sublevels of construction. Then, emerging a few at
a time, those hiding NVA and VC troops could have easily melted
back into the flood of returning refugees. Either way, they would
have lived to fight another day. In a war that was eventually lost
by the Pentagon, such a large boost to the enemy's manpower pool
is unacceptable.

The latest Vietnam War documentary in September 2017 ac-
knowledges that all remaining NVA fighters—of whom there were
thousands—simply complied with their headquarters directive to
"retreat."[49] This is not the first time in the annals of American
combat that large numbers of enemy defenders may have slipped

away undetected. After removing by ship a perfectly healthy (albeit hungry) contingent from Guadalcanal,[50] the Japanese were never suspected of using their massive new cargo submarines to evacuate the wounded from Iwo Jima.[51] Then, the scarcity of visible enemy fighters on Iwo,[52] became a common occurrence again in Vietnam. After each of several heavily contested ground assaults in 1968, one U.S. company commander wondered what had happened to all the people who had just been shooting at his unit.[53]

Effect on the Local Population

Even in the free-fire zones of Vietnam, there were innocent villagers who preferred not to abandon their own land. To the extent that they then escaped bombardment, they still enjoyed an acceptable lifestyle.

19 A MINIMALLY DISRUPTED ENVIRONMENT

● How is a battlefield altered by preparatory bombardment?

● Do any such changes then lessen the chances of peace?

The whole place doesn't have to be leveled by an initial shelling.

(Source: http://search.usa.gov public-domain image from this url: http://www.history.army.mil/images/artphoto/pripos/wwii-tideturns/BackRoad.jpg.)

If a Lasting Peace Is the Aim

As with sin in everyday life, indiscretions in combat can gradually grow more serious. Though both sides strive to fight humanely, deep-seated animosities develop. Where there is concurrent civil war, this unhappy trend becomes particularly pronounced. Then, as at Beirut from 1975 to 1990 or in Syria today, further atrocities become almost impossible to quell. If the war goes on long enough or has a less-than-equitable resolution, future generations may seek retribution (like how the Germans felt about the Treaty of Versailles in 1918 that eventually led to WWII).

To forestall such a syndrome, wouldn't it be better to do as little damage to each future battlefield as possible? Ultimate peace might be better served by not pulverizing every possible source of enemy resistance, traumatizing civilian holdouts, and ruining the local infrastructure.

Such Reasoning Seldom Followed

Deployed U.S. military personnel have been paying too little attention to their wartime environments for a couple of different reasons. One is misplaced loyalty to their organization, and the other is a mistaken impression of how best to make a difference. Tall top-down organizations require the fairly strict obedience of all subordinate elements. If a lower echelon attempts a more situationally appropriate action, it can be accused of disloyalty. That's a perception that most career-oriented members would rather avoid.

Then, there's the importance of killing to the actual winning of an ongoing war. In one-on-one combat, killing most decisively determines the outcome. But, this is not always the case in a widespread conflict. History (particularly recent U.S. history) is replete with examples of when the side suffering the most losses still came out on top (North Vietnam in 1973 for example). While political, economic, or psychological factors may have helped to achieve that end, the war is still technically lost. So, when it is argued that U.S. forces regularly inflict more casualties than they suffer, something other than final victory is being discussed. The professional soldier is expected to put the ultimate outcome of a war above all other considerations. In the age of 4GW, that may require more societal empathy than killing expertise.

Other Cultures Need Not Mirror That of the U.S.

A veteran of the war in Afghanistan who later served on the staff of the National Security Council may have put his finger on why America never seems to get any more proficient at its overseas involvements.

The people who wrote our tactics for Iraq and Afghanistan

were scholars of the Vietnam War. . . . And yet, we repeated the [same] errors over and over again [in Iraq and Afghanistan].[1]

    — Lt.Col.O'Connell USMC (Ret.), *NPR,* April 2017

As the economy-enhancing Pentagon continues to purchase "the best equipment possible," many GIs have become overly gun oriented. They assume that whoever has the most sophisticated weaponry in a war will automatically win it. Despite ample evidence to the contrary, this belief has become so deeply embedded in the American psyche that it is now part of the culture. That's why the *NPR* interviewer points out that Lt.Col. O'Connell has come "to believe that there is something cultural about the way Americans fight wars, . . . [and] the way they try to win hearts and minds."[2] Unfortunately, without pursuing both ends in a way acceptable to the beleaguered society, it's almost impossible to win a 4GW conflict overseas.

Such a conclusion, though logical, is not all that easy for many Americans to accept. How could their "freedom-loving culture" not be the best model for all things? Lt.Col. O'Connell's warning to the contrary is not his only insight. Forfeiting the countryside to the Taliban didn't work for the Soviets in Afghanistan, and it's not going to work for the Americans now. That's because insurgencies and democracies both depend upon rural support. For the country folk to forsake insurrection in support of a central government, they must first enjoy local security.

[T]he bulk of the . . . [U.S.] resources, should go towards governance—towards building up the institutions of a state. But there's a first precondition for all this, and that's [nationwide] security.[3]

    — Lt.Col. O'Connell USMC(Ret.), *NPR,* April 2017

Foreign Troops Can't be Trained as GIs Are

The way most American instructors have been preparing their overseas surrogates for battle has been following far too much U.S. custom. Every culture has its own ways of fighting. While some of these ways might look a little strange to a Pentagon planner, they nevertheless work in that region (and for the local enlistee's temperament). What a GI would readily accept as constructive (albeit public) criticism might cause an Asian soldier to lose so much face as to want to switch sides. Instead of trying to correct what that foreign fighter has been doing badly, perhaps the U.S. trainer should be focusing more on his potential strengths. After all, the underlying goal is that he be able to defeat his immediate adversary, not how he goes about doing so. Absolutely essential to that task would be a strong self-image. After all, a good short-range infiltrator has no real need be an expert marksman.

> I think we have pretty good evidence now, both from Iraq and Afghanistan, that the massive assembly-line attempt to produce capable, professional national security forces has not worked well.[4]
> — Lt.Col. O'Connell USMC(Ret.), *NPR*, April 2017

The traditional "cookie cutter" approach to military training inside the U.S. has had a few problems as well. Among the most glaring are a complete lack of learning dynamic with regard to small-unit maneuver (automatic path toward better squad tactics). If that path existed, U.S. commanders would soon discover a whole new range of tactical options for companies and above—like how totally to surprise an enemy counterpart.

There's More Than One Kind of Offense and Defense

Because the Pentagon still practices a "higher-tech" version of 2GW, most Americans have come to associate all military operations with a massive application of missiles, bombs, and bullets. In their eyes (and the eyes of the contemporary GI), every U.S. attack involves three things: (1) an indirect-fire bombardment; (2) a machinegun sheaf to achieve fire superiority; and (3) all carried weaponry on full automatic during the ground assault. Then, for the standard U.S. defense, about the same thing is assumed: (1) engaging the attacking force at maximum range with all available ordnance; (2) forcing its assault element to move through interlocking bands of machinegun fire; and (3) finally shooting the few who get through the previous fire storm.

Unfortunately (for the U.S. arms manufacturers), neither the offense nor defense needs to look like that to be effective. In fact, neither requires the expenditure of much ammunition at all. One historical example per combat phase should be enough to make this clear.

On offense at Guadalcanal during early WWII, Lt.Col. Evans Carlson's fire-team-sized patrols of Marine Raiders simply went out looking for enemy forces. Each time such a force was detected, all the tiny Raider elements in its vicinity had several options: (1) advance until able single-handedly to attack a soft target (like a bivouac site) and then pull back; (2) opportunistically swarm in to help another fire team in contact; or (3) simply report back to headquarters with the sighting.[5] For none of those options was much Raider ammunition required.

During the Vietnam War, there was also a U.S. defense that needed little ordnance. The protection plan for a CAP unit involved no final defensive fires (no last-minute indirect-fire preregistrations or interlocking bands of machinegun fire). The safety of each village (and its enclosed CAP compound) instead depended on a series of tiny ambushes that continually roved its outer periphery. Then, when one ambush patrol made contact, others moved in to further restrict the enemy's advance toward the village.[6] While such a plan may seem overly risky to firepower enthusiasts, it nevertheless worked. From 1965 to 1971, only about two dozen of over 200 CAP villages were entered by an enemy unit and none came under permanent VC control.[7]

Collateral Damage Need Not Be a Chronic Problem

Any overapplication of firepower creates more chance of collateral damage. In recent years, American forces have made huge strides in reducing the amount of "accidental destruction" that their traditional methods inflicted. Yet, no matter how well directed, a U.S. missile, bomb, or shell will invariably do some unintended harm. Nearby will be unexpected civilians, fragile watersheds, planted fields, or important infrastructure. Then afraid of returning to their fields or other sources of livelihood, local residents will have their loyalties affected.

The only way totally to preclude collateral damage is to cease waging 2GW altogether, whether "high-tech" or otherwise. Even within the martial arena of 4GW, one need not depend upon attrition warfare methods. Below are some examples (not all American) of how 3GW procedure can more than suffice.

Other-Nation Use of 3GW

A practitioner of 3GW will intentionally bypass a foe's manpower concentrations to more easily get at his strategic assets. In Vietnam, enemy sappers regularly destroyed American aircraft on the ground without ever harming a U.S. sentry. They would crawl onto the tarmac at night to plant timed satchel charges on their targets and then lob in a few hastily aimed mortar rounds at dawn. Firepower-oriented base commanders then usually attributed such equipment losses to lucky mortar hits. Around 1968, the in-country "Stars and Stripes" newspaper carried a story about how six or seven helicopters had all being destroyed at the same time in Da Nang's Marble Mountain Air Facility by a "lucky string of mortar rounds."[8] Of course, the odds against such a multiple direct hit are prohibitive. The same enemy ruse appears to have worked at Bien Hoa Airbase in 1964. Within 20 minutes, 27 U.S. aircraft were supposedly damaged or destroyed by three Viet Cong mortar tubes.[9] It's not likely that over two dozen flying machines would be sitting out in the open in a tightly packed group. Most would have had their own revetments.

East Asians are not endowed with some hereditary aptitude for this level of sabotage. Just to survive at the bottom of a strict military hierarchy, many American nonrates develop enough patience and chicanery to easily do as well. The real question is whether their leaders are culturally capable of tapping into this valuable natural resource.

Sabotage, by itself, is a wonderful wartime strategy because it tends only to harm materiel. But, when a little deception is thrown in, something truly special emerges. Then, that materiel can be damaged over and over with the same unimpeded trick. The one above does not require a *ninjutsu*-qualified commando, only a couple of truly light infantrymen—those who regularly practice short-range infiltration. In Rhodesia, a pair of Selous Scouts (in black face) once entered an African village, shot the enemy commander from close range at a public rally, and then calmly walked back into the night—all at a place many miles behind enemy lines.[10] Of note, this maneuver involved no collateral damage, and very little apparent danger. Instead of disrupting the local population's everyday life, it may have actually enhanced it.

One Fairly Rare U.S. Example from the Iraq War

The following is a firsthand account from the Iraq War and the period leading up to it. It has been only slightly edited to preserve important detail.

From 1999 to 2004, there was a Scout Platoon from a Marine Tank Battalion that was able to do some fairly amazing things. It had two sergeants who were close buddies in charge—one of South African descent, and the other was of Korean. . . . Those in charge of the platoon truly believed that as a whole, they were only as strong as the weakest link. Their training was completely out of the box and focused on bottom-up training. Twice a year [all members of] the platoon would conduct the "Scout Package." . . . This would always be followed up by a detailed after action brief in which every member of the platoon['s] observations could be heard. They were trusted by their command and allowed to work autonomously.

During Egypt's multinational Bright Star Exercise of 2001 this platoon easily infiltrated multiple Allied screen lines. Often times while dismounted they were able to walk into Army camps and even right up to armored vehicles undetected. On one of the infiltrations they located the Joint Headquarters and destroyed it with notional artillery. . . .

While functioning as OPFOR (Opposition Forces) at Fort Irwin in 2000, the 16 men of this platoon were credited with over 700 KIAs and 140 destroyed vehicles. This was accomplished through the following: (1) holding hostage all those manning the Combat Operations Center while capturing their operations plans and "Z-ing" out all of their radios (those plans were turned over to the Army's Main OPFOR who used them to destroy the majority of the division-sized unit); (2) infiltrating the Army's main troop staging area and detonating fake explosives around hundreds of sleeping troops; and finally (3) conducting multiple fire-team-size raids/and infiltrations simultaneously against a spread-out division sized unit. To escape the opposition camp, they popped a smoke grenade and tooted the horn on an Army HUMMV *[sic]* three times. This caused a nearby guard tower to signal a widespread NBC alarm (Nuclear, Biological, or Chemical) signaling an attack. Then, the ingenious Marine scouts ran through the front gate claiming they were chasing the enemy while approximately 3,000 other base occupants struggled to don MOPP-4 (Mission Oriented Protective Posture) gear in the required eight minutes at 0200 in the morning.

In 2002 at Fort Irwin, this same Marine Scout platoon was "scripted" to make them less effective as OPFOR personnel. After being told to attack an objective area at precisely between 0900 and 1100 the next morning, they did so quite effectively. Scouts deployed and observation post (OP) to gain eyes on the objective. The OP reported that the place they were supposed to attack was free of personnel and vehicles. The OP also located the convoy staging area the Army was using. The Scouts "acquired" an Army 2.5 ton truck, donned their new found Army uniforms, and snuck into the Army convoy with the instructions from the 2 Sergeants to look "lazy and complacent." As the convoy left to the area the Scouts were supposed to attack that morning, it was flanked by Army M2 Bradley fighting vehicles and M1 Abrams tanks. Forward of the convoy the Army had deployed Apache and Kiowa helicopters to look for their "scripted enemy." Several kilometers short of the objective the convoy stopped "nut to butt" with no dispersion and didn't even conduct a haring *[sic]* bone formation. The South African Sgt. took his section to the front and the Korean Sgt. took his section to the rear and every vehicle in the convoy was destroyed by attaching fake satchel charges to them. Many of the Army Command Staff were in those vehicles. The Army deployed several units to search for the intruders, which had already retrograded, picked up the Scouts at the OP and made it back to their hooch and commenced to drinking beer.

But, the true potential of this platoon was not realized until the U.S. drive on Baghdad during Operation Iraqi Freedom I of March 2003. The [two] Scout sections often worked autonomously from each other but for the size and complexity of the drive to Baghdad the whole platoon worked in tandem. . . . The Scout Platoon was comprised of 8 vehicles. The Korean and South African sergeant's sections were mirror imaged . . . [and] comprised of 3 HUMMVs *[sic]* each. One truck would have a MK-19 grenade launcher mounted with a M-2 .50 in storage. The other truck would have a M-2 .50 caliber mounted with the MK-19 in storage. The third vehicle would have a TOW missile launcher mounted. . . .

The Scouts were the lead reconnaissance unit for the Tank Battalion which was the tip of the spear for the 7th Marines Regimental Combat Team (RCT7). During this drive northward after Nasiriyah, there were no friendlies to the front of the Scout platoon. The platoon ranged as far as 60 kilometers ahead of RCT 7. In fact, they had already crossed the Nasiriyah Bridge by the time the famous firefight occurred there. While conducting what can best be described as a fighting reconnaissance, it destroyed many abandoned T-55's, T-72's, and assorted other Iraqi military vehicles. Often, it would have to dismount to even approach them. Several other firefights occurred that were mostly one sided. That the Scouts were good at what it did became fairly obvious to the large-unit commanders. That's why one battalion S-3 in Baghdad felt comfortable in issuing the following frag order one morning to the South African Sgt.: "Go forth and do great things and give me a report when you get back." When this platoon got to Baghdad, it was allowed to move freely to cross unit boundaries. After a few days there, the Korean Sgt. was given the task of establishing the Iraqi Police. This was no small task because the day prior their orders were to shoot the police on sight. The South African Sgt. was tasked with gathering human intelligence and acting on it. By this time the platoon was able to capture or destroy many more armored vehicles, fight pockets of Fedayeen Saddam, find and deal with weapons caches, stop several bank robberies, and perform various other [peacekeeping] duties. The platoon use[d] captured Iraqi diesel trucks to fuel generators for hospitals and medical clinics. . . . By the actions of the Marines from Scout Platoon, several of the people of Baghdad they encountered would often come to them and offer information the Scouts could act on to make the people's lives safer, earning their trust, and still accomplish the military objectives. The South African sergeant was able to stay with this unit for five and a half years, whereas the Korean sergeant stayed with this platoon one year longer and is still serving honorably. Their willingness to get up close and personal with the enemy and use [of] compassion when needed had prevented a lot of needless collateral damage.[11]

—U.S. Marine tank scout of South African descent

Clearly, this Scout Platoon had required some force to do its job in Iraq. It had, after all, been severely outnumbered and outgunned in the above-mentioned reconnaissance. However, occasional machinegun, grenade launcher, or antitank-missile fire inflicts much less damage than what normally ensues when the main body of a U.S. mechanized force meets the slightest resistance. Then, there is an abundant and continuous application of 120mm-tank-cannon, heavy-artillery, and aerial-bomb/rocket fire against any possible enemy hideout. A wide path of destruction regularly ensues. So, the Scouts had used minimal force to make a very small footprint (relatively speaking) on the partially urban countryside. That's largely because their previous internal training had specifically stressed "brains over bronze," namely always engaging one's brain before one's weapon.[12] The Allied drive on Baghdad in which this Scout platoon participated has also been chronicled in the TV documentary "Delta Company [1st Tank Battalion]: The Push to Baghdad."[13] Here's what the section head of Korean descent now says about the leadership skills necessary to make such an accomplishment possible.

[C]are (be there for your Marines)
[L]isten (pay attention to what they are saying)
[T]eam ("working together" is everything)
[D]efend (stick up for your subordinates) [14]
— 1st Sgt. John Schmuck USMC

Another American Example from Afghanistan

The members of U.S. Marine scout/sniper team decided to get

closer to their foe than they normally would have in Afghanistan to avoid any collateral damage. By so doing, they provided another excellent insight for others. The team leader (a former "grunt" rifleman) later admitted that with a little more "scout" training any Marine infantry squad or fire team could have easily matched the feat.[15]

> Mianposhteh, Afghanistan—For seven hours, the Marine sniper team waited, crouching behind a concrete block in a dusty courtyard. . . . They were pretty sure that a group of local Taliban militants was on the other side of the compound wall. But the snipers couldn't strike until they had some proof. . . .
> Team leader Sgt. Erik Rue kept himself sharp by running scenarios in his head of what could happen next: What if the Taliban burst in, guns blazing? What if they enter unarmed? What if there are children in the way? [16]
> — *Wired Magazine* (Conde Nast), 27 August 2009

Like any good policeman, Rue had taken his team into harm's way to better protect the local citizenry. Equipped with telescopic long-range rifles, those team members could have just as easily "dinged" bad guys from a distance. But actual enemy combatants are much harder to confirm that way.

> U.S. Marines and Taliban guerrillas have battled in the villages and compounds of this farming community nearly every day for eight weeks. . . . But during most of those shootouts, the two sides have been hundreds, even thousands, of feet apart. On Tuesday, they fought at point-blank range.
> . . . By the time it [the below-described event] was over, at least two men [both gun-toting Taliban] were dead. Another [a Marine] took a bullet to the chest but escaped unharmed [because of his flak jacket]. And another [also a Marine] had his gun shot out of his hands. Four more [Marines] survived what should have been a lethal bomb blast.[17]
> — *Wired Magazine* (Conde Nast), 27 August 2009

Clearly to distinguish normal village dwellers from visiting Taliban, the Marines would soon require either a ruse or an even closer look.

After waiting for so long, the sniper team decided to try
something new to flush out their targets. . . .

Bring some helicopters overhead, he [Rue] said, and
make a low pass. . . .

But the men on the other side of the wall didn't take the
bait. . . .

Staff Sgt. Doug Webb was getting sick of waiting. . . .

He scooted into a small room, adjacent to the courtyard.
On the western wall of the room, at floor level, was a yard-
wide "mouse hole." Webb lay his chest on the floor, and
stuck his face in the hole.[18]

— *Wired Magazine* (Conde Nast), 27 August 2009

Once the sighting was confirmed, the team wanted to take up
better firing positions.

At first, all he could see were ankles and feet. All he
could hear were four male voices, speaking Pashto. Then he
recognized a single word: "Taliban." Webb looked up, and
saw that one of the men had a vest packed with ammunition.
And an AK-47. . . .

. . . "Now or never," Rue said [upon learning of the sight-
ing]. He sent three snipers to the roof, and ran out of the
courtyard with three others: Sgt. Ryan Steinbacker, Cpl.
Fred Gardner, and [Sgt. Nick] Worth. They entered an
east-west alleyway, perpendicular to the trail that Webb
had spied through his mouse hole. . . .

Almost immediately, a barrage of bullets came flying in
directly at the snipers. . . . Clearly, there were more than
four militants on the area.[19]

— *Wired Magazine* (Conde Nast), 27 August 2009

Then, after the initial gun play was over, it became time for
a partial pull back. Just as the Carlson Raider fire team after an
impromptu attack on a Japanese camp, the modern-day Marines
withdrew to slightly safer ground.

A thunderous boom rang out. A cloud of dirt engulfed
the snipers. Webb fell forward. "I saw a white flash and
stars, like I got hit in the face," he says. . . .

"... Everyone back inside!" Rue shouted. In a daze, they stumbled back to the courtyard.

Not long after, a handful of infantrymen from a Marine platoon wandered into the compound. . . .

The firefight continued. But now it was the Taliban who were outgunned. . . .

That allowed the sniper team a chance to exit the battle, nearly 12 hours after they had first slipped into that courtyard.[20]

— *Wired Magazine* (Conde Nast), 27 August 2009

Sgt. Rue and some of his men later suffered a few side effects from that enemy satchel charge or IED.[21] Yet, they had still set an important precedent. There had been no innocent bystanders hurt during their opportunistic foray—no "unintentional" targeting mistakes to stir up additional blood feuds. That's the beauty of truly close combat—*bona fide* enemy combatants are much easier to identify, and there's no time lag with regard to intelligence. That's not generally the case with long-range weaponry as directed by satellite or drone, no matter how much magnification is involved. It's through close-up views from afar that umbrellas start looking like assault rifles, and bread-carrying grandmas like late-arriving terrorist bombers. In a counterinsurgency or otherwise 4GW environment, "up-close-and-personal" contact is—by far—the most productive (despite any additional risk). Professional U.S. law enforcement personnel now bravely follow that axiom on a daily basis. Within most Muslim communities overseas, a nearby U.S. foray along the ground also carries with it much more legitimacy than standoff firepower.

Less Shooting Had Caused the Minimal Disruption

In both of the above cases, maneuver and surprise had taken the place of firepower. Yet, truly amazing progress had still been made. Why, then, does the Pentagon and much of the American public still put so much stock in overwhelming force?

Part Seven

Historical Examples of Not Killing

"What doth the Lord require of thee, but to do justly,
and to love mercy, and to walk humbly with thy God?"
— Micah 6:8

20 HARDLY A SHOT WAS FIRED

- Have U.S. forces always required a lot of firepower?
- When might less ordnance have worked a little better?

Not all wars are decided by set piece ground battles.

(Source: "Hill 609 [Tunisia]," by Fletcher Martin, U.S. Army Center for Military History, posted Oct. 2005, from this url: http://www.history.army.mil/art/A&I/Hill_609.jpg.)

U.S. History Is Full of Examples

Every U.S. war has had occasions of hardly a "friendly" shot being fired, yet the battle still being won. There was no cannon fusillade at Concord during the first military engagement of the War of Independence on 19 April 1775. All the U.S. Minutemen needed to halt the British advance was a prolonged series of well-aimed musket shots.[1]

Then, the key to defeating a more powerful foe became even more obvious. George Washington quietly crossed the Delaware at Trenton on Christmas night in 1776 to accomplish the next big victory of the

Figure 20.1: Battle of Trenton
(Source: "Battle of Trenton," by H.C. McBarron, Jr., U.S. Army Ct. of Mil. History, published by U.S. Govt. Printing Office, and deemed public domain by Wikimedia.)

American Revolutionary War. While he was to use some cannon and musket fire during the actual assault on Trenton after dawn, the results of that assault speak of minimal force being applied.

The battle pitted approximately 2,400 soldiers of the Continental Army, . . . against about 1,400 Hessian [mercenaries]. . . .

The surprise attack was made possible due to . . . crossing the Delaware River . . . [in the middle of the night] under extremely adverse weather conditions.

The Hessian casualties were 22 killed and 83 wounded. Over 1,000 Hessians were captured.

190

The American colonist casualties were only 2 killed and 5 wounded in the battle; however . . . [some] died in the days following . . . due to illness brought on by exposure and exhaustion.[2]
— *American Revolutionary War Facts*

That Washington had concurrently cut off the defenders' various routes of escape also helped with the outcome. But, the deciding factor was the extent to which the "hung over" Hessians had been deceived by the lack of shooting. When General Sullivan had sent a message to Washington about the gunpowder getting wet during the soggy approach march, Washington replied, "Tell General Sullivan to use the bayonet."[3] (See Figure 20.1.)

Then, many difficult years later, the American Revolutionary War was finally concluded at Yorktown through an even quieter assault. On the night of 14 October 1781, a small force of American light infantrymen under the command of Alexander Hamilton seized one of the two redoubts anchoring the British bastion—without the help of either cannon or small arms. This forced Cornwallis to surrender in the decisive engagement of the war.

On the evening of October 14th, two assault parties formed to attack the two redoubts, designated "Redoubts 10 and 9." A French band . . . began their attack on Redoubt 9, while [Alexander Hamilton] . . . commanded the Americans attacking Redoubt 10. Both forces numbered 400 men, and neither had loaded weapons. Instead, the troops fixed their bayonets and followed teams of sappers to the bases of the redoubts. Each redoubt was surrounded by an abatis, or sharpened tree branches tangled together similar to modern day barbed wire, which required the sappers to tear down. The Soldiers, now under heavy musket fire from the British, dropped fascines (bundles of sticks tied with yarn) into the ditch surrounding the redoubt, and placed ladders to climb the sides of the fortification.

The fighting within the redoubts digressed into violent hand-to-hand combat. Washington reported on the assault, simply stating the allies "advanced under the fire of the enemy without returning a shot and effected the business with bayonet only." The French captured one hundred and twenty British and Hessian soldiers in thirty minutes [at the other strongpoint], while the Americans captured seventy in Redoubt 10.[4]

—U.S. Army Heritage and Information Center

At the Battle of San Jacinto during the Texan War for Independence in 1836, Sam Houston's troops only needed a few small-arms rounds to decisively defeat Santa Anna's much larger army. (See Map 20.1.)

It was on April 21, that the Texans . . . rushed forward . . . upon the breastworks of the Mexicans. . . .

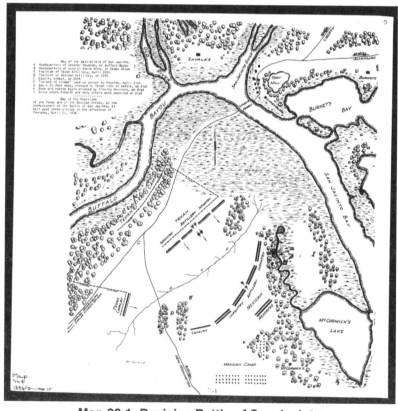

Map 20.1: Decisive Battle of San Jacinto
(Source: "Battle of San Jacinto," by A.J.Houston, Portal to Texas History, Mil. Maps of Texas Revol., pub.1938 by Anson Jones Press, deemed public domain by Wikimedia.)

The Mexican army was drawn up in perfect order, but the Texans rushed on without firing. As they approached the breastworks, the Mexicans greeted them with a stream of bullets, which however, went over their heads. Houston was badly wounded, but the Texans rushed forward. Each man reserved his fire until he could choose his target, then before the Mexicans could reload, the Texans discharged their rifles into their very breasts. Without bayonets, the Texans [then] converted their rifles into war clubs. A desperate hand-to-hand struggle all along the breastworks took place.

When the Texans had. . . broken off their rifles at the breech, they flung the remains at the enemy, and drawing their pistols. . . . When their pistols were emptied they drew their bowie knives. . . .

The little band of heroes had conquered an army superior in training and equipment and twice as large. Only three Texans lost their lives, 34 were wounded, six mortally.[5]

— Texas Military Forces Museum

During the American Civil War, Col. Chamberlain ordered a "swinging gate" bayonet charge at Gettysburg in July 1863 after his troops ran out of ammunition. (See Figure 20.2.) This was not only to surprise the attacking Confederates, but also to alter the

Figure 20.2: Looking West from Little Round Top on Day After
(Source: "View from Summit of Little Round Top at 7:30 P.M. July 3rd, 1863," from Library of Congress, Prints and Photographs Div., deemed public domain by Wikimedia.)

course of the war.[6] Then, more than one stealthy night attack was to occur during the remainder of the war. That by Union forces at Rappahannock Station in November of 1863 may have been the initial really big one.

> Spearheaded by the 6th Maine and the 5th Wisconsin, soldiers of the Federal VI Corps came out of the blackness [without any advance warning], cheering [only] as they charged the earthworks. Savage hand-to-hand fighting broke out; soldiers clubbed, stabbed and fired at close range along the line.[7]
>
> — *The Civil War: The Killing Ground,* by Jaynes

> The battle surged back and forth until a second charge [likely without shooting to avoid any fratricide] . . . gave the Union regiments a decisive edge. Broken, the Confederates fled across a bridge or tried to swim to the south bank of the river, having lost four cannon, eight battleflags and 1,303 men. In the South, the Battle of Rappahannock Station was called a "mortifying disaster." The Union celebrated a victory that marked the first successful night attack of the War.[8]
>
> — *The Civil War: The Killing Ground,* by Jaynes

No Small Coincidence

In every case mentioned above, some killing had been necessary. But it was not nearly as much death as more or heavier ordnance would have caused. Since the Middle Ages, most ground assaults have been preceded by preparatory fire from cannons, catapults, or longbow archers. Then, the assault force itself would apply as much small-arms or crossbow fire as it could on the way in. The whole idea—as is still an integral part of most U.S. infantry assault tactics—was to establish so much fire superiority that defenders couldn't contest the attack. Thus, it's no small coincidence that the most decisive battles of the American Revolutionary War, Texan War for Independence, and U.S. Civil War had all been won with less force than was customary.

The most likely reason for this scarcity of firepower was that it facilitated surprise. But, as the following more modern examples will demonstrate, there are other benefits.

20th Century Cases of Hardly Any Shooting

So far, this discussion has been at least thought provoking. But, it has probably not dissuaded any arms manufacturer or attrition warrior from believing the quickest way to victory is through eliminating all opposition. That will take additional examples of less force proving helpful during some of the most intense fighting in contemporary warfare.

Within the U.S. Marines' first major WWI action lay a fateful hint of how most safely to cross open ground against enemy machine-gun fire. The 6th of June 1918 (26 years to the day before Omaha Beach) would start out to be fairly promising. The Marines were taking part in a French offensive that had supposedly started at 03:45 A.M. Their plan to assault Hill 142 before dawn with bayonets only had been a good one, but then it got slightly delayed.[9] Just north of Paris on that date, the sun rose about 5:50 A.M. As the tall wheat being crossed became more visible to the foe, the circumstances that had made the initial plan so insightful began to change.

At 0500, the 1st Battalion, 5th Marine Regiment attacks west of Belleau Wood straightening the front and capturing strategic Hill 142 to support an assault on the wooded area. The attack was successful despite the lack of [artillery] preparation and poor timing [late start]. Twelve hours later battalions of the 5th and 6th Marine Regiments frontally assault the [Belleau] woods. . . .

The attack against the woods proper goes grimly. Crossing a wheatfield [sic] where they are exposed to machine gun fire [is the hang-up.] [10]

— "Battle for Belleau Wood," Great War Society

Luckily, that painful lesson from WWI had not been totally lost to the next generation of Marines. While WWII again called for "total warfare" against a highly capable foe, there were still occasions where a lot of preliminary bombing, shelling, and shooting were deemed counterproductive. Such was the case one early morning in the desperate battle for Iwo Jima.

The big E [Gen. Graves Blanchard Erskine] had decided now was the time to spring the predawn attack on the Japanese. . . .

Such a tactic hadn't been used on Iwo, and seldom had Marines employed it in earlier Pacific campaigns.

It might work now, Erskine felt, as it had in France against the Germans in World War I. [11]

— *Iwo Jima: Legacy of Valor,* by Ross

Apparently, this maneuver had been so appropriate to the situation that no special training was required of its participants. Normally, a loud preparatory barrage would have alerted the enemy to an impending ground assault. [12] Fully realizing the personal benefits of no advance warning, those young Marines took to the silent nighttime approach like ducks to water.

Lieutenant Colonel Howard J. Turton, the...intelligence officer,... said the troops weren't trained in the demanding skills of night fighting. . . .

Two companies from Colonel Boehm's Third Battalion of the 9th Marines [still] began moving into the lines at 3:20 A.M. . . .

Company commanders tried to orient themselves in the light of parachute flares, but the steady downpour and black night practically obliterated the landscape. [13]

— *Iwo Jima: Legacy of Valor,* by Ross

This crawling attack was not all that hard to perform, because only necessary for unit alignment was for each man to stay up with the next man closer to the center. In fact, the whole procedure worked so well that it surprised those doing it as much as anybody in the way.

They moved without detection for half an hour until a Japanese machinegun opened fire and gave the alarm. The position was silenced in seconds by a flamethrower. Now the enemy was aroused, but not before Marines had passed through the lines without being discovered and without suffering a casualty.

. . . Many Japanese had been killed in their foxholes and pill boxes. Colonel Boehm reported that K Company was atop Hill 362C [actually only Hill 331 somewhat short of 362C]. . . .

. . . Boehm's outfit wasn't alone in slipping through scores of slumbering Japanese before being detected. Lieutenant Colonel Robert E. Cushman's Second Battalion and Major William T. Glass's First [Battalion] gained several hundred yards before heavy fighting erupted around them at 7:30 A.M.[14]

— *Iwo Jima: Legacy of Valor,* by Ross

Despite the unintentional creation of Cushman's Pocket (an encircled U.S. contingent that would take a while to relieve), this nighttime maneuver had turned out rather well. Here's, how the parent-unit commander was to describe the degree of its overall success.

Colonel Boehm noted in his battle journal, "the strategy proved very sound, since it turned out that the open ground taken under cover of darkness was the most heavily fortified of all terrain captured.[15]

— *Iwo Jima: Legacy of Valor,* by Ross

Less Force During Fiercest Fighting in the Pacific

For the U.S. Marines, the three hardest-fought battles of WWII were for the islands Peleliu, Iwo Jima, and Okinawa. That's because Japan had finally perfected a "soft" underground strongpoint defensive matrix that could be hidden in rocky, vegetation-free terrain. Of the three battles, that for Okinawa contained what was arguably the most intense period of mortal combat. That struggle was for the northern end of the Shuri Defense Line in May 1945. The best evidence of this claim is the number of casualties suffered by the Allied participant during its first ten days— 2,662 killed or wounded and 1289 "combat fatigue" cases.[16] The second of those statistics is particularly indicative of the severity of the fighting. It took considerable adversity for any Leatherneck of that era to say "uncle." (See Figure 20.3.)

6th Division had initially tried to break through the Sugar Loaf Complex at the northern end of the Shuri Line. After partially capturing that Complex, the 6th then got some much needed help from one regiment of the neighboring 1st Marine Division. It had

197

Figure 20.3: Peleliu, Iwo Jima, and Okinawa as Hard as It Gets
(Source: "Closing In: Marines in the Siezure of Iwo Jima," by Colonel Joseph H. Alexander, Marines in WWII Commemorative Series, HQMC, 1994.)

done nothing really wrong with its "firepower-heavy" way of assaulting. This standard procedure for most Marine units had just failed to carry this particular objective, due to counterattacks from below ground. It would seem that by gradually refining defense methods, the Japanese had finally carpeted the perfect piece of terrain with enough flying metal and reinforcement portals. What had subsequently resulted was an area through which no attacker could travel without taking excessive casualties.

2nd Battalion, 4th Marines (2/4) was then to be assigned the hardest part of the remaining Complex—Half Moon. (See Map 20.2.) To pursue this task, it would employ a squad assault technique that had been previously improvised—when the planes were late and no other supporting arms available—while still the 4th Raider Battalion. On that occasion in July 1943, despite all that missing firepower, the young Raiders had still moved completely through

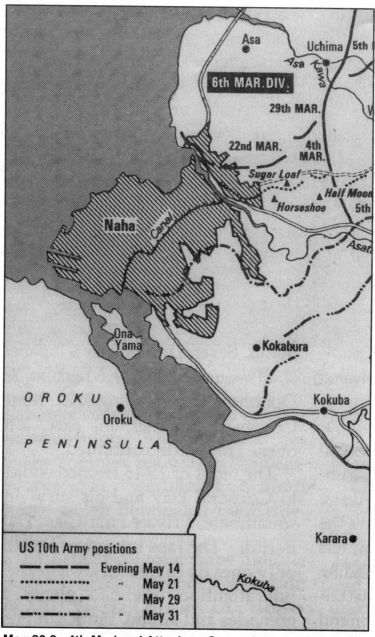

Map 20.2: 4th Marines' Attack on State-of-the-Art Shuri Line
(Source: "The Final Campaign: Marines in the Victory on Okinawa," by Col. Joseph H. Alexander, Marines in WWII Commemorative Series, HQMC, 1996, p. 38.)

three out of the four tiers of a sophisticated defense in depth that protected Bairoko Harbor on New Georgia. This bunker array may have been a slightly above-ground (but vegetation-obscured) prototype of the nearly impregnable belts that first started appearing on barren Peleliu in September 1944.

There are no detailed accounts of that piecemeal battle for the forward faces of Half Moon. Still, the nontraditional Bairoko style of assault had almost certainly come into play. The best ongoing indicator is no call for air or artillery support once the front edge of the objective had been reached (the approach march was over). 2/4 had previously objected to the use of tanks on the Orote Peninsula of Guam.[17]

Promising gains were made by both assault battalions of the 4th Marines on 20 May. Jumping off at 0800 behind heavy artillery barrages and tanks, the attacking troops moved rapidly ahead for 200 yards before encountering fierce opposition from the Horseshoe and Half Moon. . . .

Infantrymen [from 3/4] with demolitions and flame throwers followed closely behind the tanks which blasted the cave positions honeycombing the forward slopes of the Horseshoe. . . .

The attack of 2/4 on Half Moon . . . [also occurred on] 20 May. Heavy and accurate flat trajectory fire coming from the direction of Shuri heights raked the battalion's flank, and mortars firing from defiladed positions on the reverse slopes of Half Moon covered the entire zone of advance [with exploding rounds].[18]

— "USMC Historical Monograph," 1955

2/4 and 3/4 moved out in the assault on 20 May. Both battalions were supported by tanks and made rapid progress for about 200 yards, when they were brought to a halt by a torrent of enemy fire. The Japanese, who were deeply entrenched on Half Moon and Horseshoe, suddenly met the advance with a hail of small arms, machine gun, artillery and mortar fire. The enemy's artillery observers on Shuri Ridge were virtually looking down our throats, and could easily control and direct very accurate fire from hidden gun positions. . . .

On the left Col. Hayden of 2/4 . . . decided to change his plan of attack. Instead of continuing the frontal assault, he would attempt to envelop both flanks of the enemy's positions on Half Moon. . . . [T]he attack was renewed with F Company laying down covering fire, [w]hile Company G assaulted the right flank and Company E the left. . . . Company G, moving closely behind the fire of the tanks, quickly reached and secured the western end of Half Moon. Traversing more open ground and subject to enemy fire from three directions, the advance of Company E was much slower. Despite heavy casualties, and the volume of mortar fire they encountered, E Company reached the forward slope of their objective and dug in for the night.[19]

— *Dan Marsh's Marine Raider Page*

The machinegun bunkers along those steep slopes of Half Moon had been mutually supporting.[20] That means each was protected by the crisscrossing fire of two behind it. (See Figure 20.4.) Thus, 2/4 would have had fire teams moving forward (roughly on line) to try to double-envelop—through the microterrain—the bunkers in their lanes. While the most forward bunkers had priority, they could not be seized without some pressure being applied behind them. In other words, Marine buddy teams would have to provide impromptu assistance to those from different squads in other lanes. (See Figures 20.5 through 20.7.)

No frontline commander could have controlled such a convoluted "mishmash," nor would have detailed planning done much good. Capturing this objective would take "a closer look," individual initiative, and the surprise that only "micro-maneuver" can develop. Such natural flow of events must simply be allowed to happen. Only really important is the constant cooperation between teams. While prerehearsed fire team techniques might have helped with the double-envelopments, the overall maneuver required no structure other than lanes and alignment. The latter didn't need to be directed. Marines of this era knew instinctively not to get too far ahead of each other.

The closest Western parallel to a Bairoko Assault is "fire and movement with grenades added"—a decidedly "hasty" type of attack. However, that Assault had also involved "recon pull," short-range infiltration, and "swarm" characteristics. Because fire team technique would have made each bunker's double-envelopment a little easier, the entire evolution could be viewed as a "deliberate attack" of sorts. Yet, no procedural formula (or its rehearsal) could do justice to that many considerations. They must necessarily arise out of individual initiative and available microterrain. That's why this assault method was able to replace higher-echelon coordination with bottom-echelon cooperation. There is something of major tactical significance here. 2/4 had once again proven that the Bairoko Assault needed no supporting arms to overwhelm a state-of-the-art defense. Once the face of Half Moon had been encountered, the tanks had stayed behind to provide overhead fire if necessary.[21] So, the final part of that assault through the bunkers had been conducted with small arms, bazookas, flame throwers, and demolitions only.

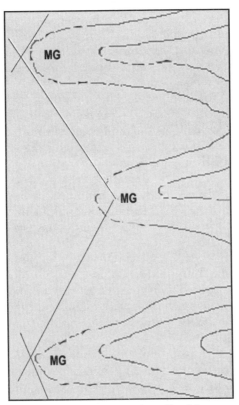

Figure 20.4: Mutually Supporting Machinegun Bunkers

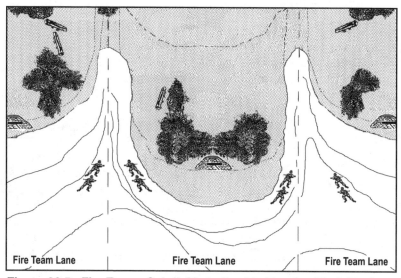

Figure 20.5: Fire Teams Subdivide to Double-Envelop Their Bunkers

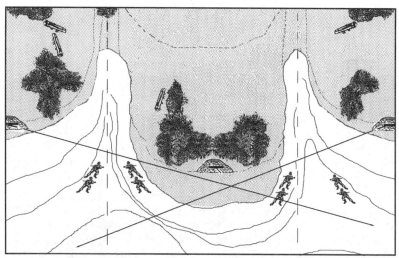

Figure 20.6: Rearward Bunkers Fire Across Front of U.S.Target

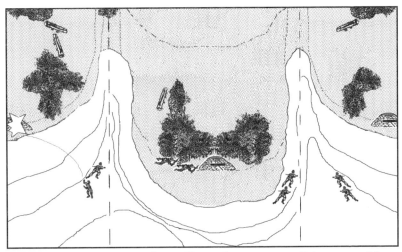

Figure 20.7: Adjacent-Lane Team Suppresses Crisscross Fire

Inherent Difficulty Behind Overwhelming Firepower

One of the biggest problems with a lot of firepower is the inevitable "short round," or some GI getting run over by a U.S. tank. Dan Marsh and his 4th Raider Battalion buddies had used a maneuver at Bairoko on New Georgia in 1943 that was just recently recognized as a key step in the evolution of small-unit tactics. Without any tanks, artillery, or airstrikes, its fire teams had cooperated between lanes to successfully attack a bunker matrix.[22] Later the same battalion (now designated as 2/4) again used small arms and demolitions only to take Okinawa's nearly impregnable Half Moon Hill in May 1945.

At the time, the U.S. War Department may have failed to attribute much importance to what had happened at Bairoko and Okinawa because of its highly unorthodox nature. Besides the lack of supporting arms, there had been no direct supervision of frontline troops in either case.

Reduced Force Too Counter-Cultural in America?

Sadly, the whole idea of less force allowing more surprise and less fratricide was badly to languish after WWII. Only recently has it dawned on U.S. war planners that fewer GIs get hurt when tiny highly secretive teams attack strategic targets, instead of firepower-spewing battalions. That may be because no U.S. military organization—commando or otherwise—has yet to produce the prerequisite degree of light-infantry assault, defense, and escape expertise. Such teams largely depend for their safety on the split-second "real-time" decisions that only they themselves can make. Too much headquarters interference invariably results from the modern-day marvels of instant communications, electronic surveillance, and precision standoff firepower.

What Tiny Teams Have Accomplished Elsewhere

Instead of the "boot camp" way in which Western recruits are prepared for combat, the fledgling Selous Scouts were simply made to live off the land (Central-African bush) for 18 days.[23] It was not long before their leaders realized their survival potential as two-man reconnaissance teams. Within weeks, there was no target within "Dakota" aircraft range that was not being reconnoitered for a possible attack by Rhodesian light infantry. A pair of Scouts had only to free-fall parachute into the potential objective's vicinity during the hours of darkness, accomplish their mission, and then walk out to a helicopter extraction site.[24]

Soon More Than Reconnaissance Became Possible

Early in Rhodesia's "war of independence," the Communist insurgents fled into the lightly populated Zambesi Valley. Like the British had in Malaysia, the Selous Scouts started sending tiny teams of trackers out in a "hunter/killer" role. (See Figure 20.8.) Soon, their quarries started taking refuge in the villages of more populated areas. It was then that a new, and quite daring, Selous Scout procedure was born. On one occasion, a tracking team (some members possibly in black face) crept unseen into a small village during a ZANLA (Zimbabwe African National Liberation Army) rally, eased their way to the front of an enthralled crowd, and then shot the speaker. As the crowd and ZANLA bodyguards broke for cover, the pair of Scouts quietly slipped back into the darkened countryside. They were only later to learn that this speaker had been the local ZANLA commander.[25]

Again, killing had been necessary. But, only the head miscreant had ended up dead. That would not have always been possible with a precision missile strike from an overflying drone. In a guerrilla-type war, not harming civilians takes precedence over eliminating rebels. That's because of such a conflict's inevitable nonmartial (4GW) aspects. Selous Scouts also allowed former adversaries to join their ranks.

Figure 20.8: The 4GW-Oriented Selous Scout
(Source: Courtesy of Orion Books, from "World Army Uniforms since 1939," Part II, Plate 98, © 1975, 1980, 1981, 1983 by Blandford Press Ltd.)

21 MAKING FRIENDS OUT OF ENEMIES

● Has America demonized its wartime adversaries?

● Does so doing have any negative side effects?

The local children provide an avenue toward adult acceptance.

A Perfectly Logical Strategy

If an enduring peace is the ultimate goal of war, then there is adequate justification for starting the reconciliation as soon as possible. Among the warring factions of Northwest Pakistan and Afghanistan, allegiances are easily shifted. Militias locked in mortal combat one day may be allies the next—all based on the whims of their tribal elders. Most soldiers are "a-political" anyway. They fight for each other, not an ideology. So, why not try to convert opposition fighters in any guerrilla-like conflict. One of the most convincing examples has come from the Selous Scouts of Rhodesia.

How the Selous Scouts Planned to Succeed

While the Scouts worked for a country in which Apartheid was rampant, they did not personally participate in the discrimination. They belonged to a tiny, semi-autonomous organization that had been allowed to form its own internal policies. Among those policies was to join four blacks for every white and then give them equal opportunity in all things.[1]

Each member of the Selous Scouts, down to the lowest ranking White soldier, speaks at least one African language—necessary for communication with their Black comrades-in-arms with whom they work in the closest possible context as equals.[2]
     — *Pamwe Chete,* by Lt.Col. Reid-Daly

The Selous Scouts' saying of *Pamwe Chete* meant "all together" in the native Shona dialect. It was much like the U.S. Marine motto of *Gung Ho* ("working together" in Chinese). Both *mantras* implied the harnessing of collective wisdom from the lowest echelons of the outfit. Rhodesia had been a British possession, so its governmental agencies were more apt to be hierarchical and "top-down." But, the Selous Scouts must have gotten the "bottom-up" approach from the *krygsraads* (war councils) of the Boers, or the communal thought processes of their Maoist adversaries. However they arrived at the formula, it worked. And when the Selous Scouts tried then to build enough all-around unison to win a very difficult war, they naturally included their battlefield opposition.

The key to the Scouts' success was the extensive reliance on turned, or "tame" insurgents. A constant inflow of these insurgent recruits kept the intelligence on guerrilla security procedures up-to-date. At its zenith, turned insurgents comprised over 50 percent of the Scouts' fighting force.[3]
     — *Defense Watch,* 17 September 2003

The way they made this many "combat conversions" was truly amazing.

How did they recruit from this pool of seemingly fanatic,

dedicated guerillas *[sic]?* Retired Lt. Col. Ron Reid-Daly, a former commander of the Selous Scouts and author of "Pamwe Chete . . . ," put it this way:

"It was simple and direct. He [the terrorist] had the option of being handed over to the police, after which he would be prosecuted for . . . offenses related to terrorism. If found guilty he would be hanged. He could, however, change sides and work with the security forces against his former comrades. After a short period of intensive contemplation, the capture elected to change sides. He was immediately given back his weapon, but unknown to him, its firing pin had been removed. The fact that he had been given a weapon astonished . . . him. [I]t was a shrewdly calculated move designed to sow the seeds of trust. . . .

According to Col. Reid-Daly, despite their vaunted fanaticism, insurgents were relatively easy to turn. They generally lived a tough, hand-to-mouth existence and were acutely aware that while they were putting their lives on the line every day, their leaders were often living in lush accommodations, far removed from any danger, traveling in high diplomatic circles and pilfering the money and supplies intended for them.

Many of the turned insurgents went on to become some of the Scouts' most loyal and decorated soldiers. That the Scouts' formula is an effective counter-insurgency technique is beyond question. Their successes speak for themselves.[4]

— *Defense Watch,* 17 September 2003

Profound Similarities

The most incredible part of the Selous Scout methodology had been routinely turning a battlefield adversary into a trusted companion. In a religious context, that's not too different from "loving one's enemy." But, for winning a conflict with distinct 4GW overtones, it was nothing short of brilliant. Among its attributes were the following: (1) it gave the Scouts a unique source of real-time intelligence; (2) it countered the Scouts natural temptation to dehumanize their foes; (3) and it helped to win the hearts and minds of the population through which all insurgents must swim.

Constantly adding turned terrorists, the Scouts kept abreast of current terrorist terminology, identification procedures, and operations; often they were better informed about terrorist procedures than the terrorists themselves.[5]
— *Dirty Wars,* by Thompson

No U.S. Sequel So Far

The American military has, on occasion, tried to befriend battlefield adversaries. During the Vietnam War, the U.S. Marines launched a concerted effort to utilize enemy defectors. The Chiêu Hoi ("Open Arms") Program had been a Saigon initiative since 1963 to offer sanctuary and pardon to VC fighters. Then, in 1966, the Marines started to turn some of those enemy fighters into Kit Carson Scouts. Of course, not all Chiêu Hois were eligible. From 1969 to 1970, roughly 79,000 conversions were recorded, but less than 17,000 turned out to be genuine.[6]

Most of these Kit Carson Scouts were attached to U.S. infantry battalion S-2 (Intelligence) Sections with an accompanying interpreter. There, they helped to uncover information about the part of Vietnam in which they had previously worked for the VC. Such Scouts then mostly helped with the following projects: (1) to identify VC guerrillas and political cadre among the civilian populace; (2) to offer insights into how the VC moved among, and interacted with, civilians; and (3) to locate traps, caves, tunnels, and ordnance caches.[7]

While some Chiêu Hois may have reverted back to their old ways, the overall program was still considered a resounding success. Almost 200,000 enemy combatants had been removed from the battlefield through VC defection by 1972.[8]

Significant progress in "turning battlefield foes into friends" was also made during the Iraq and Afghan wars. This came when U.S. forces found out how easy it was to sway tribal allegiances through a large cash payout.

The Sometimes Forgotten History

That mortal combat can create animosities that will persist for generations comes as no particular shock to anyone. But, the suggestion that wars should be fought in such a way as to limit this "payback" syndrome is not easily embraced by U.S. war planners. Revolutionary as it may seem to them, it is far from new to the rest of the world. The leaders of ancient armies used to fight each other in a one-on-one joust to the death instead of subjecting their respective subordinates to senseless slaughter. For a while during the Middle Ages in Europe, the army that could outmaneuver the other was declared the winner (without ever coming to blows). Through it all was a code of ethics in which a man's word was his bond, a helpless enemy spared, and wholesale capitulation honorable under a variety of circumstances. Besides limiting the bloodshed, such a strategy also respected the losing side enough for it gracefully to accept the defeat.

Then, the Clausewitzian concept of "total war" came along. It was a term that would become closely associated with the greater degree of destruction from the latest technology.[9] An unfortunate ramification of such a connection would be less attention to the already established rules of war.[10] Though initially occupying the moral high ground, famous German warrior/statesman Otto von Bismarck did make a few overly punitive demands of his defeated opponent following the brilliantly fought (and relatively short) Franco-Prussian War of 1870.

The French emperor, Napoleon III, declared war on Prussia on July 19, 1870, because his military advisers told him that the French army could defeat Prussia and that such a victory would restore his declining popularity in France. The French were convinced that the reorganization of their army in 1866 had made it superior to the German armies. They also had great faith in two recently introduced technical innovations: the breech-loading *chassepot* rifle, with which the entire army was now equipped; and the newly invented *mitrailleuse,* an early machine gun. . . .

[After quickly winning that war,] Germany's annexation of Alsace-Lorraine aroused a deep longing for revenge in the French people. The years from 1871 to 1914 were marked by an extremely unstable peace, since France's determination to recover Alsace-Lorraine and Germany's mounting imperialist ambitions kept the two nations constantly poised for

conflict. Their mutual animosity proved to be the driving force behind the prolonged slaughter on the Western Front in World War I.[11]
— *Encyclopedia Britannica*

Then, at the Treaty of Versailles in 1919, the French negotiators were to make the same mistake as Bismarck had, thereby paving the way for WWII.

Many historians [from European nations] claim that the combination of a harsh treaty and subsequent lax enforcement of its provisions paved the way for the upsurge of German militarism in the 1930's. The huge German reparations and the war guilt clause fostered deep resentment of the settlement in Germany.[12]
— *Encyclopedia Britannica*

Other Parts of the Equation

While it may be nearly impossible to shift the allegiance of an enemy combatant, that combatant will be of more use to the Allied war effort if not afraid of execution or abuse should he surrender. Not only will he exercise less determination during the really difficult fights, but—as a possible captive—he may constitute the only source of valuable combat intelligence. For example, only a low-ranking infantryman would fully understand the intricacies of a state-of-the art "surprise assault" technique.

Seasoned policemen have long realized that someone in their custody will attest to almost anything to avoid too much "extracurricular" attention. For precisely the same reason, military torture is not a reliable way of uncovering important battlefield information.

In any guerrilla-like conflict, enemy fighters must get the majority of their support from the surrounding civilian population. If that entire population is being treated—by a foreign occupier—like sympathizers, then it will not only support those fighters, but also produce additional rebels. Therefore, every attempt must be made to treat all ordinary citizens well, regardless of their political preferences. That makes the job of the contemporary American rifleman very much like that of a policeman. Both must be the guardians of local society, and both must show occasional mercy to its disruptive elements.

22 BATTLEFIELD ACTS OF MERCY

- Must everything in war be brutal?
- What might an act of mercy accomplish?

The "merciful" NVA shooter may have gotten some angelic guidance.

(Source: http://search.usa.gov public-domain image from this url: http://usarmy.vo.llnwd.net/e2/-images/2010/04/27/71395/size0-army.mil-71395-2010-04-27-090410.jpg.)

Hard to Identify

Battlefield acts of mercy can only be totally verified through those who have made them, yet they still appear to occur among highly professional soldiers. Such may have been the case when a U.S. Marine lieutenant found himself fully exposed within 20 yards of an NVA-occupied trench one morning in March of 1967. An enemy machinegun from this same location had just oversprayed the sunken road up which the American platoon leader and his men had approached. Then, the young Yank got shot in the leg with a single bullet.

This particular spot on the trail between Gio Linh and Con Thien had previously seen so much action as to be already nicknamed "The Three Gateways to Hell." But, on this sunny Spring morning, that rather average "brown bar" would be spared from almost certain passage.[1]

Shortly after that NVA machinegun first made its presence known, the young American officer had ducked through the intervening hedgerow and tried to lead an assault against its operator across a small pockmarked clearing. Unfortunately, he had forgotten to give his lead squad leader a full warning order. So when he said "follow me," nobody did.

Halfway across the clearing, he noticed two enemy officers to his left front just standing there watching the area (later determined to be a trench) from where the following action would ensue. Tall bushes had obscured them from the rest of the platoon, so only the "shavetail" could see them. Now at a complete loss on what to do next, he attempted to shoot them from a kneeling position. After emptying the first magazine of his pistol with no effect on either target, he tried so rapidly to insert a second that he failed to pull the slide far enough to the rear to chamber a new round. As he was "holding and squeezing" off the next nonexistent shot, everything went blank for a few moments. When he awoke, he was lying on his back with a neat little black-rimmed hole at the very top of his right pant leg. Suspecting additional interest from the nearby foe, he squirmed backwards—with an obviously shattered femur—to the last big shell hole he recalled. As he dove in, several additional bullets came whizzing by. When he looked up, he saw no fewer than five Chicom grenades in the air coming his way from the trench. The closest was to land right at the lip of his hole. After a short Marine mortar barrage, the fighting died down, and the lieutenant was eventually "medevacked." (See Figure 22.1.) For years afterwards, he attributed that series of occurrences to good fortune. Then, after developing a rather unusual gift of tactical insight, he began to wonder what had really happened.[2]

While shattering the young officer's femur outward, that NVA bullet had not harmed the big femoral artery that runs up the inside of the leg right next to the bone. Any damage (however slight) to that artery just below the torso generally proves fatal because the resulting leak recedes back up into the pelvic girdle and cannot be tied off. But near misses are common in combat. What had made this whole affair somewhat different was that the fledgling Marine leader had been shot with only one round from a rifle, instead of a whole string of rounds from the already active enemy machine-gun.[3]

Therein lies the mystery. A vindictive opposition soldier might have tried to shoot him in the "private parts" to maximize the pain and suffering, and then—through divine intervention—missed his intended target by two inches. Near-death experiences are easily attributed to God's constant need for worldly instruments. Or, some NVA veteran who had already killed scores of tactically challenged GIs may have mistaken that foolhardy act for heroics or suicide. From that range, it doesn't take much of a marksman to shoot somebody in the leg, instead of center mass. Armchair analysts have often claimed that only wounding a GI in combat causes more of a drain on the U.S. war machine than killing him. But, most combat veterans have seen far too little evidence of this in actual practice.

Figure 22.1: "God's" New Instrument Departs the Area
(Source: Courtesy of former Marine Michael Leahy, © n.d. by Michael Leahy)

That's why this particular Vietnam era survivor now believes that some highly experienced and "a-political" enemy sergeant had shown him mercy.

No fan of atheistic Communism, that same Marine has since discovered that the NVA army was not only better at small-unit tactics than its American counterpart, but also at 4GW in general. As already mentioned, 4GW draws much of its strength from limiting the extent of inconsequential killing. So, he who is now arguably the U.S. authority on small-unit tactics harbors no grudges against his former foe, nor would he support a "war of retribution."[4] In effect, whatever mercy had been shown him ended up making a far greater contribution to the NVA war effort than his fully justified death, for it had helped to achieve a lasting peace.

Hard for Attrition Warriors to Accept

America has any number of exceptionally brave and determined service branch members. Unlike the above-mentioned officer, they would not have stopped fighting until every NVA soldier in that trench had been destroyed. This quality is to be highly admired in them, because not all men have it. Yet, all such "natural finishers" must additionally realize that their only real purpose in the U.S. Armed Forces is to help win a war. Should winning that war be more easily accomplished through bypassing or otherwise sparing the lives of enemy fighters, then that is what they must continue to try.

One's Humanity Definitely at Stake

According to Saint Thomas Acquinas (the well-respected Catholic theologian), "Justice without mercy is cruelty."[5] That's why American warfighters must not put too much stock in martial invincibility. That the battlefield is still called a "field of honor" should serve as adequate warning of moral pitfalls. Despite the onset of "total war" and continuation of "life-or-death" struggles, all participants are still expected to behave honorably. Anything less would be an affront to the vast brotherhood of those who have already paid the ultimate price for their good names.

And what does the Lord require of you? To act justly and to love mercy.[6]
— "Micah 6:8," *St. James Christian Bible*

Conflict Resolution Also in Play

In any armed conflict, the term "mercy" normally refers to a lesser degree of force being applied during any particular confrontation. In other words, someone has wounded instead of killing an adversary, or taken a healthy prisoner instead of first injuring him. In a 4GW struggle, hostage taking actually contributes more to the overall war effort than any other option. According to the U.S. father of 4GW theory, such a struggle is fought on three previously unrecognized levels: (1) the physical; (2) the mental; and (3) and the moral.[7]

Physically, capturing the enemy is harder and more complicated than killing him. Mentally, it may be less frightening [to potential enemies within the general population] and thus less effective. But morally it works in our favor because the strong appear merciful (so long as prisoners are treated well), and a suspicion of cowardice hangs over anyone who surrenders.[8]
— *4th Generation Warfare Handbook,* by Lind

While Lind's levels of warfare are certainly insightful, his explanation of the mental influence of more surrender is a matter of opinion. Actually being less frightening to the overall population may be a good thing, with an *aura* of common sense hanging over those who surrender. Getting an opponent to give up also proves helpful in the three classic stages of 4GW: (1) strategic; (2) operational; and (3) tactical.[9] On occasion, people are even captured with strategically vital information.

[A] capture is equal tactically to a kill as a win, operationally it is still just attrition, but strategically it is a plus because captives are useful chips in bargaining de-escalatory deals.[10]
— *4th Generation Warfare Handbook,* by Lind

Does Allowing the Foe to Get Away Qualify?

In Vietnam, American "search-and-destroy" sweeps used so much firepower as regularly to encourage all enemy soldiers to run away or "go to ground." Little attempt was then made by U.S. forces to catch up with them. In a sense, that might be considered a "merciful" way to fight, but it was to prove decidedly nonproductive. Not only did it perpetuate the local insurgent threat, but it also produced too few captives to obtain enough intelligence for future operations. In other words, it did nothing to further the war effort from the standpoint of 3GW or 4GW. The occasional "cordon operation" might have helped to correct that shortfall, had the opposition not been so proficient at underground hiding and above-ground exfiltration.

Essentially, the well-oiled American "sweep machine" had made a magnificent "sight-and-sound" impression on the local residents, but caused very little real damage to the easily displaced and deeply embedded opposition soldiers among them. A slower on-line movement by U.S. troops skilled at mantracking, tunnel entrance identification, and sapper defense would have made more of a difference.

PART EIGHT

ENOUGH SKILL TO MAKE LESS FORCE POSSIBLE

"SUPREME EXCELLENCE CONSISTS OF BREAKING THE ENEMY'S RESISTANCE WITHOUT FIGHTING." – SUN TZU

(Source: Attributed to Sun Tzu.)

23 SUFFICIENT TINY-ELEMENT ___ ABILITY ON OFFENSE

- In which wars have tiny units made the most difference?
- Was it through their use of firepower or surprise?

How safely to "fire and move" up parallel two-man lanes takes practice.

(Sources: FM 22-100 [1983], p. 84; FM 7-70 [1986], p. D-24.)

A Good Place to Start

At Quantico (and probably Benning as well), the mostly commissioned "infantry experts" now regularly apply complicated mental gymnastics to all research on tiny-element tactics. Their conclusions subsequently mention everything from "outward focus" to "inner cohesion." Yet, one would think a less philosophical frame of reference would not only be possible, but also easier to pursue. The first Marine Corps Commandant—Gen. John A. Lejeune—once said something to the effect that "small-unit tactics are more properly the purview of infantry NCOs (noncommissioned officers)."¹ Corporals and Sergeants don't deal in esoterics. After several years where "enemy contact gets made," their thought processes are far more direct.

Many Marine NCOs would first point out that according to their new MW doctrine, firepower and surprise are practically interchangeable in combat. Then, they would share that no more than 14 people (the average rifle squad) can normally sneak up on anyone. In other words, to use less firepower on offense, the Corps would need squads that are better at secretly approaching a prepared enemy position. That would, in turn, take maneuvers that are sufficiently advanced in the evolution of squad tactics worldwide. If their own doctrine, established procedures, or regular habits currently preclude such maneuvers, then that limitation will have to be somehow superseded.

A Cultural Blind Spot?

The U.S. Army's Field Manual (FM) 100-5 divides the waging of war into three stages:² (1) strategic (employment of national power); (2) operational (campaigning); and (3) tactical (procedural).³ In the West, modern wars are thought to be won or lost at the strategic stage rather than the two others.⁴ That's because "the operational level is concerned with employing military forces . . . through . . . major operations,"⁵ while "tactics deal in the details of prosecuting engagements."⁶ Also at the tactical level are "techniques"—procedures that only squads and below are small enough to perform automatically (without any concurrent direction from internal leaders).

So, within the highly stratified and rank-conscious U.S. military, a definite hierarchy of importance seems to have been assigned to all wartime issues. Many career-oriented commanders then come to the mistaken conclusion that small-unit tactics are the least of their worries. In other words, it doesn't really matter what the squads and below do (or know how to do), as long as the companies, battalions, and regiments keep doing the right kinds of things. Besides the effect that such a belief might have on the final casualty count, there is also the little matter of many Eastern adversaries (most notably the Communists) not seeing things that way. They prefer to operate from the bottom up—by deriving operational and then strategic insights from which tiny-element tactics seem to be working. For them, tactics is no longer a science (as in the West), but more appropriately an art. Such an art would rely just as much on deception as stealth.

One self-described Western "professional and expert at the tactical level" recently made the mistake of speaking too freely through the public forum of Amazon's review process.

> [This is] a book on tactics, written within the context of the tactical level, which, as any practitioner of war will know, is the lowest, simplest, most mechanistic level. . . . I find much more value in higher-level studies of the phenomena that drive the adaptation of tactics: strategic and geopolitical studies. . . . TTPs [Tactics, Techniques, and Procedures] are fluid, and are obsolete as soon as you have adapted to them. Understanding the process is more important than understanding the tactics.[7]
>
> — a probably career-oriented U.S. military officer

One's TTPs only become obsolete when the enemy has correctly surmised what's just happened to him. East Asians have so well masked some of their small-unit procedures as to be able to use them over and over throughout an entire war. There is nothing in the U.S. doctrinal literature than would prevent American forces from repaying the favor.

A Common Misconception About Attacking

After powerful Allied maneuver elements were needed to push Hitler's invading armies back into Germany, most Americans still believe all battlefield offensives must look like that to be successful. Yet, the campaign by the NVA/VC to remove pro-government Western occupiers from Vietnam certainly did not. Instead, local contingents—often no bigger than a single man—repeatedly penetrated Allied encampments to destroy strategically vital materiel. Then, it became the overall amount of expensive U.S. equipment lost that finally forced the American Congress to stop funding the war. Not until most American ground units had already departed the theatre of war did large motorized NVA forces sweep down from the north to take control over all strategically vital infrastructure in the South.

While this version of what finally happened 40 years ago in Vietnam might not please all American veterans of that war, all that it really lacks is proof of the repeated sabotage of U.S. equipment by thousands of tiny elements.

The Necessary Evidence

Professional saboteurs do not generally claim responsibility for their mischief. Like criminals, they leave as few clues behind as possible. A really good one will make the damage look like a self-inflicted accident. As just described in Chapter 19, enemy sappers had a lot to do with most of the "lucky mortar hits" within U.S. installations.

Such a connection would be much harder to establish, if something similar had not occurred inside the huge Henderson Field perimeter on Guadalcanal during the early stages of WWII. Its Marine defenders first began to wonder why "low-tech" Japanese nighttime aircraft and out-of-sight surface cannons so easily hit major targets. Soon, they realized that many of their base infiltrators were actually forward observers. NCOs had told Chesty Puller of intruders using rifle shots to signal each other when their radios failed.[8] While General Vandegrift's Chief of Staff estimated that hundreds of Japanese had gotten through friendly lines, he saw no incongruity in the fact that only one Marine had been killed by a sniper.[9] Then, on 13 October 1942, Pistol Pete (an enemy long-range artillery piece) was "registered . . . with slow and methodical precision."[10] But too much precision can mean not only forward observers, but also concurrent sabotage. The Japanese had already been seen bangaloring the Marine's barbed wire during one of their own artillery barrages.[11] So, there was always the possibility of intruders attaching explosives to hard-to-get-at U.S. equipment during one of their own (and increasing frequent) bombing or naval-gunfire attacks.

At the time, this suspicion was never fully substantiated. The airfield did come under aerial or naval bombardment almost every day and night (often at predictable hours). Well-dispersed and revetted aircraft, ammunition, and fuel did routinely fall victim to those attacks. After American sentries had taken cover below ground, the command posts, equipment, and stores they were guarding would have been much easier to approach along the ground. Yet, most evidence of sapper sabotage on Guadalcanal remains to this day circumstantial. Only through a mathematical-odds study might that suspicion be finally confirmed. The number of direct hits on pinpoint targets were far too numerous to itemize here, and the number of incoming rounds seems to have increased with every retelling of the story. Yet, even for closely observed fire, the limits of probability still appear to have been exceeded. One can only conclude that Japanese infiltrators had been afixing explosives to some of the most "difficult-to-reach" targets. The best time to do so would have been during an incoming barrage when most Marine sentries were diligently searching for a new corner in the bottom of their hole.

There is one additional indicator of such an enemy trick on Guadalcanal. Enlisted Marines have always been quick to spot an enemy ploy, and will on occasion decide to copy it. Some of Chesty Pullers' men may have used the same diversion to relieve a recently arrived Army unit of some of its oversupply of machineguns right before John Basilone's famous perimeter stand.

> Enterprising members of the regiment [7th Marines] may also have scrounged some extra machine guns from wrecked aircraft or other sources [like perhaps the Army's recently arrived 164th Infantry Regiment, a North Dakota National Guard outfit].[12]
> —official Marine historian, *World War II Magazine*

Returning to More Recent History

All of the above makes what happened at An Hoa in 1969 no longer such a mystery. When that Marine base's ammunition dump went up shortly after dawn on 23 February, it was like a miniature nuclear explosion. The whole episode was soon attributed to indirect enemy fire. However, one independent researcher claims enemy troops entered the wire and lobbed satchel charges into the dump with a bamboo catapult.[13] While satchel charges were undoubtedly involved, such a dangerous delivery method would have lacked the necessary precision.

Conclusively known is what is in the 5th Marines' *Command Chronology*: "Incoming rounds had hit around the ammo dump at 0140, but the dump did not blow until 0610."[14] The *Command Chronology* of 3rd 155mm Gun Battery shows enemy rocket and mortar attacks in the vicinity of the ammo dump at 0130, 0700, and 0730.[15]

All the while, Golf Company, 2nd Battalion, 5th Marines had been bivouacking some 20 clicks north of the action. Its personnel witnessed a number of tiny flashes during the night and then the massive explosion around 6:30 A.M. At the time, those initial flashes had been attributed to either fireworks (which had occurred at Christmas) or U.S. H&I fires just outside the wire. But then, with the subsequent detonation, the full extent of the tragedy began to sink in. That big a blast would have killed anyone in its general vicinity through concussion alone. The very morning before, Golf Company (as the designated regimental reserve) had been itself manning that sector of the An Hoa perimeter that protected the dump.[16]

This An Hoa explosion has to have been the work of a VC sapper. Only he could have reached the revetted munitions. It has since been discovered that the residents of An Hoa's nearby village had secretly tunneled right up to the edge of the Marine base's barbed wire.[17]

Then, at Biên Hòa Air Base in 1972, after witnessing several "overly effective" mortar attacks against American aircraft over the years, U.S. Air Force Police finally connected the dots. On this particular occasion, it was supposedly the bomb storage area under attack, but there were no indirect-fire impacts being reported at that location.

> A sapper attack took place on 12 Jan. 1972, resulting in the explosion of the ammo dump at Biên Hòa Air Base. On that fateful night, explosions began at the bomb dump. . . . We initially thought it was another rocket attack but no one reported impacts or explosions except in the ammo dump.[18]
> — USAF 3rd Security Police Squadron report

Where There's Too Much Smoke

The total number of parked planes and ammunition dumps lost throughout the entire Vietnam conflict would give the reader a better idea of the drain on U.S. funds. But, such statistics are hard to find. What is known is that indirect enemy fire damaged "too many" aircraft at Biên Hòa Air Base in 1964 and Da Nang Air Base in 1967. Then, it destroyed both the ammunition dump and too many aircraft at Camp Evans in 1968. While all this was happening, sappers are officially acknowledged to have gone after aircraft at Camp Holloway Airfield in 1962, Da Nang Air Base in 1965, Marble Mountain Air Facility in 1965, and Kontum Airfield in 1968. At Chu Lai Air Base and Marble Mountain Air Facility in 1965, Chu Lai Air Base again in 1968, and Cu Chi Army Airfield (near the tunnels) in 1969, enemy mortars or rockets landed while those sappers attacked.[19]

Still, the fully refined enemy ruse took a while to develop. At Chu Lai in 1965, the planes had not been prerigged with explosives, but rather sprayed with "Tommy Gun" fire as satchel charges were tossed up their tail pipes.[20] The use of timed satchel charges did not become readily apparent until the seven-helicopter-ruining lucky mortar string of Chapter 19, and the An Hoa blast as superfluous mortar shells landed.

U.S. artillery and their pallets of shells were also a favorite target of the NVA. Satchel-charge-throwing sappers were involved in the destruction at Firebases Maury I in May 1968, Airborne in May 1969, Henderson in May 1970, and Mary Ann in March 1971. At Henderson and Mary Ann, foe mortar rounds are known to have preceded the sappers.[21]

In all of the above cases, enemy commandos had managed to sneak undetected through U.S. perimeter guards. Of course, there were many other more forceful base penetrations by the NVA that were basically the equivalent of a WWI German Stormtrooper assault.

More About Those Squad-Sized Penetrations

In Vietnam, there were many "seemingly futile" attempts to enter American bases by force (as opposed to quietly sneaking in). After U.S. close defensive fires would be briefly applied, one or two enemy bodies (normally of non-uniformed VC) would be found in the wire the next morning.[22] That's when limited explosive damage to targets inside the base would also be discovered—like to American command posts, equipment, or supplies. But, because the penetration attempt had been preceded by a brief mortar barrage, nothing of particular significance was attributed to that interior damage. The enemy had tried to get in and failed, whereas any harm to base assets had simply been the coincidental result of his preliminary mortar bombardment.

That would be the end of the story, if not for the German Storm-trooper squad assault technique from late in WWI. The U.S. military (one of the method's initial victims during the Germans' Spring Offensives of 1918) has never formally acknowledged its power. However, a few Asian armies may have. Some 50 years later, most NVA/VC satchel charges contained no shrapnel.[23] They—like the German concussion grenades—could have easily created the impression that U.S. lines were only under an indirect-fire attack.[24] The NVA/VC also had bangalore torpedoes. Some made out of bamboo were photographed after the NVA assault on Con Thien in May of 1967.[25]

That WWI Stormtrooper squad first entered Doughboy lines by bangaloring the barbed wire during a precision artillery barrage and then shifting that pinpoint barrage slightly forward.[26] That some Germans had gotten in undetected didn't save any Doughboys in their way from getting bayonetted.[27] Years later, a "Chicom" fragmentation grenade could have more covertly accomplished the same task (as its explosion and crater would have resembled that of a 61mm-mortar shell). Thus, what happened over and over in Vietnam to unsuspecting GIs could have been easily prevented by simply alerting them to the ongoing state of the art for "noisy surprise assault." Unfortunately, veterans of that war remember no such briefing. That America's most elite fighters still cannot fully describe this 100-year-old technique is so gross, that the continuing lack of headquarters' emphasis on this subject now borders on willful negligence.

An Old Chinese Standby

Finally, there is the traditional way for attacking a prepared enemy position that was used extensively by the Chinese during the Korean War. It is openly to "demonstrate" with most of one's forces at the front of an assault objective while secretly entering it with a tiny element from the back.[28] But that initial feint is not without teeth. If not properly defended, it just keeps on coming to reinforce those already inside. To any Westerner in Korea, it looked like enemy companies, each in extended-line formation, coming in one after the other. It actuality, it was a single row of Stormtrooper-like columns. Each column would have then been responsible for its own breach in the protective barbed wire.[29] Something similar apparently happened at Cam Lo II in Vietnam (possibly with several shared breaches). Here the often-Mao-emulating NVA were out to destroy a U.S. howitzer park, its ammunition, and its Fire Direction Center (FDC).

The Specific Action at Cam Lo II

During the early morning hours of 26 August 1966, the official U.S. Marine Corps chronicle for 1966 reports no fewer than "five outposts" from Alpha Company, 1st Battalion, 4th Marines notic-ing two NVA companies heading toward their perimeter at Cam Lo II. All outposts were then withdrawn and an illumination bar-rage supposedly readied to try to catch a large number of enemy troops coming through the wire. The chronicle goes on to put this wire an improbable 90 meters to the front of the Marines' fighting holes. Normally, there would have been up to three rows of wire, with the closest being just beyond hand grenade range (about 20 meters) from those holes.[30] So what happened next is still a matter of conjecture.

When those illumination flares went off according to the chron-icle, the closest enemy troops were still "40 to 50 meters in front of the Marine positions [foxholes]." That would still more logically be outside the wire. However, it admits to some "infiltrators" being already inside the perimeter doing considerable damage.[31] How that apparent paradox was resolved is not entirely satisfactory. According to the Battalion Commander, the first wave had been so skilled as to pass unseen around the fighting holes of his fully alert frontline infantrymen.

> They [the NVA] snuck on through before we even illumi-nated the area. . . . [A]s you know, they're real[ly] proficient at moving at night . . . very silently, very slowly, and very patiently. . . . [The NVA] did get through even though our people were waiting for them. They crawled in between the

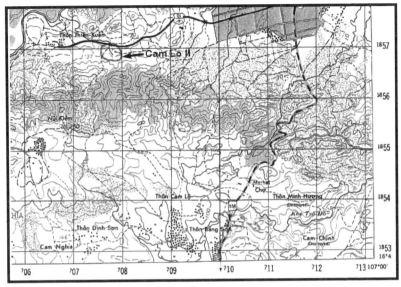

Map 23.1: Exact Location of Cam Lo II
(Source: Part of 1:50,000 USGS map, Vietnam Series L7014, unknown map sheet number.)

holes, and our people never really realized that they passed through their positions.[32]
— Lt.Col.Jack Westerman at the time of the attack

There is little doubt that several hundred NVA regulars eventually entered the Marines' perimeter, for somebody proceeded "to place explosive charges all over the positions, blowing up tents, trailers, and one tank retriever."[33] But, the ones already inside at the time of the illumination had probably snuck in from a different direction while their parent unit intentionally telegraphed its approach. All hands of that parent unit must have been in a fully upright formation when spotted—possibly like a "human wave" from the Korean War. So, there's a good chance that many members of the attacking force were still outside the Marines' protective wire when the illumination went up. That overall force had probably been battalion sized.

232

The Marines captured one NVA soldier. He identified himself as a member of the 812th Infantry Regiment . . . which in coordination with a local VC unit, had made the attack. Had this unit been able to join with the battalion from the 803rd NVA Regiment as originally planned, the attack . . . might well have been much more serious.[34]

— U.S. *Marines in Vietnam: Expanding War — 1966*

That would firmly establish the maneuver as a frontal feint that just kept coming. This was no impromptu NVA effort. Cam Lo had been providing much of the artillery support to western I Corps for quite some time. (Look back at Map 8.1.)

The official chronicle then shares what might be construed as some good news: "[T]he destruction could have been much more extensive. Just the previous day, the 155mm howitzers had moved to new revetments further *[sic]* west, . . . and the 3rd Battalion, 12th Marines had also changed the location of its fire direction center."[35] What the chronicle had meant to say was that those howitzers and FDC had just been moved from Cam Lo I to Cam Lo II, and only the heavily armored 155's had been hard to hurt. At the time of the NVA assault on Cam Lo II, all of the following had been present: (1) three tanks and one tank retriever from Charlie Company, 3rd Tank Battalion; (2) two self-propelled 155mm howitzers from Hotel Battery/3/13; (3) Headquarters Battery/3/12 (to include its FDC); (4) the 105mm howitzers of Hotel Battery/3/12; and (5) two 81mm mortars from H&S Company/1/4. Manning the perimeter were all three tanks, two platoons of A/1/4, and some people from both Hotel and Headquarters Batteries of 3/12. The third A/1/4 platoon was still back at Cam Lo I.[36]

First Hints of the Foe's Tactical Genius

There's a good reason the defenders of Cam Lo II became so nervous right before the attack. Tankers in those days had better "night vision devices" than the infantry.

One Marine manning a listening post (LP) "remembers that night . . . [of the attack] he was on the only LP for the Platoon. He was asked to return in or around 2330 hours because the tanker on the west side of the road spotted movement to the south with their binoculars. (This same Marine later remembered those tankers having infrared night vision capabilities.)"[37]

—Mike Rask, member of A/1/4 manning an outpost

The next recollection brings into doubt whether the entire response to an impending attack had been already worked out with battalion. It also shows the CP's (command post's) initial impression of the type of attack in progress.

Sometime either on the 24th or early 25th of August 1966 a NVA Soldier in civilian clothes (Gook) was caught by one of the platoons . . . east of the new fire support base Cam Lo II. . . . [H]e was making a map of the area where everything was located, all color coded showing our positions. The bunkers and positions where we had the radios & 2-9'er-2 antenna[s] set up was highlighted. . . .

The official USMC history claims that it was known that it was going to happen and that we were prepared for it with a plan and I find that hard to believe considering what happened the night of the 25th of August.

On 25 August, about dusk . . . I was at the sandbagged command bunker standing the radio watch on the battalion net and just as it was beginning to get dark some of the Marines on the perimeter began tossing fragmentation grenades at noises. . . . [Then everyone noticed that] it became real quiet.

The Battalion call sign was Permission and my being with Alpha Company I became Permission Alpha. So there I was, listening to nervous grunts on the perimeter saying something was out there, command folks saying at most it was a probe. . . .

[Then] all Hell broke loose!

My first reaction was to hit the ground and get inside the bunker . . . lots of explosions and gunfire . . . and I let Battalion Headquarters know we were being hit. . . .

It wasn't too long before the bunker was full of folks; Lieutenant Galvin [acting A/1/4 CO] in his underwear and glasses, Lieutenant Sewell [the Air Officer or Forward Air Controller] came barreling through the door immediately telling me, "Call for Puff and a Flare ship," which I did. . . .

Lieutenant Roach came in and I had my reality check when I heard him answer the question of why he was at the bunker and not with his people on the perimeter. . . . [H]is answer was, "What perimeter?" . . .

. . . Lieutenant Galvin was . . . trying to get a good feel of what was going on, I was on the horn with Lieutenant Colonel Westerman relaying orders and information back and forth. . . . Lieutenant Jeff Sewell was plotting where he wanted the gunship and flare ship to begin their runs when they arrived. . . . We knew we were in big trouble, but not the extent and the word was passed for everyone to get into their holes and shoot anything that moved. It was about that time that an Air Forces Puff the Magic Dragon, a C-47 gunship, and the Marine Corps Smokey Bear, the flare ship, arrived on station. . . .

Soon after the sun was up a convoy came from Dong Ha bringing the Battalion Commander, Lieutenant Colonel Westerman . . . to try and piece things together to formulate an After-Action Report.[38]

— Don Cuncio, battalion radioman during attack

After a few of the initial festivities, it soon became apparent that at least part of the southern side of the perimeter had been compromised.

At 260340H [0340 on 26 August]. Company A, located at the artillery positions at Cam Lo, began to receive heavy incoming mortar and S/A [small arms] rounds. During the next 1-1/2 hours, Company A's lines were penetrated by an estimated 2 Companies of VC and NVA.[39]

— *1st Bn., 4th Marines Command Chronology*

Full Details from Frontline Defenders

The precise method of this attack can only be pieced together through more firsthand accounts. The initial account takes particular note of the initial throwing of satchel charges to emulate an indirect-fire attack Then, it reveals definite enemy interest in the side of the perimeter opposite to the one eventually assaulted (where the silent infiltrators had probably entered).

At 0300 hours, I woke [Mike] Strickland who took over the watch. . . . I was just laying there for about 20 minutes or so when I heard a blast followed quickly by a second and third blast. . . . [S]everal more blasts went off . . . near the center of the perimeter. . . . Mike realized that the blast was not mortar rounds impacting as they were throwing an inordinate amount of sparks; they were grenades or satchel charges.

Suddenly, trip flares started going off, mostly on the southern and southeastern edges of perimeter. . . .

. . . The NVA and VC attack was supported by heavy automatic weapons fire. . . .

At one point, there was a heavy rate of enemy fire . . . to our right front near the main gate. . . . Our machine gun was in just the right position to respond to this outburst and . . . suppress the NVA assault near the main gate. . . .

As the sun began to arise from the east, the NVA began to slowly disengage and move southwest.[40]

—Peter Mancuso, A/1/4 machinegunner at Cam Lo

The second remembrance of events that night talks again about satchel charges to imitate mortar fire. As the WWI German Storm-troopers did likewise, this account should reinforce the hypothesis that (like the Chinese in Korea), the NVA had launched a "not-so-stupid" human-wave simulation against the objective's southern flank.

Our position was on the northwest side of the perimeter [at Cam Lo II]. . . . The perimeter was very hasty to say the least. There were three rolls of very rusty concertina wire [probably in a triple-concertina pile] to our direct front about 20 yards out. This wire ran around full length of the perimeter.

. . . A little after 0300 hours in the morning . . . there was a series of blasts to the south east of our position which was behind us. . . .

From our position we could see the trip flares going off behind us. . . . Just by observing the incoming tracer rounds we knew a large force was attacking us.

Almost immediately there was an 81mm mortar tube that was sending our rounds to provide illumination for the fire support base. . . . We could make out all kinds of shapes moving around and that the NVA was attacking the south side of the perimeter.

About 30 minutes to 45 minutes into this attack our Platoon Sergeant, Staff Sergeant Szymanski, went from position to position to grab one Marine from each position to counter attack the NVA as they were coming through the lines. . . .

The force was less than 20 Marines, and we gathered near the Company Command Bunker. . . . Gunny Winebar took charge of us and moved us to a position on the East Side of the perimeter near Route 9. From there we got on line and started to sweep south toward the attacking NVA. About 50 to 60 meters into this sweep we were told to stay on line. Then word was passed to . . . get into firing positions and shoot the NVA as they came in our direction. . . . We stayed on line for about one hour firing at the NVA as they move[d] in our direction. . . .

. . . When dawn almost arrived, the Gunny Winebar told us to get up and start our sweep of the perimeter toward the south. . . .

The dead and the fast dying NVA lay everywhere in and outside the perimeter. As we swept through the perimeter one could no[t] help notice that legs, arms, heads, and torsos were lying all over the place. Sergeant Price went on to explain that the NVA tied C-4 plastic explosives to there [sic] bodies. . . . The body parts that you see are the ones that were wounded that could not make there [sic] assigned objective. . . . Price said once [in] a while a stray round would hit the blasting cap and the NVA would be blown apart. He also mentioned that the NVA would take these blocks of C-4 and as they came close to the perimeter . . . throw them at the fortifications. The Marines in the fighting positions would believe it was incoming 82mm mortars rounds and crouch down and not see the NVA coming into the lines. Sergeant Price explained that is what the NVA did in the early part of the attack. It was not mortars rounds that were hitting the perimeter. . . . He was right. I do not remember the popping sound the mortar makes as it leaves the tube. . . .

Later that morning I saw Tag [Guthrie] . . . in the center of the perimeter where the NVA destroyed tents with the

C-4 explosives. . . . Tag told me that the Marines that were
manning the FDC were killed or severely wounded.[41]
— Larry Schorr, 2nd Platoon member of A/1/4

A veteran and longtime historian of Cam Lo explains how the
NVA could have still been using a modified version of the German
Stormtrooper technique, though their machineguns eventually came
into play. After simulating a mortar attack with an overabundance
of satchel charges, some of the enemy squad columns might have
run into too much resistance coming through the wire. Then, the
rising terrain to the south of the base would have permitted pinpoint
overhead NVA machinegun fire (green tracers) to counter its U.S.
equivalent (sources of red tracers). After so visible a display, the
assaulting troops could have more easily avoided both sources of
automatic fire.

Cam Lo I was at grid 113575 and Cam Lo II . . . at Grid
078568.
The perimeter [at Cam Lo II] was OVAL shape where
the center was at Grid 078568 and 2nd Plt. was . . . on Route
9. One squad . . . facing east . . . one . . . north . . . and the
other. . . west. . . . All the positions were 15 to 20 meters apart
with two Marines to position. The only exception was the
[machine]gun team[s] and they were three Marines to each
position. 1st Platoon was facing east and south. The area
in which they were [emplaced] . . . was wide open . . . like
an open field. There was a hasty triple-concertina [row of]
wire. It was installed by grunts and not by combat engineers
[possibly without all lateral strands and upright posts that
would keep it from being too easily crushed]. The [machine]
guns were facing north and west and the tanks were on the
military crest of the hill facing south and west. On that
portion they had their . . . [own] fighting positions.
The NVA came from the south and south east from the
hill which was about 800 feet high. It has foliage from the
base all the way to the top.[42]
— Charles "Tag" Guthrie, 2nd Platoon, A/1/4

The most revealing details come from that part of the Marines'
perimeter that was forcibly penetrated—namely, the defensive

sector of 1st Platoon/A/1/4. One watchstander confirms what Mike Strictland had originally observed from the highest point in the compound. Enemy satchel charges had been going off in the artillery positions before mortar rounds started landing on the front lines. He also remembers an American radio insertion by the opposition to shift defenders away from part of those lines. That's where the order for all Leathernecks to stay in their respective holes initially came from.

The attack came from the east and southeast and was aimed at the artillery at Cam Lo. Explosive charges were put in [the artillery's] trailer and tents. Hearing [them], we received incoming mortars around 1:00 A.M. and our position [that of 1st Platoon/A/1/4] was penetrated [from beyond the wire].

Prior to being overrun, let me give you some things that were done.

We ran . . . [concertina] wire around our perimeter where the tanks 105 Howitzers and 155 Guns were positioned. We placed Claymore Mines out by the wire.

We set up Aiming Stakes to the right and left of our foxhole where we lived. This was done to keep us from shooting our own men on both sides of us.

The .50-caliber machine gun was set up on the point of our perimeter facing the mountains. . . . .

August 26, 1966. Approximate time: 1:00 A.M. to 2:00 A.M. The word came down that we were on 100% ALERT. Also, . . . we had to attach our bayonets to our rifles. . . . We thought it was just a drill.

The NVA broke into our radio frequency trying to make us think it was our men. They were trying to get some of us out of our foxholes and move to another part of the perimeter. We were told not to get out of holes and disregard those messages on the radio.

At approximately 1:00 A.M., two NVA companies from the 324B Division broke through the wire and were inside our perimeter. Their goal was to take out our tanks and big guns. By the time we got illumination, they were already in our compound.

The . . . [gunners] on the .50-caliber opened up and

steadily fired where they were coming through. With illumination now lighting up the area, we could see them better. They were all over the place. . . .

The fighting was so loud with everyone shooting and the .50-caliber machine guns added. . . . What was scary was not being able to see them due to the delay time of the illumination coming in. You would lose sight of them for a minute or so. It was total darkness.

The firing lasted a few hours, it was a long and scary night. When the firing ceased, there were Marines wounded, crying out for Corpsmen. Their cries for help were so loud and we could do nothing for them until the fight was over.

When it was light of day, approximately 6:00 A.M., we were given the order to get out of our foxholes and assess the damage and see who was wounded and needed help.

When I went towards the wire where the gunner of the .50-caliber shot from, I could not believe what I saw!!!! There were NVA soldiers stacked on top of each other and their bodies were so mutilated that you could not identify what they looked like. . . .

To my knowledge, we had about 9 Marines KIA and several other WIA [wounded in action]. I believe if the wounded were taken care of sooner, they might have survived. This is no fault of the Corpsmen the fact is that no one was allowed to be out of their foxhole. They could have been missed for the enemy due to the darkness. . . .

I feel that the gunners on the .50-caliber were so awesome. If it wasn't for them, we would have lost many more Marines. They never stopped to change the barrel even when it was getting warped and needed to be changed.

I don't remember much more after that incident. [This Marine was knocked in the head by an NVA soldier who came at his position from the side. He later awoke to continue the fight].[43]

— Dennis Mansour, 1st Platoon member of A/1/4

The Extent of Minimal Force by This Particular Enemy

Some degree of violent persuasion is necessary in most battles, but this attack on a well-defended Allied bastion had not included much preparatory bombardment. Before the ground assault, only the section of the perimeter to be breached had been briefly "dusted" by mortar fire. The Stormtrooper method employs a few such rounds to mask the bangaloring of the wire and create the impression that all subsequent explosions are just part of the same indirect-fire attack. So far, the only confirmation of any mortar attack comes from the Company CP's initial call to Battalion, the *1/4 Command Chronology*,[44] and S.Sgt. Joys' Navy Cross Citation. Four frontline fighters became more interested in the fact that most explosions were from satchel charges and grenades: Sergeant Price, Mike Strickland, Larry Schorr, and Dennis Mansour. The following is from a note left on the Vietnam Memorial Wall for Sgt. Donald Allen Lewis, one of the 3/12 defenders killed in the attack. It too forgets to mention any mortar impacts.

> The 3/12 Chronology contains the following entry: "At approximately 0330H the Battalion (fwd) [forward] position was attacked by an enemy force of at least Company strength. The attack came from the east and southeast and was obviously aimed at the FDC . . . and the howitzers. . . .

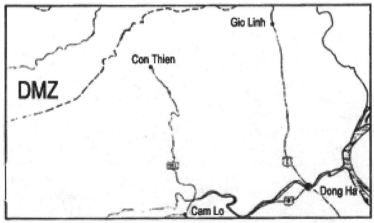

Map 23.2: Cam Lo Was Only 10 Miles from the DMZ
(Source: Map based on illustration designator "amtrac.org - bullalo03.jpg," from official website for 1st Amtrac Battalion.)

Initially, small arms and automatic weapons fire and numerous grenades were received by the security rifle company [Alpha 1/4] defending the position. . . . . In spite of the heavy fire and the commitment of a reaction squad composed of members of Headquarters Battery in order to reinforce the line, several of the attackers managed to penetrate the [3/12] position, placing explosive charges in trailers and tents."[45]
— Note left for Lewis on Vietnam Memorial Wall

The award citation for S.Sgt. John William Joys, the Platoon Sergeant of 1st Platoon/A/1/4 that got partially overrun reveals an initial smattering of mortar rounds, and then a veritable deluge of satchel charges and grenades.

The President of the United States takes pride in presenting the Navy Cross (Posthumously) to John William Joys . . . for extraordinary heroism while serving . . . in the defense of a forward tank and artillery position at Cam Lo in Vietnam on 26 August 1966. Employing satchel charges, hand grenades and a heavy concentration of automatic weapons, the enemy launched a fanatic assault against the Marine perimeter, penetrating the First Platoon's lines. Staff Sergeant Joys, the platoon sergeant, was wounded by mortar fire during the initial phase of the attack. In spite of his painful wound, he proceeded to organize and coordinate the defenses in his sector. . . . He made repeated trips carrying desperately needed ammunition to the men on the line, stopping briefly to spot and shift targets while encouraging adamant determination of his men to stop the penetration. At one time, while moving across the open area between holes, a Viet Cong satchel charge exploded beside Staff Sergeant Joys, lifting him completely off the ground and slamming him down again. Bruised and battered . . . he picked himself up . . . and continued without hesitation. . . . Noting that the momentum of the enemy's assault was endangering the safety of tanks in his area, he immediately organized part of his platoon to counterattack the enemy from the flank. While leading the assault, Staff Sergeant Joys was wounded for the second time. Although seriously injured and in intense pain, he courageously pressed the attack, and continued to

move from man to man, uttering encouragement, helping the wounded, and directing fire until he himself fell mortally wounded by an enemy hand grenade.[46]
                    —Part of S.Sgt. John W.Joys' Navy Cross Citation

Final Analysis of What Happened at Cam Lo

It would appear that the enemy at Cam Lo was primarily trying to destroy the Marine artillery, but to do so it also had to defeat the U.S. armor. After breaching the wire with bangalores, NVA fighters may have had to widen the holes with cutting shears.

> The enemy troops, estimated at 300 to 400 men, hit the [Cam Lo] outpost from all sides with automatic weapons fire as North Vietnamese soldiers armed with grenades and satchel charges cut through the wire and charged the tent area. . . .
> "They were definitely North Vietnamese regulars," said Lt. Col Jack Westerman. They were well equipped and determined to get the tanks and artillery."[47]
> —*Democrat-Tribune* (Johnstown,PA),August 1966

At the time of this attack on Cam Lo II, the enemy had enough long-range artillery in the DMZ and heavy-mortar assets nearby to have heavily bombarded this entire base before any ground assault. But, their tactical scheme was sophisticated enough that they decided not to waste the ammunition or prewarn the defenders. Also of note was Dennis Mansour getting hit with a rifle butt instead of a bayonet. This was probably not to save his life. A bayonet stab might have helped U.S. investigators to trace the surprise assault technique back to its WWI prototype. A regular researcher of foreign military literature explains such behavior in this way. "All Asian Communist writers protect their small-unit infantry methods like they were nuclear secrets."[48]

According to the lone POW (prisoner of war), his superiors had only wanted to interrupt the base's artillery function, not permanently erase it. From that standpoint, they had enjoyed limited success by destroying the following: (1) the 3/12 FDC; (2) various artillery supply tents and trailers; and (3) one tank retriever. Even

MAIN ASSAULT FORCE COMES NONE TOO SECRETLY FROM THE SOUTH

SAPPERS USE THE DIVERSION TO SNEAK INTO TARGET FROM THE NORTH

SAPPER SATCHEL CHARGES SIGNAL THE SOUTHERN ASSAULT

A FEW MORTAR ROUNDS COVER SOUND OF BANAGALORES IN THE WIRE

ASSAULT TROOP SATCHEL CHARGES SIMULATE MORE MORTAR IMPACTS

ELEVATED FOE MACHINEGUNS FIRE ONLY AT RED-TRACER SOURCES

Table 23.1: The Natural Flow of an Asian Infantry Attack

after taking 78 casualties, the American penetration of an equally well-defended NVA firebase north of the DMZ would have been considered an accomplishment.

Still, the individual defenders of Cam Lo II deserve a lot of credit for their performance that night. (See Table 23.1.) Unlike later in the war when the supposed effect of supporting arms on withdrawing attackers was often added to the enemy casualty totals, the outcome of this battle was strictly on the up and up. There had been nine friendly KIAs, 27 friendly WIAs, possibly one friendly MIA (Missing in Action), 78 enemy KIAs, and one enemy POW.[49] That's a clear-cut victory for the American side, though it had been dealing with a much more tactically advanced adversary. Here, the noncommissioned "fabric" of Alpha Company/1/4 (sometimes called the enlisted chain of command) had obviously made the difference. Everybody from Gy.Sgt. Winebar, to S.Sgt. Joys and S.Sgt. Szymanski, on down to the various NCOs like Sgt. Price had collectively set a determined example. Their combined leadership had been at a high enough level that less-experienced Marines (of whatever rank) tried to do everything in their power to maintain the Marines' magnificent record.

Truly sophisticated infantry tactics involve a lot of built-in deception and automatic signalling. This Cam Lo attack definitely qualifies. (Look back a Table 23.1.) The Asian Communist attack unit does not force its way into the natural flow of things; it waits for an opening. Suffice it to say that any American infantry company—if ever sufficiently allowed by its headquarters—could develop just as much small-unit tactical skill to secretly enter a prepared enemy position.[50] For some U.S. unit finally to do so, however, it—like its East Asian counterpart—must first reject the false promise and dangerous illusion that all good things come through fire superiority.

A More Recent Case of Enough Tiny-Element Ability

There exists at least one contemporary example of sufficient small-unit American ability to exercise minimal force in battle. Not surprisingly, it comes from the U.S. Special Forces community. When NATO was still wisely trying to maintain a presence at the village level in Afghanistan, one U.S. "Green Beret" team put on a clinic on how to do it.

While those U.S. Army special operators certainly knew how to fight, they instead took more of a 4GW approach to their assignment. They started regularly to converse over tea with all community leaders (some of whom were undoubtedly Taliban). Well enough versed in Asian culture to know "there was a game being played," they carefully studied its parameters. Soon, they became able to insert their own agenda on a regular basis. While the specifics of this agenda have since been lost to history, its underlying wisdom was not. Village elders were probably told that the Americans only wanted to provide a pro-government presence, not to kill or arrest anybody.

While all this palaver was being tactfully accomplished by students of Afghan custom, it was still straight forward enough to get the job done. This same Special Forces team was then able to occupy this village for several months without any major incidents. Shortly after it was replaced by a more traditional (openly aggressive) NATO entity, a big ambush of that entity occurred outside the village, thereby dooming any further governmental representation.[51] The new unit had either been overly aggressive toward the local population, or lacking in protective behavior.

24 SUFFICIENT TINY-ELEMENT ___ ABILITY ON DEFENSE

● Why can't a GI watchstander keep out Asian infiltrators?
● How much does his firepower help him?

Expert defenders are generally obscured from the front.

(Sources: FM 7-11B/C/CM [1979], p. 2-5; FM 5-20 [1968], p. 31.)

The Same Misconception on Defense

Nor do viable defensive operations strictly require a good-sized manpower contingent or fire superiority. The recent buildup of American armor in Poland is supposed to deter any future Russian aggression in that region. Yet, more than once over the last 80 years, large urban areas have been successfully protected by tiny, loosely controlled, and under-equipped infantry elements. In a kind of "rubble swarm," reinforced Soviet squads were able to keep a fully supported German division from reaching the Volga River at Stalingrad in late 1942.

The Battle of Stalingrad

The classic 3GW defense of an urban area occurred at Stalingrad as 1943 rolled around. After backing the Russian troops into several narrow enclaves along the Volga, the German mechanized phalanx was not able to finish them off. Within the exploits of those enclave occupants lie the seeds of advanced defensive technique. Of note, that technique was predicated on decentralized control. It gave each Soviet soldier the chance to make a tremendous difference. As every Russian replacement boarded the ferry for the dangerous crossing of the river, he was handed a pamphlet entitled "What a Soldier Needs to Know and How to Act in City Fighting." Among "light-infantry" enthusiasts, its contents have become something of a tactical treasure.

This leaflet listed the individual methods with which Lt.Gen. Vasily Chuikov's battered 62nd Army had successfully contained the vastly superior (in numbers, conventional training, and materiel) German 6th Army. Chuikov had allowed his men to function on their own initiative in cleverly improvised small-unit actions that took advantage of the heavily rubbled terrain. The pamphlet's instructions were concise: (1) to neutralize German artillery, "Get close to the enemy"; and (2) to escape German observation and small-arms fire, "Move on all fours," "Make use of craters . . . ," and "Dig trenches. . . ."[1]

As with any good defense, this one had a number of offensive characteristics. They were not the mandatory "do or die" counterattacks that one might expect from a large Soviet unit, but widely dispersed, loosely controlled, and initiative-reliant small-unit stratagems. Their first target was the German outpost line. Each night, small packs of Soviet snipers would creep forward to do their damage. In the morning, they would pull back to secret vantage points. Meanwhile Soviet scouts formed killer teams with a more personal approach.

> Parties of three to five scouts used the . . . ravines . . . to infiltrate enemy lines . . . [and] pounce on outposts.[2]
> — *Red Army Resurgent,* by Shaw

When the Germans then blindly advanced, their maneuver elements were swarmed by reinforced Russian squads. Partially by necessity, those squads had mastered the art of annihilation.

SUFFICIENT TINY-ELEMENT ABILITY ON DEFENSE

These [squad-sized] "storm groups" would creep close to their target, wait . . . and then charge.[3]
— *Red Army Resurgent,* by Shaw

One wonders why Chuikov focused more on the techniques of the individual than the squad. Perhaps, he wanted to make sure his squad leaders followed suit in delegating authority. He went so far as telling each Russian soldier how to penetrate a contested space: (1) throw a grenade; (2) enter; (3) throw other grenades into every corner; and (4) direct submachinegun bursts at anything left while moving forward.[4]

Within each Soviet enclave were matrices of "strongpoint" buildings connected by trench. Relatively flat areas between the buildings were covered by antitank and submachinegun fire from basement or first-floor apertures. Uneven areas between the buildings were protected by mines, mortars, and plunging machinegun fire from upper-story windows. Until the heavy fire was needed, Soviet snipers kept the Germans at bay (presumably from somewhere else) while stronghold defenders stayed hidden. Each little matrix of bastions then created an impenetrable island. Protected by interlocking fields of fire from rearward positions, small bands of resolute Russians could and did hold off much larger German forces "almost indefinitely."[5]

Chuikov expected his troops to turn every occupied house into a fortress, complete with barrier plan and covered routes of reinforcement or egress. His men seeded the surrounding areas with mines and dug trenches between the buildings. Then, they occupied positions most advantageous to their weapon. Artillerymen watched the distant approach avenues, while heavy machinegun and mortar crews covered the closer open areas. Submachinegunners defended each structure's immediate access to lower floors. All withheld their fire until a German unit entered their kill zone. In one such ambush, two machinegunners at a crossroads house brought a closing German battalion under fire (apparently along its entire length). The logical combination of technique and trust had made it possible for two Russian privates to kill scores of enemy troops and still live to tell the tale.[6]

Published on 1 November 1945, the U.S. War Department's *Handbook on U.S.S.R. Military Forces* may reveal how many of Stalingrad's buildings were actually defended. (Figure 24.1 even

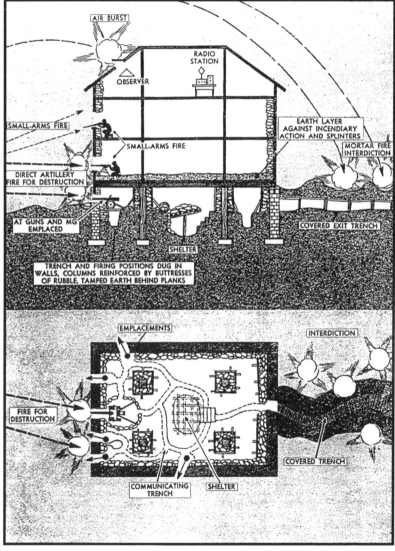

Figure 24.1: The "Soft" Eastern Building
(Source: "Handbook on U.S.S.R. Military Forces," TM 30-340 [1945], U.S. War Department, p. V-124.)

250

sports an underground escape route.) As a result, contemporary Russian soldiers may be quite adept at utilizing urban microterrain.

Still Smaller Elements Stymied the Germans at Warsaw

Urban areas have always been a good place for rebels to operate. That's partially because of the greater degree of popular support they can provide. But it's also because of the terrain itself. From a tactical standpoint, urban terrain is unique; it favors even the untrained defender. Different rebel groups have tried various tactical stratagems over the years, but there are several common threads. For example, Warsaw ghetto rebels could easily move backwards through the crawl spaces that naturally occurred in building construction. The Irish rebels of 1920 instead had strings of safe houses they could use during a retreat.

How the Warsaw Ghetto Was Finally Defended

The Warsaw Ghetto fighters got their initial baptism of fire in early 1943. Poorly armed, they only had 143 revolvers, one machine pistol, and seven rounds of ammunition per weapon. There were 650 rebels, divided into groups of 30.[7] Their principal secret to success was a clever escape and evasion network. It could also be used to sneak up on the enemy.

> The Ghetto fighters constructed an intricate network of underground cellars and tunnels. Concealed retreats and passages for shifting and distributing the defense forces were also devised.[8]
> — *The Holocaust,* by Levin

This invisible underground city was then fully outfitted with utilities.

> All inhabitants of the Ghetto prepared for what they realized would be their final fight. Hundreds of camouflaged bunker shelters were dug under the houses (including 618

air raid shelters), most connected through the sewage system and linked up with the central water supply and electricity.[9]

When the fighting finally broke out, Jewish freedom fighters poured a hail of bullets, grenades, and bombs down on the German infantry. Against Axis tanks, they tossed a barrage of gasoline-filled bottles. The battle raged from 19 April to 16 May 1943. Then, realizing the Ghetto could not be captured by any standard clearing method, the Germans started to dam up and flood the sewers. Their commander subsequently destroyed the entire residential area by setting every block on fire.[10] Unbeknownst to the Germans, one of the two insurgent organizations had a tunnel from the central stronghold at Muranowski Square to the Michalin Forest outside the Ghetto.[11]

Despite the monumental destruction, hundreds of Jewish fighters nevertheless survived in the sewers and rubble. There was sporadic shooting throughout the summer of 1943, and then things turned quiet.[12] In August 1944, the underground Polish army attempted to liberate Warsaw from German occupation. The remaining rebels joined in, and the fighting soon turned brutal. At one point, an encircled Jewish enclave managed to secretly join another through the sewers.[13] This time, the Germans had to burn down 85% of the city to restore some semblance of order.[14]

Defensive Precedent Had Much Do with Smaller Scale

The Jewish fighters had started to work at a scale in which the Germans were unaccustomed. While the occupiers tried to clear rooms and buildings, the rebels had already moved into the walls, ceilings, and sewers. To make more urban E&E possible through a building's construction, one must remember two things: (1) the effectiveness of a hiding place and its secret exit will depend on how well the entrance is obscured; and (2) the enemy isn't stupid. In the Warsaw Ghetto, there is no proof that the Germans ever summoned mantrackers, but they did call in dogs. And then they did a lot of shooting into suspicious walls, ceilings, and floors. Another of their tricks was to bust out all of a building's windows from the inside. If any window then seemed unbroken from the outside, it marked a hidden chamber.[15] The valiant Ghetto defenders responded in kind—using some truly amazing ingenuity to disguise their work. As with Anne Frank's hiding place in Amsterdam, many of Warsaw's "extra rooms" remained unknown to the Germans for a very long time.

Soon an underground city began to emerge beneath the Ghetto. All persons capable of helping to build it, did so. Not having to be excavated from virgin soil, its larger spaces were created by walling off "feeder" portions of the existing sewer system. Some could house dozens of people. With water, drainage, and wiring readily available, they had bunk rooms, kitchens, and lavatories. While their lights usually required a generator, the phones would work for short periods of time on batteries alone. Of course, there were a fair number of above-ground improvements as well—some 50,000 secret entrances to false rooms in subfloors, closets, eaves, and attics. The floor entrances varied from loose tiles and rug-covered trapdoors to toilets on hinges and removable hearths. The wall entrances consisted of everything from holes behind picture frames to false backs in cabinets and bookcases.[16] Of all the portals to a secret space, the removable toilet was probably the best thought out. The only tunnel not found by the Germans at Stalag Luft III POW Camp after the legendary breakout of WWII's "Great Escape" was the one with a partially submerged entrance. The Allied fliers had brilliantly created a bathroom sump that did not properly drain (or leak beyond a certain point). Though its movable side began just above the surface of the standing water, the Germans never suspected the optical illusion.

"Tom" went from the dark corner of a hut corridor; "Harry" began under a stove. A tiled base was lifted to one side, revealing the top of a tunnel shaft. "Dick" started in a washroom beneath the drain cover. Hiding the tunnel entrance in a sump where dirty water collected was a master stroke. The Germans never did find "Dick."[17]
— *PBS's* "Nova," 5 June 2007

While cellars could hold more supplies and their entrances be easily concealed, attics provided better communication and escape routes. From those attics, Jewish fighters could sneak out onto the often connected rooftops. Their tormentors weren't anxious to follow, and many who did soon took a terminal tumble over the roof's edge.[18]

The tenements did not provide the only refuge. In stores and bakeries, Ghetto dwellers hid under counters, in unfired ovens, and beneath tubs. Some even tried to remove the stuffing from couches. False backs to packing crates provided discreet ways to enter secret rooms, and outside garbage piles made a perfect place to fabricate tiny niches.[19]

One way to gain rooftop access in the Warsaw Ghetto was to climb a rope ladder to a trapdoor in the attic ceiling. When wishing to move from one roof to another one story lower, the fighters often positioned a mattress to soften their descent. Then, they stood on the edge of the first roof, jumped, landed on their feet, and fell forward onto the waiting mattress.[20] Though not formally trained in UW, they had nevertheless become masters of a full sixth of its content for infantrymen. From their exploits, one might logically conclude that the best UW methods are born from experimentation at the small-unit level.

Tiny Groups Can Also Provide a Good Rural Defense

There are plenty of places for one or two people to hide in nature as well. A tiny element can hold up a massive enemy formation in the countryside just as easily as the two Russian privates did at Stalingrad.[21] But, small defensive groups need not be part of a strongpoint matrix in rural terrain.

To limit the extent of Allied interference in Vietnam, the North Vietnamese may have used a variant of the Russian double-encirclement strategy.[22] While technically an offensive maneuver, this dual cordon also had great defensive possibilities. Basically, the enemy continually drew U.S. maneuver forces to the outer circle to give themselves more freedom of action along the inner circle (around strategically vital transportation centers and Allied installations).[23] As former Marine Raider Samuel B. Griffith once put it, "The enemy's rear is the [Maoist] guerrilla's front."[24] The NVA/VC's ultimate goal was to destroy enough strategic assets within U.S. camps, that the American Congress would stop funding the war. They could best do that through secretive sabotage. Then, the same stratagems would work over and over.

How they dealt with the U.S. maneuver forces on the outer circle will first be discussed. There is no enemy literature on the subject, just a few fleeting references.

> For the inner circle, task forces units, commandos, special-ized mortar gunners, [and then for the outer circle] guerilla *[sic]* forces on the "anti-U.S. snipers rings" attacked the U.S. forces wherever and whenever it was possible.[25]
> — *Tet Mau Than 1968 Event in South Vietnam*
> The Gioi Publishers, Hanoi

The VC had three kinds of troops: main force, regional force, and local militia.[26] The first two were primarily offensive in nature; and the third, defensive. Embedded—each within the next—were five tactical areas of operation: (1) hamlets (or villages); (2) communes; (3) districts; (4) Bases; and (5) Zones.[27] The self-defense forces (or militia) furnished local security, intelligence collection, and policing. Some may have also provided combat service support to maneuver elements passing through.[28] Within their respective areas of responsibility, they additionally monitored enemy activities, guided NVA forces (sometimes through opposition wire), and guarded infiltration routes.[29]

The "anti-U.S. sniper rings" mentioned in the above (and very rare) Hanoi reference were undoubtedly cells of skilled VC snipers. Their precise role can only be surmised. They first would have countered any American sniper activity. Then, every time they managed to kill a U.S. leader, they would disrupt the Allies' command and control apparatus. But, such snipers could also have defended a small piece of vital real estate from afar. Their shots might easily have caused a U.S. maneuver element to slow down or even change direction. The North Vietnamese battle chronicle for the Tay Nguyen Campaign of 1975 brags about the ability to "attract the enemy forces in the direction of our choice, keep them moving according to our will and hold them back."[30] Why couldn't VC snipers have done the same thing on a smaller scale? Just by knowing where the underground staging areas and ammunition caches were in their home region, they could have protected the entrances. Any American patrol that got too close was about to lose its senior member.

The Inner Circle Also Had a Defensive Role

All U.S. installations were surrounded by an inner circle of "fighting villages, political pockets, guerrilla zones, and anti-U.S.

snipers rings."[31]   In concert, these four forms of enemy alignment
could cause U.S. forces to assume a more defensive or passive posture.[32] They did so by giving U.S. "search-and-destroy" sweeps little
to show for their offensive effort. Some facilitated enemy attacks on
U.S. installations, while others helped to draw U.S. security patrols
away from the staging areas for such attacks. Many of those staging
areas must have been hidden within plain sight of (or right next to)
U.S. perimeters. While adjacent-hamlet residents were thought to
be there for protection from the guerrillas, some had been doing a
lot of digging toward the U.S. wire. The more distant staging areas
were probably in hamlets inhabited by sympathizers, protected by
boobytraps, and surrounded by snipers. To find an active antagonist, American patrols would have avoided any supposedly secure
or mined area.

Most "fighting villages" were hamlets that were slightly more
distant from the Allied camps. They were heavily fortified, and ostensibly deserted. While concealed by vegetation, their peripheral
trench lines were long enough to protect the random occupant from
aerial bombardment. As with today's North Vietnamese "Military
Fortress" barrier along the Chinese border, these fortified villages
must have formed a "soft, strongpoint defense." They were, after
all, mutually supporting bastions that were little effected by the
loss of a few. As with the "combat villages" of the modern Military
Fortress, all "fighting villages" of the 1960's must have had their
own "vanish underground" facility.[33]

> The [Duong Minh Chau] Base [northwest of Saigon] was
> divided into 13 districts, each district was divided into com-
> munes and hamlets having their own fortifications, tunnels,
> and trenches; they formed a closed front line able to help
> one another when necessary.[34]
> — *Tet Mau Than 1968 Event in South Vietnam*
>   The Gioi Publishers, Hanoi

Flatland Base Areas

Mao had written about the flatland guerrilla needing shifting,
yet relatively secure, "base areas" (different from the capitalized
subsection of a Zone).[35] The guerrilla base area for each commune

must have rotated among (and existed beneath) that commune's ten or so fighting villages.[36] This was, after all, the same way that maneuver elements quickly disappeared from view.

Few permanent camps [existed], especially within South Vietnam itself. In Laos, North Vietnam, and Cambodia, there were permanent camps, although as the war went on even these camps in "safe areas" tended to be underground. Within South Vietnam, each Viet Cong or North Vietnamese unit had several entrenched camps. Communist units would constantly move around, rarely staying in one place more than a few weeks, and usually never more than a few days.[37]
— *Dirty Little Secrets of the Vietnam War*
by Dunnigan and Nofi

However, these flatland base areas could not have survived without some way of staying beyond view of the Allies. Their "rear-support" establishment was generally in the less-accessible forests and mountains. Yet, just northwest of Saigon, the subterranean status of many base areas permitted them to be very near to the action.

[Within the Duong Minh Chau Base] were concentrated officials, personnel in government services, schools, factories, hospitals, storehouses, broadcast stations. . . . These centers [were] built along dried streams, below the forest foliage, and at half-underground level.[38]
— *Tet Mau Than 1968 Event in South Vietnam*
The Gioi Publishers, Hanoi

Early in the war by Communist admission, these centers had been located within a vast network of communications trenches to obscure their exact whereabouts.[39] Later on, many were connected by tunnel.

Enemy's Above-Ground Defensive Array Had a Name

As shown in Map 24.1, the interspersion of fortified villages and guerrilla zones resembled a leopard's skin. Not surprisingly, that's precisely what the North Vietnamese called the formation.[40] At the center of every ten or so spots was an underground guerrilla base camp.

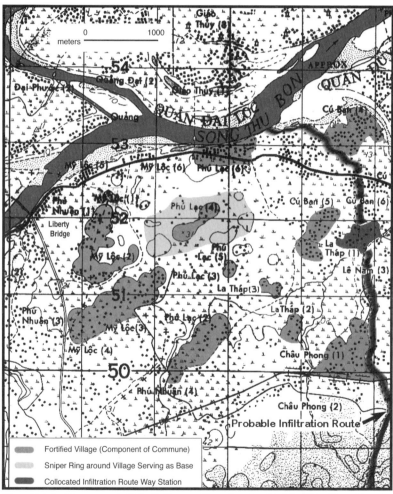

Map 24.1: "Leopard Skin" Formation Protected Infiltration Route
(Source: Further refinement of Map 10.1 from "The Tiger's Way," originally constructed from 1:50,000 USGS map, Vietnam Series L7014, of area just northeast of An Hoa.)

We controlled many areas in the mountains and plains alike, and had established our bases in the towns.[41]
— Gen. Hoang Van Thai

Along the inner circle near some place like Da Nang Airfield, their would have been a surrounding belt that looked like this. Further out from Da Nang, like down across the Song Thu Bong River at the base of the Que Son Mountains, such a formation would have been linear and deployed along either side of the major infiltration routes. One Marine company spent many months operating in this region. That's why such a map is now possible. (Look again at Map 24.1.)

In Memoriam to a Dutiful NCO

Sadly, a squad leader from Golf Company, 2nd Battalion, 5th Marines (2/5) would have to pay the ultimate price for some of this knowledge in July of 1968. While his name has since been obscured from history by the loss of so many other wonderful Leathernecks, his gallant service to God, nation, and Corps must now be formally recognized.

With a full head of blond hair and mustache, this fine young warrior looked hauntingly old the day his company commander asked him to "get back on the same horse that had just bucked him off." He and his squad had just come back from a daytime patrol to an arbitrarily chosen point some 1500 meters southeast of the G/2/5 outpost at Liberty Bridge (on left side of Map 24.1.) After learning the patrol had taken small-arms fire from several sides and one very big mortar round from the mountains, his Commanding Officer (CO) had helped the squad leader to call in and adjust an artillery mission from An Hoa. That mission had opened up an "escape lane" from what had apparently been an enemy encirclement. Unfortunately, U.S. intelligence briefings in those days didn't include where the infiltration routes were, or how they might be defended. So, on a well-intended yet situationally naive impulse, the company commander had then asked his squad leader to briefly reaffirm Marine control over the same area the next day. *En route,* this consummately professional Corporal was then killed by a single shot from a VC sniper rifle.[42] Like thousands of American infantrymen before him, he had done his utmost to accomplish an overly dangerous mission. His death in the performance of that mission therefore makes him a true hero in every sense of the word.

On 18 August of that year, a heavily contested assault by G/2/5 on the tiny hamlet of Lap Thap 1 would firmly establish it as an infiltration route waystation. (See the right edge of Map 24.1.) Soon thereafter, a large cache of medical supplies would be discovered right next to the trail leading south, as was the site of a previous battle (bits and pieces Marine 782 gear all over the place). That battle had happened at the north end of Chau Phong 1. There was little doubt at this point that a major infiltration route had been located leading out of the Que Son Mountains and heading towards Da Nang.

Whether or not any higher headquarters S-2 section ever realized the existence of this infiltration route is doubtful. For, that same company commander continued to work in this general area for eight more months without being apprised of it. Only years later did all the pieces of what had happened in this tiny Vietnamese backwater begin to build a plausible picture.[43] Farther north, those NVA and VC personnel traveling this route to and from Da Nang would have had little trouble crossing the Song Thu Bon River in either direction, because much of it was shallow enough to wade most of the year.[44]

When the precursor to Map 24.1 was first drawn in 2003, Phu Lac 4 was arbitrarily chosen as the village serving as the local VC's "base area."[45] At the time of this magnificent Marine corporal's death, the rotating base area location must have been either at My Loc 2 or My Loc 3. That would explain such prolific and sadly accurate rifle fire (most VC fighters were notoriously bad shots). Those anti-U.S. sniper ring members would have been safeguarding the entrance to the chosen hamlet's underground hide facility.

This Much Small-Unit Success Just as Possible for GIs

Among those still living ground-combat veterans of WWII, most agree their fight was largely one bunker at a time. In fact, throughout U.S. history, every serious adversary from the Sioux to the Japanese and Germans had eventually to be confronted by tiny groups of well-experienced American infantrymen But that was then. At present, the idea of losing a single ground combatant to close combat has become so aberrant to the American public that it no longer appears to recognize an inescapable truth. Even the most modern of wars cannot be successfully prosecuted without some risk to U.S. life and limb. As with WWII, they all require some close combat at the small-unit level.

A tiny element's success in battle can arise out of necessity as it did for the initial survivors of Omaha Beach, or be previously instilled through more comprehensive GI preparation. But, in a world in which low-intensity 4GW has now become the norm, it must somehow happen to avoid too much collateral damage. Whatever people of Russian, Jewish, or Vietnamese descent could do in history, any present-day American can do just as well after a little of the right kind of training. That it may be a bit more risky than stand-off bombardment is just an unfortunate fact of life. Without fully intending to win a foreign war, Uncle Sam should stop embarking on them. For then, every American life lost from the outset may be in vain.

For the U.S. rifleman, a good place to start that preparation is all the little warnings of impending trouble. They are just as prevalent in the city as in the woods.

PART NINE

INCREASING THE GI'S SITUATIONAL AWARENESS

"THERE IS NO UNIVERSAL LANGUAGE IN THE JUNGLES; EACH SPECIES HAS ITS OWN LANGUAGE, AND THOUGH THE VOCABULARY OF SOME IS LIMITED (AS IN THE CASE OF PORCUPINES AND VULTURES), THE LANGUAGE OF EACH SPECIES IS UNDERSTOOD BY ALL THE JUNGLE-FOLK." — JIM CORBETT (SUCCESSFUL HUNTER OF DOZENS OF MAN-EATING CATS, 1910 TO 1930)

(Source: Edward James Corbett, from "The Man-Eating Leopard of Rudraprayag," as retrieved from this url: https://www.goodreads.com/author/quotes/43681.Jim_Corbett)

25   URBAN WARNINGS OF
___ IMPENDING TROUBLE

- What kinds of things alert city dwellers to nearby danger?
- Can someone from the country learn to detect them?

Unnaturally cluttered furniture may indicate an interior bunker.

(Source: FM 7-8 [1984], p. P-6.)

Most U.S. Troops Now from a Built-Up Area

Urban combat seems more natural to the modern-day American snuffy than the rural kind. Unfortunately, staying alive in a heavily contested city also takes a higher degree of sensory awareness. The barren and more three-dimensional nature of a built-up area offers too many ways of getting shot. Just to appreciate the degree of increased danger, one needs imagination. A section of street can be so fully covered by separate sectors of plunging fire that it becomes impossible to cross. Picture 20 sharpshooters, each on a table well back from the open window of a darkened room, and each with about 36 square feet of pavement to defend. Without the benefit of muzzle flashes, how could there be any way to return their fire? Such a nightmare scenario has already occurred along Hue City's Phase Line Green during the Vietnam War.[1]

Easier to Get Cut Off from Parent Unit in the City

Within a built-up area, there's no dense vegetation or muddy ditch into which to disappear. There are only occasionally perforated walls, floors, and ceilings. That makes "tactical withdrawal" far more difficult. As the first Russian armored column into Grozny more than adequately demonstrated in 1994, it's also easier to get separated from one's friends in urban terrain. Then, there are only two options: (1) fight until assistance arrives (which it never did at Grozny [2]); or (2) work one's way back to friendly lines. While a town offers any number of separate conduits for E&E, they must normally be combined for a journey of any duration. (See Table 25.1.)

The urban U.S. soldier (particularly when part of a point element) would therefore be wise to keep track of all available "exit" routes as he advances. (See Figures 25.1 and 25.2.) His job is to fight, not to throw his life away unnecessarily. The same holds true for any badly outnumbered policeman in a carefully laid trap. Once one's buddies have been accounted for, there is no dishonor in temporarily departing the premises. Isn't that what the President's Secret Service detail does every time he is attacked?

Nor Is Being with a Moving Unit Healthy

The taller structures and scarcity of vegetation in urban terrain permit more observation than on unimproved ground. That's why the side that tries to shift location in a city is at a disadvantage. Their personnel can be "attrited" in a myriad of ways. Even if it were possible to cover every possible source of enemy fire, each of its fighters would still have to avoid the first bullet through his actions at the time. (For the general categories of what he faces on the street see Table 25.2.)

Minimally meeting this multifaceted threat would take con-

Figure 25.1: Typical City Street

Figure 25.2: Urban Point Men
(Source: Courtesy of Sorman Info. & Media, illustration by Wolfgang Bartsch, from "SoldF: Soldaten i falt," *p. 289*, © 2001 Forsvarsmakten and Wolfgang Bartsch.)

RETURN OF SECURITY TEAM TO UNIT OR TACTICAL WITHDRAWAL

EACH ROUTE SEGMENT MUST OFFER SOME COVER/CONCEALMENT

SUBTERRANEAN:
- SUBWAYS AND TRAIN TUNNELS
- STORM DRAINS AND AQUEDUCTS
- CATACOMBS AND PREVIOUS-HABITATION LEVELS
- SEWERS AND UTILITY CONDUITS

AT SURFACE LEVEL:
- CULVERTS
- PARTIALLY COVERED DRAINAGE DITCHES
- CRAWL SPACES BENEATH HOUSES
- NARROW BREEZEWAYS BETWEEN BUILDINGS
- ROADSIDE GUTTERS IN LOW LIGHT
- SPACES BETWEEN WALLS AND BUSHES OR TRASH
- FENCED-IN AREAS BEHIND BUILDINGS
- SHADED SIDE OF AN ALLEYWAY

NATURALLY OCCURRING CORRIDORS WITHIN BUILDINGS:
LATERAL
- BASEMENTS
- SPACE ABOVE SOME SUSPENDED CEILINGS
- ATTICS
- EAVES
- VENTILATION DUCTS
VERTICAL
- WELL-ATTACHED DRAINAGE PIPES
- "DUMB-WAITER" OR LAUNDRY SHAFTS

LIKELY AVENUES BETWEEN ADJACENT BUILDINGS:
- SIDE ENTRANCES
- JUXTAPOSITIONED WINDOW OPENINGS
- TELEPHONE LINES AFTER DARK
- ROOFTOPS

OTHER ABOVE-GROUND PATHWAYS:
- SPREADING TREE BRANCHES
- GUIDE WIRES AFTER DARK
- STREET SPANNING SIGNS OR WALKWAYS AT NIGHT
- ELEVATED TRAIN TRACKS AFTER DARK

SEGMENT COMBINATION MUST ADEQUATELY BYPASS ENEMY

Table 25.1: Urban Escape and Evasion Components

stant rehearsal, total focus, and manual dexterity. Heavily committed SWAT members may have assimilated some of this inherent ability, but recent military or police recruits would need special preparation. For starters, each must be told all the different ways of getting shot on the street, so they can at least recognize the need for rehearsal.

Then, when the U.S. street warrior decides to enter a building, his task becomes even more complicated. After making the initial breach, he must now worry about separately defended hallways and rooms. As on open ground, each floor might then offer its own strongpoint matrix. When stacked one upon the other and all connected by some means of communication and reinforcement, such matrices would then resemble a nightmarish three-dimensional bees' nest. (See Figures 25.3 through 25.6 and Tables 25.2 and 25.3.)

In other words, each building could be so fully defended as to make it nearly impossible to seize by force. Such an example exists in *The Last Hundred Yards*.[3] Again, the fledgling rifleman or cop must be told of these additional risks. Though not yet familiar with all appropriate procedures, the adequately warned fighter will still do a better job. Those who would argue this point have badly underestimated the courage, intelligence, and potential of young Americans.

An Adequate Response Would Take Constant Rehearsal

A seasoned SWAT member would have already experienced a wide variety of street frontages, door latches, building interiors, and room obstacles. Few future scenarios would catch him by complete surprise. But for his infantry counterparts, building enough muscle memory to instinctively do the smartest thing takes continual practice at handling the most often recurring combinations of urban variables. Then, whatever tactical technique they decide to use, they can more easily transcend it to account for unforeseen circumstances.

Because moving with any measure of safety through urban terrain takes concurrently compensating for multiple threats, each student must first accept responsibility for his own learning. For the best results, he works on one or two threats at a time and

THINGS TO NOTICE WHILE MOVING UP A CITY STREET

SEARCHING GI CAN BE EASILY SEEN COMING.

HE CAN BE SHOT FROM SEVERAL DIFFERENT SOURCES:

BY BULLETS DEFLECTED ALONG WALLS
BY LONG-RANGE MACHINEGUN AT EITHER END OF THE STREET
FROM UPPER STORIES TO THE FRONT, SIDE, OR REAR
FROM SPACES BETWEEN BUILDINGS
FROM OPEN WINDOWS AND DOORS
FROM TINY WALL APERTURES (LIKE AIR VENTS OR DRAINAGE HOLES)
FROM CRACKS OR BULLET/SHELL HOLES IN THE WALLS
FROM SEWER OPENINGS IN THE GUTTERS
FROM OTHER GRATES IN THE SIDEWALKS
FROM MANHOLE COVERS OR SOMETHING OVER THEM (LIKE A JUNKED CAR)
FROM PARKED VEHICLES
FROM TRASH CANS OR PILES OF REFUSE ON THE SIDEWALK

THINGS TO NOTICE WHILE ENTERING A BUILDING

SEARCHING GI CAN BE EASILY SEEN APPROACHING THE STRUCTURE

UPPER-FLOOR ENTRY THE BEST, THEN VIA ANY ROUTE BUT FRONT DOOR

IF HE WANTS TO USE MAIN ENTRANCE, HE MUST PAY ATTENTION TO

WHETHER THAT DOOR IS WOOD (RIFLE CAN SHOOT RIGHT THROUGH IT)
WHETHER THAT DOOR CONTAINS A TINY WINDOW OR PEEPHOLE
WHETHER SOMEONE AT DOOR IS VISIBLE FROM ANOTHER WINDOW
WHETHER DOOR HAS A LOCKED STORM, SCREEN, OR SECURITY COVER
WHETHER DOOR OPENS INWARD OR OUTWARD
WHETHER ENTRANT HAS PRIOR EXPERIENCE WITH THIS TYPE OF LATCH

Table 25.2: Ways to Get Shot While Moving Up a Street

Figure 25.3: Entering an Urban Structure
(Source: Courtesy of Sorman Info. & Media, illustration by Wolfgang Bartsch, from "SoldF: Soldaten i falt," p. 289, © 2001 Forsvarsmakten and Wolfgang Bartsch.)

Figure 25.4: Walking the Halls
(Source: FM 90-10-1 [1982], p. B-12)

271

Figure 25.5: Door Kicking Not Always a Good Idea
(Source: FM 90-10-1 [1982], p. B-27)

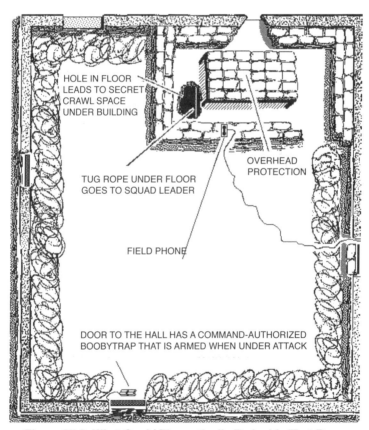

HOLE IN FLOOR
LEADS TO SECRET
CRAWL SPACE
UNDER BUILDING

TUG ROPE UNDER FLOOR
GOES TO SQUAD LEADER

OVERHEAD
PROTECTION

FIELD PHONE

DOOR TO THE HALL HAS A COMMAND-AUTHORIZED
BOOBYTRAP THAT IS ARMED WHEN UNDER ATTACK

Figure 25.6: What Could Theoretically Be Inside That Door
(Source: FM 90-10 (1979), p. C-5)

THINGS TO NOTICE WHILE MOVING ALONG A HALLWAY

ADVANCING GI CAN BE DETECTED THROUGH:

A CAVITY IN THE WALLBOARD AND PINPRICK IN THE WALLPAPER
PEEPHOLES IN THE DOORS
CREAKY FLOOR BOARDS
PERISCOPE-LIKE SERIES OF TINY MIRRORS
MAN IN LIGHTED HALLWAY CASTS SHADOW UNDER DOOR OF DARK ROOM

HE CAN BE INJURED FROM SEVERAL DIFFERENT LOCATIONS

THROUGH THIN WALLS, FLOORS, OR CEILINGS
OUT OF VENTILATION DUCTS
FROM DISTANT DOORWAY BY AUTOMATIC WEAPON AT ARM'S LENGTH

THINGS TO NOTICE WHILE ENTERING A ROOM

ADVANCING GI CAN BE DETECTED THROUGH:

DOOR-OPENING NOISE OR CREAKING FLOOR BOARDS FROM BELOW
ENTRANT CAN BE EASILY SEEN FROM OUTSIDE IN A LIGHTED ROOM
EVEN WITH SHADES DRAWN, HIS SHADOW WILL STILL BE VISIBLE
OPPOSITE-SIDE WINDOWS WOULD SILHOUETTE HIM IN ANY LIGHT

HE CAN BE INJURED FROM SEVERAL DIFFERENT SOURCES/LOCATIONS:

DOOR OR ANY INTERESTING OBJECT MAY BE BOOBYTRAPPED
SOMEONE (NOT NECESSARILY AN ENEMY) COULD BE HIDING
IN CLOSET
IN CUPBOARD
BEHIND AIR-CONDITIONING OR HEATING VENT
BEHIND CURTAINS
BEHIND FURNITURE
ABOVE FALSE CEILING OR IN SECRET ROOM
OUTSIDE WINDOW
WITH AK-47 ON OTHER SIDE OF THIN ROOM SIDE OR DOOR

Table 25.3: Ways to Get Shot While Moving Through a Building

then several in combination. All can be done as he runs through a makeshift "street movement" course. At the end of each run, he gets feedback on how well he did against simulated fire. By then having to repeat the course, he automatically improves.

Easiest Way of Providing That Training

No "hard-to-reserve" base combat town is needed for such a course. It can be quickly set up in any little-used portion of a base business area or small town. The prerequisite rehearsal for a proficient urban warrior then most logically takes the form of daily physical-fitness exercises. Below are the construction and operating details of such a street-negotiating "fun run." Others for moving through hallways or even rooms could be established the same way.

First, a pair of instructors find a deserted city block like one in the current war zone. Then, they issue 20 or so students rubber rifles. Each takes half the student body and two aggressors to opposite sides of the street at one end of this block. (See Figure 25.7.) Their subsequent operation will be completely separate. Each then deploys his aggressors to the other end of the block to provide casualty simulation from two different perspectives. He then starts sending one student (who is trying not to get shot) at a time up the store fronts. He and his pals are about to get successive tries against three pairs of threats.

During the first evolution, one aggressor sits in the middle of the street to simulate long-range machinegun or sniper fire, while the other stands next to the store fronts to simulate wall-following bullets. Both will count three-second sight pictures against each runner. Then, that runner is told how many times he died and is sent back — behind the buildings — to the end of his original column. After everyone has had two chances, they must face a less obvious challenge.

This time, the aggressors "obscurely" provide examples of the third and fourth threats. The instructor tells his students to avoid fire from between the buildings and any upper stories. After each student's score has been relayed by cell phone to the instructor, he informs the appropriate party before launching him on his second try.

Finally, the aggressors move to provide the fifth and sixth threats. The instructor advises his runners to elude fire from open windows or doors and any tiny wall aperture. Again, all get a chance to improve.

One or two days later, the same instructors deploy six aggressors apiece and work on four threats at once, then all six. For a particularly motivated group, other threats from Table 25.2 can subsequently be added. Only one man can run the gauntlet every five minutes, so each column should be no bigger than 10 people. For more students, the command should set up duplicate courses at other locations. Similar packages can be easily designed for interior movement. They may even be possible for particularly risky pieces of rural terrain.

Figure 25.7: Waiting Their Turn at Street Movement Practice
(Source: Courtesy of Sorman Information and Media, Illustration by Wolfgang Bartsch, from "SoldF: Soldaten i falt," © 2001 Forsvarsmakten, Stockholm, pp. 22, 23)

More Than One Way to Skin a Cat

If one's Command cannot be convinced to provide such training, then a 10 or so proactive nonrates could easily provide it for themselves. Their only inconvenience might be checking out and then recleaning their rifles. How better might they wile away a long weekend on an isolated infantry base? For additional motivation, some prize (like a sixpack of some bubbly beverage) could be awarded to the person who gets killed the least number of times. He who has the most to lose must often try a little harder. The average Command would welcome such a display of enlisted initiative and possibly donate a prize.

26 ___ RURAL HINTS OF NEARBY OPPOSITION

● How aware are most GIs of their surroundings in the field?
● What should they be looking for on patrol?

Ground sign will often provide warning of an enemy presence.

(Source: Courtesy of A.E. Taras, from "Podgotovka Razvegchika: Sistema Spetsnaza GRU," p. 173, © 1998 by A.E. Taras and F.D. Zaruz.)

Most U.S. Citizens No Longer Familiar with Nature

When America's young men answered the call to arms after Pearl Harbor, many were from the Appalachians and others the Civilian Conservation Corps. While one had helped to feed his family through hunting, the other had worked on remote public-service projects. Today's youth are much more digitally oriented. Even if fully outfitted and provisioned, many would have difficulty operating for long in their local countryside. Within Chapter 9 was what became of some fairly woods-wise Soviet troops during the Finnish winter of 1940.

Most of the world's current aggression is by nonstate actors who can ill afford fancy gear. Instead, they have come to largely rely on their natural instincts. Thus has developed a dangerously widening gap between the survival capabilities of the average U.S. soldier and his miscreant adversary. Advanced surveillance and targeting equipment may help the modern-day GI to shoot a fully visible quarry, but any self-respecting criminal will seldom expose himself to that extent. Neither does all that expensive U.S. gadgetry do anything to obscure the approach or location of its current owner. Thus, the loosely controlled foreign terrorist, insurgent, or drug runner has little trouble devising a more than adequate response to his overly controlled and firepower-oriented tormentor. As far back as 1942, U.S. Marines had difficulty spotting their opposition in heavily vegetated terrain.

> There must be training in difficult observation, which is needed for the offense. It is my observation [on Guadalcanal] that only 5% of the men can really see while observing.[1]
> — Col. Merritt A. "Red Mike" Edson

Nor could they see those adversaries three years later on the nearly barren island of Iwo Jima.

> Seldom on Iwo, from D-Day until the battle was over, did you see the enemy—just the sights and sounds of deadly fire from his weapons.[2]
> — *Iwo Jima*, by Ross

Thus, today's more "city-and-electronics-oriented" U.S. infantrymen and special operators would be unwise to believe their preparation for spotting rural trouble had been adequate. Formal training hours are expensive, so many of the more sophisticated "woods-wise" detection skills must be acquired either on the job or through personal study. For additional sensory ability of this kind, one must first have the imagination to identify which battlefield occasions might require it. (See Tables 26.1 through 26.5 for a few suggestions.) To ignore such things out of an overabundance of pride could easily lead to a premature trip to the State veterans' cemetery.

Throughout the Eastern World, "visualization" has long been recognized as a way to prepare for what has not been properly rehearsed. In this case, all contemporary GIs would do well to visualize what more they might need to know to stay safe in freewheeling combat.

The Ever Present Headquarters Distraction

The U.S. military is a decidedly top-down organization. That means every member must pay fairly close attention to what his or her immediate superior appears to want. Unfortunately, so doing at the bottom echelons makes nonrates not only less aware of enemy aggression, but also slow to react to it.

This overemphasis on following orders has created some serious shortfalls among the true gladiators—namely, that proud system's lowest-ranking infantrymen and special operators. When up against one of America's usual "bottom-up" foes, they are in the best position to notice any new enemy initiative. Yet, they are not being shown how to spot it, counter it, or even quickly report it up the chain. Instead, they have been unintentionally conditioned to do exactly as told no matter what the situation. Wars are not won that way, nor are casualties limited.

Here's what fills the mind of the average U.S. "snuffy" in combat: (1) is he in the right part of the formation; (2) what is his overall mission; (3) on which parts of that mission can he ask questions; (4) when can he take cover; (5) when can he fire his rifle; and (6) who can he shoot at. That young rifleman has been too seldom apprised of the following vital information: (1) his "commander's intent"; (2) the strategic ramifications of the battle; (3) what he might personally do to win it; or (4) any detailed instructions. No wonder his bosses have so much trouble winning wars.

So, when that snuffy stumbles upon something of strategic significance, he is generally at a loss on four very important matters: (1) what qualifies; (2) how best to report it; (3) whether slowing the unit down would be worth it; and (4) what he might personally be authorized to do before leaving the location. He has often been rebuked for far less of an interruption to the mandates of a "superior." So, when confronted by any decision-requiring dilemma, he will normally just move on without ever telling anyone (except maybe a close buddy later) about what he has seen.

One time during a Marine operation north of Chu Lai in early 1967, the point man for a returning squad-sized patrol from A/1/4 told his platoon leader he had just seen a AK-47 toting and pajama-clad man without shooting at him.[3]

Then, to compound the average snuffy's reluctance to take nondirected action, his patrol or sweep is never properly debriefed for possible intelligence discoveries. That's because neither his Company officers nor the Battalion S-2 generally knows enough about the evolution of squad tactics or the Asians' bottom-up way of operating to conduct such a probe.

Things Only a Snuffy Will See

The combat rifleman does not live in a world of "big-picture" esoterics, where people with rank routinely ignore many local details. His is one of small rocks, stumps, and depressions in the soil. That's where he may soon have to take cover. Ground anomalies of this size are not discernible from aerial surveillance. They are only visible to the nearby eye, and even more so to an "experienced" eye (like that of a longtime mantracker).

Ever since Iwo Jima, the 38th Parallel Stalemate in Korea, and Vietnam, the Asian enemy has been operating extensively below ground. That means many of America's expeditionary base camps have been actually attacked from within, its tanks disabled from right beside them, and the defenders of its combat objectives able to disappear. Without regularly collecting the firsthand observations of the lowest-ranking infantrymen, U.S. forces will continue to have trouble with such threats. They will also have difficulty locating the enemy's infiltration routes, protective strongpoints, and caches of supplies/equipment (as in Chapter 24). This means that more foreign adventures will drag on for years, and eventually have to be abandoned.

The Name of the Game Is Winning Wars

Imagine how many times some U.S. rifleman has trodden across glaring evidence of such things in Vietnam without either the will or the authority to do anything about it. One grenade per cache entrance might have been finally sufficient to win the war. But, once that golden opportunity to destroy strategically vital assets had been forfeited, rediscovering that hole in the ground would have been like looking for a man overboard in a choppy sea. The fault is not that of the snuffy himself, but of a system that has doggedly refused to decentralize any control whatsoever over its training and operations.

Good light infantry doesn't need any expensive ordnance or equipment to get the job done. Neither can its every action be orchestrated from above. Unfortunately, the first flies in the face of the military industrial complex, while the second makes nervous the disciplinarians. During the Vietnam War, one U.S. general went so far as to say something to this effect during a public speaking engagement: "He would not do anything to jeopardize America's military heritage and traditions just to win a war." Similarly, the funding-and-control-focused Pentagon may never relax enough of those self-defeating restrictions on lowest-echelon initiative and ingenuity (through its codes of conduct).

In the meantime, each U.S. infantry private must become more alert to enemy clues and then strive to share them with his leaders. Asian forces will often feign a Western-style attack formation and then penetrate a U.S. perimeter with tiny elements from a different direction. Such "bottom-up" overtures are most obvious to those of least rank in a Western defense (as was the case in Chapter 23). All the latest advances in electronic surveillance—whether by drone or satellite—does not alter this basic truth. The ground observer has his former experience to draw upon, is only inches away from the suspicious sighting, and can more accurately counter it. In a 4GW war, where no civilian casualties at all can be tolerated, such a personal touch on the battlefield is absolutely essential. How can a drone possibly tell if the four-square-foot hole it sees is actually the entrance to a civilian-occupied bomb shelter?

Things for Present-Day Nonrates to Start Observing

The role of the U.S. defensive watchstander is not an easy one. For what may easily distract him from his mission, see Figure 26.1 and Table 26.1. Nor is the job of patrol security team a "slam dunk." Then, what he somehow detects can make the difference between the life and death of many people. (See Figure 26.2 and Table 26.2.) At times, the two-man point team may have to look for (and then

NOT QUITE SURE OF WHAT HE JUST SAW OR HEARD

CONSTANTLY TOLD HOW EASY IT IS TO IMAGINE THINGS AT NIGHT

NOT ALLOWED TO GIVE AWAY HIS POSITION BY FIRING

CAN'T REACH HIS IMMEDIATE SUPERIOR BY RADIO OR LAND LINE

WOULD HAVE TO WAKE UP HIS PARTNER JUST TO REPORT A SIGHTING

DOESN'T WANT TO BOTHER HIS SUPERIOR AGAIN

GOT CHEWED OUT LAST TIME HE REPORTED SOMETHING UNUSUAL

WOULD RATHER NOT BELIEVE THE ENEMY IS SLOWLY CLOSING IN

IS MORE USED TO TAKING ORDERS THAN MAKING A DECISION

OFTEN PUNISHED FOR SHOWING TOO MUCH INITIATIVE

HAS FALSE SENSE OF SECURITY WHEN WITH HIS PARENT UNIT

NEVER TOLD HIS FOE IS GOOD AT SNEAKING THROUGH U.S. LINES

CONSTANTLY REMINDED HIS UNIT IS THE BEST IN THE WORLD

NOT TRAINED IN SHORT-RANGE INFILTRATION HIMSELF

UNAWARE THAT ALL SENTRIES HAVE VULNERABILITIES

NEVER WARNED OF ALL THE DISTRACTIONS TO VISION

NEVER WARNED OF ALL THE DISTRACTIONS TO HEARING

NEVER WARNED OF ALL THE DISTRACTIONS TO PERSONAL FOCUS

SO OVERCONTROLLED, HE FEELS LITTLE RESPONSIBILITY FOR UNIT

BECOMING EMASCULATED BY TOO MUCH DEFENSIVE COMBAT

WOULD RATHER BE HOME

SIGHTING HAS ALREADY STARTED TO BLUR IN HIS MEMORY

HASN'T SLEPT FOR MORE THAN THREE HOURS AT A TIME IN WEEKS

Table 26.1: Detractors to a U.S. Watchstander's Ability to React

Figure 26.1: The Average U.S. Perimeter Guard
(Sources: FM 7-1181/2 [1978], p. 2-II-B-3.3; Corel Print House, Plants; Gallery Graphics, Mac/EPS, Flowers, Trees, and Plants.)

Figure 26.2: Lead Man on a U.S. Point Security Team
(Source: FM 21-75 [1967], p. 8)

SECURITY TEAM MUST DETECT ANYTHING OUT OF THE ORDINARY

FORMATION: LEAD MAN LOOKS NEAR, REAR MAN LOOKS FAR

MISSION:
    MAIN CONCERN IS AMBUSH AVOIDANCE
    NEXT WORRY IS ENEMY SCOUT ENCOUNTER

THE SIX SENSES:
    SIGHT:
        ANY FRESH DIRT COULD DENOTE ENEMY POSITION
        RECENT FOOTPRINTS MIGHT MEAN FOE PRESENCE
        INVERTED "V" IN FOREST CAN ONLY BE LEGS
        TRIP WIRE NORMALLY ATTACHED TO BOOBYTRAP
        UNNATURALLY DISTURBED GROUND MAY MARK MINE
        ELECTRICAL WIRE CAN LEAD TO CLAYMORE
    SOUND:
        AK-47 COMING OFF "SAFE"
        FAINT THUD OF RIFLE BUTT AGAINST GROUND
        SOFT "JANGLE" OF MILITARY EQUIPMENT
        COUGH OR WHISPER
        BRANCH RUBBING AGAINST STIFF CLOTHING OR GEAR
    SMELL: GUN OIL, CAMPFIRE, CIGARETTE, FECES, GARLIC
    TASTE: SALTY AIR, POISON GAS
    TOUCH:
        RESIDUAL WARMTH FROM HUMAN BODY
        HARDER TO DETECT WHEN FULLY SHOD AND CLOTHED
    SIXTH:
        EITHER SUBLIMINAL COMBINATION OF OTHER SENSES
        OR GUARDIAN ANGEL (ACCORDING TO JIM CORBETT [4])

THE EFFECTS OF LOW LIGHTING CONDITIONS:
    MANY THINGS NOT EASY TO SEE STRAIGHT ON AT NIGHT
    THEY ARE BEST DETECTED THROUGH PERIPHERAL VISION
    VERY SLOW MOVEMENT IS IMPERCEPTIBLE IN MOONLIGHT

THE ADVERSE EFFECT OF SENSORY ENHANCEMENT DEVICES:
    HEIGHTENING OF ONE SENSE REDUCES THE OTHERS
    ANY OCULAR DEVICE LIMITS PERIPHERAL VISION
    ANY BRIGHT LIGHT NEGATES MOST NIGHT VISION DEVICES

THERMAL-IMAGING LIMITATIONS:
    HEAVY PRECIPITATION OR FOG INTERRUPTS
    BUSHES SCREEN WARM OBJECTS

Table 26.2: Rural Warnings for U.S. Patrol's Security Element

remember) ways to get back to its parent unit safely. (See Figure 26.3 and Table 26.3.) Many of the most fruitful discoveries occur off trail, like on a unit sweep. (See Figures 26.4 through 26.6 and Table 26.4.) Then, during the assault of an enemy strongpoint, U.S. snuffies start to see things for which their formal training never prepared them. (See Figures 26.7 through 26.9 and Table 26.5.)

Figure 26.3: U.S. Point Man Trying to Get Back to His Own Unit
(Source: FM 5-12B3 [1977], p. 2-308.)

1. POINT ELEMENT MAY HAVE TO E&E BACK TO PARENT UNIT
   WHILE RECONNOITERING THE FAR SIDE OF BIG DANGER AREA:

   A. IF ASSUMED DEAD, IT COULD END UP UNDER FRIENDLY BOMBS
   B. WITHOUT A RADIO, IT MUST STAY WITHIN VIEW OF MAIN BODY
   C. ALWAYS BE AWARE OF CLOSEST COVERED ROUTE BACK TO UNIT
   D. CRAWL THE LAST 50 YARDS INTO THE SUSPECTED TREELINE
   E. COVER EACH OTHER, WHILE CHECKING THAT AREA FOR ENEMY
   F. IF FIRING BREAKS OUT, MUST STAY BELOW SURFACE LEVEL TO
      AVOID FIRE FROM EITHER SIDE WHILE RETURNING TO UNIT

2. NATURAL WAYS OF DISCOURAGING PURSUIT:

   A. LEAVING NO SIGN DURING EACH CHANGE OF DIRECTION
   B. MAKING FALSE TRAILS TO THE SIDE
   C. RETRACING ONE'S FOOTSTEPS TO THE REAR
   D. MOVING ALONG TREE LIMBS, ROOTS, ROCKS, FALLEN LOGS
   E. FOLLOWING STREAMBEDS UNTIL CAREFUL EXIT

3. IF FRIENDLY PATROL GETS SURROUNDED:

   A. WAYS TO ESCAPE AN ENCIRCLEMENT IN THE DAYTIME

      (1) MOST MEMBERS HIDE WHILE ONE ADVANCES TO CREATE A
          LOUD DIVERSION AND THEN CAREFULLY CONCEAL HIMSELF
          (MAJORITY THEN LEFT OUTSIDE CLOSING CORDON).

          (A) HASTY HIDING PLACES: IN NATURAL DEPRESSION
              WHEN COVERED WITH LEAVES, IN ROOTS OF
              UPENDED TREE, DEEP INSIDE THORN BUSH

          (B) FOOLPROOF HIDING PLACES: IN MURKY MARSH
              WITH HOLLOW REED, HIGH IN BUSHY TREE WITH
              NO TELLTALE FOOTPRINTS AT ITS BOTTOM

      (2) CREATE THE IMPRESSION OF BEING INSIDE A MINEFIELD

   B. WAYS TO BREAK OUT OF AN ENEMY CORDON AFTER DARK

      (1) SHORT-RANGE EXFILTRATION
      (2) SIMULATED MORTAR ATTACK (GRENADES ONLY)
      (3) SILENT RUSH TOWARD PART OF CORDON WELL AWAY
          FROM FUSED FIRECRACKERS GOING OFF

Table 26.3: Rural Escape and Evasion for a Squad or Smaller

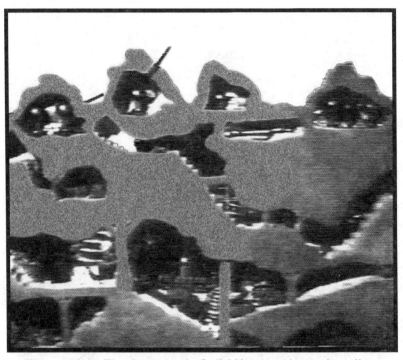

Figure 26.4: The Apparently Solid Hummocks on Iwo Jima
(Source: "A Tribute to WWII Combat Cameramen of Japan," Nippon TV, videocassette.)

Figure 26.5: The Hollow Haystacks in Europe
(Source: Courtesy of "*Podgotovka Razvegchika: Sistema Spetsnaza GRU,*" pp. 374, 375, © 1998 by A.E. Taras and F.D. Zaruz.)

GROUND ANOMALIES SPOTTED DURING RECENT U.S. CONFLICTS

WWII IN THE PACIFIC:

TINY RECTANGULAR BUNKER APERTURE IN HEAVY FOLIAGE
UNNATURALLY BUSHY AREA NEAR TOP OF TREE HIDING SNIPER
UPPER PORTION OF ROTTEN TREE TRUNK CONTAINING SNIPER
REVERSE-SLOPE TUNNEL OPENINGS
SPIDER HOLES FOR UP CLOSE TANK KILLING
HOLLOWED OUT HUMMOCKS

WWII IN EUROPE:

SIMULATED STUMP, ROCK, MOUND, OR HAYSTACK HOLDING FOE OP

KOREAN WAR:

COVERED TRENCHES AND REVERSE-SLOPE TUNNEL OPENINGS
THREE ABOVE-GROUND PRONGS OF BOUNCING BETTY MINE

VIETNAM WAR:

ANY GROUND OPENING MIGHT HOLD FOE ORDNANCE OR MEDICINE
PARALLEL MOUNDS OF PLOWED FIELD MAY CONTAIN BAGS OF RICE
RECTANGULAR INDENTION IN GROUND COULD BE ENTRANCE LID
ROUND COLOR DIFFERENCE IN SOIL CAN DELINEATE MINE
WEAPONS AND AMMO OFTEN BURIED IN FLOOR OF FOE BUNKER
UNDERWATER TUNNEL ENTRANCE IN WELL OR RIVERBANK
TRAILSIDE SPIDER HOLE FOR PULLING MINES UNDER TANKS

WAR IN IRAQ:

COVERED COURTYARD HOLE (LIKE WHERE SADDAM HUSSEIN WAS)

WAR IN AFGHANISTAN:

ENEMY COMPOUND ESCAPE TUNNEL

Table 26.4: Rural Discoveries by the Member of a U.S. Sweep

Knowledge Is Power

Staying alive in combat takes constant vigilance and focus. Experience is, of course, the best teacher. But if the mentoring of seasoned veterans is not easily available, a little personal inves-

Figure 26.6: Low-Ranking Member of a U.S. Unit Sweep
(Source: U.S. Air Force Clipart Library [www.usafns.com/art.shtml], image designator "1-4e.tif.")

MINIMAL NOISE:

    QUIET ALL WEAPONRY AND GEAR BEFORE THE ASSAULT
    APPROACH OBJECTIVE DURING DISTANT SHELLING OR "HELO" NOISE

DEFEATING ENEMY NIGHT VISION CAPABILITIES:

    ASSAULT WITH DISTANT FLARES, MOON, OR OTHER LIGHT AT REAR
    DENSE FOG, RAIN, OR BUSHES WILL BLOCK THERMAL IMAGING

THINGS TO WATCH OUT FOR DURING THE ASSAULT:

    ELECTRICAL WIRE LEADING TO CLAYMORE
    THREE PRONGS OF ANTIPERSONNEL MINE
    TRIP FLARES OR FLAME TRENCH
    CAMOUFLAGED SEGMENTS OF BARBED WIRE
    PEBBLE-FILLED TIN CANS OR LISTENING DEVICES

MOVEMENT VARIATIONS WHILE MAINTAINING LINE FORMATION:

    STAGGERED LINE IS BEST WITH LOTS OF SPACE BETWEEN MEMBERS

        NO FRIENDLY SHOULD EVER BE IN FRONT OF ASSAULT MAN
        NOR SHOULD A FRIENDLY EVER MOVE BEHIND ASSAULT MAN

    WHEN LATERAL MACHINEGUN FIRE IS ENCOUNTERED

        WATCH THE TRACERS
        CROUCH OR CRAWL BENEATH THE STREAM OF BULLETS

    OVER UNEVEN OR CLUTTERED TERRAIN

        SKIRT MOUNDS TO KEEP FROM BEING SILHOUETTED
        KEEP SOME OBJECT BETWEEN SELF AND FIRST DEFENDER

    IN FULL MOONLIGHT

        ANY DEEP SHADOW WILL HIDE MOST MOVEMENT
        VERY SLOW CRAWLING IS INDISCERNIBLE IN LOW LIGHT

USE OF FORCE:

    ANY SHOOTING COMPROMISES SURPRISE, EXPLOSIONS BETTER
    DOUBLE TAPS FROM THE HIP, BUT ONLY WHEN NO OTHER OPTION

Table 26.5: Rural Dangers for a U.S. Assault Member

tigation can help. Then, if the individual infantryman lives long enough, what he observes—over time—in battle will make him fairly self-sufficient. Among the things he can now avoid is capture.

As might be expected, Asia's UW fighters have any number of ways to discourage pursuit. Turkish militiamen may have held something of a clinic on British Regulars during a battle on the Anafarta Plain behind Suvla Bay on the Gallipoli Peninsula during WWI. Beneath a self-imposed smoke screen, couldn't a row of defenders have hidden in the soft sand to the front of their fighting holes and then quietly risen up behind the parallel line of attackers trying to overrun those holes? The Sandringham Company of the 5th Norfolks (the famous "lost company" of WWI) may have experienced just such a trap.[5] As those defenders quietly arose in unison through the thick smoke, each had only to shoot the closest British soldier in the back and then dispose of the body.

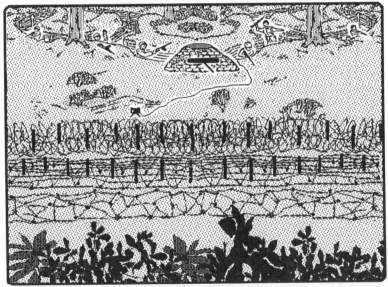

Figure 26.7: What GI May Face at End of His Approach March
(Sources: FM 7-8 [1984], p. 3-28; MCO P1500.44B, p. 14-18.)

Figure 26.8: Typical U.S. Assault
(Sources: FM 5-103 [1985], p. 4-7; FM 7-8 [1984], p. 3-1; FM 7-11B1/2 [1978], p. 2-II-A-5.2; FM 90-10-1 [1982], p. E-18.)

Figure 26.9: Bad Time to Stop Looking for Defensive Particulars
(Sources: FMFM 1-3B [1981], p. 4-19; FM 90-10-1 [1982], p. B-4.)

U.S. Snuffies Must Stay More Alert in Asia

When fighting any Eastern foe, U.S. troops must be especially watchful. They must keep a running count of the number of bushes to their front at night. They must be ready for an opponent to hide in plain sight, rise up out of the ground, or drop out of an overhead tree. Some such opponents are so skilled that they can hide behind a big tree trunk and then move backwards along its base as their pursuer traverses its front. Under such conditions, the GI's best chance is to remain constantly alert for attack from an unexpected quarter. However, if he is careful, he may avoid such a lopsided confrontation altogether.

PART TEN

CONTACT AVOIDANCE

"TO ADVANCE IRRESISTIBLY, PUSH THROUGH THEIR GAPS."
— SUN TZU

(Source: Sun Tzu, *The Art of War*, trans. Thomas Cleary, p. 105.)

27 MOVING AROUND MORE DISCRETELY IN THE CITY

- How hard is it to stay alive in urban combat?
- What must the U.S. rifleman know how to do?

In any way silhouetting oneself in a contested city is dangerous.

(Source: FM 90-10-1 [1982], p. E-13.)

Where No Enemy Contact Is Perfectly Acceptable

American troops have been traditionally conditioned to "wade into their opposition," not sidestep possible engagements. Still, the latter seems perfectly logical during the approach march to a critical attack objective, while on a reconnaissance patrol, or upon entering a sniper's lair. Sentry/listening posts are routinely withdrawn from the peripheries of U.S. bases as soon as a large enemy attack unit is spotted. Any direct force they might have applied to the first visible enemy soldiers would have risked their annihilation.

Well-Traveled Tourists Agree with the Concept

Contact avoidance is also the mindset of any U.S. tourist who has traveled alone of late through dangerous countries. Within some of those countries (like many in Africa), all travelers instantly become the lowest thing on the food chain. Those who attempt to take a taxicab from the airport to their hotel (instead of the hotel van) will be lucky to lose only their wallets. In such places, ethnic background, political affiliation, and religious orientation have very little to do with who gets killed. It's more about how well they are able to avoid compromising circumstances. In fact, this environment is much like that of the nearsighted wildebeest. On the open savannah frequented by lions, he travels with farsighted zebras. While crossing a crocodile-infested river, he does so in great numbers. Human beings are theoretically smarter than animals, so they should have more ways to elude trouble. Here are just a few things that a seasoned tourist will almost never do: (1) go into a practically deserted place; (2) accept rides from strangers; (3) walk around much after dark; (4) establish movement patterns; (5) enter the first cab to come along; or (6) fail to watch for someone following him. To help in this regard, he has several tricks: (1) remembering faces; (2) occasionally scanning store window reflections; (3) watching the eyes of any loiterer; (4) listening to what locals say to each other; and (5) staying alert to all that goes on around him.

After three days at a hotel on the western (or Muslim) side of Beirut around 2003, the male member of a U.S. tourist couple, happened to notice no fewer than three separate groups watching the entrance. A man he had seen at breakfast had later tried to pick him and his wife up in a taxicab, so he decided it might be a good idea to leave for the airport a bit early. Feigning an after-dinner sightseeing ride to the center of town, the two Americans instead took a circuitous route to the aerodrome. Needless to say, *Hezbollah's* headquarters lay at its southeastern corner. It was that same organization involved in the Marine barracks bombing just to the south of the terminal and the hanging of Colonel Higgins at the Israeli border.

As the tourist pair wended their way through the darkened back streets of West Beirut on this final leg to their plane, they couldn't help but notice three or four young men hanging around the parking lot of every high-rise building. As is often the case in tense situations, this American and his wife had enjoyed the help of a local resident—namely, a particularly alert female desk clerk at their hotel. When the couple prematurely checked out, she had—on her own accord—summoned a cab driver by the name of Joseph. After glancing one time in his rear view mirror, it was Joseph who had decided to get off the main thoroughfare to the airport. Upon his eventual arrival at its heavily guarded gate, he had offered a very enthusiastic Muslim greeting. Then, following some barely audible "roadrunner" joke between two rather large Muslim men at baggage security, the U.S. couple happily roamed the otherwise deserted "departure terminal" for the remainder of the night.[1]

Such is the life of a contemporary American tourist. While never getting actually mugged, he does—on occasion—pay some fairly hefty "tips." Nor do U.S. embassy security guards now take many chances during their off-duty wanderings. In other words, simply coexisting with the ever present foreign danger generates plenty of self-esteem.

The Military Version of Sidestepping Trouble in the City

For an infantry unit in transit, there are more ways of getting ambushed in an urban area than in the country. That's largely because it's harder in built-up terrain to avoid lines of drift and danger areas. To change location, the unit often has little choice but to use the streets. Not to constitute a danger area, each street must then be well indented with tiny alcoves or lined with cars. Alleyways would often be too smoothly walled and clutter free to offer enough cover. Due to this limited number of route possibilities, it becomes very difficult for the unit to take an unexpected path. To compensate for the additional risk, it must be quite alert to enemy sign.

The point element of any U.S. unit moving around on foot in the city could usefully take its inspiration from the most effective tracking formation for this type of terrain—the "Y." With flankers slightly ahead and on either side of a trained mantracker, it primarily looks for evidence of an IED (Improvised Explosive Device). Behind that mantracker walks his controller (who should also be the detachment navigator and commander). (See Figure 27.1.) Amidst multistory buildings, each flanker keeps a particu-

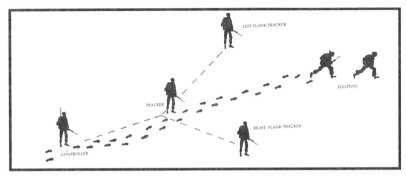

Figure 27.1: The "Y"-Shaped Tracking Formation
(Source: Courtesy of Paladin Press, from "Tactical Tracking Operations," p. 63, © 1998, by David Scott-Donelan.)

larly close watch on the windows directly above any cross-street counterpart. As in the country, it's also wise to add a fifth "optics man" behind the controller. Through binoculars, he can look for trouble far ahead and to the side at all intersections. That's because there's more risk of long-range machinegun or sniper fire in the city. A sixth security man could try to preclude ambush from the immediate rear, high overhead, or some subsurface location.

The main body of the unit should then move up either or both sides of a structure-lined street, but not its center. (Chapter 25 has already covered the finer points of individual movement.) Every wall opening *en route* must be carefully, but still expeditiously, crossed; each alleyway or intersection treated as a caution area; and each park or vacant lot considered a potential danger area. In the daytime, any fully exposed friendlies should be in the process of running.

Ferreting Out Any Bombers

The areas between buildings are only partially covered with pavement. Following footprints there is like doing so across occasional patches of rock—something that only highly skilled native Americans used to be able to do.

Hard surfaces are not as easily disturbed as soft ones. If they hold any traces of human passage, they are on the order of a dislodged pebble, modified residue, shoe dropping, or scuff mark. In the city, an intervening street, alleyway, parking lot, or sidewalk would still pose little problem if not encountered in too big a series. One would only have to spot where similar footprints continued on its far side. Unfortunately, such a surface is often quite long or heavily traveled, so the tracker must commit to memory the unique characteristics of his quarry's shoe print. He should also be adept at judging a track's age.

Luckily, most urban surfaces provide an aid to mantracking that is not normally available in the woods. That aid is dust, and it is even more prevalent where there has been recent combat. Because of the particulate-matter imprint (or transference) possibility, one should not disturb any paved or cement area that has been likely crossed by the quarry. With sufficient side-lighting (like from a flashlight at the end of a stick), the trail may become astoundingly visible.

How Human Sign Look in Urban Terrain?

In most built-up areas, dust is everywhere. What hasn't been caused by crushed dirt, falls out of the smog. When that dust is disturbed or transferred onto another surface, it leaves a mark. Yet, dust is not the only thing that can be "transferred." There is also mud, blood, water, oil, tar, and refuse. Thus, the city is full of trails. (See Figure 27.2.)

The principal difference between following a person here and in the country is what to do when the trail goes cold. In urban terrain, the tracks often come to an end because the quarry has passed over an ostensibly clean and impenetrable surface. Finding them again may take a more extensive search than in rural terrain. Chapter 14 of *Terrorist Trail* reveals the most helpful search patterns. The next visible track need not come from a dust imprint.

Urban "Track Traps"

A "track trap" is an area of any soft material (soil, sand, dust, vegetation, etc.) that has left distinct evidence of human passage.

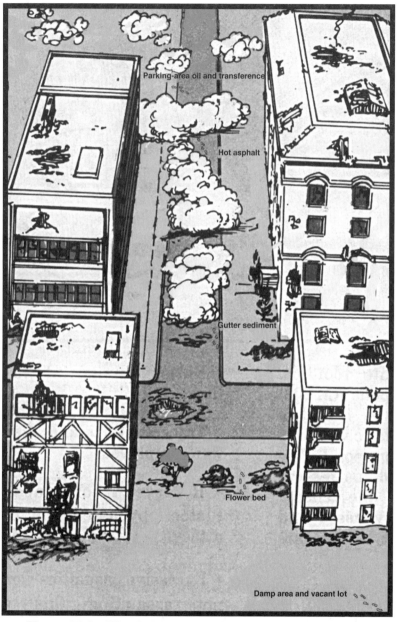

Figure 27.2: "Track Traps" and Sources of Transference
(Source: FM 90-10 [1979], p. G-4.)

Any one of the following would qualify: (1) lawn, (2) flower garden, (3) crop area, (4) just watered plot, (5) park, (6) vacant lot, (7) bicycle/foot path, (8) dirt road, (9) muddy street, (10) roadside shoulder/dust, (11) mud puddle, (12) gutter sediment, (13) steep incline, (14) gravel embankment, (15) slippery stream bank, (16) construction site, (17) garbage dump, (18) alleyway refuse, (19) parking-area oil, (20) molten asphalt, (21) sewage pipe seepage, (22) drainage ditch runoff, (23) community water point spillage, (24) industrial-site residue, or (25) children's playpen/sandbox. In addition, any urban surface becomes a track trap when covered by residual dirt, fallen leaves, pollen, dew, frost, or snow. Upon their addition, even a brick/concrete wall, paved street, or railroad track/tie could be included in the list.

Some will be more obvious than others. Through grassy areas will exist depressed blades. In gardens and cultivated patches, there will be the compacting of soft soil. Both mediums also attract dew and frost. Additionally, people often slip while negotiating steep inclines or road embankments, leaving a characteristic skid mark. In dump sites, cardboard, paper, styrofoam, and trash bags leave footwear impressions wherever stepped upon. As fallen leaves are crossed, some get crushed. The tops and sides of brick/concrete walls are easily scuffed.

Then, there will be an excellent chance of transference of material onto the next hard surface as one's quarry leaves a track trap. (Refer back to Figure 27.2.) Near a gutter, there will be traces of mud or water. Where a street abuts a vacant lot, there will be dirt particles or grass stains.

More Emphasis on Print Peculiarities

In the city, the tracker must be thoroughly familiar with the "search image" of what he is looking for. Much of his success will depend on his knowledge of local habits and footwear. Some outsole patterns will be more common than others due to current fads and shared designs. Wherever an IED has been detonated, all print peculiarities must be carefully recorded. Was the probable bomber wearing an unusually soled shoe? Did his left foot pitch out, or right foot drag a toe? As in police work, these are the things that will eventually lead to his apprehension.

Wherever there are twist/pivot marks, the quarry may have abruptly changed direction. This happens quite often in the city—like when someone turns a sidewalk corner.

Where some person has squatted (with his feet apart and fingers on the ground) or dug, there may be an observation post or impromptu toilet. Evidence of kneeling (knee impressions between toe- and foot-prints) has far more significance. A nearby row of up-turned soil might contain a wire, or a patch of dry grass be hiding a mine. Needless to say, any hint of fabrication should be taken seriously.

Third World Cities Are Different from Those in the U.S.

Throughout the Developing World, the most heavily populated regions are often a conglomerate of old and new construction. Throughout that construction are patches of unimproved land. Beyond the ancient inner cities are streets with very few sidewalks. Amidst the taller vegetation along such "streets" are the same signs of human transit as one might expect in the woods: (1) broken twigs, (2) displaced root bark, (3) stripped leaves, (4) changes in foliage color, (5) crushed/bent/scratched/intertwined branches, (6) broken spider webs, (7) disturbed ant trails, and (8) dislodged insect nests.

In addition, any quarry will likely brush dust or dew from the plants he encounters. Once he reenters a paved area, the art of trailing him becomes again of the newer variety.

Security Patrols Have More Responsibility in Urban Areas

Sometimes, the object is not to catch up with the individual who has made a trail, but just to see where that trail goes. When the recent footprints of many people lead into a dead-end corner between two buildings and then suddenly stop, there is something funny going on. Near their termination may be a spider hole or buried cache, from which important intelligence or vital supplies may be retrieved. Or, that makeshift trail may lead to the secret entrance to a large, underground hide facility at which something of considerable strategic significance exists—like the subterranean waystation on one of the enemy's major infiltration routes. Within that underground facility, there would be a further need for tracking procedure. By "side-lighting" the floors and walls with a flashlight, one might find a hidden trapdoor to an even deeper thoroughfare. Along that thoroughfare might lie other waystations, arms storage spaces, escape corridors, and safe-house access ladders. Of course, such a discovery would be far more likely if every American infantry unit had its own formally trained mantracker. But, any U.S. security patrol could follow the initial trail, providing its leader had been bold enough to ask permission to leave his preplanned route for a few minutes. Without so doing, would he have thoroughly accomplished his security mission?

All that has happened above ground is more obvious to an experienced mantracker, but not completely lost on everyone else. There may be 40 ways to detonate an IED, but only one way to position it. By sending a "sign-cutting" patrol up both sides of a frequently used road each morning, a unit could usually determine if that road had been mined overnight. But this is not possible for every street in a recently captured city, so security patrols must continually look for such things. Any suspicious string of footprints leading away from street-side construction may indicate an IED to be carefully avoided and then later disarmed. After every IED detonation, there is a trail to be followed. It leads initially to the perpetrator and eventually to the manufacturer. Due to the climate, most Middle Eastern cities are extremely dusty. That should make unusual sole patterns easier to follow.

Finally, to escape almost certain bombardment, most of America's adversaries prefer to fight at close quarters in all types of terrain. As a result, there exist subtle signs of an enemy presence before any short-range encounter in the city. All American troops should therefore be trained on what those signs might be and how silently to report them up their chain of command while the parent unit is still on the move. Not doing so would compromise their security mission.

Just because a traveling military unit attempts—through sophisticated movement techniques—to preclude a violent encounter does not mean it can ignore hard evidence of an enemy presence. Not until all IED implantation has been stopped can any neighborhood be declared pacified. The same holds true for mines in a tract of rural land.

28 NONCONFRONTATIONAL RURAL LAND NAVIGATION

- Are some forest hikes less likely to run into opposition?
- Through which parts of those woods do they run?

It's easier to avoid any confrontation on a very dark night.

(Source: FM 19-95B/CM [1978], cover.)

The Four Choices for Cross-Country Travel

When a U.S. unit wanted to change location in Vietnam, it simply took off in the same general direction as its map indicated and then looked for all recognizable map relief along the way (mostly hamlets, streams, and hills). (See Figure 28.1.) Not surprisingly, that unit sometimes ended up on a terrain feature near its assigned objective that was similar in appearance. No harm was really done, however, because that interim location would often work as a base of fire for more easily assaulting the actual target.[1] Patrols, on the other hand, moved more reliably between major

Figure 28.1: Movement Route Planning
(Source: FM 22-100 [1983], p. 66.)

landmarks (like long existent trail junctions). Either way of getting around would now be labelled "Terrain Appreciation." That's
not the same as its more sophisticated successor—"Terrain Association." To practice Terrain Association, one must pick all route
legs before the checkpoints, and then take a zigzag path along permanent linear terrain features—like roads, draws, and fingers. So
doing will more consistently reach the proper destination. It offers
ridgelines for speed and defensibility, and long narrow draws for
obscurity. Yet, it sometimes also channelizes the user into a "path
of least resistance"—i.e., one also traveled by his opposition. In
other words, neither Terrain Appreciation nor its predecessor tries
to avoid enemy contact. This is unfortunate, because most wars
are won through the destruction of enemy wherewithal, and any
armed clash between adversaries makes that more difficult. That's
why not only all American reconnaissance patrols currently evade
enemy contact, but so do all U.S. approach marches to an attack
objective.

Upon the development of certain technologies, Terrain Associa-tion—with its destination accuracy and landscape utilization—has fallen out of fashion. Yet, to move across a battlefield with any hope of regularly doing well at chance contact, American units must still focus on the terrain and all composite "microterrain." That's because a one-foot-deep dip in the earth's surface can either hide a lone soldier or protect his parent element from enemy fire. Legendary Marine general Lew Walt credited much of his success in combat to what he had learned about microterrain from Chesty Puller.

> Being under Puller in Basic School did more for me than anything I experienced until I got to Guadalcanal. He taught us the use of terrain like a master, how to use the tiniest bit of cover to our advantage.[3]
> — former Raider and Vietnam era CAP proponent

In peacetime, fledgling land navigators tend to overlook all the tiny folds in the ground. Without real bullets whizzing over their heads all the time, they have much less reason to keep track of those folds. That's a real shame, because most of the attack ob-jectives on Vietnam's Coastal Plain had a shallow and partially vegetated drainage ditch leading right up to them (namely, an en-velopment route that crawling GIs would have much preferred to a cross-paddy rush).[2]

Now well anchored in the 21st Century, most American units just move off toward their assigned objective, and then periodically check their interim location on a GPS (Global Positioning System) device. For sidestepping an enemy *en route,* this is not a bad way to operate as long all lines of drift are carefully avoided. In fact, this "GPS Land Navigation Hybrid" is very much like the way U.S. enlistees are first trained to traverse a battlefield—i.e., through "Dead Reckoning." While ostensibly simplistic, Dead Reckoning has some definite advantages over its "more terrain-oriented" trav-el alternatives for certain missions.

Most of the following discussion has been based on lessons learned along the coastal lowlands of North Carolina with a 1:24,000 scale map. As many overseas military missions occur near the ocean shore of a semi-tropical nation with similar latitude, those same lessons widely apply. For example, most of Southeast Asia is like that.

Figure 28.2: Dead-Reckoning More Useful Than Once Thought
(Source: FM 90-6 [1980], pp. 1-4, 1-5.)

Dead Reckoning

As in seafaring, Dead Reckoning across rural countryside involves following (on a compass and for the prescribed distance) the Grid-Magnetic (G-M) angle conversion of a map azimuth. (See Figure 28.2.) While so doing with a randomly selected direction, one has little chance of making enemy contact in heavily vegetated terrain. That's because such a procedure effectively avoids all lines of drift (like the flat streambeds through precipitous terrain). As long as the checkpoints between azimuths are of no particular interest to the enemy, the Dead Reckoning traveler is unlikely to encounter any other human being. Most of the following are too risky: (1) trail or road junctions; (2) any tall object with a good view; (3) major draw or ridge intersections; (4) the very end of a big draw or finger; and (5) a stream ford or bridge. Better choices would be: (1) any place at which the desired route hits (but does not have to cross) a road or stream; (2) where two inconspicuous linear terrain features intersect (like a trail and draw); and (3) the near side of any map-indicated break in the vegetation (like a power line corridor).

310

Not being observed while crossing any major brush interruption (like a road, burned-off spot, or firebreak) would also help to prevent an encounter. The necessary mechanics will be later discussed.

In many ways, forestalling an armed confrontation while on the move takes the exact opposite of searching for one. Just as passing through observation points and movement conduits helps to locate enemy, staying in terrain with lots of concealment and no channelizing effect tends to avoid them. Of course, the latter can be quite strenuous.

Dead Reckoning Limitations and Electronic Assistance

Land navigation is more of an art than a science. It involves constantly compensating for several margins of error. For example, any direction to be followed on a compass must first come from measuring the grid azimuth from start point to destination on a map, and then arriving at its magnetic equivalent. While most maps clearly show this conversion formula, whether to add or subtract the G-M angle to the grid azimuth can be hard to remember. Further distortion to the magnetic direction can arise out of "map error" at either end of a planned route.

Even recently published maps contain "map error" with regard to the exact shape of permanent terrain features. This type of mistake does not result from the map's age, but its construction process. Many maps come from photographs taken during a few airplane fly-overs. While such photos are somewhat distorted by the different exposure angles, they are still manually connected by some technician. To help him put the collage of photos into better perspective, a surveyor will occasionally traverse the area. Finally, the map maker sits down and—with pen in hand—creates a reasonable facsimile of the suggested terrain. Minor errors often result. If the aerial photos have been too rapidly pieced together, hundreds of yards of terrain can vanish. If tree cover has obscured ground relief from the camera, the map will show draws and fingers of the wrong length, or hills of the improper height. Smaller draws, fingers, and hills won't appear at all. Recent technological advances make identifying minor changes in ground elevation below a leaf canopy possible, but many decades will pass before the entire world is remapped through this new procedure.

Add any possible hardships in distance estimation to the "detractors" of proper azimuth, and one is definitely dealing with an art form.

Distance Estimation

In the strictest interpretation of Dead Reckoning over a non-watery surface, distances are computed through pace counts. After the desired distance has been measured by using a map's "bar scale," the appropriate number of paces are taken. The average man does 60 double steps every 100 meters. An implicit prerequisite to the pace count method is absolutely level terrain—something that only happens once and a while in nature (like on the Salt Flats of Utah).

A more accurate way of determining distance during Dead Reckoning over "nearly flat" ground is to keep track of all permanent terrain features passed, and then estimate the distance of the target from the last one or to the next one. Due to the irregular surface and possible map error in the area, there is no real reason to attempt any more precise measurement than that. Because of the importance attributed by the U.S. military to individual marksmanship, most GIs are still good at guessing distances up to 500 meters.

There now exists a computerized GPS module, with which one can theoretically determine his exact location at any given time. It could be used to determine how far one has traveled along a Dead Reckoning azimuth. Unfortunately, that electronic module mostly depends for its bearings on radio signals from satellites. That means there must exist a direct line of sight between the user and several skyward objects at once. This only reliably happens where there are no tree branches to obstruct that line of sight—like out in a desert or prairie. In heavily wooded terrain, the module must be inconveniently moved to a large clearing. Moreover, not enough satellites may yet exist to cover every corner of the world 24 hours a day.

The GPS version that uses earthbound signals has even more limitations. Now, higher ground will interrupt the line of sight between user and points of reference, so the module will have to be moved to a hilltop. Prior to any landing or offensive, transmitters must also be placed in enemy territory.

Like radios, GPS modules are delicate and apt to get shot or wet in combat. While now widely available to small-units, their degree of utility has been overestimated. Most paper maps still do not match the computerized (or "virtual") version of the earth's surface. So, an infantry squad at a map-generated grid coordinate cannot depend on totally accurate supporting-arms fire from a GPS-oriented artillery battery. In heavily jungled or precipitous terrain, where the distance to an explosion cannot be accurately judged by ear, such a discrepancy could result in "short rounds." Still, GPS-generated smoke shells could be used as location markers by a disoriented American patrol.

Yet, those GPS limitations are not the main reason small-unit U.S. leaders must continue to wend their way through the rural maze of linear terrain features, just as a city dweller would follow streets. That's because of an ever present enemy. Only through Terrain Association will those leaders be able to take full tactical advantage of the existing ground.

Too Little Provision for Enemy Contact

Unfortunately, Dead Reckoning provides very few ways to handle enemy contact (should it improbably occur). In fact, all straight-line navigation tends to ignore the large obstacles and danger areas along the way. But, that's not its only problem with regard to possible contact. Having to scale the sides of ravines, slog through bogs, and climb over tree falls will make well-conditioned troops with reasonable loads too tired to handle much fighting. (See Figure 28.3.) Similarly, directly trekking through any large danger area (like an overgrown field) is just asking for trouble. Even a dense stand of pine saplings will not stop .50-caliber machinegun bullets. Under either set of circumstances, the whole unit could be annihilated.

Still Taking Some Tactical Advantage of the Terrain

There exists one "terrain-linked" safety option with Dead Reckoning. It offers more chance for overhead covering fire (due to the steeper inclines encountered). Yet, taking full advantage of the landscape takes either loosely paralleling some overall azimuth

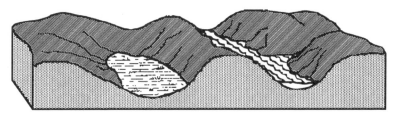

Figure 28.3: Ground Relief Can Be Either Problematic or Helpful
(Source: FM 21-76 [1970], p. 49.)

or precisely following a series of linear terrain features (fastidious Terrain Association). For example, one could stay fairly well hidden in the daytime by moving along a continuous string of overgrown fencelines and runoff gullies. That's why a deer will use a ditch to cross a cornfield.

To avoid foe contact through anything but Dead Reckoning, the overland hiker must actively seek out places that will totally obscure him. Their amount of "cover" (protection from bullets) will depend upon the abundance of man-made structures, trees, rocks, and depressions. Their extent of "concealment" will be a function of all those things in combination with other foliage, weather, and light.

No traveler—however hard he attempts to mind his own business—can always avoid a chance meeting with the opposition. The terrain most favorable to coming out on top during such a meeting is that which provides both cover and concealment from direct-fire weapons, without sacrificing any observation or fields of fire. Unfortunately, cover and concealment are generally enhanced by heavy vegetation, whereas observation and fields of fire are not. That's why during any random get-together, the U.S. unit would like to find itself near a treeline or ditch, while its opponent is still out in the middle of a field. Under such conditions, friendly automatic weapons fire would almost certainly dissuade a much bigger adversary from frontally attacking.

Another important piece of real estate from the standpoint of chance contact is the "military crest" of sloping ground. This is any place from where a person can face downhill and see all of the earth's surface out to beyond grenade range. To keep from being silhouetted at night, "Terrain Associators" will often follow the military crest of a ridgeline.

Discretely Crossing a Danger Area

As previously mentioned, Dead Reckoning more greatly risks a large unexpected clearing in the way. Most small breaks in the vegetation do not require extensive reconnoitering. Excessive caution will demoralize any unit, so tiny openings are simply caution areas to be most productively handled with the "Bump Method." But, any extremely wide one (however narrow) cannot be crossed by many increments in this way without giving away the parent unit's presence. (See Figure 28.4.)

Big fields present the greatest problem. But, to qualify as a genuine danger area, one would have to be crossed by the whole unit at once. Totally to escape detection while negotiating such an area

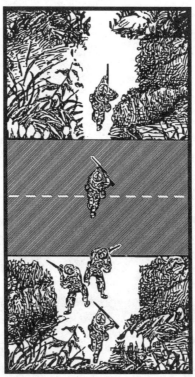

Figure 28.4: Bump Method No Good for Long Observation Lane
(Source: FM 5-103 [1985], pp. 4-4, 4-6.)

Figure 28.5: Full Moon Creates Enough Shadow to Hide In
(Source: FM 7-11B1/2 [1978], pp. 2-11-A-4.2 , 3-11-A-4.2; OPNAV P34-03 [1960], p. 40.)

in sun or bright moonlight, everyone would have to crawl the entire way. If not in good enough shape to do so, they could also traverse the field through several slowly walking increments (all covered in the appropriate foliage). As long as only a few crossed at once, the whole unit could not be targeted.

But, what if the enemy is too woods-wise for such a ruse? There is a way completely to circumvent all but the biggest obstruction or danger area. First, the navigator chooses a distinctive steering point on its far side—like, a large dead oak at the end of a mangrove swamp. Then, he walks around the edge of the swamp until he reaches the tree. Next, after estimating the straight-line distance back to the start of his bypass, he continues on with what's left of his ongoing leg.

In starlight, that whole unit can both hide and maintain some semblance of momentum by remaining upright and moving very slowly (in no particular formation) across a somewhat bushy field. Through only partial light, its adversary will have great difficulty distinguishing vague and slowly moving shapes from the existing shrubbery. Deep shadows in bright moonlight can also obscure an entire unit, as will an inky background. (See Figure 28.5.) After having to deal with so much fully illuminated ground, the human eye cannot see into either type of blackness.

Artillery illumination rounds can also help to screen all human movement on really dark nights. In forest or jungle, flares swinging from airborne parachutes create dancing shadows along the ground that look just like moving combatants. Plus, the bright light from those flares will temporarily blind any foe wearing Night Vision Goggles (NVGs).

Needless to say, Dead Reckoning routes should not be planned through places with lots of concealment but very little cover (like fields of tall grass or crops). Nor should they be plotted across difficult obstacles (like cliffs, marshes, or fallen trees). For either one, a formal 90° offset may be possible—namely, moving off at a right angle to the assigned azimuth for a measured distance, continuing on in the same direction as before, and then moving back an equal distance to the original route. But, offsets take extra effort, so enough time must be available.

Other Contact Avoidance Measures

During any travel through enemy-controlled countryside (whether by Dead Reckoning or some other means), setting a pattern can be extremely dangerous. While the actual transit may not be observed, its occurrence will be obvious to a rural foe from the footprints and other sign. That means even an arbitrarily chosen azimuth through virgin territory may contain an enemy ambush the next time it is used. By the same token, any linear terrain feature (Terrain Association leg) must only be followed once, and the way back to the patrol base differ from the exit route. U.S. troops manning listening or observation posts right outside huge American bases have been ambushed while trying to reuse the same "watch relief path."[4]

As risky as any enemy contact can be running into unexpected friendlies. By taking too long exiting their own barbed wire, nighttime U.S. patrols have been grenaded by replacement watchstanders.[5] Before planning any new trip, all U.S. unit leaders should first check their parent-unit's "daily-activity overlay" to see which sister contingents may be operating nearby. Well-meaning security patrols will occasionally stray from their assigned routes. But, the easiest units to run into are the two-man sentry posts that routinely lie just outside every encampment.

Figure 28.6: Evading Contact Takes Staying off the Horizon
(Source: MCRP 3-02H [1999], fig. I-3.)

Less Enemy Contact During Terrain Association

Many patrol routes require a combination of legs from Dead Reckoning, Terrain Appreciation, and Terrain Association. For a good balance of cover/concealment and observation/fields of fire in the daytime, they should not include any large interruption to the carpet of vegetation (like a road, firebreak, streambed, or hilltop). Such features are still valuable as reference lines/points as long as they are never actually crossed.

A night patrol might more successfully stick to the lower areas along its approximate route. Otherwise, friendly soldiers may end up being silhouetted against the sky. (See Figure 28.6.) Low areas will not only better conceal the GIs, but also increase their powers of observation. Obviously, a shallow ditch would provide better cover than a narrow gully. (See Figure 28.7.) But most low places in the microterrain offer a unique advantage at night. Security outpost members (whether moving or stationary) will more easily spot enemy during the hours of darkness when located in a slight depression or near the base of elevated terrain. (See Figure

28.8.) By occasionally laying their heads sideways on the ground and looking up, they can easily distinguish movement against one of the now visible horizons in the microterrain. (See Figure 28.9.) At the same time, those security personnel remain nearly invisible themselves. That's because enemy travelers tend to watch for other moving humans, while all stationary anomalies are assumed part of the landscape.

Low ground offers a skilled opponent the same opportunities at night. Therefore, a good case can also be made for the American unit hiking just above the military crest of fingers and ridgelines during all hours of darkness. (See Figure 28.10.) That way, its members will never be silhouetted from the adjoining draw bottom yet still enjoy good observation and fields of fire over any opponent below them.

Figure 28.7: A Poor Choice for Low-Ground Transit
(Source: FM 7-8 [1984], p. B-2.)

Figure 28.8: Being Between Mounds Has Advantages at Night
(Sources: FM 7-11B1/2 [1978], p. 2-III-E-8.2; FM 5-103 [1985], p. 4-4; FM 22-100 [1983], p. 22.)

Even at night, friendly patrols should stay well clear of barren ground, standing water, and light backgrounds. Instead, they should gravitate toward jumbled ground, deep shadow, and dark backdrops. That's because just a few objects in an otherwise open

Figure 28.9: Best Way to Spot Microterrain Skylines
(Source: FM 21-76 (1957), p. 38)

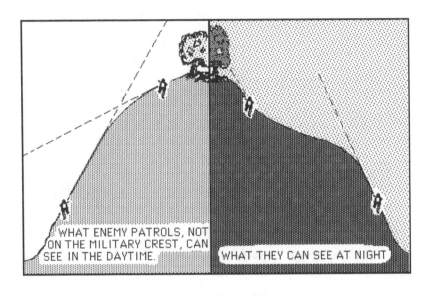

Figure 28.10: Where to Travel Relative to the Military Crest

area tend to draw unwanted attention; water reflects movement; and all light backgrounds will act as an artificial horizon after dark. From starlight alone, black asphalt roads appear almost white at night. "Want-to-be" shadow walkers sometimes forget this. (See Figure 28.11.) Yet, any long artificial horizon can also act as an asset. The unit wise enough to move parallel to—but just barely within sight of—a road can often spot the enemy moving along its very edge without ever being noticed itself. (See Figure 28.12.) The same holds true for not too closely skirting a field or body of water. The very edge of many such terrain features is also a series of linear segments, so those segments can be incorporated into a (Terrain Association) route. While some may in theory constitute a line of drift, how loosely they are followed would make an enemy encounter unlikely.

One's degree of concealment can be improved by wearing enough natural camouflage; and one's powers of observation by night vision technology. But, both come with their own inherent handicaps. Covering one's self with large twigs will make it much harder to move around quietly, while night vision devices are blinded by flares and cannot see through fog or brush. (See Figure 28.13.) As

Figure 28.11: Shadows Must Be Combined with Dark Backdrop
(Source: MCRP 3-02H [1999], fig. I-5.)

Figure 28.12: Good Way to Catch or Evade Enemy on the Move
(Sources: FM 7-11B1/2 [1978], p. 2-III-E-8.2; FM 90-10-1 [1982], pp. B-3, B-4; FM 5-103 [1985], p. 4-4.)

a result, even a modern-day Asian commando might prefer donning a loin cloth, painting himself black, and then solely relying on his "practice-enhanced" natural senses. The only way to eliminate any motion signature whatsoever is to crawl in low light. But, only on very short patrols will most light infantrymen have the strength and patience to move around on their bellies. Still, there is evidence of such patrols by the Japanese just outside the Henderson Field perimeter on Guadalcanal.[6]

Further to research this nonconfrontational art form, one has only to watch a deer move through different types of "predator-infested" terrain. Lighting conditions, foliage density, and ambient noise all appear to affect its movement decisions. For example, in broad daylight, a small group of deer will take turns sprinting across a road, whereas after sundown an entire group will slowly walk across that same road in single file.

Figure 28.13: NVGs Are of Little Use in Heavily Foliated Terrain
(Source: FM 7-8 [1984], p. G-4.)

Non-Electronic Nighttime Techniques

As in urban driving, cross-country routes that have been negotiated hundreds of times during the day can look so alien at night as to invite error. Still, there are ways to compensate for this different way that everything appears.

During all after-dusk and moonless trips, the land navigator should be at the very head of his column with any point men right behind him. To find a target location under such conditions, he must rely on a combination of Dead Reckoning and Terrain Appreciation (though the only visible collecting features will be roads and streams). Any azimuth can be placed on a compass in complete darkness by counting clicks of the bezel ring, but actually following

324

that azimuth may be disconcerting. Anyone too good at obeying orders must remember that the luminous north arrow will invariably point in a direction other than he wishes to go.

For the best indicators of cross-country progress, the nighttime navigator mostly depends on his feet. If they are atop an embankment or in soggy soil, he is nearing a waterway. If the ground is starting to rise to his front after crossing a swampy watershed area, he has reached the finger or hill mass at its edge. In other words, for all Dead Reckoning in low light, he more completely relies on collecting features for all distance estimation. In deep woods, his GPS device cannot make enough satellite communication to be of help.

The "aiming-off" procedure is also very useful at night. Falling into a chilly stream sends an unmistakable message to the navigator that he has overshot his objective. If he had initially headed toward a place on that stream that was to one side of his ultimate destination, eventually reaching that destination would have been greatly simplified.

Terrain Association still has some utility after the sun goes down, but mostly while paralleling unmistakable map features—like roads, power lines, railroad tracks, or major waterways. To Terrain Associate along fingers and draws in total darkness, the navigator would have continually to monitor all changes to his elevation. For example, if he can't go right or left without moving downhill, he is on a finger or ridgeline. If he starts to climb in any direction but forward, he is in a narrow draw. In all places where it regularly rains, he can usually identify draws large enough to show up on a map by some of runoff water in their bottoms. If his march objective is then up a side draw, he can find it by walking along the original rivulet's bank until he feels other dampness underfoot. None of the "fake draws" (draw-like openings that only extend a short way) will produce such moisture.

Concurrent Considerations

Needless to say, the whole matter of concealment during a unit transit is much more complicated after dark. Any area bathed in bright moonlight becomes a caution area, whereas any area devoid of vegetation but in heavy shade may be able to conceal moving personnel.

Figure 28.14: Enemy Ambushers Are Not Hard to Hear
(Source: FM 7-8 [1984], p. 5-22.)

Any "trial-and-error" assessment of the ground relief must be done very quietly. Complete silence is the friendly outfit's best protection against ambush. That's because flankers and NVGs often cannot see through the intervening vegetation. On more than one occasion, particularly stealthy U.S. patrols have walked right through enemy ambushes without ever triggering them.[7] Only by hearing the waiting assassins, could they have known this. Most combatants lying in wait for an adversary will get a little nervous when he finally shows up. Here are the types of noises they then make: (1) a weapon coming off safe; (2) a rifle butt hitting the ground; (3) a tiny twig snapping as someone shifts position; (4) the brushing of a branch on rough clothing or gear; or (5) a stifled whisper. (See Figure 28.14.) A wild animal will not step on a twig or make any sound as it closely passes a bush.

As a result of this natural detection capability, one of the best ways to move around undisturbed after the sun goes down is for every unit member of a single-file formation to walk exactly in the footsteps of the person ahead of him. Between footfalls, all must then carefully listen for any sound that may not be common to the area.

Even Head-On Encounters Can Be Defused

If the point security men for a U.S. patrol get down after each advance up its nighttime route, they will first see any enemy counterpart coming their direction. Then, they can either signal for a hasty ambush or for everyone to get out of the way. (See Figure 28.15.)

Should that U.S. point team be unlucky enough to approach a prepared enemy position by accident, no enemy sentry will probably shoot at them before asking a superior for permission. Those few seconds should give the American patrol time to crawl back out of danger.

Discretely Reestablishing One's Bearings

GPS devices get wet, shrapnel damaged, or otherwise dysfunctional in all types of terrain. That's when a unit's land navigator

Figure 28.15: Almost Any Exchange of Gunfire Can Be Avoided
(Sources: FM 90-3 [Aug. 1977], p. 4-9; MCWP 3-35.3 [Apr. 1998], p. A-1.)

Figure 28.16: Inconspicuous Culverts Make Good Attack Points
(Source: MCRP 3-02H [1999], p. IX-1.)

(who should also be its leader) might get irretrievably lost. But when every U.S. officer/NCO is also adept at traditional land navigation, such a disheartening (and risky) situation can be avoided. The difference between a lost novice and a lost expert is what happens next. The novice tends to panic whereas the expert doesn't. Nor does the expert ever admit to his people that he is confused. He is simply "feeling around for a gap in the enemy's defenses." More often than not, so doing will produce an unexpected bit of military intelligence or position of tactical advantage. That expert then has several ways of discretely reorienting himself: (1) using a cloverleaf search pattern to investigate the surrounding terrain; (2) backtracking to the last checkpoint to try another way to his objective; or (3) shooting an escape azimuth to a know collecting feature to help find a preplanned "attack point."

Similar to rally points, attack points are places the land navigator is certain he can find if lost. Should he not want to backtrack, he can head for an attack point. The best ones are not likely to be occupied by opposition soldiers: (1) unusual bends in a road, trail, or ridge line (like a 90° dogleg); (2) where major watersheds pass beneath roads via culverts; and (3) any object tall enough to be seen from a distance. (See Figure 28.16.) That the first two lie along linear terrain features makes them easier to find. The lost navigator simply heads toward one end of the feature (by aiming off) and then turns in the appropriate direction. Tall objects can be more easily spotted by climbing a tree.

The astray navigator has one other option. Any tall/pointed feature that exists on both map and ground can provide a valuable frame of reference from a distance. Where the back-azimuths from two such widely separated features (after the appropriate and G-M angle conversion) come together on a map marks his precise location. If there are none visible after dark, artillery illumination rounds can often serve the same purpose. (See Figure 28.17.) Where an enemy follows, such a trick might prove highly deceptive.

Figure 28.17: Finding One's Location Through Flare Resection
(Sources: FM 7-11B1/2 [1978], p. 3-II-A-4.2; OPNAV P 34-03 [1960], p. 40.)

29 GIVING THE "SLIP" TO A SIZEABLE PURSUER

- How can one best elude a determined hunter?
- Which things are done differently than imagined?

Leave no footprints and then hide in soft soil or debris-filled ditch.

(Source: OPNAV P34-03 [revised 1960], p. 394.)

No Need to Save the Last Bullet

American reconnaissance inserts and rifle squads have on occasion found themselves badly out-matched by their opposition—particularly while trying to move around alone on Asian soil. This has had more to do with the enemy's tracking and stalking ability than their own lack of stealth. On Operation Maui Peak at the south end of Da Nang's infamous Charlie Ridge in late 1968, a U.S. Marine ambush squad one night radioed back to its company CP that it was being pelted by small stones.[1] Four months before, while on a daytime patrol southeast of An Hoa's Liberty Bridge, a sister squad had reported small-arms fire from several different directions at once and a very large artillery impact of unknown origin. In other words, tiny contingents from the world's most technologically advanced military were still finding themselves in "deep *kimchi*."

Nothing then happened to that first squad because the whole area had been considered too dangerous to allow a foray beyond the base of the company-occupied hill. Its sibling was subsequently sprung from the apparent encirclement by a corridor-clearing (and this time friendly) artillery barrage (as per Chapter 24). But, such stories do not always have happy endings. Of late, American commando contingents have once again been getting into untenable situations.

Among the SEALs' (U.S. Navy's "Sea, Air, and Land" commandos') most honorable traditions is never becoming a POW. But, such a heritage can prove difficult for a tiny commando team that suddenly discovers skilled enemy soldiers all around it. Most U.S. adversaries like to "hug" their quarry, so no pinpoint bombardment can be summoned. Then, fighting to the death may seem the GIs' only option. But, it really isn't. All the Yanks have to do is last until the sun goes down and then covertly slip away. Most ISIS, *al-Qaeda,* or other insurgent factions don't carry any night vision equipment. So, a tactical withdrawal is well within the capabilities of the average American commando team. U.S. special operators need only look at how their Asian counterparts have regularly accomplished such a feat. In effect, all that technologically sophisticated gear and on-call firepower can only do so much to save a tiny group of trusting GIs from a more numerous and tactically oriented pursuer.

Planning the E&E

Sometimes, a reconnaissance team becomes encircled right after insertion into enemy territory, due to its none too stealthy means of transportation or some intelligence *faux pas*. But, more often, the enemy cordon occurs after the American squad has already accomplished its mission. In other words, that squad gets followed from its point of attack. Either way, its initial efforts to disengage take priority.

Obviously, the best way to escape encirclement is not to let any sizeable pursuer catch up. Speed helps, but so will leaving no easily discernible trail. So, first on the agenda must be a good escape route. It must provide the most promising combination of three things: (1) speed; (2) land navigation; and (3) obscure movement. The first and second are best accomplished through Terrain Association (following linear terrain features). But too much Terrain Association can lead to an enemy-expected "line of drift." For example, in Okinawa's northern jungles, all reasonably quick movement must be accomplished along a limited number of narrow streambeds or thin ridgelines. As a result, Dead Reckoning provides the safest form of movement. However, such movement would be strenuous and slow to achieve much straight-line distance.

In less precipitous terrain, one way to accomplish a quick and covert version of Terrain Association would be to stay barely within view of a long-existent road or powerline or just inside its accompanying woodline. Any such route would, after all, still constitute a series of straight-line segments.

If the Enemy Is Too Close Behind

The best way to break immediate contact with unwanted company is to get wet. (See Figure 29.1.) Standing water will not only obscure footprints, but also discourage comfort-seeking enemy feet. While streambeds might seem a viable option, they are still lines of drift. Shallow ponds, swamps, and open-air sewers would better disguise one's withdrawal. Don't be dissuaded by the supposed territorial nature of certain snakes in water. A fully submerged Marine scout/sniper once had a "cotton-mouth" brush by his cheek without biting.[2] Thus, the deep swamp makes a perfect way to disappear.

Most of the 2000-3000 NVA troops to escape the Hue City Citadel in 1968 are thought to have first floated with debris across the Perfume River, then swum a side canal, and finally crawled up one of the adjoining rivulets of waste. (Refer back to Chapter 18.) Stealth swimming and flotation pots *(suijutsu)* have been among the *ninjutsu* "water escape arts" for centuries.[3] So, the watercourse strategy is perfectly viable. Thermal imaging doesn't work well against wet or defiladed human beings.

There are several places to hide along such a watery outlet:

Figure 29.1: No Ordinary Enemy Soldier Will Follow Him Here
(Source: FM 21-76 [1970], p. 43)

(1) the occasional culvert; (2) constant vegetation; and (3) the ever present opportunity to submerge. With some way to breath, the latter is not all that farfetched. A hollow reed was also part of *ninjutsu* methodology.[4]

Then, once the pursuit has been sufficiently slowed, one might risk a few quick Terrain Association legs. In full moonlight for example, one can run fully upright in the deep shadow of a highway adjacent treeline without being noticed.

Every Escape Should Include Deception

Once some space has been created between hound and hare, more attention can be paid to not leaving behind any recognizable trail. To keep from being tracked, the withdrawing element has two choices: (1) make as few "signs of passage" as possible; or (2) leave behind a false trail. For the first option, the UW chart for rural E&E in *Dragon Days* suggests walking atop surfaces that are either firm or elastic. Among its recommendations for the second strategy is breaking branches in the direction opposite to that traveled.[5]

In other words, minimizing one's human sign involves more than just avoiding full footprints. There are other above-ground giveaways, like bent twigs, bruised leaves, and displaced dust. To avoid footprints, the quarry can move between rocks, roots, and tufts of grass. When they run out, he can walk on the harder ground at the base of each bush.[6] To the extent he can travel on tiptoes, he will leave no heel marks. Additionally, he has various ruses at his disposal. He might move past a tree, retrace his steps, and then jump to the blind side of that same tree (a method used by some animals).[7] Or he might move 20-30 meters back along the stream he has just come up and then carefully exit through a feeder creek or thick brush.

One of the oldest ways to throw off a pursuer is to pretend to move away without ever leaving. This might be particularly helpful during a daylight search. Within the Orient, this ruse is normally accomplished by making departing footprints and then secretly doubling back to climb a very bushy tree. But, if one harried traveler were to simulate many by doing a lot of backwards walking, then the rest of his group might not have to do anything but climb.

That aforementioned UW chart also suggests hiding somewhere and then moving in the opposite direction after the enemy passes. There are more places for a single person to hide in the woods than one might suspect. They include, but are not limited to, the following: (1) in the upper portion of a hollow tree trunk; (2) within a rotting log; (3) under the roots of an upturned tree; (4) within a narrow runoff ditch; (5) near the top of a leafy tree; (6) in an irrigation canal or deep streamlet; (7) beneath an impassable tangle of vegetation; and (8) under a pile of leaves in a tiny depression. Within the methodology of *ninjutsu*, there are even more ways to "appear not to exist": (1) hiding in the gap between two objects; (2) conforming to the crook of a tree; (3) balling up like a stone; (4) hiding under soft soil; (5) using low vegetation for concealment; and (6) standing motionless before obvious cover.[8] Young Americans should not attempt the latter without first experimenting with various camouflage and poses. The Asian will often use a makeshift cape for this type of thing.

There may also exist a few very promising man-made modifications to the local landscape. They generally have to do with irrigation, electrical power transmission, or highway construction. Few enemies will fully investigate the small culverts that occur whenever a dirt road crosses a tiny draw. They are in no hurry to meet the *fauna* that may inhabit such a cramped space. Nor will they take the time to investigate all the shallow ditches that cross farmers' fields. Such laziness creates opportunities for any living thing willing to do a little crawling.

Natural Ways of Discouraging Pursuit

As might be expected, Asia's UW fighters have a full portfolio of "nonmechanical" ways to permanently discourage pursuit. One of the most daring is to hide in soft soil by the side of a trail and then come up quietly behind one's tormentor. In fact, the British "lost company" at Gallipoli may have moved on line in heavy smoke across a parallel string of Turkish defenders lying just beneath loose sand.[9] Another is dropping in on an unwanted visitor from an overhead branch, or positioning oneself behind a big tree's trunk—just to move backwards along its base as the visitor crosses its front.

There are also ways to slow down unwanted followers. An experienced mantracker will look for sign up to 15 yards ahead. For the quarry regularly to alter direction and then not leave much sign before and after each modification will greatly hamper his efforts. Most effective is nearly reversing direction, for the tracker must waste many minutes looking for the next print to each side of the expected line of travel. An occasional false trail to one flank will further delay his progress.

Countering a Mantracker

The ways of countering a tracker thus fall into four general categories: (1) increasing the time/distance gap; (2) disguising/concealing sign; (3) leaving less or confusing sign; and (4) counterattacking.[10]

Least efficient is paradoxically the first. Moving faster leaves more perceptible clues with which a seasoned tracker can leapfrog ahead. To insure the widest possible gap during the French and Indian Wars, Rogers' Rangers would keep moving until dark.[11] As truly light infantrymen, their pace may have also been somewhat accelerated. Just below are the other three ways to frustrate sign cutting.

Concealing or Disguising Sign

Tracks can be hidden or veiled in several ways. After an area is brushed out, it will be devoid of all ground sign and weathering. However, when a leafy branch is used too long for this purpose, it can turn into a bundle of twigs that will leave an unmistakable trail. Another way to eliminate any evidence of one's passage is to lead a small herd of farm animals over the same ground. Initially choosing a heavily traveled human footpath would make any mantracking much more difficult.

By precisely walking in each other's footsteps, the pursued can lower their apparent number. Then, to travel more obscurely, such a column can follow a streambed or hard ground. But, in the process, it may create long-lasting underwater footprints, crushed/broken water plants, unnaturally wet rocks, and stream bank skid marks. (See Figure 29.2.) The muddy water alone will alert anyone

Figure 29.2: Streambeds Do Not Obscure All Sign
(Source: Courtesy of A.E. Taras, from "Podgotovka Razvegchika: Sistema Spetsnaza GRU," pp. 144, 145, 152, © 1998 by A.E. Taras and F.D. Zaruz.)

downstream to the ploy. On *terra firma,* the last man in column should try to restore any displaced vegetation to its natural state and then cover his and his comrades' tracks with leaves. When the Truong Military Corps No. 559 took over responsibility for the Ho Chi Minh Trail in 1959, its construction crews had a clever way to keep their mission secret. While in single file, the lead man would gently separate all leaves and grasses with a stick, and then the last man walk backwards to restore them to their original state (also with a stick).[12]

Various foot coverings can also be employed. They will disguise one's sole pattern, but also add width to the imprint. Among the more ingenious coverings are leaves. Shoes can be removed or interchanged with wide pads or animal feet. Another trick is to walk backwards. Unfortunately, as the foot's initial pressure shifts to the toe, soil particles will reveal the actual direction of movement. On soft ground, the heel print will also be deeper and the pace shorter.[13]

Leaving Confusing Sign

Next, there are ways to make existing sign more difficult to follow. While traveling across swamps or soft ground, Rogers' Rangers used to spread out abreast.[14] Why couldn't a withdrawing group of contemporary GIs simply subdivide and then rendezvous later? Individuals could drop off the back of the moving column (using rocks or sun-baked ground to exit covertly), and then go their own separate ways to the assigned meeting location. To simulate a less complicated exodus, every other man could carry a companion piggyback. Only in soft soil would this make his footprints noticeably deeper.

A lone quarry can also befuddle a tracker. He can crawl off on his hands and knees or roll along on the ground. While only hand prints, boot toe indentations, and weapons/equipment drag marks will be left behind, his pursuer must still waste valuable minutes locating the new trail. Or a fugitive may swing away from his expected route on a vine or low-hanging limb. Again, there will be clues to the event—the sudden disappearance of tracks, broken branches, and missing or scuffed bark. But, the tracker must still take the time to "connect the new dots." Finally, there will be places in the forest where a particularly agile quarry can virtually disappear. He does so by carefully following a zigzag route across horizontal limbs, surface roots, fallen logs, and rocky ledges.

Counterattacking

On occasion the pursuing mantracker can just be eliminated altogether. This is most easily done through a sniper, boobytrap, or ambush. While raiding the Viet Minh's rear areas, the German contingent of the French Foreign Legion in the first Vietnam War would simply snipe—from several hundred yards away—anyone who appeared (through binoculars) to be following them.[15] The commander of Rogers' Rangers instead advised circling back on one's route to ambush those doing the tracking.[16] That way, there would be fewer mistakes. During the Banana Wars in Haiti and Nicaragua, Marine legend Chesty Puller simply dropped off a tiny welcoming party.

Sufficiently Hiding If the Foe Catches Up

All is not lost if he who is fleeing gets seemingly cornered. Encirclement becomes much more difficult if the following force never determines the withdrawing element's exact location. Nor can it guarantee an annihilation with any gaps in its cordon. (See Figure 29.3.)

At the east end of Henderson Field on Guadalcanal, Lt. Joe Terzi asked for six volunteers for a "suicide mission" one hot night in September 1942. He and six stalwart Marines were to man an LP directly in the path of a huge Japanese attack force. With wisdom far beyond his training, Lt. Terzi had correctly surmised that 3rd Battalion, 1st Regiment's best chance to stop that enemy horde was to interrupt its momentum beyond the perimeter wire. (If the Nipponese unit had too easily reached Marine lines, its "German-Stormtrooper-like" squad assault technique would have probably breached them.) When the first Asian skirmishers showed up well after dark, all seven Americans began shooting their Thompson submachineguns. The enemy commander, believing his lead units had reached the Marines' main line of resistance, became both con-

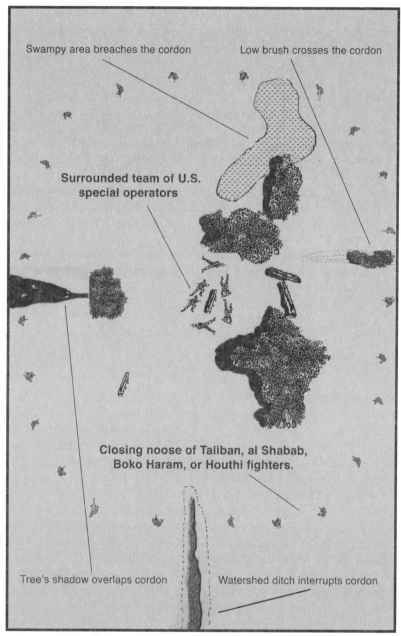

Figure 29.3: A Few of the Nighttime Gaps Between Encirclers
(Source: FM 5-103 [1985], p. 5-10;TC 90-1 [1986], cover.)

fused and resolute. His soldiers then did everything they could to penetrate the Marines' supposed row of machineguns. But, quite possibly through the grace of God, Terzi's overcommitted Leathernecks then did something one of them must have just seen in an old cowboy movie. They all jumped into a deep stream and begun breathing through hollow reeds.[17] Little did they know that this native American trick had also been practiced by Japanese *ninjas* and their mainland predecessors many eons before.

Asian commandos are so infrequently captured for a reason. They will either climb a tree or "go to ground." (See Figure 29.4.) Westerners don't expect to find people in trees or beneath their feet.

Figure 29.4: Many Trees Offer Too Little Foliage
(Source: FM 21-76 [1970], p. 29.)

U.S. Techniques for Escape from Rural Encirclements

If an opposition cordon still forms around an American contingent, there are several ways to avoid capture or death. The safest involve no use—whatsoever—of U.S. supporting arms. They instead depend on deception and the full use of all available microterrain. All should be rehearsed in a similar landscape before being attempted in combat.

The first is exfiltration, or quietly sneaking between enemy cordon sentries. It generally requires darkness, but with enough tall grass or low brush, it might also be possible during the day. When ready to attempt such an escape, the tiny group of GIs divides into two-man teams. Each heads for a different quadrant of the enemy circle to look for a viable gap. After dark, there should be many. (Look back at Figure 29.3). Then, in the sleepy predawn hours, all Yanks silently penetrate the enemy encirclement in their respective sectors and then move to a rendezvous point. If any become the least bit nervous during that final breach of enemy lines, they have only to wait for a natural diversion. More than a few are possible: (1) the moon going behind a cloud; (2) a distant illumination flare fizzling out; (3) the enemy line being checked; (4) the enemy watchstander getting relieved; (5) a passing helicopter; (6) etc. Such things will either interrupt the sentry's night vision, or otherwise distract him. The exfiltration technique is almost exactly the same as that pictorially described for infiltration in *Strategic Rifleman*.

The Lone-Party Diversion Ruse

America's tiny ground combat elements have been so overcontrolled of late that they don't miss what more leeway would have made possible. As a result, America's foes won't expect much bottom-echelon initiative. That makes them susceptible to a little trickery.

There are places in wooded terrain where a single person can virtually vanish and several people at least hide from view. The former include short cracks in the earth, murky watercourses, and hollow tree trunks. The latter include treetops, large bramble bushes, and the root systems of overturned trees. Of course, the group refuge would better work if the enemy could be somehow lured past its location by the actions of another member. And that member's personal sacrifice would be less permanent if he could then move unseen from the place of diversion to a foolproof hide-out.

In Figure 29.5, from a distant stream bank, a well-seasoned U.S. volunteer fires a few ineffective small-arms rounds past the base of a big bushy tree his five buddies have just climbed. As all approaching enemy then converge on the source of that fire (which they believe to be the last stand of the American team), they pay little attention to trees they pass. As soon as that volunteer thinks his buddies safe, he crawls/swims to an inaccessible part of the same murky or vegetation-choked stream to begin breathing, as necessary, through a hollow reed.

Yet, neither ruse will work against an experienced mantracker unless all evidence has been carefully erased. While Asian armies generally enjoy more trackers than the U.S. military, not every unit has one. But, it may have a woods-wise local guide.

A More Old-Fashioned Breakout

To succeed, not all escape attempts need be totally silent or confusing to the enemy. As in rural assault methodology, it has only to deceive the foe as to its exact place of execution. Thus, any encircled American force that can hold out until dark, should then be able—fairly safely—to conduct a special kind of frontal assault. That assault will not be as dangerous if it can meet a single, non-traditional condition—no shooting of unsilenced small arms. All killing must be done by grenade or bayonet. Because of America's traditional love for indirect fire, the enemy will associate any closely spaced explosions with a mortar barrage, and not a ground attack.

The infiltration sequence in Chapter 13 of *Strategic Rifleman* is followed until the two-man teams are within grenade range of the enemy holes in their lanes. Then, they toss grenades in those holes, widen the breach as necessary with more grenades, and then escape. (See Figure 29.6.)

There is a variation to this scheme from the Asian UW chart in *Dragon Days*. While a string of firecrackers is going off on one side of the opposing cordon, all in the cornered party quietly rush

Diverter finds hard and barren place on streambank, brushes away all nearby footprints, and occasionally shoots back towards base of hiding tree. Before encirclers see him, he carefully slips into stream and crawls along it to a deeper part with heavy vegetation in and around it. Then, with a hollow reed for breathing, he submerges when the foes show up and waits until they give up looking.

Five GIs already at the top of this very bushy tree after carefully brushing away all footprints at its base.

Figure 29.5: Five Hide in a Treetop as One Diverts at the Stream
(Source: FM 5-103 [1985], p. 5-10;TC 90-1 [1986], cover.)

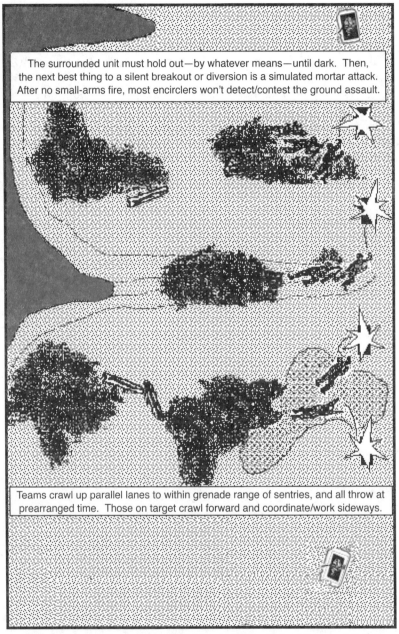

The surrounded unit must hold out—by whatever means—until dark. Then, the next best thing to a silent breakout or diversion is a simulated mortar attack. After no small-arms fire, most encirclers won't detect/contest the ground assault.

Teams crawl up parallel lanes to within grenade range of sentries, and all throw at prearranged time. Those on target crawl forward and coordinate/work sideways.

Figure 29.6: Best After Dark Back-Up Is Fake Mortar Attack
(Source: FM 7-70 [1986], p. 420; FM 5-103 [1985], p. 4-6; MCI 03.66a [1986], p. 2-8; FM 23-30 [1988], p. 2-8; FM 7-1183 [1976], p. 2-VII-C-4.4.)

another. The tiny explosions sound to the enemy like small-arms fire, and only those right next to them consider themselves in any danger.

None of the escape techniques so far presented have involved improvements to the microterrain. Where time is available to do some digging, much more in the way of escape and diversion is possible. After watching an enemy sapper disappear from 50 yards away in an area no bigger than a household living room, a Marine lieutenant in 1966 could find no tunnel or spider hole entrance.[18] With a little practice, Americans could also prepare a nondetectable escape cavity. Criminals do it all the time.

PART ELEVEN

IDIOSYNCRASIES OF 21ST CENTURY CONFLICT

"[O]NE WHO IS SKILLED IN WARFARE . . . TAKES THE ENEMY'S WALLED CITY
WITHOUT ATTACKING [FROM ITS PERIPHERY], AND OVERTHROWS
THE ENEMY QUICKLY, WITHOUT PROTRACTED WARFARE." — SUN TZU

(Source: Attributed to Sun Tzu.)

30

FOE MORE PRODUCTIVELY
CONSIDERED A CRIMINAL

● Could a policing operation better handle 4GW issues?

● How would the distressed population benefit?

Unlike insurgents in mufti, civilian lawbreakers have rights.

(Source: FM 7-8 [1984], p. N-1)

America's Usual Way of Handling a Foreign Adversary

The U.S. military has been so far conducting most of its overseas "wars of liberation" through an Attrition Warfare methodology. Enemy elements are deemed too prevalent and powerful for Americans to safely pursue the perpetrators of any separate act of aggression. The population in which opposition agents and their insurgent proxies regularly "swim" is considered sympathetic to one or both. And any locals who fail to abandon their normal place of residence after it has been declared a "free-fire zone" must do so at their own risk.

Then, each time the U.S. military phalanx rolls through an inhabited area with all of its inherent firepower, there occurs some collateral damage. Some of the indigenous society's economic and political infrastructure gets depleted, along with its overall sense of psychological/religious well-being.

Yet, most 21st Century wars no longer require this forceful a solution, despite adversaries who often pretend to be more mighty than they really are. This limited martial threat that they actually pose, in turn, allows for more of a 4GW approach to their eviction. The most productive of the available options is a carefully targeted policing action.

Is ISIS Crazy or Just Clever?

ISIS is the first large nonstate actor to use fear as a main part of its wartime strategy for hundreds of years. It was largely that fear that caused the Iraqi Army to collapse on 2014. Now, all too fresh in every American's memory is the Jordanian pilot who was publicly burned alive, and row of red-jump-suited Coptic Christians who were simultaneously beheaded with pocket knives. Other U.S. opponents have done things just as grotesque, but what makes this modern-day butchery so terrifying is the extent of its media coverage. Getting shot in the groin by an enemy machinegun in WWI Europe was probably no picnic either. But, it didn't stop America from again sending her sons against fully prepared German and Japanese defenses on many different fronts during the next world war.

None of this recent media-enhanced trepidation appears to have been lost on U.S. leaders (both civilian and military). Already aware of the political ramifications of losing a single American life in combat, they easily imagine their livelihood slipping away should so much as one GI be captured. As a result, what was once a life-saving wish—"no more boots on the ground"—has since become standard procedure. After all, no amount of future success in war is worth a government career. So, from now on, America will fight her wars with local proxies and U.S. airpower. That most of those conflicts will be almost impossible to win that way no longer enters the discussion. So, in a way, such leaders have already caved in to the terrorism.

Its Possible Intent

ISIS is a historical anomaly. It has seized petroleum facilities for a source of income, and placed volunteers into enemy equipment for an army, but still has no central structure. Its only real chance at survival is for the West to now blame all of Islam for the deranged behavior of a fringe element. In actuality, the mainstream Muslim has no more chance of reining in ISIS than the average U.S. citizen has of lowering America's growing number of serial killers.

ISIS does have supporters in many nations around the world, but not the hordes of well-trained fighters that the Pentagon seems to expect. Thus, it could be treated like any widespread prison gang or organized-crime family. Death means very little to either type of organization. Both are more interested in absolute loyalty and the "equitable" distribution of all proceeds. That makes them particularly susceptible to internal disruption. For example, after a load of heroin had mysteriously disappeared from a cartel's refining lab, it wouldn't be all that difficult to make it look like an inside job. That's when crime element members who have long embraced an illicit lifestyle might start preying upon one another.

The Law Enforcement Approach

Standard U.S. counterinsurgency procedures weren't designed to curtail criminal behavior. They more strive to generate loyalty to the central government than bring violators of local laws to justice.

Yet, the struggle against a potent Communist insurgency in Malaysia in the 1950's was largely won through sending a special tracking team after the perpetrators of each terrorist act.[1] Thus, the case for a different counterinsurgency paradigm in America can be quite compelling.

What if someone were to set off a big IED in New York City? Would the New York City Police Department (NYPD) do any of the following: (1) stomp all over the detonation site; (2) not look for implantation tools; (3) not collect bomb fragments or residue; (4) not search for where the lookout or trigger man stood; and (5) not scour the area for foot- and finger-prints? Upon learning—from an unknown bystander—"who in the neighborhood might have been sympathetic to the bomber," would they have further: (1) kicked in the door of the suspect's supposed residence; (2) brashly interrogated any males they found present though the women and children seemed terrified; and then (3) taken those males into extended custody for under-regulated interrogation? If the NYPD operated that way in Brooklyn, there would be an armed uprising in that location.

As a result of the sectarian divide between Sunni and Shiite, standard counterinsurgency procedures could become a recipe for disaster almost anywhere in South Asia. That's because those procedures pay almost no attention to civil law. They may comply with military law and the Geneva Conventions, but they generally ignore locally established rights and customs. At some point, the opposing sects may try to discredit the foreign occupier. As soon as one sect falsely accuses the other, that occupier's credibility can be compromised. A tip from a lone bystander is not enough to justify a military-style raid on a resident's house. That's the reason for search warrants in New York City. To get one, a legal expert has to be convinced that there is sufficient evidence to warrant such an intrusion of privacy. Such evidence usually comes from several corroborating sources at once—to include physical evidence from the crime scene.

Then can easily ensue a seemingly endless cycle of miscues. Order-oriented U.S. service personnel receive a nebulous intelligence report that *al-Qaeda* is about to attack again. Fully motorized, they roll like sitting ducks out of their cozy base and into their assigned neighborhood. The inevitable occurs. They soon destroy—or not look for—the physical evidence that would have led them eventually to the perpetrators. Their apparent preference for intimidation over investigation further alienates the local population. And then, those GIs return to their bases more convinced than ever that any Muslim who won't fully answer their questions is an insurgent sympathizer.

Bystanders won't always level with NYPD detectives either. That's usually because they are scared of retribution from whoever conducted the crime. But the detectives don't conclude that all who remain silent are trying to aid or abet a criminal. Where local citizens are hesitant to help, those detectives simply dig deeper for physical evidence and other leads. That's the way professional policing is done. In other words, the civilian residents near the scene of the crime are always given the benefit of the doubt. Until U.S. military units are able to develop more of this mutual respect between flock and shepherd, they will continue to have trouble quelling insurgencies.

U.S. Police Already Operating in a 4GW Setting

To succeed, U.S. law enforcement agencies must pay close attention to the sensibilities of neighborhood groups. So, they try to minimize the political, economic, and psychological fallout of every case. Many of their methods of investigation and apprehension would be of great help to the GIs who must operate in a similar environment on an overseas deployment. Many law enforcement personnel are not expert tacticians (e.g., the "feds" at Waco). But neither are they naive enough to think that valuable leads can be obtained through coercion.

To be of much 4GW help at a host nation outpost, the members of a contemporary U.S. squad would have to undergo somewhat of a paradigm shift. Instead of "those who close with and destroy the enemy," they must get used to viewing themselves as "protectors of the weak" and "public servants." No longer would all suspects be possible targets.

To survive alone as police augment, such a group of fourteen GI's would also have to master some of the more obscure light-infantry skills—e.g., sensory perception and urban escape. Too much armament and technology might make such things appear superfluous. But, with the constantly rehearsed techniques of a *ninja,* no GI would ever again be surprised, much less captured.

Law Enforcement Objectives

As a matter of normal protocol, U.S. police personnel protect not only innocent bystanders, but also suspected offenders. This law enforcement *mantra* just happens to coincide with the most credible formula for battlefield morality ever composed. Contrary to what most U.S. troops are being told in training, the answer is to kill as few enemy soldiers as possible—according to Pope John Paul II.[2]

That's because killing for killing's sake serves no strategic purpose in war, and the more allowed can lead to irreconcilable animosities and unattainable peace.

How Police Procedure Accomplishes Such Goals

U.S. policemen are not allowed to preemptively fire at any suspect. Routinely assumed be innocent, that suspect cannot be harmed until he (or she) makes some life-threatening gesture toward the arresting officer or another human being. Only in those rare instances where the person of interest is known to be a convicted murderer, can he (or she) be legitimately fired upon while fleeing the police officer.

The most successful detectives don't maltreat detainees. They have learned over the years that information obtained through forceful interrogation is generally a fabrication. The idea that the suspect is innocent until proven guilty shapes their every action. To acquire justice for a "bad guy," they must first prove beyond a reasonable doubt that he (or she) is guilty. That takes far more investigative effort that most American infantrymen are allowed. For an in-depth discussion of what they could do, see Chapters 9 through 12 of *Dragon Days*.

How ISIS Might Be More Easily Combatted

Because ISIS—despite all of its bluster and atrocity—remains a tiny fraction of each plagued society, its composite elements can be more safely confronted piecemeal.

Only in the cities that ISIS members have occupied are U.S.-led forces hesitant to run enough localized raids to root them out. That's because of the "skedaddle"—out of sheer terror—that city's former military garrison had demonstrated. But, what a host nation security force does as a result of an Islamic feud should in no way dictate what Christian-led rescuers attempt. In effect, the previous occupiers' Shiite identity had helped to foment the terror.

Yet, these new ISIS occupiers may still constitute less than one percent of the total population of that city, so its recapture must be conducted like a hostage rescue operation. Such a nontraditional kind of urban assault will be thoroughly detailed in the next chapter.

31 RUINOUS URBAN ASSAULT NO LONGER NECESSARY

- Must Allied armies still level every contested city?
- Is there any alternative to this much devastation?

Heavy rubbling makes a cityscape much more difficult to seize.

(Sources: FM 90-10-1 [1986], p. H-7; MCI 03.66a [1986], p. 3-11.)

When the Enemy Uses a Civilian Shield

Over the years, the U.S. War Department (or subsequent Pentagon) has often fought insurgents. It did so in the Philippines around 1900, at the Caribbean Banana Wars of the 1920's/30's, during the 1960's/70's Vietnam conflict, and throughout Central America in the 1980's. It has most recently done so in Iraq and Afghanistan. Throughout this period, collateral damage has been often attributed to the foe's use of local inhabitants as "human shields."

Most insurgencies follow the Maoist model, wherein members

357

of the rebel faction "swim like fish" throughout the civilian population. So, finding the two segments of society in close proximity is to be expected. Whether those guerrillas have been intentionally hiding behind women and children is a matter of opinion. But, America has on occasion levied the same charge against organized armies. When the last Japanese defenders of Manila broke out of the Intramuros Fort in February of 1945, they did so without any interference from the attacking U.S. troops—by blending in with a horde of refugees.

Did Japanese Soldiers Also Hide Behind Noncombatants?

By 12 February 1945, the U.S. 37th Infantry Division and 1st Cavalry Division had encircled Manila.[1] Upon reaching the 16th Century Intramuros Fort (the most probable last stand for any diehard defenders), they encountered little resistance. Most of the Japanese marines had either given their lives for the Emperor or complied with their initial instructions to abandon the city.[2] But, having the Nipponese Naval Defense Force commander and his staff commit suicide in no way proves that all frontline fighters did likewise. The Japanese Army was still poised north of Manila to defend Luzon.

Shortly after the Intramuros' 40-foot-thick walls were breached, U.S. assault troops were deluged by 2000 refugees. That flood of civilians almost certainly included Japanese soldiers in mufti. Needless to say, the Americans were too busy to check all identification papers. The same thing had occurred when U.S. forces crossed the Pasig River (the defender's principal barrier in front of Manila).[3] At that point, resistance within Intramuros intensified. Ancient fortresses of this vintage had secret passageways that led under their walls from royal chambers. Many members of the Japanese rear guard could have escaped that way. Others had only to dress like GIs.

> The hardest fighting in Intramuros was the 129th's effort to capture Ft. Santiago in the northwest corner of the old wall. They fought room to room, and then through subterranean dungeons and tunnels . . . The regiment did not secure the last of the fort's [most obvious] tunnels until 1200 on 25 February (U.S. Army, *The 129th Infantry in*

World War II, 1947, 108; Smith, *Triumph in the Philippines,* 1963, 298; U.S. Army, *37th Infantry Div. Report after Action,* 1945, 83).

During the fighting in Intramuros, some Japanese troops attempted to exfiltrate wearing U.S. uniforms and carrying M1 rifles.[4]

— U.S. Army Combat Studies Institute research

The Korean Experience

A little-known American movie—"One Minute to Zero"—about the Korean War begins with a U.S. commander using artillery to stop an approaching refugee column that supposedly contains enemy infiltrators.[5] Little additional research was needed to come up with similar events in 1950 when South Korea was being rapidly overrun by the North Korean Army. Most famous is the so-called No Gun Ri Massacre that occurred on 26-29 July, when many refugees were killed by an American airstrike and subsequent small-arms fire from a U.S. Cavalry Regiment. Most Americans were unaware of the incident until an Associated Press (AP) story in 1999 used U.S. veteran recollections to corroborate various survivors' accounts. That article also claims to have uncovered declassified U.S. Army authorization to fire upon approaching civilians after any report of enemy soldiers joining refugee groups.[6] The U.S. Army now only recalls a "regrettable accident," and what really happened is no longer at issue. The occurrence is only mentioned here to show that organized armies have also been accused of deploying human shields.

Endangering foreign civilians in this manner was at the time thought to violate Article 28 of Geneva Convention IV of 1949: "The presence of a protected person may not be used to render certain points or areas immune from military operations."[7] Since then, article 51(7) of the 1977 Additional Protocol I has given additional guidance on the subject.

The presence or movements of the civilian population or individual civilians shall not be used to render certain points or areas immune from military operations, in particular in attempts to shield military objectives from attacks or to shield, favour or impede military operations. The Parties

to the conflict shall not direct the movement of the civilian population or individual civilians in order to attempt to shield military objectives from attacks or to shield military operations.[8]
— Article 51(7), Internat. Committee of Red Cross

Yet, some civilians are always going to be present during most forms of ground combat, so both sides could be accused of preventing their departure. In Vietnam, U.S. forces simply declared huge swathes of the intermittently populated coastal plain to be "free-fire zones." Then, after receiving warnings to leave, all remaining civilians were considered enemy relatives or sympathizers. While they could not be intentionally targeted, they might still wander beneath a nightly H&I artillery barrage or where U.S. planes "pickled" unwanted bombs. Or, they might just get hit by a stray bullet from one of the many firefights in the region. Either type of casualty would stretch the rules of engagement. To be on totally solid moral footing, American forces will have to start treating all civilians still present on future battlefields as if they are enemy hostages.

U.S. Law Enforcement Rules for Hostage Rescue

In any hostage-taking situation, the attending police department can't do anything that might further endanger the captives until they are in immediate danger of being murdered. ISIS is as criminal an expansionistic entity as has ever existed. It loves occupying a congested urban area just to scare more people into doing its will. So, one could reasonably obey this prisoner-saving axiom while trying to recover a Middle Eastern city from its clutches. ISIS is not militarily strong in those metropolises it "captures," just unbelievably brutal.

Why, then, does it take a rock-crusher-like 1950's assault (like Operation Ripper) to remove ISIS from a big built-up area? Wouldn't a secretive infiltration to the center of town be more fitting? It would automatically create a safety zone for the largest concentration of hostage residents. That's how the North Vietnamese Army or a modern-day police force would solve such a problem. The best example was the recapture of an ambassador's residence at Lima in 1997.

The Peruvian Masterpiece

On 17 December 1996, 14 members of the Tupac Amaru Revolutionary Movement (MRTA) took more than 400 high-level diplomats, government officials, and business executives captive in Lima. Those victims had done nothing more risky than attending the party at an ambassador's house. Unfortunately, that structure had already been converted into a veritable fortress by the Japanese government. It was surrounded by a 12-foot-high wall and had doors that could withstand a grenade explosion. All of its windows were covered by grates, and some had bulletproof glass. Once inside, the Marxist rebels had little trouble defending the place. Their principal demand was that the 450 MRTA prisoners in Peru's prisons be freed. Without giving in to the rebels, Peruvian authorities finally won the release of all but 72 of the hostages. Then, at the request of Fujimori (Peru's president of Nipponese descent), they made a thorough study of how safely to rescue the remainder. Within their findings may lie the key to "hostage friendly assault"—a topic of interest to every U.S. military and police detachment. That key involves non-Western tactics.

After being held captive for 126 days, the 72 dignitaries were finally rescued on 22 April 1997 by Peruvian commandos. During the raid, 25 hostages were superficially wounded, and one died of a heart attack. Additionally, two of the commandos were killed by enemy fire, and all 14 MRTA militants died.[9]

The final attack to free those prisoners was launched in mid-afternoon. Its initial thrusts were made through tunnel openings in the embassy's tiled floor and outer courtyard. After the Peruvian press had predicted a nighttime helicopter assault, those daytime penetrations must have come as quite a shock to the militants. At the time, the entry vestibule to this multistory building had contained the guerrilla leader. That his "temporary headquarters" was first targeted makes this very much like the North Vietnamese "Blooming Lotus" maneuver. If it can work on a town, why couldn't it also work on an urban compound?

This methodology was developed in 1952 in an assault on Phat Diem. Its key characteristic was to avoid enemy positions on the perimeter of the town. The striking columns move directly against the center . . . seeking out command-

and-control centers. Only then were forces directed outward
to systematically destroy the now leaderless units around
the town. . . .

This approach contrasts sharply with Western doctrine,
which traditionally would isolate the town, gain a foothold,
and systematically drive inward to clear the town. This sets
up a series of attrition-based battles that historically make
combat in built-up areas such a costly undertaking.[10]

— *Marine Corps Gazette,* April 1999

In addition to initially striking at the compound's center, the
Peruvian troops had also used encirclement and "swarm" tactics.
Western police will seldom attempt either, and Western infantrymen never do. In fact, for fear of fratricide, U.S. military doctrine
makes no provision for a multidirectional entry to any objective.
Still, the encirclement maneuver has been regularly used by Asian
Communist forces. To be done relatively safely, it requires only a
little natural cover, carefully positioned personnel, and well-aimed
shots. Concussion grenades and low-velocity munitions also help.
So does having all attackers crawl in at the same elevation and then
shoot upwards.

With regard to the swarm stratagem, there were some 14 concurrently moving maneuver squads when the operation kicked off
in Lima. All may have attacked from different directions—four
from beneath the compound floor and 10 more from beyond its outer
confines. But, it's more likely that some squads were working in
tandem. At least two could have easily blasted their way through
the front gate and main building entrance while other pairs "vaulted"
over side and rear courtyard walls following diversionary explosions.
(The guerrillas had blown a hole in that wall to enter the compound
initially.) Each tunnel contained 10-12 men, so all other squads may
have consisted of the same number. In most locations, a follow-on
squad would have permitted a feigned building breach or shuttled
out the wounded.

The key to the success of the mission was the tunnel that
reportedly led to three points within the compound—the
main reception area where the terrorists were playing soc-
cer, the kitchen, and under the tent that had been set up
way back in December.

A Lima newspaper reported that professional miners had started building the tunnel in January. Four-man teams worked in four hour shifts.[11]
— Emergency Net News Intel. Rpt., 24 April 1997

Details of the Final Assault

From each tunnel inside the building, there was first a floor-breaching detonation. Over 40 men then emerged from all four subterranean passageways. Through the front gate came another squad and its backup to assault the building's main entrance. Concurrently explosions went off elsewhere, and other contingents climbed over the compound walls at five to ten different places. So many cross-wall excursions would then mask the number of actual attempts to enter the ambassador's residence. Again, such a multiple assault is probably Asian in origin.

After ladders had been placed against the rear of the residence, a squad from the backyard tunnel climbed to the second floor to blow open the door that led to the hostages. Another squad (of indeterminate origin) ascended to the roof to blow open a hole through which any terrorist who came near the hostages could be shot. Some of its members must have subsequently dropped down into the building, because hostages were soon seen exiting by way of its windows and roof. As waiting columns helped them down the ladders and into ambulances, many of the 10 wall-crossing squads must have had that as their subsequent mission.

Commandos were seen at just before 3:30 p.m. running along the tree-lined streets surrounding the Japanese compound. Shooting began. A small team of special forces stormed through the double doors of the compound's outside wall. The shooting increased at the front of the building.

Two teams of commandos, each with 12 men, attacked the front and rear of the building. A loud explosion rocked the front of the house. The soldiers had blown open the front door and burst inside, guns blazing. Another explosion occurred on the right side of the building and then another from the rear. Soldiers attacked from the rear.

Within seconds, hostages began climbing out windows and down ladders. Inside of the building, gunfire could be

363

heard. Soldiers had ordered the hostages to drop to the floor to avoid being shot. More explosions shook the building. Hostages began appearing on the roof. On hands and knees, they crawled along the flat roof to a side stairway where more soldiers escorted them to freedom.[12]

— Emergency Net News Intel. Rpt., 23 April 1997

What Was Theoretically Learned in Peru

The massing of rebels within full view of the front entrance of the ambassador's house is what gave the Peruvian authorities such a good chance at success. They were also fortunate that the hostages were being held elsewhere in a group. As it turned out, all but three of the 14 terrorists were killed by the initial explosions and fighting near the front of the building. Those other three could not be immediately located.

The MRTA guerrillas had made two mistakes: (1) establishing a routine; and (2) leaving all hostages together. While the rescuers were to capitalize on those errors, the final assault remained rife with danger. Several Western special operations commands had been consulted, but the final approach to the problem remained unmistakably Asian. It was a combination of Blooming Lotus, encirclement, and swarm tactics. With the latter, the Peruvians had hoped to confuse the guerrillas, while still reinforcing the two-part main effort (one at the front rebel hangout and the other at the upstairs hostage area). Of particular note, the hostages were already being saved while the front-entry fight was still going. Such a stratagem is almost nonexistent in Western tactics. After all, the Japanese ambassador's residence was technically on Japanese soil, and the green light for the assault had been given by the Japanese government. When Fujimori (the Peruvian leader) met with Japan's Prime Minister in Canada, the two leaders had agreed on how to handle the hostage situation.[13] So, the Japanese military likely provided operational advice. Its light-infantry tactics had evolved from the same ancient Chinese formations as those in North Vietnam. And its forefathers knew enough about tunneling to allow 300 soldiers to assault an airfield on Iwo Jima two weeks after that island had been declared secure.[14]

That no hostage was slain by commando or kidnapper during the rescue was more than coincidence. The Peruvian assault had been so well designed that it should now serve as the model for attacking all contested buildings (or even cities) containing noncombatants. The key elements of that assault are as follows:

° Prepositioning surveillance devices to monitor activity.
° Killing or stunning most kidnappers in the initial blow.
° Confusing those left as to the direction of the assault.
° Moving immediately to protect hostages.
° Coming to close-quarters combat with every foe.

The Retaking of Mosul

Sadly, Coalition forces made no attempt to save the citizenry of Mosul in this manner. With the exception of an outer encirclement and several concurrent thrusts toward its center, their approach has been strictly of the 1950's "meat-grinder" variety. When ISIS first entered Mosul in October of 2014, its population was over two million. Most residents of West Mosul and its Old City were Sunni Muslim, whereas those of East Mosul were Kurdish.[15] Since then, about a million of those residents have fled the city, leaving almost the same number behind. Of that remaining million, up to 750,000 may have been in West Mosul, where the final most bloody part of that battle occurred.[16]

> The pre-ISIS population of Iraq's second-largest city was approximately 3 million. Current estimates of the number of people still living in the city vary from 700,000 to over one million.[17]
> — Kurdish media network, 17 October 2016

Meanwhile, the number of ISIS fighters inside Mosul since the Coalition first attempted to retake it in October 2016 has been only about 6000.[18] This measly total could not have grown, because the city was surrounded. That's six tenths of one percent of the total remaining population, or one ISIS fighter per every 167 inhabitants. Granted, some were suicide bombers, others skilled in the use of VBIEDs (Vehicle Borne IEDs) or armed drones, and still others homicidal maniacs. But no police department in its right mind would have leveled a full housing project to get at one criminal for every 167 hostages. The U.S. has already admitted to killing over

100 civilians by airstrike in the al-Jadida District within two miles of the Old City,[19] so the following may have "unintentionally" killed many more.

> Eight months of airstrikes [have] largely leveled Mosul's Old City.[20]
> — *Defense One,* 7 July 2017

Might the West have become a little too comfortable with the complete destruction of contested cities to limit its own casualties? Just as the Tank Battalion Scout Platoon had approached Baghdad ahead of its main body in Chapter 19, so too did Iraq's Counterterrorism Service "advance so far so quickly" and then operate alone in East Mosul for a month.[21] That's because overwhelming force had not been necessary in either case.

There's no doubt ISIS has been throwing some Mosul's less cooperative citizens off the tops of buildings since it arrived in 2014, but the Coalition's recent "human-shield-oriented" offensive has probably cost more innocent life.

> By March [2017], the effort to free Mosul had killed more than 7,000 Iraqi civilians and wounded another 22,000, estimated Middle East observer Joel Wing, who has been tracking developments in Iraq since 2008.[22]
> — *Defense One,* 7 July 2017

A Different Approach May Have Been Possible

U.S. military professionals readily admit that their civilian leaders in Washington worry too much about every GI killed in combat. Nobody likes casualties, but it's almost impossible to decisively win a war without some risk. If that conflict drags on and has to be abandoned, then every young American lost from the outset will have been in vain.

What if 2000 elite Iraqi troops had quietly filtered into Mosul's Old City, just as the 12th VC Sapper Regiment did to the Hue City Citadel in 1968 before the main NVA assault on that city.[23] (Look back at Map 18.7.) Then, those Iraqi troops would have been virtually immune to attack (due to the close confines) from ISIS's gun-toting jeeps, VBIEDs, and armed drones.

Old Mosul, it's just a different landscape. It's very tight.
Vehicles can't fit in there. It's a dismounted fight."[24]
    — *Defense One,* 7 July 2017

By then manning the very edge of the Old City, those Iraqi
commandos would have accomplished two things: (1) saving all
Old City dwellers from further harm; and (2) creating an extensive
"safety zone" for other refugees. For all West Mosul residents wishing to escape the fighting, one of the gradually narrowing streets
and alleyways into the Old City would have been far safer than a
suburb boulevard.

Knowing full well how the firepower-heavy West likes to operate, most of the 6000 ISIS defenders would have been either at
Mosul's outskirts or along its most likely avenues of entry. Any
who then tried to charge back into the Old City in their pickup
trucks could have been easily shot. Even a hastily assembled urban defense is well known to have the edge over a traditional offense. Inside the Hue City Citadel, the NVA defenders of Phase
Line Green had created an almost impregnable barrier in just a
few days. It then took a fully supported U.S. assault battalion four
days to cross a 50-foot-wide street.[25]

In addition, the new Allied occupiers of Mosul's center could
have been easily resupplied by old-fashioned airdrop. There must
have been one or more existing hospitals in that area to handle casualties. If the way the Coalition attacked West Mosul is still the
state of the art, then God help all future city dwellers.

How ISIS Had Occupied Mosul in the First Place

From the very start, the threat posed by radical Sunni ISIS
to the Middle East has been an illusion—albeit a particularly terrifying one. Its so-called Caliphate had been devoid of infrastructure, and its army lacking in substance. Yet, that army had still
succeeded through what might best be described as Maneuver
Swarm Tactics with "technicals" (pickup trucks or HMMWVs with
bed-mounted guns). Its tiny vehicle-borne contingents had covered a lot of ground, stolen what they needed, and then alternately
swarmed or bypassed all who stood in their way. Meanwhile, their
well-publicized atrocities so shocked the Shiite-led Iraqi Army that
many of its soldiers would later desert. Just as a 80,000-man Sin-

gapore garrison had surrendered to 20,000 seemingly unstoppable Japanese light-infantrymen in 1942,[26] Mosul's defenders would mostly skedaddle. So many quickly left their posts in that city (up to 25,000 [27]) that the West may have—from the very start—overestimated the number of Coalition troops it would need to evict ISIS.

> At 2:30 A.M. on June 6 [2014], [Lt.Gen.] Gharawi and his men returned to their operations room after an inspection of checkpoints in the city of two million. At that moment, convoys of pickup trucks were advancing from the west, driving across the desert that straddles Iraq's border with Syria. Each vehicle held up to four IS[IS] fighters. The convoys shot their way through the two-man checkpoints into the city.[28]
> — *Reuters,* "How Mosul Fell," 14 October 2014

Why near panic was to set in among many of the city's police and Iraqi Army contingents may never be understood. After rumors of an impending ISIS attack, Baghdad had refused to send reinforcements. Mosul had before been a hotbed of *al-Qaeda*-inspired Sunni insurgency, so the age-old fear and animosity between the opposing sects must have played some role. Like sister units throughout Iraq, Mosul's Shiite-dominated security forces (including its police) had almost certainly committed a few prisoner abuses and extrajudicial killings.[29] The man responsible for the city's long-term protection may have simply become too worried about retribution.

> A member of the country's dominate Shi'ite sect, he [Gharawi] alienated Mosul's Sunni majority before the battle, according to the provincial governor and many citizens. That helped to give rise to IS sleeper cells inside Mosul.[30]
> — *Reuters,* "How Mosul Fell," 14 October 2014

Before the attack, ISIS had not intended to take over the whole city. But, once that opportunity arose, it was loosely enough controlled to rapidly take advantage of it. The truly amazing thing is how few fighters were ultimately involved.

> As IS[IS] fighters raced towards Mosul before dawn on June 6, the jihadists hoped only to take a neighborhood

for several hours. . . . They did not expect state control to crumble. They hurtled into five districts in their hundreds, and would, over the next few days, reach over 2000 fighters, welcomed by the city's angry Sunni residents.[31]
  — *Reuters,* "How Mosul Fell," 14 October 2014

While the extent of Sunni discontent in West Mosul is now difficult to ascertain, it is extremely doubtful that the entire population of that part of town was happy to see ISIS in charge. By that time, ISIS was already known of be very hard on suspected defectors. During May of 2016 in a nearby portion of Nineveh Province, it would bury 45 of its own fighters alive after they had run way from a firefight.[32]

But shortly after ISIS first penetrated Mosul in June of 2014, through whatever means (to include sleeper-cell disinformation), each Iraqi soldier/policeman was told either to flee or that his leaders had.[33] To help him make up his mind on what to do next, he was then treated to a few explicit previews of hell. The rest is history.

As the militants infiltrated the city, they seized military vehicles and weapons. The sergeant based there said they also hanged soldiers and lit them ablaze, crucified them, and torched them on the hoods of Humvees.[34]
  — *Reuters,* "How Mosul Fell," 14 October 2014

By 3:30 A.M. [on 6 June], the militants were fighting inside Mosul. Within three days the Iraqi army would abandon the country's second biggest city to its attackers.[35]
  — *Reuters,* "How Mosul Fell," 14 October 2014

How Mosul Was Later Defended by ISIS

As Coalition forces first attempted to take Mosul back in October 2016, ISIS started sending a lot of captured and makeshift artillery shells down range. But none of those shells were very well aimed. The militants had also laced many of the best entry routes with car bombs (some mobile and some not). So, though widely spaced and not very well coordinated, these various explosive charges still made a lot of noise. To a Western attacker preoccupied (for political reasons) with force protection, that posed enough of a threat to cause him to proceed more cautiously. In effect, the city had been partially mined, and ISIS drones had raised the unlikely specter of more accurate artillery fire. But, like everything else about ISIS, the extent of its protective actions had been largely a mirage.

After all, how many defensive strongpoints can 6000 people who like to ride around in little trucks really create in a sprawling urban area? Yet, ISIS had still gotten its way. It had forced the U.S.-advised attack force into a slow-moving, collateral-damage-producing, rock-crusher type of military operation. Even a token dosage of pinpoint preparatory firepower will still rubble adjacent buildings. And then their falling rafters and stone will still harm local residents. So there was a good chance that—as news of all that heavy Western ordnance spread to other Iraqi citizens—many would be reminded of their Islamic duty to expel invaders and revenge the death of family and friends.

There had been a similar example at Fallujah in 2004. By the end of that bloody summer, American warplanes had already bombed its neighborhoods for quite some time.[36] On 6 July alone, they dropped two tons of bombs—four 500 pounders and two 1000 pounders—on a purported militant safehouse.[37] As a result, many Fallujans must have come to see Americans more as destroyers than liberators.[38]

Then, shortly after the November 2004 U.S. ground assault on Fallujah, rebels in Mosul attacked nine police stations and executed a number of National Guardsmen.[39] In response to insurgent bands openly roaming the streets of Mosul,[40] the U.S. military again resorted to airstrikes.[41] Though 1200 American troops then entered Mosul to restore order, the attacks against its police stations continued. So, in December 2004, U.S. planes dropped at least one more 500-pound bomb within its city limits.[42] From that point forward, Mosul residents knew what to expect should the militants return.

Aftermath of the 2017 Assault on Mosul

When the most heavily populated parts of Mosul were finally reoccupied by Coalition forces in mid-July of 2017, drone photographs of the area revealed the true extent of the structural devastation.[43] It was, quite frankly, difficult to tell whether West Mosul's residents had been rescued or punished. The rift between Sunni and Shiite that had been fueling much of the Middle Eastern discord certainly seemed no closer to resolution.

The Case for Technology

On the assumption that more technology would facilitate the assault on Mosul, the West did two things. First had come the reconnaissance and combat drones—some capable of dropping a hail of 40mm grenades.[44] Then (possibly by tracing the previous paths of detonated car bombs through photographic records), it had located some suspected VBIED "factories." After conducting airstrikes against more than 100 such targets, it greatly reduced its bombing campaign after the errant strike.[45]

While technology can lead to the destruction of many enemy soldiers, it could also help with nonconfrontational tactics. With Coalition headquarters closely monitoring various routes into the Mosul's Old City through U.S. thermal imaging, any number of infiltration teams could have sidestepped ISIS strongpoints. Might an assault like that be a more proper in a 4GW urban environment?

Once a City Is Captured

After whatever degree of rubbling, the new owner still has to control a sizeable urban area as it rebuilds. Otherwise, guerrilla activity may jeopardize his victory.

32

CONTROLLING THE
URBAN EXPANSE

- How can the DoD best monitor neighborhood progress?
- What might keep tiny dismounted U.S. delegations safe?

This U.S. outpost is at a local law enforcement substation.

(Source: "The Hizara Province," by SFC Elzie Golden, U.S. Army Center for Military History, from this url: http://www.history.army.mil/art/Golden/Image-12.jpg.)

Two Most Common Ways to Watch an Urban Area

A liberating army has two means of quelling all remaining resistance in a recently captured city: (1) run motorized patrols through its various sections and arrest/shoot anyone who still poses a threat; or (2) outpost those sections and try—through nonmartial means—to limit any remaining discontent.

The first has been widely used by U.S. forces in Iraq and Afghanistan, whereas the second is most frequent with Communist armies in Asia and the Iranian Revolutionary Guard Corps (IRGC) in the Middle East. Both options are dangerous and roughly the

373

equivalent from the standpoint of battlefield ethics. That's because the Eastern version often entails more "public persuasion". Still, these two ways of pacifying a built-up area are quite different in intention. While the outposting method strives to prevent any armed confrontation whatsoever, the patrolling routine almost encourages it.

That makes the Chinese/Iranian solution to urban consolidation much more of an advanced-warfare evolution. To more easily access the enemy's most vital strategic assets, it avoids killing his soldiers (3GW). Such assets primarily lie in the economic, political, and psychological/religious arenas (4GW). While a few may be material in nature, most have only to do with how the societal infrastructure will subsequently function. The Eastern model additionally permits more occupier interaction with the general public.

The Occasional Variation to the American Theme

Not all U.S. commanders have been satisfied with the largely ineffectual patrolling routine. Something quite different was tried when Gen. David Petraeus contained al-Sadr's Mahdi Army and other revolutionary elements during the Baghdad Surge of early 2007. The good general may have been following the advice of a civilian small-unit tactics expert by dividing all contested parts of the city into scores (if not hundreds) of tiny TAORs—each with its own contingent of GIs or friendly (often Sunni) militiamen. Through vehicular and pedestrian security checks at all TAOR entry points, he could have kept all opposition factions from launching an offensive operation very far away from their home turf. Then, as Allied forces gradually encroached upon that turf, he may have established more such TAORs at its edge.

The rest of that civilian recommendation was to operate at a scale smaller than even an irregular-army foe would be comfortable. It specified TAORs of only a few square blocks in size, with ways for their few defenders to hide when threatened. One such way might have been an obvious headquarters, and then various escape routes to an obscure safe room.[1] That final destination could have been so thoroughly prepared as to be virtually unassailable (like the room in Figure 25.6).

To what extent that outside advice was followed may never be known, but it's clear that something completely out of the ordinary for the American military was then tried successfully in the capitol of Iraq.

> The 30,000 additional [American] troops they used in a new way to provide more security inside Baghdad and in the rings around Baghdad.[2]
> — John Nagl, U.S. Army advisor to Gen. Petraeus

Such a stratagem would not have endangered as many American lives as the standard Asian version. A single squad of GIs could have handled each separate enclave, and Sunni militiamen would have manned most of them. Plus, the plan would have generated additional thinking on how to keep tiny groups of Americans fairly secure—like maybe stationing them with a local police detachment.

But, so clever a way of consolidating a Third World city had no more chance of being institutionalized by America's military establishment than its engineer had of becoming her next vice president. Its brilliance lay in the extensive compartmentalization of urban terrain, use of both GIs and local militiamen to man all segments, and decentralized control over the entire assemblage. So loose a logistical and communications network would be far too politically risky to be normally tried by the leaders of a "top-down" Western culture.

Purpose of So Widely Spread an Occupier Presence

Whether Communist or Iranian, each of those Asian outpostings of an urban area was accomplished by a single squad of regular military personnel (with at least some training in the nonmartial aspects of 4GW). In effect, that squad was attempting to establish a regime-loyal political cadre within its respective zone of operations. The details of the Iranian model are far more accessible than the other, so it will be discussed first. With guerrilla roots and a dual, "quasi-political" mission, this new Iranian Revolutionary Guard entity was about to change the power balance in the Middle East.

Birth of a New Type of Government Agency

In 1979, Ayatollah Khomeini designated—as "guardians of the Revolution"—the *Pasdaran*.[3] This unusual organization subsequently came to be known as the *Sepah* or IRGC. Its role was to preserve the new Islamic State. "The *Sepah* was [at first] a diverse group of guerrillas who [had] initially fought against the Shah's regime but then joined . . . the successful insurrection of 11-12 February 1979."[4] Subsequently, its role expanded to include the following: (1) dislodging other guerrilla factions and restoring order to the cities; (2) suppressing ethnic uprisings in the countryside; (3) providing internal security to expand the Ayatollah's control; and (4) prosecuting the war with Iraq.[5] Implicit within the first four missions was a very important fifth—the gathering of "human" intelligence.

IRGC Unit's Dual Role Required Public Interaction

Each Guard detachment was concurrently to promote religious doctrine and political stability. That's much the same as a Western military delegation setting a good ethical example and then looking for political allies.

Neither government entity would appear to be an intrusive occupier. Yet, in enough quantity, they could still spot possible flash points and keep any from flaring up into open hostility. Collectively, they also would have considerable influence over public opinion.

> In rural regions . . . [Iranian] Guard bases [are] located in individual small towns. In more urbanized areas . . . a subordinate headquarters, which may even be a storefront or large house, overseas further subdivisions of the city ("Duties, Aims, Policies of the Guard," *Tehran Kayhan,* 14 February 1984, 167). The intention and result is that the Guard achieves maximum penetration of the civilian population *(Defense and Foreign Affairs Handbook,* 1989, 514).[6]
> — *Warriors of Islam,* by Katzman

IRGC Units Delegated a Lot of Authority

In suppressing anti-government sentiment, this local IRGC

contingent was authorized to take almost any corrective action it deemed appropriate. It thus had the chance to experiment with various options and then pick the most effective. Unfortunately, some of that experimentation in the realm of civil-law or religious-doctrine enforcement may have led to moral error.

> There is . . . no evidence that the Guard has ever had to await orders from the civilian leadership to disperse or arrest demonstrators, but rather the Guard appears to have assumed the authority to suppress demonstrations when they occur. . . .
> . . . The Guard . . . has never hesitated to use force against demonstrators, even when those demonstrators were clerics, apparently believing that any opposition to the regime constitutes treason against Islam.[7]
> — *Warriors of Islam,* by Katzman

On a more positive note, each Guard detachment could train their recruits anyway they wanted. This type of leeway had a better effect on the overall security of the country. Many IRGC units may have developed—through trial and error—some fairly sophisticated light-infantry techniques. Shiite Iran has a long tradition of small-unit action. As such, it still encourages initiative at every echelon. In an ancient war with the Indian Army, Persian forces mounted small cannon atop camels. When ready to fire those cannon, they had the camels kneel. Soon, many of their heavily armed adversaries had toppled with their elephants. Two paintings commemorate this lopsided victory at the Sa'ad Abbad Military Museum in Tehran.[8] When asked about them, the government host for foreign visitors extolled the virtues of "ingenuity" in battle.[9] Against a mechanized adversary in either mountains or city, decentralized control and lower-echelon initiative might make a commensurate contribution.

What Makes IRGC Units Different from Communist Ones

Each neighborhood Guard detachment (whether at home or abroad) has intelligence gathering responsibilities. That gives their civilian overseers something that most Western governments now lack—enough "human" intelligence to successfully conduct 4GW overseas. At present, there are IRGC detachments in Syria, Iraq, and Yemen. They are almost certainly being used to outpost urban areas recently captured by the side most friendly to Iran. From deep within these recently liberated neighborhoods, the Guard detachment then does the following: (1) enforce Islamic law; (2) collect intelligence; (3) quell anti-government sentiment; and (4) recruit/train soldiers for a "people's army." Meanwhile, their Communist counterparts have more strictly functioned in a counterguerrilla role.

While Communist countries also have people's armies, their "outposted squads" do not recruit and train civilians for anything but local security duty. Furthermore, they are not deployed throughout the parent nation, though its paramilitary police detachments may vaguely resemble them. Instead, the special military squads are spread throughout any area of a foreign country that has just been invaded or the target of Communist subversion. As such, their mission is more political in nature.

Rare Insights into the Communist Model

As the NVA pushed the regular Khmer Rouge forces out of Cambodia in 1979, they left squad-sized outposts in every village.[10] While such soldiers retained their small arms, they enjoyed no supporting-arms umbrella. Thus, it was their previous training in guerrilla E&E that kept them from piecemeal annihilation. Unfortunately, their precise method for building up a pro-government cadre in each location can now only be surmised. It almost certainly involved more coercion than any Western nation would permit. So, one of the best indicators of its possible extent comes from Africa.

As two Communist armies (one Soviet backed and the other Chinese) strove to "liberate" Rhodesia, here's how the Chinese-sponsored Zimbabwe African National Liberation Army (ZANLA) liked to operate.

> The ZANLA commissars . . . promised the tribesmen, that in return for their support, when ZANLA came to power all the good things belonging to the white men would be theirs. . . .

The commissars would conclude these meetings by giving clear warnings as to what would happen to the villagers collectively, family units or individual persons, should anyone decide to become a "sellout" by reporting their presence to the authorities. . . .

The people would then be invited to tell the commissars who the stooges and puppets of the government were. . . . They were also collectively ordered to indicate the families of serving soldiers and policemen. . . .

Sometimes a man, a wife, a mother or a father, or a whole family would be pushed to the front by the crowd and would be publicly put to death by the commissars. . . . Sometimes the insurgent commissars, wishing to bind the tribesmen to them by a pact of blood, would order the villagers to kill the sellouts or stooges themselves. . . .

Afterwards . . . the commissars would select and nominate various members of the population . . . to act as contact men and "policemen."

The contact men and policemen played a vital role in the insurgent network and a chain of these men was gradually created until they stretched from inside Mozambique to the farthermost reaches of the operational area. . . .

By order of the insurgents, it became and was the duty of every person in the Tribal Trust Land concerned to pass every scrap of information relating to the security forces to the local contact man. . . .

In addition to collating intelligence, the contact men were responsible for the selection of bases and the collection and provision of food for the insurgents. They were also responsible for the transmission of letters and message between detachments and sections, and arranging and setting up security procedures for meetings between various groups. . . .

The policemen worked with and under the contact men and were responsible for maintaining the insurgents' system of law and order. They could not, however, discipline or punish anyone themselves. Any suspected sellout . . . would be taken by them to the local insurgent leader.

The contact men and policemen were later supplemented, as the war progressed, by the *mujiba* system. . . .

Although too young to fight they [the children] could still
act as ears and eyes, or as messengers or go-betweens with
the civil population. . . .
And so, by these methods, Mao Tse Tung's dictum that to
be successful, a guerrilla must move through the population
as a fish does through water, was satisfied by ZANLA.[11]
— *Pamwe Chete,* by Reid-Daly

Then, after the Chinese-backed army had persevered over its
Soviet opponent in Rhodesia, here's how it managed to consolidate
its holdings at election time.

Some 7,000 guerrillas had gone to ground in the tribal
areas on the orders of ZANLA commander, Rex Nhongo.
He told them to ignore the cease-fire, hide their weapons,
and persuade the people to vote for ZANU P/F (Zimbabwe
African National Union Patriotic Front) (Verrier, *The Road
to Zimbabwe,* 86). . . .
When ZANLA first infiltrated its political commissars
into the Rhodesian tribal areas in 1972, they embraced
the . . . methods of the [communist] Orient to politicise the
tribesmen. On entering villages, they selected people for
execution. . . . Their objective was to rid communities of
their leadership and destroy the *bourgeois.*
Executions were conducted in an exemplary [local]
fashion. . . . ZANLA's reign of terror has had few parallels
in recent African history.
Not surprisingly, it took little persuasion to get villagers
to set up informer networks, report on the activities of the
security forces, feed and look after incoming guerrillas, and
spy and report on [unseemly] reports of their fellows. . . .
After Lancaster House [the cease-fire conference], . . .
[ZANLA] guerrillas were able to live openly amongst the
villagers without fear of attack by the Security Forces. . . .
[T]he unsophisticated tribesmen took this as a signal the
guerrillas had "won." . . .
So when ZANLA guerrillas insisted that ZANU P/F
would win the independence election and announced that
their first task afterwards would be to open the ballot boxes
and identify those who had voted against them with the help

of a special machine imported from Romania, the villagers believed them. They also accepted that those who voted against ZANU P/F would afterwards be put up against walls by ZANLA and shot (Sutton-Price *[sic], Zimbabwe,* 63).

. . . Britain's quaint idea of stationing British bobbies in uniform at polling stations to ensure fair play, was at the least naive. . . .

An admission that ZANU P/F used its notorious political commissars to intimidate the indigenous people into voting for them came during Granada Television's *End of Empire* series when Edison Zvobgo said: ". . . [W]e had a very large army left (outside the assembly points), who remained as political commissars . . . simply to ensure that we would win the election (Flower, *Serving Secretly,* 255-256)." . . .

So much for the democratic process, African style.[12]

— Peter Stiff, renown South African historian

For GI Squads to Outpost Urban Parts of an Alien Land

Obviously, none of the immoral coercion of the Chinese or Iranian models would be appropriate for any American version of the same strategy. And, as was implicitly the case in Vietnam, any moral excess by host country authorities would have to be immediately reported up the U.S. chain of command.

Next would come the biggest stumbling block—force protection. The isolated squads worked well for the Communists and Iranians because all outpost participants had undergone either formal or on-the-job guerrilla training. This allowed them quickly to disappear when annihilation threatened. But American squads could still accomplish a similar mission as long as they put some initial thought into how best to hide if necessary. After all, there has already been a very successful precedent for this type of thing—namely, the U.S. Marine CAP initiative in Vietnam. No CAP village ever permanently reverted to Viet Cong control, and a member of at least one overrun CAP compound now freely admits to having hidden before retaking his tiny base.[13]

Additionally, no American squad would as actively try to create a friendly political cadre. Its only visible role would be providing a host government presence. A beleaguered society often needs some counterbalance to the Islamist, Maoist, or drug commissars who frequently reside in its villages and neighborhoods. Local officials are too often corrupt, so a reasonable alternative would be a few visiting GIs. They could at first mimic some of the commissar's least objectionable protection ploys. Then, just by buying all supplies locally, they could easily enter into the main stream of everyday life. Before long, they would locate the prospective nucleus of a pro-regime faction.

To come anywhere close to what the Iranian version of 4th-Generation counterinsurgency achieved, each tiny U.S. contingent would have to do all of the following: (1) be a part of the local security establishment; (2) live off the local economy; (3) be proficient at UW; (4) provide basic services; (5) have its own intelligence and community watch networks; and (6) be able to train local militiamen for any contingency. Such a broad undertaking would be far too ambitious for the GIs at first. But, such a list offers ways for them later to expand.

How They Would Defend Themselves

Such outposting Yanks could have no on-call artillery concentrations or relief force. If too large an enemy force came after them, they and any collocated militia would have to hide locally or exfiltrate the cordon. While such actions may seem "unmanly" to the average American, they are perfectly legitimate forms of tactical withdrawal. Both are heavily practiced by Eastern soldiers. Whatever the official defender of another nation can do successfully, so can a GI. Still, without sophisticated early warning, he and his buddies would not know when to disappear.

In any overseas setting, a squad of visiting Yanks cannot hope to enjoy the societal acceptance of a more culturally harmonious group. Yet, for early warning, they must still depend on the good will of the local population. Even the highly militant Muslims of the Pakistani/Afghan border region have a heritage of "being hospitable to strangers." Similar traditions exist throughout most of the world, providing the foreign visitors are few in number and well behaved.[14] So all American contingents must act like guests in a friendly neighborhood. To do so, all members of the squad must be strongly committed to minimal force, interrogation etiquette, and local customs regarding women. Additionally, no cruelty by host nation personnel would go unreported up the U.S. chain of command.

Before long, members of the American contingent would start to receive "offhanded" hints from local residents regarding possible threats or how better to proceed with their mission. Then, over time, the GIs' own intelligence-gathering and community watch network (one beyond the purview of local authorities) would begin to function. To expedite this process, squad members could contribute to the local economy by hiring guides or tutors on how to do certain things. It is in this more humanistic and peace-loving way that one best accomplishes the "monitoring" of contested territory in a modern 4GW environment.

The U.S. Squad's New (Yet Still Logical) Role

The Allied presence would not be to kill anybody or lure local miscreants into an act of aggression, but unobtrusively to provide a host government influence. Just as the U.S. Special Forces team did in the Afghan village in Chapter 23, it would simply interact with the founding fathers, and not try to change (or arrest) any of them. Its underlying mission would, of course, be to monitor the extent of anti-regime activity.

For early leads, most police investigators depend on civilian informants. Some of those informants do what they do as a public service, but most are being paid or working off a legalistic favor. These outposting Yanks will require similar *confidantes* in the community to ascertain local-commissar intentions. They will also need lookouts, should any of those intentions not be discovered in advance.

A lookout is much easier to recruit than an informant. The lookout's role is defensive, so less risky. Still, he may be subjected to bribes, threats, or even death prior to an enemy attack. Some may be stationed far enough from the GI headquarters to collect other types of intelligence. Needless to say, all lookouts must be carefully hidden. It is from *Sepah*, *Hezbollah*, and Asian Communist procedure that one most easily learns how to obscure them from view in a semi-active war zone. For a further discussion of Islamist and Communist security elements like street corner sentinels, inside-of-building watchers, secret-station occupiers, roving sentries, and public-intelligence harvesters, see Chapter 16 of *Tequila Junction.*

Nothing Must Be Altered in the Neighborhoods

The success of any future U.S. "liberation" effort will largely depend on a minimal footprint. That means as few aerial assassinations, resupply visits, commanding-officer tours, and public dedication ceremonies as possible.

Throughout the Eastern world, the principal axiom of urban security is not to alter the appearance of any area to be defended. Among other things, there must be hidden lookouts to discretely sound the alarm.

Now Possible Is Constant Vigilance at Every Location

Aerial electronic surveillance will locate unusual activity and intercept suspicious communications, but it can't positively identify all participants, their motives, or their movement plans. As a result, it offers a poor means of monitoring the pacification of any built-up area. Nor is it the best way to limit collateral damage from drone strikes against militant leaders. In a struggle for the hearts and minds of a population, one can more productively act on what a local contingent of GIs can sense or otherwise determine. That the American military has traditionally put such a low priority this type of information may help to explain why it has had so much trouble defeating guerrillas. One of the biggest strengths of the CAP concept in Vietnam was that it facilitated the collection of local intelligence.

The most useful local intelligence doesn't come from detainees. It comes from paid informants and the civilian population as a whole. As a detainee's level of discomfort grows, so will the extent of his imagination. That is the least blatant of all 4GW reasons to treat him humanely. The most blatant is that he and his extended circle of family members and friends will someday be voters who could quickly reverse any amount of Allied success on the local battlefield.

Nor will drones provide enough surveillance along the rural approaches to a city. There, only well-positioned pockets of "human intelligence" will be able to spot the more sophisticated forms of enemy infiltration.

33 COUNTRYSIDE CANNOT BE PACIFIED BY DRONE

- Do cameras stop crime or just record its occurrence?
- Can drones effectively watch every gully and treeline?

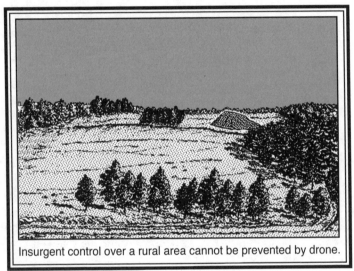
Insurgent control over a rural area cannot be prevented by drone.

(Sources: FMFM 6-4 [1978], p. 356; FM 90-3 [1977], p. 4-70.)

History of U.S. Pilotless Planes

Since Operation Desert Storm in 1995, America has launched Tomahawk cruise missiles against militant elements in Iraq (1618), Serbia/Montenegro (218), Libya (112), Afghanistan (110), Syria (106), Bosnia (13), Sudan (13), Yemen (7), and Somalia (2).[1] Then, around 2004,[2] Predator and Reaper drones started to do more than just reconnoiter enemy positions. Their ordnance is known to have hit targets in Iraq, Yemen, Somalia, Afghanistan, and the Federally Administered Tribal Areas (FATA) of Pakistan.[3] During the Baghdad Surge, Predator-fired Hellfire missiles were even sent against particularly lucrative targets in al-Sadr neighborhoods.[4] Not surprisingly, many of the civilian residents in such areas objected.

> [M]any of the leading candidates in the May [2013 Pakistan] election ran anti-drone campaigns, including winner Nawaz Sharif. Pakistanis say their national sovereignty has been compromised; they feel emasculated in their inability to stop the intrusion.[5]
> — *Christian Science Monitor,* May 2013

4GW Allows For Very Little Collateral Damage

There's no sense in trying now to establish how many civilians may have been killed in those many drone strikes. Washington's estimate is one tenth of some independent versions.[6] But against a society in which any noncombatant death can lead to an extrafamily or tribal—if not multigenerational—quest for vengeance, one errant strike is too many. The problem, of course, is not in the missiles' accuracy, but in the quality of their preliminary targeting information. The Pentagon has preferred electronic intelligence over the human variety for many years. Not only are there no more American "boots on the ground" in many locations, but no dependable informants or spies either. Aerial reconnaissance will rarely determine the intentions of suspected terrorists. Nor will the assassination of top-level leaders to a "bottom-up" organization generally lead to its demise. So, while drones may risk fewer American lives, they have not been greatly helping any current U.S. war effort. In at least one, they have proven counterproductive. A few "personalized" episodes from Pakistan should be sufficient to make the point.

South Waziristan's *TTP* (*Tehrik-i-Taliban Pakistan* or "Pakistani Taliban") has been drawing most of the Pakistani Army's offensive wrath for many years. In January 2011, a Shiite procession in Lahore was hit by a 13-year-old suicide bomber. *TTP* later told *Agence France Presse* that the "bombing [was] in retaliation for drone strikes and military operations in tribal areas." Then, according to the BBC (British Broadcasting Co.), *Fedayeen-e-Islam* (a *TTP* wing) took credit for the bombing.[7] The *Fedayeen-e-Islam* (or

Fedayeen-al-Islam) also claims to have carried out the devastating suicide attack against Islamabad's ritzy Marriott Hotel in September 2008.[8] So, its reasons for that atrocity were probably similar.

All the while, it has been the Haqqani Network that has been controlling most of the drug trade in Northern Pakistan. This is the same outfit responsible for the highest visibility commando raids on Kabul. Having targeted the elder Haqqani with drone-fired missiles since October 2008, the U.S. military and CIA then aimed a veritable barrage at him in December 2009. In September of the following year, another 21 drone missiles were launched against Haqqani targets.[9] Those ongoing strikes may not have pleased the faction within Pakistan's government that has come to depend on the Haqqani Network for political and financial support. When a U.S. helicopter mistakenly fired on a Pakistani border post in Kurram Agency in September 2010, Pakistan closed the Torkham (Khyber Pass) border crossing to NATO supply vehicles. This, in turn, sparked an all-out assault by angry militants on the gasoline tankers coming up from Karachi. The connection between the drones and Afghanistan's fuel supply would soon become evident.

Even the Pakistani Taliban have since admitted that the fuel truck attacks had more to do with the latest barrage of drone missiles than with the helicopter incident.

> A spokesman for the Pakistani Taliban, Azzam *[sic]* Tariq, told CNN [Cable News Network] that . . . the attacks were retaliation for U.S. drone strikes in Pakistan. . . .
> September saw 21 drone strikes in Pakistan, a record number, with three more strikes occurring so far in October, reports Reuters.[10]
> — *Christian Science Monitor,* 5 October 2010

In mid-October 2010, two more gas trucks were attacked by tribal factions inside Pakistan on their way to the Khyber Pass. On 11 November, an additional pair were torched *en route* to the Chaman crossing into Afghanistan. Three days later, 12 refuelers were set ablaze in Afghanistan's Nangarhar Province, to the east of Kabul. Afghan militants then promised to keep hitting NATO-bound fuel trucks until there was an end to the drone missile attacks against their tribal areas (many of which stretched well into Pakistan).[11]

Other Dangers of Excess Drone Activity

Too much reconnaissance by drone can also be risky. The following example comes from Southern Lebanon many years before. It involves an Israeli patrol of elite special operators that had likely been spotted coming ashore by radar, and then picked up a *Hezbollah* "tail." At some point, that tail was able to signal ahead where the patrol would be crossing a main road. What happened next was unexpected.

> For 10 days, . . . the MK drone—a pilotless reconnaissance plane—had flown over the fields and orange groves at the northern end of Insariyeh [in the South of Lebanon]. Ghalib Farhat had seen the drones clearly from his one-story house on the edge of the village. Their presence had

Figure 33.1: Overhead Surveillance Had Doomed the Commandos
(Source: U.S. Air Force Clipart Library [www.usafns.com/art.shtml], image designator "1-07aa.tif.")

puzzled him. Insariyeh was far from "Israel's" occupation zone and there was little that could interest the "Israelis" in the village.

The naval commandos silently emerged from the water onto a rocky beach. . . . The team had to sneak across the road and pass through a gate in a 3-meter-high concrete wall running along the east side of the highway to reach the cover of banana plantations and orange groves before continuing up the hill to Insariyeh. . . . Under the cover of a banana plantation, the team began the hard uphill march to the cliff-top village. . . .

The "Israeli" [commando] team approached the lane between Insariyeh and Loubieh cautiously. Kurakin, the radio operator and one other soldier led the rest of the team by a few meters. As they reached the gate near the lane, Kurakin motioned them to halt. He and his two companions darted across the road and crouched beside a pile of garbage. Kurakin turned to order the other commandos forward. As he did so, a massive explosion engulfed the commandos, killing several of them instantly. Barely having time to recover from the shock of the blast, the team was hit by a second bomb which exploded in a huge bubble of orange flames with hundreds of steel ball bearings ripping through the "Israeli" unit. Kurakin raced back across the road to help the survivors. Then the machineguns opened up from the orange grove to the north. A bullet struck Kurakin in the head, killing him instantly. . . .

An "Israeli" Army commission of inquiry concluded that the commandos were the victims of a chance guerrilla ambush. . . . *Hezbollah* has maintained [virtual] silence over the affair. . . . Three years after the raid . . . , *Hezbollah*'s southern commander, Sheikh Nabil Qaouk, is still reluctant to reveal the truth behind the battle. "It's still too early to tell the secrets of Insariyeh. The "Israelis" know that *Hezbollah* was aware of the operation but they don't know how. But I will say that our presence there was not a coincidence," Qaouk told The Daily Star. . . .

. . . Sayyed Hassan Nasrallah . . . perhaps gave the most accurate account of the . . . the Insariyeh battle. . . . He said groups of fighters armed with roadside bombs had

deployed throughout the South . . . in anticipation of further
commando raids.[12]
— *The Daily Star* (Lebanon), 9 June 2000

A high-level Israeli probe later determined that there had been
no intelligence leak.[13] The commandos would have been clearly
visible on radar coming ashore. Then, they had probably picked
up an accomplished stalker at the hole in the wall near the beach.
After watching them enter the natural lane running between orange
grove and windbreak, that stalker had only to relay their route to
a hilltop command post by a blinking infrared light (or some other
nonelectronic means). By the time the commandos reached the
intersecting road, a roving claymore team could have been there
waiting for them. Or, several claymore clusters may have been set
up along that road at probable crossing points. When the hilltop
observer saw black shapes crossing the whitish-appearing road,
he may have remotely detonated the nearest cluster and then told
his long-range machinegunner to fire at the same spot. Whatever
the case, the rest is history. The loss of that entire squad of special
operators so shook Tel Aviv's confidence in its own Armed Forces
that no Israeli military personnel were subsequently allowed into
South Lebanon after May 2000. (See Map 33.1.)

Ground Outposting of Every Rural Area Still Necessary

If overflying an area can't make it safe, then there is one other option. It must be thoroughly garrisoned with tiny elements.
While such a thing may seem overly dangerous to leaders steeped
in the tradition of electronic surveillance and overwhelming firepower, light-infantry experts could easily do it. Anytime the annihilation of one of those elements seemed imminent, it would be
well-enough prepared to simply disappear. Asian army outposts
have been dong this kind of thing for centuries. Not fighting is
quite often the most strategically useful response.

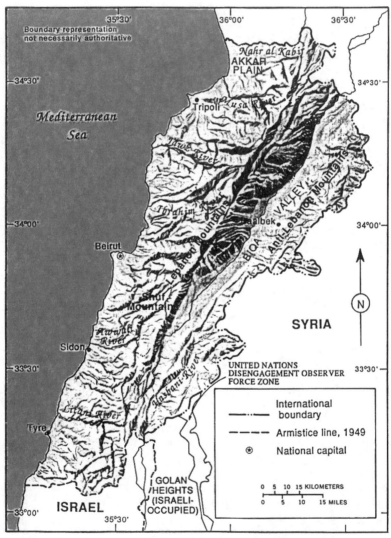

Map 33.1: Lebanon Would Reveal Several Warfare Lessons

PART TWELVE

ONLY FIGHTING WHEN STRATEGICALLY HELPFUL

"TO SUBDUE THE ENEMY WITHOUT FIGHTING IS THE ACME OF SKILL."
— SUN TZU

(Source: Attributed to Sun Tzu.)

34 THE IMPLICIT PART OF EVERY MISSION

- What is the commander's usual "intent" in modern war?
- Can accidental killing forestall a lasting peace?

Assumed in every "frag order" is the protection of noncombatants.

(Source: "Capture at Ar Ramadi," by Don Stivers, possible ©, from this url: http://www.nationalguard.mil/resources/photo_gallery/heritage/hires/arramadi.jpg.)

The Flip Side of the Coin

If police work—and warfare in general—is about the restoration of law and order to a community, why is it ever allowed to become an outlet for temperamental behavior? No well-seasoned U.S. infantryman has so far said that getting angry helped him to do his job. That's the mistaken conclusion of armchair leaders who want more easily to lead him into harm's way. If the truth be known, most short-range combat is quite surgical in nature, with the only active emotion being an aversion to unacceptable behavior.

397

Within this personal aversion may lie the crux of the problem for a formerly "attrition-based" U.S. military. Most of America's young service personnel still believe that more proficiently killing enemy soldiers constitutes optimal performance of duty. In a modern, low-intensity, 4GW kind of war, it doesn't. Even during some of America's most intense episodes of "total war," it didn't. The WWII Marines who failed to contract "combat fatigue" after fighting for weeks at the nearly impregnable north end of Okinawa's Shuri Line likely did so out of self-discipline and mutual regard.[1] Such perseverance did not result from revenge. In fact, many would later admit to holding no animosity toward their former adversaries. Like them, most Japanese soldiers had known little about politics, not personally committed any atrocities, and wanted only to do their patriotic duty.

Might this inescapable paradox—that wartime killing is not always productive—be the way to finally produce a U.S. military that can decisively win a 4GW conflict? Its acknowledgment might also help any police department now struggling with the overreaction by certain officers to suspects not complying with all instructions. In many cases, such an officer should be looking for employment elsewhere. He or she lacks the proper temperament to be the guardian of an understandably imperfect (and sometimes hard-of-hearing) society. Nor is every American infantryman well suited for the job at hand. But, in both cases, headquarters must clearly define to all frontline personnel when lethal force will be tolerated.

If Peace Is Ultimately the Mission

Not since the Marine Raiders of WWII and later outfits of U.S. Army Rangers has this county had any truly light infantrymen. All modern-day American grunts are of the heavy or "line" variety. That means they are most proficient at operating their equipment/weapons and following orders.

While so simplistic a role makes them easier to lead, it has its drawbacks. One is being so traditionally undertrained from a tactical standpoint as to get easily hurt in combat without any real chance at retribution. All the recent emphasis on "Force Protection" doesn't help. Force Protection is just another term for fighting defensively. So doing can sometimes help (like when Allied invaders used to welcome a nearly suicidal *banzai* counterattack in the Pacific), but ordinarily it does very little to win a war. Wars are mostly decided through offensive action. Consistently doing well while on the attack takes well-trained, self-assured, and opportunistic nonrates in the forward elements. Privates that skilled are seldom the product of too much upper-level resistance to their being used in tiny, semi-autonomous groups.

Sadly, this lack of trust in bottom-echelon personnel can result in more than just excess casualties. The still healthy buddies of each GI who gets hurt by the enemy will be henceforth looking for "payback." That in turn results in unnecessary enemy deaths. Such things may temporarily assuage a personal quest for revenge, but they also erode unit resolve.

While unintentionally bequeathed to U.S. enlisted personnel, such dilemmas still undermine the Pentagon's ethical foundation. In this age of 4GW, whoever can capture the moral high ground is usually the long-term victor. This creates a challenge for all military establishments that are too heavily steeped in their own tradition. If long-standing procedures and habits no longer work, they must be discarded.

"Frag Orders" Provide Only General Guidance

Frag orders are a valuable part of modern combat because they help to develop momentum. Still, the recipient of a frag order must be just as careful not to read anything illegal into his abbreviated instructions as to ignore the commander's underlying aims. A "not-so-good" example of the first may have occurred during the My Lai Massacre in Vietnam. There, "a motivational summons" may have been misinterpreted to mean authority to exercise unlimited force against not only enemy combatants, but also any "sympathizers" in the way. The unfortunate result was an explicit occasion of group excess.

Examples of the second are harder to find. They would depend on the personality of each commander, and the extent to which he had shared his battlefield "intent" with the frontline troops. Most commanders would want to seize all contested ground without any unseemly behavior by subordinates.

Now That 4GW Is Better Understood

It was Attrition Warfare that had previously put too much pressure on U.S. commanders to produce enough enemy bodies to justify their tactical decisions. Now that Maneuver Warfare has become the U.S. Marines' new doctrine, those commanders should be more interested in enemy logistics. In effect, numbers of supply caches found, food sources destroyed, and weapons captured might become the new measures of success. As for the enemy combatants themselves, their intelligence value would also override any supposed need to "permanently remove" them from the proceedings. In other words, Maneuver Warfare ambush patrols could now shoot low and then wait until dawn to search the area. That way, they could more safely capture opposition materiel and "medevac" possible informants.

The most elusive part of MW methodology has been attempting to lower the opponent's resolve. Causing him to run out of ammunition has worked pretty well in the past, but killing too many of his buddies might have the opposite effect. And killing his mother by accident could create a multi-generational blood feud. That makes the modern soldier's mission more like that of a practicing Christian. Both are attempting to limit the extent of amoral activity.

Only among those untested in combat is "shock and awe" or "fire and fury" a viable wartime strategy. Much more promising from a modern 4GW standpoint would be "turning every adversary into a friend." Where that could not be accomplished, the goal becomes preventing (as gently as possible) all suspected criminals from any more deviant behavior. As long as all martial initiatives were continually monitored for nonmartial side effects, there would be no problem. It is in the former belief that the foe must be thoroughly eliminated, that peace becomes jeopardized.

"Whatever is hurtful to you, do not do to any other person."[2]
— Mosaic Law

The Unhappy Alternative

The alternative, of course, to the above suggestion is perpetual warfare. There are too many divisive influences in today's world

400

to conduct U.S. foreign policy in any way other than Christian. Any American arms manufacturer or military organization that believes another war useful must call to mind the ultimate cost. Higher profits and more combat experience are not necessarily in their best interests. Their mutual goal should now be assuaging all warring parties before trans-generational animosities create a lasting divide. All manufacturers should therefore be trying to develop nonfatal weaponry, while the U.S. Army and Marine Corps do more experimenting at the company level with less-lethal (more surprise-oriented) tactics.

Any individual U.S. service member who would also welcome another war as a way of proving their bravery is as misguided as the police officer who uses daily danger as an excuse for outward aggression. Implicit in the average military and law enforcement mission is doing as little as possible to jeopardize the ultimate tranquility of the community.

Only Fight for What Is Strategically Important

Obviously, every American GI will fight when so ordered. But, it is during those chance or optional encounters with the enemy that he or she can purposely avoid combat that is irreconcilably lethal.

The most productive kind of warfighting is that which helps to achieve a lasting peace. Killing all enemy soldiers is seldom possible. Nor is making contact with the enemy always appropriate. Most U.S. wartime efforts should now focus on destroying enemy supplies and equipment.

35 WHAT'S STRATEGICALLY VITAL TO U.S. FOES

- Do all wartime adversaries have the same needs?
- What do the armies of Communist Asia mostly rely upon?

Communist and Islamist rebels need only a rich and "deliberate" foe.

(Source: FM 90-5 [1982], p. 5-4.)

Accepting the New Reality

America harbors no "culture of death," nor do her military and police always kill someone. Instead, both strive to limit their use of overwhelming force. Yet, around 24 August 2017, the new U.S. Commander in Chief (presumably on the advice of his generals) announced that America's strategy for Afghanistan would be not to rebuild another nation in her image, but only to kill terrorists.[1] While ostensibly less difficult than promoting democracy, the new plan had two problems. It implied that the U.S. would no longer try to wage 4GW against 4GW-adept foes, and that just killing rebels

403

would be of help to a beleaguered regime. The CIA and Pentagon have already "sent to paradise" any number of extremist leaders since 9/11, yet the world seems no more secure as a result. Could it be that the opposition's personnel (of any rank) are too easy to replace to constitute a strategic asset? If that were true, then what part of its expansionary apparatus should the Pentagon be going after?

One of the world's biggest money-makers is the trade in illegal narcotics. All war machines need funding. Perhaps, DoD should be doing more to curtail the involvement by this nation's various foes in drug trafficking. Some of the highest visibility attacks on Kabul have come from the region's largest heroin cartel (the Haqqani Network). So, there's more than enough correlation between militancy and opiates to justify an economic initiative by the U.S. military.

A quick look at America's other enemies may reveal the same overemphasis on manpower removal while drug involvement continues to fund their armed forces or undermine the U.S. homeland.

This Country's Current Adversaries?

The opponent getting most of the attention in Washington these days is ISIS. Yet, still viable or partly amalgamated by ISIS is *al-Qaeda,* despite a 16 year (largely drone) effort to assassinate its highest leaders. Then, there is a wide assortment of ISIS and *al-Qaeda* affiliates. Among the most destructive ISIS-connected groups in Africa are: (1) *al Shabaab* in Somalia; (2) *Boko Haram* in Nigeria; (3) *Ansar al-Sharia Libya*; (4) *Ansar al-Sharia* in Tunisia; and (5) *Ansar Beit al Maqdis* in Egypt. African sects likely still linked to *al-Qaeda* include: (1) *al Gamaat al-Islamiyya* in Egypt; and (2) Eritrean Islamic Jihad.[2] Of course, many additional groups from all over the world also claim ties with either ISIS or *al-Qaeda.*

Hard at work in the Middle East is not only Sunni-oriented ISIS, but also the Shiite-led Iranian Revolutionary Guard Corps (IRGC) and its associated proxies. The most proficient and active of these proxies is Lebanese *Hezbollah.* Of important note, insurgent factions of almost every description follow Mao's guerrilla model.

Then, there is the Democratic People's Republic of Korea (DPRK)—a country still technically at war with the U.S. China—North Korea's 1950's invasion partner—has retained the same ruling party. So, its love for America may also be less than officially acknowledged. Anywhere within the South China Sea, the U.S. Navy would certainly deem any People's Republic of China (PRC) ship or plane a potential threat. After Russia's annexation of an entire Ukrainian region in 2014, its army also looms as a possible opponent.

So, America's current array of ground combat adversaries runs the gamut from loosely structured Muslim militias to well-equipped Eastern armies. But, there is one thing that they almost all enjoy—more advanced squad assault-and-defense techniques than the U.S. military. That's because the Pentagon's focus on costly firepower over the years has effectively limited its access to cost-free tactical proficiency.

To What Extent Those Enemies Need Wartime Materiel

The U.S. "meat grinder" got defeated on the ground in Vietnam by an army that needed no tanks, no aircraft, and very little artillery. With units of any size able to shift quickly between Positional, Maoist Mobile, and Guerrilla Warfare,[3] it could steal most of what it needed from an oversupplied foe. ISIS has followed much the same model.

The NVA in Vietnam came to rely on more food, medical supplies, special ordnance, and well-trained recruits coming down the Ho Chi Minh Trail. So far, ISIS has been employing tactics that only require the wherewithal it can extract from those it fights. While the way to finally defeat ISIS may lie in the nonmartial arena of psychology/religion, any source of its economic solvency should still be targeted. That includes more than just oil refineries.

Are Such Foes More Affected by Killing or Drug Removal?

All Asian nations are quite populous. So, no amount of killing will limit their wartime activity. Meanwhile, America continues to be the world's largest market for illicit narcotics. That's why 4GW-adept Communist and Salafist enemies often work together to destabilize her through a surge in habit-forming drugs. This surge, in turn, raises the overall rate of U.S. crime and violence—making Washington much less likely to counter expansionary activity overseas.

While no opposition countries might solely depend on drug trafficking to fund their armies, those armies may still dabble in it themselves to augment their minimal budgets. China provides the best example. In 1998, there were 10,000-15,000 PLA-owned businesses. After conceding the criminal involvement of PLA and PAP (People's Armed Police) companies, Chinese President Jiang Zemin ordered both to cease all "commercial activities" on 22 July 1998.[4] Unfortunately, all of his wishes would not be subsequently obeyed.[5]

Additionally, the PRC and former Soviet Union have been furthering their "foreign policies" for decades through home-based criminal syndicates.

> There is a well-documented history of both Russian and Chinese organized crime organizations working as tools of their governments.[6]
> — *American Foreign Policy Council Report,* 1999

It's not likely that this seditious cooperation has ended since 1999.

> [China is still] the major trans-shipment point for heroin produced in the Golden Triangle . . . [and] source country for methamphetamine and heroin chemical precursors.[7]
> — *CIA World Factbook,* August 2017

Within the Communist Camp

Of note, the hermit state of North Korea has now become heavily dependent on narcotics trafficking to bolster its sputtering Marxist economy. In fact, it has been dealing openly with the Hong Kong syndicates.[8] The U.S. State Department cites "credible reports of North Korean boats . . . transporting heroin and uniformed North Korean personnel transferring drugs from North Korean vessels to traffickers' boats."[9]

Among the Muslim Foes

In the Islamic World, at least two of Islamabad's federal agencies have openly augmented their budgets through narcotics involvement. During the Soviet-Afghan War, much of the Afghan-grown opium was being carried to Karachi by a Pakistani-Army-run trucking company.[10] Since then, that nation's ISI (Interservice Intelligence) has been partially funded through drug route protection.[11] One of Afghanistan's biggest smuggling conduits dips down from Helmand into Pakistan's Baluchistan Province before heading for Iran and eventually Turkey. Near the end of the Soviet occupation, Stinger-protected convoys regularly ran the final stages of this passage under the joint auspices of rogue Pakistani-government elements and IRGC.[12]

The nonstate "actors" of any insurgency are almost always cash strapped. That's why so many embrace some form of illegal funding. At present, ISIS mostly prefers the income from captured oil facilities, but as a criminally oriented entity, it could at any time shift from hostage ransoming to drug trafficking. Both *al-Qaeda* and the Taliban have already profited from the worldwide demand for drugs.

> Islam forbids the use of opium . . . but the [Afghan] militants now justify the drug production by saying it's not for domestic consumption but rather to sell abroad as part of a holy war against the West.[13]
> — McClatchy News Service, 10 May 2009

So too has Shiite Lebanese *Hezbollah* long depended on the dollars it can raise from some involvement with narcotics smuggling.

> In the mid-1980's, the *Hezbollah's* use of the illicit drug trade as a funding source and a weapon against the West was sanctioned by an official *fatwa* (religious edict) issued by *Hezbollah*.[14]
> — *Funding Evil,* by Ehrenfield

Of late, *Hezbollah* has shifted much of this money-making effort to the protection of Colombian cocaine as it is transported up from Venezuela to West Africa on its way to Europe.[15] During the operation of this conduit, it has cooperated closely with the now Maoist-oriented FARC (*Fuerzas Armadas Revolucionarias de Colombia*).

> *Hezbollah* uses these operations [in South America] to generate millions of dollars to finance *Hezbollah* operations in Lebanon and other areas of the world.[16]
> — *Washington Times,* 27 March 2009

Needless to say, all of America's above-named adversaries have been forced to learn how to survive under the constant threat of a U.S. technological advantage. That survival has largely depended on an age-old way of fighting that requires little, if any, gadgetry. Through covert light-infantry maneuvers, this warfare style instead generates enough surprise to compensate for its lack of firepower and technology.

Light-Infantry Experts Make a Dangerous Foe

A proven way of war cannot be undermined by destroying its followers. So, while the highly numerous Eastern infantryman may be occasionally "attrited," his low-ranking comrades can still inflict great damage on a Western foe.

Small-unit action has long been the key to winning lengthy conflicts. It is even more important now in the low-intensity 4GW environment of the 21st Century. Adequately to consolidate a vast region "captured," every voting facility within it must be kept open to the public. That takes a military detachment nearby. Safely to perform this role, that detachment must be well versed in the UW art of hiding.

Truly light infantrymen don't just march long distances with lighter loads. Though far from superhuman, they are more tactically skilled, initiative-driven, and self-sufficient in tiny contingents than their "line" counterparts. In fact, troops skilled at Maneuver Warfare are able to: (1) silently sneak a small contingent into almost any U.S. base at night; (2) with a single squad penetrate a U.S. defensive line without most watchstanders realizing they are under ground assault; and (3) create an almost impenetrable defense matrix from squad-sized strongpoints.

While on patrol, a single light-infantry squad can: (1) ambush an enemy force of any size without that force realizing it has been ambushed; (2) handle an adversary of much greater size during a chance encounter; and (3) seek out and disrupt a big enemy force about to attack its parent unit.

In urban warfare, the same squad can: (1) clear one side of a city street more quickly than the foe thinks possible; and (2) successfully defend a small city block from successive fall-back positions.

Therefore, it's small wonder that America's military advisors around the world have been realizing only limited success of late. In essence, standoff bombardment has little effect on a widely dispersed and loosely controlled foe. Controlling him takes tiny ground elements with enough tactical ability to operate beyond any firepower umbrella. There aren't now, nor will their ever be, enough U.S. Special Operations Command (SOCOM) teams to augment local police and militia detachments throughout several developing countries at once. That will require the help of hundreds of semi-autonomous regular infantry squads with some UW training.

North Korea Has Huge Reservoir of Such Troops

North Korea has long sported a "Light-Infantry Training Guidance Bureau." Its 125,000 commando members have—as their secondary mission—to share their advanced light-infantry expertise with all regular North Korean "ground pounders" (of which there are almost a million).[17]

It was once thought that all students of this Bureau's commando school were required to sneak—by themselves—far into South Korean territory just to graduate. If enough were now to match that feat, they could severely jeopardize the opposition's defenses. Imagine 40 or so in South Korean uniform who simply showed up some morning at the center of every Allied base within 100 miles of the border.

Of particular note, North Korean infiltrators enjoy a long heritage of not only scaling obstacles, but also burrowing beneath them. "Ordinarily the primary barrier fence was climbed over or tunneled under."[18]

Hermit Kingdom Still Has a Vast Tunnel Network

Though large North Korean army units might operate fairly well with what they could seize south of the border, they would still need some way to reach South Korea safely. And thus arises the question of how many tunnels remain undetected beneath the DMZ.

To stop further U.S. incursions above the 38th parallel toward the end of the Korean War, the Chinese dug 1250 kilometers of tunnels.[19] These tunnels provided ample opportunity for spoiler attacks. In that way, they prevented a repeat performance of the impenetrable U.S. phalanxes on Operations Killer and Ripper. Some of those Communist attacks occurred at the very front of, or just behind, Allied lines.

The Chinese liked to construct tunnels and caves at launching-attack points.[20]

The Chinese would send out small teams to dominate no-man's land, take over exposed outposts, and mine daytime outposts abandoned at night, create disturbances in enemy rear. They would also keep up continuous sniping.[21]
— *Mao's Generals Remember Korea*

Other assaults unexpectedly came from beneath captured Chinese bastions.

Whether we can defend our positions is a question that was resolved last year. The solution was to hide in grottos *[sic]*. We dug out a two-level fortification. . . . Once the enemy entered the surface positions, we started counterattacks and inflicted heavy casualties on them [from below]. By this crude means, we were able to seize and take away the equipment left by the enemy.[22]
— *Mao's Generals Remember Korea*

By 1953, North Korea had developed a similar underground methodology. That country's Soviet mentors recorded the particulars of what may have been one of its mountain strongpoints just above the 38th parallel.[23] (See Figure 35.1.)

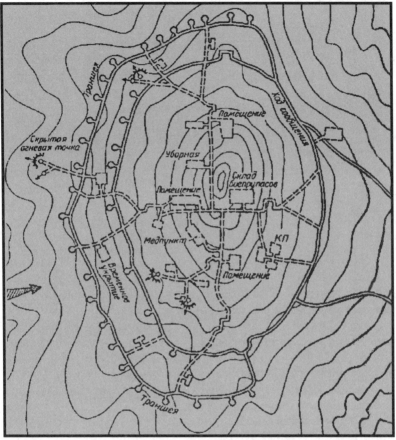

Figure 35.1: Korean Hill Honeycombed with Escape Chambers
(Source: *Voina v Korea: 1950-1953*, by A.A. Kuryacheba, © 2002 by Polygon Publishers, p. 582)

The tunnels between the hilltop's concentric trenchlines had to run just below the surface and were probably covered trenches themselves. But, their upward extensions clearly enter the hill mass. Along them are side rooms with no surface access. Those rooms are too far from the outer perimeter to be used as temporary refuge during a pre-assault bombardment. However, they could have been inhabited for quite some time by anyone having to abandon the above-ground fortifications.

411

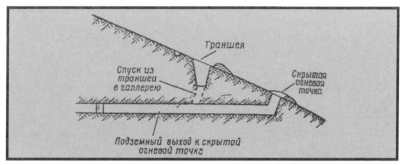

Figure 35.2: Trench Exit by Trapdoor to Sealed Tunnel
(Source: "Voina v Korea: 1950-1953," by A.A. Kuryacheba, p. 613. © 2002 by Polygon Publishers.)

In Pyongyang's massive war museum are several photographs of North Korean troops manning just such a hill. At the same location is a full-scale mock-up of its underground living area. With log-shored walls and ceilings, that area appears quite habitable. Just off the main tunnel are the following: (1) kitchen; (2) sleeping quarters; (3) bathroom; (4) separate storage rooms for food, water, and ammunition; (5) observation post with tiny viewport; (6) artillery or anti-aircraft chamber with cave-like opening; and (7) land line phone booth with surface access.[24]

In Figure 35.2, the Russian artist shows how beleaguered frontline troops could have also escaped another way. Trench bottom trapdoors led to a number of other horizontal tunnels. Within them, former defenders could have remained for many days unobserved or simply moved out beyond the front lines of the hilltop's new owners to finally escape.

Tunnels and Light Infantry Make Quite a Combination

To bypass minefields and artillery concentrations, North Korean infantry regiments would have only to invade South Korea through longer tunnels. If enough such underground conduits existed, any number of commando "beachheads" within South Korea could be quickly reinforced.

412

[I]n 1971, Kim Il-song *[sic]* specifically ordered the construction of infiltration tunnels along the DMZ: "one tunnel can be more powerful than ten atomic bombs put together and the tunnels are the most ideal means of penetrating the South's fortified line" (Republic of Korea, *Defense White Paper 2-1990,* 75).

The engineer battalion of each infantry division deployed directly on the DMZ was assigned the task of digging two infiltration tunnels. . . . Aside from the four located and neutralized tunnels, ROK/U.S. intelligence currently [as of 1998] estimates that there are eighteen suspected active tunnels in various stages of completion along the DMZ.[25]
— *North Korean Special Forces,* by Bermudez

A former South Korean general, Han Sung-chu, claims there are at least eighty-four [84] tunnels—some reaching as far as downtown Seoul.[26]
— *The National Interest,* 6 May 2017

That hermit kingdom also has a wide array of underground staging areas for large-unit attacks.

A North Korean defector disclosed that, starting in 2004, North Korea began building bunkers capable of concealing between 1,500 and two thousand fully armed combat troops near the border. At least eight hundred bunkers were built, not including decoys.[27]
— *The National Interest,* 6 May 2017

21st Century Wars Still Require Dismounted Infantry

No one can dispute the role that Allied foot soldiers played in the two world wars. But, since the Korean War, the focus of most Western armies has been on mechanized infantry. Along flat open ground (as in the deserts of the Middle East), troops in tracked vehicles can cover greater distances. But, not all terrain is that friendly, and the age-old need for truly light U.S. infantrymen has again surfaced.

In fact, while everyone was watching Iraq, there occurred an epochal shift in the evolution of warfare in the somewhat hilly southern border region of Lebanon.[28] Of significant note, it may have come as part of a Chinese and North Korean experiment in that location.[29] And it made clear how light infantrymen can operate in conjunction with advanced electronics.

> The . . . parallel disasters of Bint Jbiel and Wadi Saluki became laboratories for teaching how a well-trained insurgent force exhaustively drilled, carefully dug in, camouflaged and armed with the latest precision anti-tank weaponry could utterly devastate a modern, technologically superior Cold War armored force, even if that force commanded the air absolutely.[30]
>
> — M.Gen. R.H. Scales (Ret.)
> "Armed Forces Journal," December 2007

There is evidence that *Hezbollah's* defense line was—at least in part—of Chinese and North Korean design. The Chinese helped to arm it, and the North Koreans to dig it.[31] So, gone forever is the myth that the North Korean army has acquired no new battlefield experience since 1953. To the extent that *Hezbollah* has learned to combine light-infantry strongpoints with remotely controlled anti-tank weaponry, so too will ISIS, *al-Qaeda,* and the North Korean army.

To counter this evolutionary milestone, the Pentagon will need Marine infantry battalions modeled after the WWII Raiders and Army Ranger battalions with a renewed interest in surprise assault. It will be a long time before American aerial surveillance gadgetry will be able to spot an anti-armor matrix that is a below-ground and heat-signature-free.

36   WAGING WAR WITH TECHNOLOGY ALONE

- Do all adversaries rely upon sophisticated equipment?
- What do Eastern armies value more than fancy gear?

He could walk right past knife-wielding foe beneath loam or leaves.

Source: Courtesy of Raytheon, from "Revolutionary Soldier," by Glen W. Goodman, Jr., *Armed Forces Journal International*, October 1999, copyright © 1999 Raytheon.)

Latest Advances Create a False Sense of Security

If one were totally to believe the military gear manufacturers, no U.S. soldier would ever again get injured in combat. Near the start of the Afghan War, ground-penetrating radar (GPR) was announced. It could detect defenders behind thick walls and in underground bunkers. Then, more advanced aerial surveillance systems appeared. They would determine who were the combatants in mufti from thousands of feet overhead. Soon, ground optics were being improved. The individual GI was now able to see any antagonist in absolute darkness.

415

Next (in April 2017), the Pentagon was to employ the largest non-nuclear bomb ever dropped in combat. Its massive air blast created so much oxygen deprivation that some 40 Muslim militants suffocated inside a mountain tunnel complex of Eastern Afghanistan. Finally (in mid-August 2017), prestigious *60 Minutes* reported that swarms of tiny autonomous drones had the capability of assassinating enemy leaders after spotting their facial features through any disguise.[1] At that point, most cell-phone-toting Americans must have envisioned a whole new age of casualty-free warfare.

That may be why so many U.S. leaders believe that no American infantry "boots on the ground" will be necessary to win future wars. Unfortunately, all that money-making hype has—once again—not meshed well with battlefield reality. While the U.S. military has for quite some time enjoyed a technological advantage over most adversaries, it has not decisively won an extended conflict since WWII. So, other factors must be more important to final victory.

Ground Penetration Radar

The latest GPR devices can—to some extent—locate tunnels, bunkers, and caches, but this is from ground level (not some aerial platform) and much depends on a uniform composition of overhead medium. Within rocky soil, for example, it produces indistinct images. And the ground easiest to penetrate is often that least receptive to high-frequency radio waves. For example, in moist clay-rich (highly conductive) soil, the GPR can at best see down 20 feet, whereas in nonconductive dry sand or concrete, it can peer down 60 feet.[2]

Such GPRs are too heavy to be man carried, time consuming to use, and vulnerable to enemy fire. As a result, they have more of an application to landmine detection than infantry combat. On Iwo Jima, they would have been of little use until the entire island was in Leatherneck hands.

Aerial Surveillance

While aerial surveillance has greatly improved, it cannot yet distinguish an AK-47 from an umbrella or a suicide vest from a Afghan cartigan. Without some "real-time" human intelligence from the ground, no drone strike should ever follow aerial photography. At the instant somebody's innocent grandmother comes to clean the house of known terrorists, their hideout is no longer a valid 4GW target.

Night Vision and Targeting Devices

The night vision devices most GIs now wear on their helmets have a number of serious drawbacks. First, they all present two little "telltale" reflective surfaces about the same distance apart as human eyeballs. Any ambient light can thus be bounced back toward an antagonist. If ill fitting, those NVGs can also cause a greenish glow on the wearer's face.[3]

Next, all NVGs are made temporarily ineffective by any bright light. They eliminate not only the wearer's natural nighttime seeing ability, but also his peripheral vision. And finally, they can badly detract from his other senses. Everyone's "sixth sense" is believed by many outdoorsmen to be a subliminal combination of the other five.

The Mother of All Bombs

The above-mentioned thermobaric GBU-43/B Massive Ordnance Air Blast (MOAB) was dropped over Islamic State positions in Afghanistan's eastern Nangarhar Province in April 2017. This was "a move the Trump administration said was aimed at denying the group's freedom of movement."[4] The movement probably at issue was that which could be secretly conducted—below ground—between Afghanistan and Pakistan. Within Afghanistan's Paktia and Khost Provinces are many tunnel complexes that extend into Pakistan. Two the most famous are at "Zawwhar Kili" and "Tora Bora."[5]

However, such a massive blast may have served another purpose for America's political leaders in Washington. The North Korean dictator had just begun to "rattle" his intercontinental missiles.

> White House press secretary Sean Spicer said the
> MOAB was dropped to reach "a system of tunnels and
> caves" used by Islamic State terrorists. . . .
>   . . . [There was] speculation that the big boom in Af-
> ghanistan was meant at least in part as a warning to North
> Korea.[6]
> — *Bloomberg News,* April 2017

This first use of this MOAB bomb in wartime was encouraging
because it had been dropped in a narrow canyon filled with cave
entrances.

> The Air Force statement said that the weapon is designed
> to clear targets in caves and canyons (about the giant
> bomb).[7]
> — *Bloomberg News,* April 2017

Those canyon walls had simply magnified the bomb's effect on
all embedded caverns. Had the same bomb been deposited atop
a fortified mountain, it would have bee considerably less successful. Much of the blast would have then been dissipated down the
mountainside, and anyone deep inside the hill mass left relatively
unharmed. Such would be the average target in North Korea. Of
course, the Pentagon is also developing a Massive Ordinance Pen-
etrator (MOP) to succeed the BLU-118/B "Bunker Buster" of the
early 2000's that could go through over six feet of concrete before
exploding.[8] However, even this new MOP would probably have
a minimal effect on the North Korean tunnels deep inside one of
the many granite ridge lines that lie between Pyongyang and the
DMZ.

Needless to say, the psychological effect of such a bomb on diehard ISIS members may have been less than expected as well. Nor
were some of Afghanistan's former leaders very impressed by the
display of U.S. might.

> Hamid Karzai [Afghanistan's former leader] strongly
> condemned the attack.
> Afghanistan's ambassador to Pakistan Omar Zakhil-
> wal also protested the U.S. bombing, breaking ranks with
> Ghani [Afghanistan's new President].[9]
> — *Bloomberg News,* April 2017

Swarms of Assassination Drones?

As for the swarm of "disguise-debunking" drones targeting enemy leaders, most of America's battlefield adversaries operate within a "bottom-up" culture. In other words, how well their armed forces perform on the battlefield depends very little on top commanders.

The Associated Illusion

U.S. SOCOM has been bravely setting the proper example (through its use of semi-autonomous detachments in several nations at once), but commandos alone cannot win a major global conflict. The U.S. infantry establishment will have to get involved. To what extent America's "currently heavy" grunt units become again "light" is all that's negotiable. Being truly light means that they depend more on surprise than firepower, and have little need for technology.

After the first North Korean Electro-Magnetic Pulse (EMP) bomb gets dropped, much of that fancy U.S. gadgetry isn't going to work anyway. So, the more truly light infantrymen the U.S. military can now produce, the better. Among the oldest axioms of ground warfare is always to keep a manual backup for any automated system. To keep from losing the opening round of a third world war, the Pentagon will need hundreds of infantry squads that are tactically proficient enough to operate alone beyond any supporting-arms umbrella. They must further be authorized to pull back a little.

37   WITHDRAWAL AND THEN REBUILDING MOMENTUM

- How many U.S. foes pull back a little when helpful?
- Why don't American forces ever do this?

Tactical withdrawal can make big unit possible to attack piecemeal.

(Source: Courtesy of Sorman Information and Media, illustration by Wolfgang Bartsch, from "SoldF: Soldaten i falt," p. 220, © 2001 Forsvarsmakten and Bartsch.)

Avoiding a Fight May Require a Little Backing Up

Breaking contact with the enemy can be as dangerous as a frontal assault. It's most safely done through a series of situationally consistent and thoroughly practiced procedures. Unfortunately, U.S. forces have for so long disdained moving backwards, that their small units now lack much of the necessary expertise. To many GIs, tactical withdrawal means nothing more than a "bounding overwatch" in the wrong direction. Unfortunately, America's under-equipped foes have so far produced at least two advanced variants: (1) an elastic positional defense that so disperses an attacker as to subject him to piecemeal annihilation; and (2) a backwards moving defense that so exhausts an attacker as to make him easy to counterattack. While both are more often practiced in the Orient,[1] there is no reason U.S. infantrymen couldn't use them as well.

This search for more advanced pullback technique must necessarily start with how American's most formidable adversaries have conducted retrograde warfare. The quarry is first lured into apparent gaps in their defenses, or led through a succession of ambushes, and then—when sufficiently weakened—dealt a fatal blow. Among the foes with such a capability have been the Japanese, Germans, Russians, Asian Communists, and Afghan Taliban.

Initial Development During the World Wars

To this day, American defenders prefer a static linear or perimeter defense, containing as much weaponry as possible. The enemy is then engaged as far out as each weapon will reach, and then finally defeated by close defensive fires at the Main Line of Resistance (MLR). Not all armies have stuck with this way of repulsing an attacker. In fact, intentionally moving rearward on defense may have been part of every Asian's bag of tricks for centuries. At Sulva Bay in 1915, Turkish militiamen kept going backwards until the Allied invaders ran so short of water they could no longer think straight. Then, during an on-line assault through Turkish smoke, the members of one whole British company may have crossed over (and bared their backs to) a parallel row of occupied "spider holes."[2] What happened next was so unpleasant as to have since become a mystery.

Later in WWI, a somewhat soft, defense-in-depth began to emerge in Europe. By 1917, the Germans had abandoned the belief that defended ground must remain inviolate.[3] If that ground were penetrated, the battlefield's distance backwards would weaken the attacker, preserve the defender, and enhance that defender's chances of retaliation.[4] So instead of fighting to the death for an MLR, the Germans placed—within each shell hole of a sizeable strip—one squad with its attached machinegun. That way, the craters nearest the enemy could be sometimes abandoned for others farther back without forfeiting overall containment of the attacking force. The result was a more elastic (and durable) form of positional defense. Those shell holes would later be replaced with bunkers. But, for either kind of strongpoint, the Hun squad manning it could only move a short way rearward on its own initiative.

Then, during WWII, all German units (of any size) were theoretically able to pull back when continuing to fight lacked promise or defeat was imminent.[5] In conjunction with a simultaneous delaying action, they could further bring mutually supporting strongpoints into play.[6] When possible, such a withdrawal was accomplished at night. Soon standardized by the German Army was the shifting rearward of defense matrix elements into other fallback matrices. As in WWI, most such elements still consisted of a squad-sized strongpoint.

Meanwhile, the WWII Russian squad could only pull back from its MLR after being so ordered by its platoon leader. However, its official tactics manual still showed how to perform the maneuver.[7] Initially, its light machinegun would cover the withdrawal of the rest of the squad.[8]

Yet, continually shifting rearward through successive belt lines of manned positions didn't fully take hold until late in WWII. That's when, the Japanese in the Pacific first started referring to it as "retreat combat."

> They [the Japanese] called it [their new style of defense] "retreat combat." . . . Initially, Japanese firepower had been concentrated on the perimeter but subsequently the Army showed considerable skill at defense in depth. The offensive aspect of defense in depth was preserved by the use of underground passages from which Japanese soldiers would emerge when the ground had been overrun. . . . [T]he exits were so well camouflaged and concealed that they were not easily detected. . . . Dummy defenses . . . were used to shepherd attackers into positions well prepared to receive them.[9]
> — *Japanese Army of World War II,* by Warner

On Iwo Jima, every apparent gap in the defenders' strongpoint array was really a firesack, and almost all manning those strongpoints able to withdraw to a well-hidden reverse-slope emplacement.[10] Of course, so doing took a tunnel. Some Nipponese generals would later give credit for this ingenious style of defending against a powerful adversary to their former advisors—the Germans.

Our general retreat policy [on Okinawa] . . . was aimed at a total retreat toward fortifications at Kiyan. Our war objective, however, remained a war of attrition, looking forward to a decisive battle in mainland Japan. We intended to carry out a German-army-style, local prolonged resistance, taking advantage of the rugged terrain and numerous caves along the twelve kilometers between the Shuri Line and the new front line.[11]

> — Col. Hiromichi Yahara,
> Imperial Japanese Army survivor of Okinawa

As will be later demonstrated, there was also some "retreat combat" evident during the Nazis' extremely difficult defense of Berlin.

Further Refinement in the Korean War

Much of this "counter-intuitive" way of incrementally wearing down a powerful attacker was to carry over to the Korean War. Against overwhelming firepower in that conflict, the Chinese were also to shift their tiny bastions backwards.[12] But now, a clever trap was being laid at the end of this rearward movement to sap the attacker's momentum. While the "Closing-V" or *Haichi-Shiki* probably originated on the Asian Mainland, its name implies a

Figure 37.1: Haichi-Shiki Formation

long Japanese affiliation. (See Figure 37.1.) This formation was specifically designed for counterattacking a pursuer. That's why its swinging-door "V" always faced him. First noticed during the Korean War, its various sequels must have become part of Maoist Mobile Warfare.

> [T]he Chinese Army . . . planned attacks to strike from the rear, cutting escape and supply routes and then sending in frontal waves. The basic battle tactic was the *Haichi Shiki*, a V formation into which they allowed opposing troops to move. The Chinese then would close the side of the V while another force moved below the mouth to stop any attempts at escape and to block relief columns.[13]
> — *Korea: The Untold Story of the War*, by Goulden

During the initial stages of the U.N. "Police Action," both the North Koreans and Communist Chinese conducted special retrograde operations. While ostensibly a kind of "mobile defense," those operations were often accomplished through a succession of hastily fortified fallback positions. Then in 1953, the lines stiffened at the 38th Parallel in the face of another Allied advance into North Korea. That's when an almost impregnable below-ground version of the WWI-vintage "elastic, positional defense" appeared. Fortunately for U.S. history, the nearly futile Allied attempts to breach it were soon superseded by peace talks.

Yet, by 1994, the North Korean Army (NKA) was still using three defense options—two of which involved moving backwards.

> NKA [tactical] doctrine calls for three types of defense: position[al] defense, mobile defense, and retrograde operations. . . . The mobile defense would be used to gain time, exact losses on . . . [enemy] forces, and preserve combat strength *while losing ground.* NKA retrograde (or disengagement) operations would be used to gain time to plan for the next operation or to restore combat capability [italics added].[14]
> — "North Korea Handbook"
> U.S. Dept. of Defense, *PC-2600-6421-94*

The more recent North Korean positional warfare formation in Figure 37.2 contains elements that look like the "two-up-and-

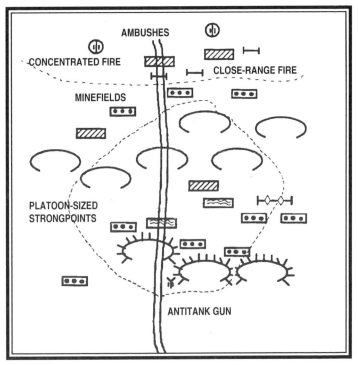

Figure 37.2: Modern-Day North Korean "Defensive Strongpoint"
(Source: "North Korea Handbook," DoD PC-2600-6421-94 [1994], p. 3-99.)

one-back" defense matrix building blocks of the WWII Germans and Russians. Such a component concurrently provides all around protection and mutual support.[15]

While capable of both mobile and positional defenses, the Chinese definitely prefer the former. Yet, the latter still makes provision for disappearing below the ground.

> Chinese Communist concept of defense includes . . . trading space for time; complete abandonment . . . of areas

of little importance; concentration of defensive strength in critical areas; conduct of extensive guerrilla activities in hostile rear areas, and . . . psychological warfare. . . .

The Chinese Communists employ both mobile defense and positional defense, but favor the mobile defense since it is best suited to the concept of mobile warfare.

. . . Mobile defense tactics are frequently employed to lure an extended hostile force into an . . . ambush.

Positional defense is employed only when absolutely necessary. . . . Where a prepared position has been overrun by the enemy, the defending forces will fall back into bunkers, call artillery fire and tactical air support onto their own position, and wait to join with counterattacking forces.[16]
— "Handbook on Chinese Communist Army"
U.S. Army, *PAM 30-51*

Effects of the Vietnam War

Throughout most of America's Vietnam experience, the enemy moved backwards in the face of overwhelming U.S. firepower. Yet, it did so in a very deliberate manner.

VC/NVA hasty defenses did not resemble Western blocking positions or perimeters. Partially designed to withstand bombardment, they ordinarily consisted of two roughly parallel lines of fighting holes. (See Figure 37.3.)

Under the dense canopy of vegetation, two lines or belts of fortifications were constructed fifty to two hundred meters apart. . . . These belts of defensive positions followed the outline of an L, U, or V so as to offer the possibility of a crossfire.[17]
— *Inside the VC and the NVA,* Lanning and Cragg

The forward-most line apparently contained a built-in firesack. So, its center must have been only partially manned by fighters able to pull back rapidly to the second line. Such a formation would again resemble the three-element strongpoint grouping of the WWII Germans and Russians.[18]

At Ia Drang in the autumn of 1965, a U.S. Army relief column encountered a "Flexible Horseshoe."[19] Then, on Operation Buffalo

Figure 37.3: North Vietnamese "Double-Line" Pull-Back Defense

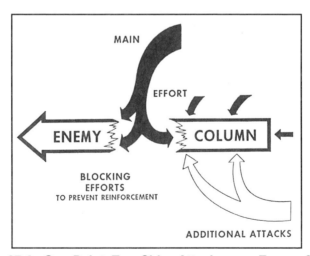

Figure 37.4: One-Point, Two-Sides Attack on an Enemy Column
(Source: "Handbook on the Chinese Communist Army," DA Pam 30-51 [1960], p. 24.)

in 1968, a U.S. Marine column got methodically segmented by what was more obviously a *Haichi-Shiki* from Mao's Mobile Defense.[20] (See Figure 37.4.)

How Much Did America's Cold War Opponent Adopt?

Within the outpost and forward-defense zones, contemporary Russian infantry units also systematically withdraw to fallback positions. They use deeply echeloned defenses with interlocking fires and obstacles to sap the attacker's strength.[21] Then, their forward detachments generally conduct a mobile defense in the security zone. To preclude encirclement, those detachments would need withdrawal routes and exfiltration technique.

In fact, to the modern-day Russian, pulling partially back or outright retreating are as much a part of the defense as holding ground. He sees the defense not as a positional tool but as a temporary condition on a dynamic battlefield.[22] Even behind the MLR, he constructs a defense in depth ultimately consisting of platoon groupings of squad strongpoints.

> The main defensive position comprises a series of defensive belts arranged in depth (Ionin, "Modern Defense," *Voennyi Vestnik*, 1981, 4:16).
> ... Defensive belts are organized along defensible terrain and comprise a series of mutually supporting defensive positions or strongpoints reinforced by obstacles and supported by fire.
> ... A motorized rifle company may occupy a strongpoint 1000 meters wide and 500 meters deep, with 300 meters between platoons. Platoon positions are self-contained and are organized so that the company and the platoon can fight in any direction. ... [Second] echelon units may be placed to provide defense in depth in gaps between first echelon units. ...
> ... A platoon strongpoint is up to 400 meters in frontage and 300 meters in depth and comprises squad positions (Merzylak, "IFV's on the Defensive," *Soviet Military Review*, 1983, 8:20). ...
> ... The final step is to prepare communications trenches

for supply and evacuation and to permit covered movement within the platoon strongpoint.[23]
— *Soviet Airland Battle Tactics,* by Baxter

Within the main defensive position, the Russian relies on maneuver as well as dominant terrain and firepower.[24] He pulls back to avoid destruction by superior enemy forces, to trade space for time, or to redeploy forces to another axis.[25] If the plan calls for withdrawal, he does so on his own initiative. If it does not, he will need the approval of the commander at two echelons up his chain of command.[26]

To this day, the post-Soviet defense is probably still predicated on strongpoints and firesacks.[27] To disguise a firesack, the center portion must be lightly manned and then evacuated. The Soviet defender had, as his first priority, to construct obstacles and barriers. He did so to channelize his foe. Then, he prepared strongpoints with the emphasis on deception and digging.[28] Finally, he worked on "communication" routes for easy access and egress.[29] His squad-sized strongpoint was of a design that can be easily hidden and shifted within a network of communication trenches.

Current Use by the Afghan Foe

Whatever the *mujahideen* could do in the 1980's, the current crop of Taliban, *al-Qaeda,* and ISIS combatants in Afghanistan can probably still accomplish. After deploying to Afghanistan, the Russians soon realized that even nonaligned political movements understand the value of tactical withdrawal. The *mujahideen* pulled back from almost every major engagement with the Soviet army. They normally did so over prerehearsed routes,[30] or through fog or darkness.[31]

The Afghan *mujahideen* practically never conducted positional warfare and, when threatened with encirclement, would abandon their positions.[32]
— DoD-published Soviet military academy study

Each *mujahideen* ambush formation was uniquely tailored to the terrain. To hold enough enemy vehicles to make the ambush worthwhile, the kill zone was seldom less than one to two kilometers in length.[33] Whether the Afghan assault groups attacked from one or both sides of the road depended on the availability of cover. It was from a single side when a roadside streambed obstructed enemy counterattack and aided friendly withdrawal.[34] But mostly it was from both sides. Then, the assault groups would sit across from each other only when both were situated above the road.[35] Thus, the *mujahideen* "U-shaped" ambush was again highly reminiscent of the East Asian *Haichi-Shiki*. It generally occurred where the road entered a side valley.[36] The quarry would then take fire from three different sides.

At least once, the *mujahideen* set up several anti-vehicle and antipersonnel ambushes in exactly the same place.[37] Soon, they were enjoying so much success with this scheme that they began to bait the Soviet armored columns. That's when Abdul Haq would pioneer the concept of using dummy *mujahideen* convoys to lure them in.[38]

The Possibility of a U.S. Infantry Sequel

Except for the "two-up-and-one-back" strongpoint firesack and *Haichi-Shiki* inverted "V", there is not enough information to construct a model for how those retrograde operations were conducted. However, for various ways a U.S. infantry company might still defend rural terrain by gradually giving way to a powerful attacker, see Chapter 18 of *Global Warrior*.

Concurrent Rise of a Retrograde Urban Defense

All above-named opponents—except for the *mujahideen*—have also been noticed maneuvering rearward in the face of a determined urban assault.

As the Soviets were taking Berlin in 1945, they discovered "cellar escape routes" from some of the outer-ring defense bastions.[39] On the walls were the German inscription, "We withdraw but we are winning!"[40] While the Germans were pulling back to the center of the city and blowing canal bridges *en route*,[41] they were also trying to soften up their opponent sufficiently to counterattack him. In more than one neighborhood, they had already taken offensive action.[42]

During the Korean War, Seoul changed hands several times. While attempting to counter the first Allied onslaught on that city in September 1950, the North Koreans made the U.S. Marines "fight for every inch of ground" and launched spoiling attacks [43]—all while moving rearward. As the Japanese had done in Manila, Seoul's defenders succeeded—with roadblocks—in blunting the Allies' momentum. However, this time a specially trained rear guard was to capitalize on each barrier interruption.

> Even as air reconnaissance revealed the main body of Kim Il Sung's [North Korean] army fleeing northwards, Communist rear guards fought on to delay the advance of [Marine Gen. O.P.] Smith's regiments, extracting their price, yard by yard at each rice-bag barricade. [44]
> — *The Korean War,* by Hastings

Just as "retreat combat" had become Japan's most formidable way to defend jumbled rocky ground near the end of WWII, [45] so too did sequential withdrawal come to define the Maoist Mobile Defense of a built-up area. This Communist pullback from Seoul was not an impromptu "skedaddle," but rather a carefully choreographed way of overextending and exhausting a powerful attacker. A slightly different account of the North Korean pullout shows a much more orderly event. Unfortunately, its precise method is still a little vague.

> [A]lthough the bulk of the KPA [Korean People's Army] forces in the city were withdrawing, units were left behind to fight a desperate rearguard action. Fighting behind a succession of street barricades, they exacted a heavy toll among the ranks of the U.N. forces for every meter of territory they yielded. Against such bitter resistance, it took the U.N. forces three days to gain complete control of the town. [46]
> — *The Korean War: History and Tactics,* by Rees

Some 18 years later, when the NVA finally decided to abandon Phase Line Green in the Hue City Citadel after four days of fighting for it, their squads and fire teams did something fairly unique. They provided much of their own covering fire as they moved two blocks back to the next hastily fortified street. [47] Again, the precise details of this maneuver are sketchy. But, a tactical pattern had definitely emerged—one of evolutionary significance. That's too many major armies conducting a moving (or soft) defense for the Pentagon not occasionally to do likewise.

For similar maneuvers through which an American infantry company might better defend urban terrain through a retrograde operation, see Chapter 21 of *The Last Hundred Yards*.

Those NVA units could not have tactically withdrawn so well, if their individual soldiers had not been adept at reverse "fire and movement"—one of the hardest maneuvers for any squad to master going forward.

PART THIRTEEN

WHEN ONE'S LIFE HANGS IN THE BALANCE

"DEATH, BEFORE DISHONOR."
— CODE OF THE JAPANESE SAMURAI WARRIOR

(Source: Attributed to the Japanese Samurai, from the following url: http://www.historynet.com/death-before-dishonor-the-samurai-of-japan.htm)

38 THE ONE-ON-ONE CLASH WITH ANY ASIAN SOLDIER

● What makes the Eastern combatant so dangerous?
● How much standardized procedure can the GI risk?

This lopsided encounter occurred late one night in Korea.

(Source: "Corporal Hiroshi N.Miyamura, Korean War," by George Akimoto, U.S.Army Center for Military History, from this url: http://www.history.army.mil/art/A&I/0507-3.jpg.)

The Alarmist's Warning

Posterity Press has been often criticized for overstating Eastern capabilities at the small-unit and individual level. Clearly, not every soldier the GI encounters in Asia will be a *ninjutsu* master. Nor will he always be tactically sophisticated. But, as a routinely under-equipped combatant, he has had to compensate for insufficient firepower. Most U.S. veterans of Far Eastern wars remember him as not only extremely elusive, but also fighting by different rules. So which would more help the contemporary U.S. inductee: (1) being continually told he is the best in the world at all things;

or (2) being advised to carefully handle any foe of Oriental descent, from a place once occupied by Asians, or following Maoist doctrine (like most insurgents)? At least with the latter assessment, the fledgling GI would be more watchful. The price for too much confidence could be high.

During one of the most fiercely contested battles in world history (on the tiny island of Iwo Jima late in WWII), the invading Yanks rarely saw one of the 22,000 defenders.[1] Yet, those well-experienced and exceptionally determined "Jarheads" still suffered 26,000 casualties.

American Troops Are the Best at Pentagon Priorities

GIs have the best equipment, training, discipline, and leadership in the world. Their Communist Asian counterparts not only use the same old weaponry, but enjoy less headquarters direction during both training and battle. Nor are soldiers' lives as precious to the Chinese and North Korean regimes, as in Washington. Most insurgent foes follow similar Maoist principles/tactics. So, the average U.S. infantry enlistee now feels pretty good about his chances in open combat against a lone Asian regular or Third World guerrilla.

But, things may not be as rosy as they appear in the technology-driven Pentagon. It's true that U.S. infantrymen are continually issued the most modern equipment. But, then they must spend an inordinate amount of time learning how to operate that equipment, often at the expense of some other subject (like small-unit tactics). That, in itself, makes them the best trained in the world (in using their new gear and following orders). Of course, excellent unit discipline also ensues, but not necessarily enough self-discipline and personal initiative at the bottom echelons. Might that be why a Communist Asian infantry company will use a less standardized (and more bottom-up) way of tactically training its frontline personnel?

What Else Might Such Training Produce?

Another benefit of "following the collective suggestions" of

NCOs and their nonrates would be situationally tailored and continually refined tactical techniques. Such techniques might make it possible for a tiny element to continually surprise a much larger unit. Perhaps, that's how Red armies have so easily compensated for less ordnance As in MW, they have simply substituted small-unit momentum for the missing bombardment.

With a further requirement to study guerrilla warfare,[2] Chinese and North Korean troops get much more practice at tactical-decision making than U.S. riflemen. Such a thing might make quite a difference during a "one-on-one" fight to the death. After all, the American's edge in firepower would only guarantee victory if his adversary were to remain fully visible throughout the encounter.

While the U.S. no nonsense "do-as-you're-told" style of leadership may get the job done in garrison, routine success in combat requires more bottom-echelon initiative. That's probably why Eastern officers are so different from their Western counterparts. The PLA platoon leader makes no attempt to teach his men what he learned at "Basic School." He instead determines what they already know how to do. Then, in combat, he tries to place them into a similar situation.[3]

While Western cultures tend to solve problems from the top down, Eastern cultures do so from the bottom up. That's how Asian Communist armies more easily create a "world-class" light infantryman.

Different Kinds of Light Infantrymen

Several levels of light-infantry expertise exist. There are GIs in America who still call themselves light infantrymen, yet ride around all day and then fight mostly at standoff distance with supporting arms. To find true light infantrymen from this nation, one has to go back in time. Rogers' Rangers of the 1700's could live off the land while covertly traveling great distances on foot. Edson's Marine Raiders of early WWII carried lighter loads and marched farther than their heavy or "line" counterparts. And Carlson's Raiders of the same era became superbly agile and versatile by conducting Maoist Mobile Warfare with semi-autonomous fire teams.

A New Western Model for This Kind of Soldier

Now proposed by William S. Lind—U.S. father of 4th Generation Warfare—is the European kind of light infantryman who follows MW precepts. In other words, he attacks by infiltration, and defends by ambush.[4] Consistently to do so, he adopts a "Jaeger" or hunter mindset along with all of its associated skills. Mr. Lind understands that light infantrymen still require "techniques."[5] But, those reading his new handbook might erroneously conclude that because light infantry "does not adhere to any type of proscribed methods," it never develops the drills of a line infantryman.[6] This is not true. In fact, the most sophisticated squad "surprise assault" technique still requires a specific sequence of steps from various members. If those members haven't practiced other drills for common battlefield scenarios, their tiny unit won't be able to operate alone.

Less rigidity is what makes this kind of drill different from a line infantry drill. In other words, it allows more adaptation by individual members to unforeseen circumstances. But, without a drill of some kind, there can be no practicing of the solutions to recurring group problems—none of the planning process that Sun Tzu so valued before actual battle.

History has already confirmed a natural fit between light infantry and advanced tactical technique. The highly opportunistic Stormtrooper squad was the tip of the German spear in late WWI, yet few Western military men consider it comprised of "heavy" infantrymen. While carrying very little ammunition, those Stormtroopers became virtually unstoppable because of their familiarity with two evolutionary procedures: (1) how to mimic an indirect-fire attack while actually assaulting along the ground; and (2) how to single-handedly man a defensive strongpoint that could be later abandoned at their own discretion.

It is this latter example of a tactically adept or "super" light infantryman that would be most helpful to modern war—especially, if he had a number of squad maneuvers instead of just two. Then, Bill Lind's suggestion to train all light infantrymen in flexibility, free play, ordnance proficiency, land navigation, stealth/stalking, and survival would be the initial part of their preparation.[7] No first-stage graduate could then be allowed "to build from scratch" the solution to a common battlefield scenario.

That would not only take too long and ignore various lessons of history, but possibly conflict with his own squad leader's plans. Short of dropping everything to defeat an immediate assailant, the young American warrior must still function as the member of a larger team.

So, the second part of the super light infantryman's training would most logically consist of enough tactical technique to quickly handle the most common challenges. Such techniques are best designed through a two-step procedure: (1) he and his peers imagining how best to handle the event; and (2) their practicing/refining of this collective choice against simulated casualty assessment. Each fighter would then enjoy the same tiny playbook of personal moves that meshed with the maneuvers of his buddy team, fire team, and squad. Without such a playbook, his longevity would be as fleeting as squad momentum. Bill Lind would almost certainly support such a suggestion.

> Tactics combines. . . techniques and education. Techniques are things you can do by formula, like . . . unit battle drills. Excellence in techniques is very important to Maneuver Warfare. But good techniques are not enough. . . . Tactics includes the art of selecting from among your [assortment of] techniques . . . for [current circumstances]. Education [or group experience] is the basis for doing that.[8]
> — W.S. Lind, father of Maneuver Warfare in U.S.

How to create a future U.S. "grunt" with this much ability has already been fully chronicled in *Strategic Rifleman*. Needless to say, the process would come far more easily to an Oriental military.

How Asian Armies Do It

Because a cultural background in "bottom-up" progress, many Far Eastern societies already possess this higher caliber of light infantryman. While it's not easy to show that their lowest ranks help to design their own techniques, it is not impossible. As early as the 1930's, Mao's troops were publicly criticizing their leaders' tactics via *"Gung Ho* Sessions."[9] Then 30-40 years later, North

Vietnamese soldiers did the same thing through "*Kiem Thao* Sessions."[10] So, both sets of frontline combatants had been implicitly "critiquing" existing technique.

Still, the discerning reader might need additional evidence of nonrate input. Part of the proof is in the relatively greater importance attributed to the individual fighter in Communist armies — not of his life *per se,* but of the strategic difference he might make. North Vietnam's tactical genius makes this clear.

> Whether in guerrilla . . . or limited regular warfare, . . . it [armed Communist struggle] is fully capable of . . . getting the better of a modern ["high-tech"] army. . . . This is [through] the development of the . . . military art, the main content of which is *to rely chiefly on [the] man, on his patriotism and . . . [individual] spirit.* [Italics added.] [11]
> — Gen. Vo Nguyen Giap

A Defense Intelligence Agency (DIA) handbook further describes "the average [Chinese] soldier as . . . able to . . . improvise under a wide variety of conditions."[12] One of those conditions might be during his tactical "work up" for a specific objective. Chinese light infantrymen have depended heavily on the resulting battledrills.

> The [Chinese] armies [entering Korea] had two phases of drills before going into battles. . . . The first phase focused on the exercises of small-group combat tactics, including shooting, throwing grenades, demolition, anti-aircraft training, and nighttime anti-air-raid practice. The second phase stressed courses of [larger] group-attack tactics . . . These exercises were aimed at the demolition of enemy defense works under enemy fire.[13]
> — *Mao's Generals Remember Korea*

Within each NVA line company, subordinate elements also practiced many maneuvers. There were drills for almost every aspect of the offense and defense.

> Sapper units were also considered light infantry and were taught how to operate as an infantry unit. . . . [S]apper units trained hard so that they could do these small unit drills

better than regular infantry units. Such tactics covered how to deploy on the battlefield for various types of operations (deliberate attack, hasty attack, meeting engagement, withdrawal, hasty and deliberate defense, regular patrolling, etc.).[14]
　　　　— *Dirty Little Secrets of the Vietnam War*
　　　　by Dunnigan and Nofi

Contemporary North Korean infantrymen operate through the same kinds of battledrills. All dedicate two months a year to squad-level-and-below training from the commandos of their Light Infantry Guidance Bureau.[15]

Each [unit's biannual] cycle consists of approximately 760 hours of training, which progresses from individual . . . exercises to joint service maneuvers.[16]
　　　　— *North Korean Special Forces,* by Bermudez

Besides possibly running into a super light infantryman, what other surprises might the average GI face in a personal encounter anywhere east of Istanbul?

The False Face and Art of Delay

Mongols controlled what is now Iran, Iraq, and Afghanistan for over 200 years. When Genghis Khan became the emperor of China in 1227 A.D.,[17] his armies all learned of the *36 Stratagems of Deception.* Dating back to 200 B.C.,[18] most are based on the *yin-yang* antitheses of the *I Ching* (Book of Changes). Thus, like Chinese regulars, Southwest Asian insurgents may still practice the "False Face and Art of Delay."[19] First, they show the Westerner what they want him to see. Then, they wait for him to make the first, incorrect move. Finally, they secretly launch a maneuver he would not choose under similar circumstances. Most Vietnam War veterans can attest to this ploy.[20]

With John Boyd's highly respected "Observe, Orient, Decide, and Act" (OODA) Loop theory, the modern-day American commander attempts to think more quickly than his opponent. However, during the initial stages of any Asian unit clash, such a rush to judgment can be extremely dangerous. Initially, the Western commander may see his foe in a Western-like formation that is either slow moving or static. But that apparent disposition is visible for a reason. It is either a holding attack or feint. That Asian unit's main attack will be launched from somewhere else as soon as there is sufficient opportunity. So while the Western commander is quickly thwarting the enemy's supposed intentions, he is actually just opening himself up to a decisive blow from an unexpected direction.

In a less carefully controlled Communist army, this same kind of deceptive fighting could carry over to one-on-one engagements between individual fighters. That may be why studies on this subject have shown the average Asian infantryman to be better prepared for the rigors of close combat than his Western counterpart.[21]

Carlson's Advice on Close Combat

Lt.Col. Evans Carlson heavily focused on giving his WWII Marine Raiders' the edge in any one-on-one contest. He first created the requisite level of individual initiative, by not always demanding a standard procedure. "Carlson's system . . . was . . . for . . . the attainment of objectives by unorthodox and unexpected methods."[22] This vision initially shaped the curriculum at Camp Pendleton's Raider School—with guerrilla warfare classes supplanting those on more traditional skills. Freewheeling aggressor duty also took the place of "canned exercise" participation.[23]

Then, Carlson showed his Raiders how more consistently to win personal encounters with an enemy counterpart. Initially, he had wanted only Marines who were prepared to kill or be killed at close range with a knife. Then, he gave them more close-combat insight and endurance. His troops learned to watch for an attack against their person from any direction, and then—through various ruses—how instantly to gain the upper hand against an onrushing assailant.

While the command guidance was "always to expect the unexpected,"[24] most Raider deception appears to have been limited to personal-defense methods. Yet, those Raiders were additionally trained in how to cross man-made barriers—wall scaling, barbed-wire crushing, and invisible-obstacle vaulting (like over a stream of machinegun bullets).[25] So, those same close-combat tricks may have also had an influence on small-unit maneuvers.

What This Means to the Present-Day "Snuffy"

Evidently, standardized close-combat training makes its recipients too predictable in combat. It has been long recognized that Asian Communist countries study U.S. weaponry and procedures. Must all such efforts be to steal or copy something? Why couldn't one just discover the U.S. rifleman's first move in close combat? While Washington continues to offer all of its infantry manuals on the open market, Beijing, Pyongyang, and Hanoi protect theirs like they hold nuclear secrets.

Many Pentagon thinkers have now concluded that advanced optics make an assault or defense by complete surprise no longer necessary or possible. Such is not the case. Squad-carried optics are too easy to defeat. Firstly, the modern-day GI's helmet-mounted night vision device effectively limits how well he can fare against a maneuver-oriented, opportunistic, and less-encumbered Asian soldier. Most glaring of its side effects is the loss of peripheral vision. So, while the peepers-wearing GI is moving clumsily forward trying to spot his supposed target through all that intervening foliage, another enemy soldier is rising up unseen on his flank. (See Figure 38.1.) Secondly, all optics (as well as the wearer's natural after-hours eyesight) are effectively negated by any bright light—to include distant flares. The most modern thermal imaging cannot see through fog, rain, bushes, or hull defilade. Still, the profit-oriented manufacturer of such things will not easily abandon his inflated claims. How much less gear would the still mortal U.S. grunt prefer to wear? All those fancy electronics don't make his whereabouts any less obvious to the enemy.

So, the average GI wanting to return home in one piece from an overseas deployment must look for ways occasionally to deviate from his standardized training. Only then will he become sufficiently nonpredictable to forestall injury. In the process, he must remember two things: (1) no getting down during an assault unless specifically authorized; and (2) no moving backwards in the face of the enemy unless implicitly allowed by a "noncontact" mission.

Figure 38.1: A Potential Threat to Sensory Balance
(Source: FM 20-32 [1976], p. 60.)

The Public's Perception

While U.S. citizens have long suspected their offspring sent into combat with hands tied, the Pentagon insists that such tight control was necessary to prevent atrocities and ensure a unified effort. It's true that—without any military training at all—the 18-year-old Pride of Portland might do fairly well during a chance encounter with his Pyongyang counterpart. But, for consistently winning that one-on-one contact while still meeting parent-unit responsibilities, he will need three things: (1) more than one way to comply with fire team technique; (2) several close-combat moves for enough muscle memory to handle a skilled assailant; and (3) a personalized opening feint for that struggle. Once the foe is off-balance, a more standardized regimen can be applied. All football players and martial artists are familiar with such prerequisites for momentum. But, within the U.S. military, the young inductee is rarely considered agile or smart enough to do more than follow simplistic orders. It's no wonder he has trouble lasting a full combat tour.

39 LIVING LONG ENOUGH TO __ CARRY ON THE FIGHT

- What kinds of things would get a "new guy" hurt?
- How might he minimize that risk?

Before shooting back, one way to avoid injury is to get down.

(Source: "Preventive Maintenance: M203 and M79 Grenade Launcher" [pamphlet reproduced by U.S. Army Armor School, Fort Knox, Kentucky].)

Problems Already Noted

Junior enlisted Americans have so far been warned of too little daring/initiative, hidden combat risks, less humanity, a defensive mindset, not enough tactical technique to perform 3GW/4GW, and one-on-one contacts in Asia. Such a list could result in a little self doubt. Because confidence has long been important to longevity in combat, this chapter will show each rifleman how gradually to chip away at the shortfall while continuing to do his job. That additional effort should, in turn, increase his or her chances of survival in combat.

The Basic Limitation

Most combat injuries are caused by tiny pieces of flying metal (bullets or shrapnel). Those tiny missiles can come from small arms, grenades, bazooka-like weapons, mines, bombs, or indirect-fire shells. Whether intentionally generated by an enemy or mistakenly by a friend, they are equally deadly. Thus, anything one can do to minimize exposure to them will extend battlefield tenure. Among the most common remedies are: (1) digging in at night; (2) running instead of walking; (3) crouching instead of staying erect; (4) crawling instead of crouching; (5) using all available cover while changing location; (6) zigzagging where not enough cover exists; (7) never silhouetting oneself; (8) staying in the shadows wherever possible; and (9) stealthily moving.

Unfortunately, the U.S. infantry private has not been the master of his own fate for a very long time. He first and foremost function is as part of a parent unit. If that unit's commander prefers 2GW (Attrition Warfare) to 3GW and 4GW, then that's what the private must help to conduct. All three are valid under appropriate circumstances, and his commander may be aware of a few that make a 2GW solution preferable. He cannot always take the time to explain them to subordinates, so all must follow his orders. Only when the prerequisite detail of execution is missing (as in a "frag order") is there much room for interpretation. If that commander has further restricted his small-unit training to the singular 2GW procedure for each battlefield scenario in the official manuals, then the amount of leeway still available to nonrates may be extremely limited.

At that point, the young GI must be extremely careful about what he does differently in combat. He should not get down or move rearward the face of the enemy unless specifically instructed to do so. He will have to find some other—less profound—way to survive a seemingly illogical or risky order. War is inherently dangerous, so the best he can hope for is to recognize some small way to lessen his exposure to harm while fully contributing to the team effort.

Luckily, the manuals are not very explicit about how fire teams, buddy teams, and individuals actually perform their respective roles in many squad maneuvers. For example, they fail fully to describe how point security team members cooperate during a unit move.

Figure 39.1: Snuffy Can Now Follow the Spirit of His Orders
(Source: "Army/Marine Clipart," U.S. Air Univ. [www.au.af.mil/au/awc/awcgate/cliparmy.htm], image designator "1-07a.tif.")

So, the modern-day U.S. rifleman has ample opportunity to enhance his staying power through a little personal planning. Having to comply instantly (and without any thinking) with every order of his NCO should now be just a vestige of his 2GW background. So doing isn't necessary (or even helpful) for most 3GW and 4GW missions. (See Figure 39.1.) Granted, when the foe is yards away and aware of the Americans' presence, all squad members doing precisely as told or in the same sequence practiced is still important. But, when that foe is farther away or the Yanks not yet detected, then there's more room for individual initiative. Still, the contemporary American grunt should only attempt the safest thing where enough procedural leeway exists.

There's Always Room for Self-Improvement

The recent U.S. inductee has only been formally instructed in the most elementary aspects of the three basics—"shooting, moving, and communicating." Should he be first assigned to a mechanized or motorized infantry outfit (now virtually the only kind), his knowledge of more advanced individual movements will come quite slowly. He will mostly learn how to enter and exit the vehicle under various circumstances and to cross unobstructed terrain on

449

foot. Then, if sent to a special-operations unit, he will be immediately thrust into more complicated endeavors—like swimming, fast roping, and parachuting. Meanwhile, the fellow commandos without any prior infantry experience (like from a combat support or combat service support unit) may be almost completely lacking in all the little actions that permit personal agility in open combat.

Due the enemy soldier's relative lack of equipment, he spends much more of his time on "micro-basics": (1) microterrain appreciation; (2) harnessing the senses; (3) night familiarity; (4) nondetectable movement; (5) guarded communication; (6) discreet force at close range; (7) combat deception; and (8) one-on-one tactical decision making.[1] Examples of all are not necessary here. From just one, the average U.S. private should be able to surmise what he's been missing. As he was being shown how to walk the battlefield during various missions, his adversary was learning how to crawl it. While the Yank private was concentrating on how to move stealthily through woods with a full load of gear (to now include helmet electronics), his adversary enjoyed a much broader curriculum. Without much gear at all, he was practicing how covertly to negotiate the following: (1) dry leaves; (2) mud; (3) water; (4) several rows of barbed wire; (5) a mine field; and (6) aerial flares in series.[2]

To some American officers, the modern-day U.S. rifleman might be more useful if he were just to accept his limited introductory training and then do exactly as told. But, no future-combat commander would object to that same snuffy working—during his time off—on a few subcategories of the standard basics. That "fledgling snuffy" might then become a little harder to lead, but he will also be more capable of the self-sufficiency required for a 3GW or 4GW mission.

The Survivor's Agenda

The initial prerequisite for surviving any series of dangerous circumstances will be complete alertness and an opportunistic outlook. (See Figure 39.1.) Yet, no U.S. private is going to risk any action that might bring shame or discredit upon himself. He will thus follow all instructions to the letter and only chance a little "personalized technique" where it has not been specifically disallowed. He knows he should try something a little different in the midst of any standard U.S. maneuver. Yet, he must still keep up with his squad's formation and contribute to its mission. So, any alterations (on his part) to its movement patterns must be limited. Without causing too much of a disruption, a squad member might be able to slightly vary his own speed and approximate whereabouts. He could also manage a quick feint before personally engaging an enemy defender. Throughout the contact, he can additionally expose as little personal body mass as possible.

Just as with larger infantry elements, the U.S. ground pounder must further guard against channelization. Even during something as small as a single-squad assault, what initially appears to

Figure 39.2: A Long Heritage of Never Quitting

WHEN ONE'S LIFE HANGS IN THE BALANCE

be a gap may end up being a firesack. So, he must keep track of every possible piece of cover while moving forward. As in stalking, most helpful would be some object between himself and his most likely assassin. Or, it may be just a tiny fold in the ground. Few combat commanders would object to subordinates "hitting the deck" after encountering fire from three sides at once, or even pulling back a short distance to continue the assault along a slightly different path.

Producing Commensurate Technique

Obviously, the more things each U.S. rifleman knows how to do, the better he is able to do his job in combat. Traditionally, not all of those things have been committed to writing. Does having them passed down from generation to generation over a campfire make them less valid? Most are just common sense anyway, so the fledgling infantryman should be able to resurrect a few on his own.

A tactical technique is a "move" that tiny infantry elements practice ahead of time to be able to do by virtual instinct in an emergency. To become less predictable during a standardized parent-unit maneuver, the U.S. snuffy would ideally like two or three alternatives to any assumed action that is not precisely specified. In fact, consistently to confuse an observant foe, he will need such options for his role in all common scenarios. But, that would be too tall an order, so he starts small by slightly altering one example of predictable behavior at a time.

First, he works on the routine things he can do less well than his peers. For example, a man with a bad leg might substitute a free arm during his urban duck walk. Then, he develops personalized procedures for whatever has not been fully explained to him, like how most expeditiously to flop down during a "fire and movement" exercise. Those who regularly participate in such a drill will seldom resort to a painful swan dive.

To design other helpful techniques, U.S. privates need not wait for permission. They can get together (with a case of refreshment during their off-hours) to develop a few as a type of game. Or each can simply visualize what might work better for him, and then experiment with it outside the barracks. No commander in his right mind would object to that much dedication. Isn't that about what a football team's running back does on his own to improve his yardage?

The Involvement of Others

Surviving for long in heavy combat is necessarily a group pastime. That's because the threats to one's body may come so fast and from so many different directions that only his buddies can thwart them. Thus, two Marine Raider mottoes from WWII—"working together" and "looking out for the man on one's right and left"—are good rules of thumb.[3]

While the U.S. rifleman may not personally like every one of his peers, he still has the responsibility to assist that person in combat.

Fratricide Prevention

No battlefield formation or maneuver is run exactly as practiced because of various things in the way—like rocks, trees, etc. That's why participants can slightly alter their behavior to save a friend.

Obviously, no U.S. rifleman can stop in the midst of a contested assault to administer first aid. But, he can slightly change his position in the on-line formation to where no peer will be directly behind or in front of him. In this way, he greatly reduces the chances of an accidental shooting.

During a poorly defined chance contact, he can also take only well-aimed shots from behind good cover. That way, he more easily identifies the opposition, and runs less risk of being hit by friendly fire. (In an active war zone, American units clash with each other more often than one might think, particularly at night.) Downwards and upwards aimed shots also tend only to hit their intended target.

To give the American rifleman a few more ideas on how to avoid injury to himself and nearby pals, the most common U.S. maneuvers will now be reviewed. This is not to bring discredit upon any of them, only to show where a participant might slightly deviate from the procedure.

During the Usual Patrol

New guys are sometimes awarded a march security mission. This is supposed to be a two-man job. While on point, the lead man watches nearby for trip wires, landmine prongs, and regularly shaped indentations in the earth, while the follow man looks for other trouble farther up the trail. They and the main body often move in leapfrog fashion to keep the latter from completely entering an unchecked danger area. Flank security also walks in staggered column while keeping the patrol leader barely within view. Meanwhile, rear security stays far enough back so that no opposition machinegunner can take the entire patrol under fire from behind.

The patrolling mission often entails moving through stifling heat with a load almost as heavy the man who carries it. While it's much safer to slog through marsh or rice paddy than to follow trails or dikes, only the most hardy GIs can regularly force themselves to do so. That's how many get wounded. A patrol member must try not to take any path of least resistance, or rummage through abandoned gear in search of intelligence. He must also regularly check the status of his rifle. On a live-fire training mission at Camp Lejeune, an exemplary Staff NCO (SNCO) was found to be suffering from heat exhaustion with an live unauthorized round one trigger pull away from being fired. He may have accidently chambered it while pulling his rifle through the thick vines.[4] Nor does a U.S. service member use a rifle to pull a friend out of the marsh. The Marine Raiders of WWII carried toggle ropes for that purpose (among others).[5] Whatever safety habits the patrolling unit appears to lack, the survival-oriented private should develop on his own.

At the Average Chance Contact

During an opposition encounter, the friendly unit normally comes on line facing the enemy force, and then advances toward it. At some point, its "covering and stalking" of the foe by two-man teams up parallel lanes turns into a "fire and movement" exercise. (Look back at the first Chapter 23 picture.) Then, each rusher must realize "it's up he sees me I'm down" (three seconds) on only the first dash from a new location. Should he attempt another run from where he was last seen, "it's up he see's me I'm dead." However, that runner can give himself a slight edge by waiting for someone in another lane to create a diversion. Some leeway also exists in how the "hit and roll" at the end of each sprint is accomplished. Rolling sideways may be not only disorienting, but also take the rusher into someone else's lane. So, more productive would be flopping down forward and immediately crawling to the next piece of cover in one's own lane (whether it be a projection or depression). All the while, his buddy will have to try to suppress all enemy fire coming back along their joint lane. That may sometimes require shooting "around" a running pal. This should not be attempted without knowing his movement idiosyncrasies.

On a Standard Ambush

The normal U.S. ambush is linear and conducted at night. One squad enters the ambush site from the back and then spreads out facing the kill zone. As soon as the squad leader detects enemy in the zone, he triggers the ambush.

The average squad member has only to follow the man to his immediate front into the site, turn to his right or left, and then get down. Yet, there are still a few things he can do to enhance his personal safety. At some point there may be bullets whizzing through this location from the kill zone. He should therefore try to set in behind some solid object—like a tree, rock, or mound. If there are none to be had, a slight depression may be quietly scooped out in the soil. Next, he must not give away the ambush through some last-second sound—like taking his weapon off safe, breaking a twig while shifting his weight, or inadvertently bumping the ground with his rifle butt. If asked after a sprung ambush to check the kill zone for intelligence in total darkness, he should do so very carefully and only while crawling. That's because a wounded foe can be doubly dangerous. Finally, on the way out, the U.S. rifleman cannot lose contact with his former neighbor, or part of the column may get separated from the rest.

Throughout the Most Common Assault

Most common in the U.S. ground attack arsenal is the stand-up, on-line, daylight assault. All the new optics have only produced a nighttime version of the same risky procedure. Besides being careful not to mask the fires of any other assault member, the U.S. private has only a few ways to minimize his own risk. He can crouch instead of standing perfectly erect, or conduct little darting motions instead of steadily moving forward. But, other than that, he must generally "stay the course."

How well that private now shoots within his assigned area of responsibility must be his next focus. Just picking a fire lane that is appropriately shaped takes practice. Ideally, all lanes together should stay as wide as the initial formation. But, unit members who don't regularly practice such things tend to converge toward the center. That, in turn, generates narrowing fire lanes and more chance of a friendly getting shot in the back. It may also leave opposition soldiers at the very edge of the assault sector to fire freely.

Among the U.S. snuffy's most effective shooting techniques is the "double tap from the hip" (where he shifts the first bullet's impact onto the target just as forward observer would a mortar blast). Another is "snap shooting" (where he stops momentarily to acquire a hasty front sight picture and then hurries to catch up with his pals).

Though seldom mentioned in the manuals, the initial assault may not cover the entire objective. So, every assault member must be mentally prepared to "fire and move" (upon direction) across the remainder of the enemy position. During the Faulkland War, at least one such evolution took the better part of a day.[6] Neither do the manuals discuss the likely presence of claymore mines. Coming upon one of these ball-bearing-spewing monsters would be more than enough justification for the U.S. private to temporarily suspend his forward motion. Removing the blasting cap or turning the mine face down takes just a second. No ground assault can withstand the full force of such a mine. During a heavily contested Vietnam War assault, a Marine company commander had to personally disarm one.[7]

While Manning the Normal Defense

To take full advantage of the firepower advantage, the Pentagon has doggedly stuck over the years with either a linear or perimeter defense. Unfortunately, either formation often depends on a thin line of fighting holes for its Main Line of Resistance. For those having to man such holes, there are a number of ways to better their overnight chances. Most important, of course, is staying alert. After patrolling all day with a heavy pack, this can be easier said than done. Normally, it results in the defender being somewhere else mentally with his eyes still open. While such a trick may be enough to prevent a court martial, it will not protect the encampment.

America's perpetual foes like to attack by short-range infiltration. That's why the survival-oriented defender should devise a few games to keep his brain focused on the here and now. Among them might be repeatedly counting the number of indistinct shapes to his front. If that number ever started to grow, he would have to take immediate action. Yet, too heavily concentrating on any one thing to his front might be equally dangerous. That can lead to a type of hypnosis an infiltrator uses to capture a defender's attention long enough for his partner to pass him. Most distinctly to see an object after dark without any electronic assistance, the defender will have to look to one side of it anyway.

With or without NVGs, the enlisted defender must still protect his natural ability to peer into the darkness. That means keeping one eye shut during any bright light (to include a cigarette puff, distant flare, suddenly uncovered moon, or NVG image). Then, he will have to be especially vigilant during any natural diversion— like a passing helicopter, distant shelling, thunder, gusty wind, or rain shower. Nor can he allow himself to be distracted by a watch change or commander visit. He is often one of the last bastions on a very thin U.S. defense line, and the enemy knows it.

Contributing as Much as Possible to the War

Throughout all of these dangers, the U.S. fighter must not lose sight of the fact that regional peace is his ultimate goal. To be of most help, he must appropriately acquit himself on the "field of honor." That means never resorting to meanness, and where possible showing mercy. Even in the heat of battle, he remains the local representative of America.

PART FOURTEEN

HOW MODERN WARS ARE MORE EASILY WON

"ALSO I HEARD THE VOICE OF THE LORD SAYING, 'WHOM SHALL I SEND?
AND WHO WILL GO FOR US?' THEN SAID I, 'HERE I AM; SEND ME!'"
— ISAIAH 6:8

(Source: King James version of the Bible, Isaiah 6:8)

40   An End to All Fighting Is the Goal

- What is the ultimate purpose of most wars?
- Can all opposition soldiers be killed?

Is any collateral damage involving children ever really justified?

(Source: http://search.usa.gov public-domain image from this url: http://www.jointbasemdl.af.mil/shared/media/ggallery/hires/AFG-100730-021.jpg.)

A Still Glorious Military Heritage

For most U.S. war veterans, the service branch to which they belonged was comprised more of people than methods. In fact, many have—on occasion—had to ignore an organizational procedure just to accomplish their mission. Despite all this extra effort, some of the wars didn't turn out well. Yet, all responsibility for that outcome belongs atop their chain of command. And no aspersions should now be levied against any individual veteran's degree of training or performance by those who were not there to share his hardships.

461

But, what of the contemporary American rifleman? Doesn't he now deserve the benefit of all those lessons learned by previous generations—all the little ways of staying alive that big bureaucracies tend to ignore? While his instructors should never impugn the advisability of a past leader's questionable tactical decision, they must still help that modern-day GI to weather similar circumstances. Otherwise, he may one day find himself not fully prepared for his job.

Accurately to assess what has occurred in battle, high-ranking officers must first accept the difference between unadulterated truth and hastily written after-action reports. Then, all U.S. units must be shown how to counter any known organizational drain on their performance. Any headquarters that does not agree to this will be implicitly dishonoring all who have bled for its heritage and endangering those who still serve.

Who Decides to Go to War?

Active combat is something that politicians with no personal experience within a nation's Armed Forces consider a viable way of countering foreign aggression. Yet, the very prospect of open warfare remains subliminally abhorrent to most military professionals (particularly in the ranks that do most of the dying). Their main reason is its uncanny way of lasting longer than anyone expected. At that point, unimaginable evils and trans-generational blood feuds have a way of cropping up, as they did in Germany after WWI and Lebanon in the 1970's. Beirut's Green Line became no longer a front line between organized antagonists, but rather a glimpse into hell. All women and children unlucky enough to fall under a snipers' gaze anywhere near there paid for their innocence in blood. Soon, all battlefield etiquette by either side had fallen by the wayside.

Where men are willing to stoop to any indiscretion to counter perceived evil by their battlefield adversary, the "field of honor" to which all professional soldiers secretly aspire becomes just a pipe dream. So, they study war and constantly prepare for the next one, but most would rather not face the threat to their humanity that killing constitutes. So, they quietly applaud any return to the bargaining table.

U.S. Politicians Are Not Solely to Blame

Within Washington, most elected officials honestly expect an accurate assessment of America's chances against any foreign aggressor from their intelligence agency briefers and military brass. Unfortunately, neither segment of U.S. society has reached such an exalted status by too often "rocking the boat." If so directed by superiors, both would gladly declare a nuclear-armed light-infantry Goliath to be no more dangerous than a petulant school child. Yet, they are not trying intentionally to deceive anyone through such unfounded optimism. A positive outlook is simply how their parent agencies have managed over the years to acquire such big budgetary payouts. Both also try to handle all claims of organizational ineptitude in-house. Hard proof to the contrary seldom reaches their own top echelon, much less Congress or the President. As a result, all departments remain officially capable of handling any security challenge. No amount of historical evidence will change that because each governmental entity is thought to have already assimilated its value. To further compound the illusion, both the intelligence and expeditionary force representatives tend to report a world situation that is much the same as their Commander in Chief already perceives. They are not doing so to please him *per se,* only to comply with their DoD-directed focus of main effort.

The Underlying Problem

Despite a proud heritage, the U.S. Department of Defense is still made up of several "overly tall" governmental bureaucracies. A "bureaucracy" is more than just a type of institutional structure; it is also a way of managing institutional members. The Western version entails so many echelons that the highest seldom receives any input (positive or otherwise) from the lowest. Within this strict a hierarchy of "top-down" direction, some level invariably short-stops any attempt to delegate enough authority downward to achieve peak performance.

A system of administration marked by *officialism* [lack of flexibility and initiative combined with excessive adherence to regulations], *red tape* [official routine or procedure

marked by excessive complexity which results in delay or inaction], and *proliferation* [organizational expansion].[1]
— definition of "bureaucracy," *Webster Dictionary*

For an American military service branch, such an inflexible system leads to less success where the "rubber meets the road" against any "bottom-up-operating" adversary. Since 1900, most of America's wartime opponents (even the Germans) have been of this cultural persuasion.

How Tall Bureaucracies Fare in Combat

Of course, Western-style bureaucracies do have a few advantages. How else might a peace-loving nation quickly multiply the size of its army? But, some of that procedural standardization must at some point be replaced by situationally consistent action, or too many young GIs are going to get hurt. Among the most often reported problems of a Western military bureaucracy is battlefield inertia. That's why particularly insightful U.S. commanders have over the years striven to compensate for this "built-in" drain on their unit momentum. By all accounts, too strenuous an effort in this regard by Marine legend Chesty Puller is why he was never awarded the Congressional Medal of Honor. Because most officers get praised for being "team players," many come to realize such organizational pitfalls after already suffering unnecessary casualties. Thus springs forth a continual (yet routinely suppressed) push toward military reform. The battlefield has changed. Their equipment has changed. So, why shouldn't their tactical procedures as well?

But that is not the way of a big Western bureaucracy. It will staunchly resist any structural or procedural change, however useful. That organization runs on existing structure and established procedure—the virtual equivalent of a *status quo*. Small wonder "lessons learned in combat" are slow to be added to both manual and school, and the tactical wheel to evolve. If no weakness is publicly acknowledged, then what—if anything—needs fixing? Even longtime organizational heads have been unable to make major changes to their internal chains of command and methodologies. The new MW doctrine that General Gray introduced to the Marine Corps in the late 1980's has yet to be fully practiced. Why is that? HQMC has simply not been willing (or able) to decentralize enough control to produce squads that are as self-sufficient as the Germans enjoyed late in WWI. Without more bottom-echelon autonomy, there can be no true MW.

A Chronic Problem with Bureaucratic Roots

Not enough leeway at the bottom echelons is completely consistent with the British and French way of doing things that the U.S. military bought back from WWI. During WWII, the U.S. Marines' SNCO Corps tried valiantly to overcome this tactical shortfall at the squad level. Their job was to keep often inexperienced commanders (whom they were supposed to mentor) informed of any aspect of troop training that had yet to be performed. This totally honest and quite close relationship was to focus more on troop welfare, than pleasing headquarters. As such, it had much to do with the final outcome of the war. So too did the fact that the American military establishment had been allowed to retain its own culture.

Throughout the Vietnam War, top-echelon civilian leaders in Washington privately voiced concerns about whether or not that conflict could ever be won.[2] All the standard excuses came into play: (1) fighting in someone else's back yard; (2) Communist influences on the U.S. media and public; (3) poor leadership in the ARVN; and (4) whether tiny soldiers of another race could fight hard enough. But at no time—throughout this long soul-searching episode—was there any mention of the degree of bureaucracy within the U.S. military contributing to the problem. The U.S. Armed Forces were thought to be doing as much as humanly possible, and thus sacrosanct from suspicion.

Fortunately, DoD now enjoys a leader with a thorough understanding of military history. He has promised to "rapidly rebuild the warfighting readiness of . . . [all] Joint Forces." The only thing the least bit worrisome about this promise is its apparent emphasis on "lethality."[3] But deadly force is still one if the tools for the martial component of 4GW, and its repeated reference may have been only in that context.

First, [to] restore military readiness as we build a more lethal force. . . . This line of effort prioritizes . . . the field-

ing of a decisive conventional force, and retains irregular warfare as a core competency.[4]
— J.N.Mattis, DoD Memorandum, 5 October 2017

The good general would be the first to admit that to be "decisive," a conventional force must somehow consolidate all battlefield gains (successfully occupy them to prevent a follow-on insurgency). He must also realize that any "core competency at [IW]" necessarily involves truly light infantry expertise (as in the Asian tradition) at several of DoD's ground commands.[5] That means squad-sized units that can physically assault or defend against a much bigger opponent—by complete surprise—without the help of any supporting arms or other technological crutch. According to the former commandant of the Army War College, such a (micro-basics-oriented) tactical superiority at the small-unit level will be prerequisite to winning modern 4GW conflicts. (Suffice it say, it would have also helped in Vietnam.)

Our own experience in Iraq and Afghanistan tells us that we have no choice but to meet him [the enemy] on his terms, on the ground in the close and all too often fair fight.[6]
— M.Gen. R.H. Scales (Ret.)
"Armed Forces Journal," December 2007

The Latest Internal Threat to National Security

While two U.S. Service Branches must share in the blame for this shortfall in small-unit tactics, their overly strict control over all subordinate elements may have been largely dictated from above. Congress has also been preventing the transfer of funding from programs those Branches deem unsuccessful, to new ones. And, all of America's Armed Forces are now facing the replacement of a well-refined military culture with one that is more civilian oriented. Modern-day recruits are issued stress cards with which to avoid growing up in boot camp. Recent infantry trainees aren't allowed to "road march" very far without taking a nap. Women and men are placed side by side in combat units without any thought of possible favoritism or other damage to unit cohesion. The list goes on and on.

Figure 40.1: Oldest Infantry Professional in Every Company
(Source: FM 12-75Z3/4 [1979], cover.)

Yet, an even bigger crack has started to appear in the very foundation of the U.S. military. That crack started in the late 1980's with the students at Quantico's Infantry Officer Course being warned by an instructor that their SNCOs were not to be trusted.[7] Then, several years ago, the E-7 participants of one of the Corps' most prestigious SNCO leadership courses were told that their job was to "perpetuate the organization."[8] Only a well-experienced Gyrene or Dogface would fully appreciate the dangers of such an assignment. (See Figure 40.1.) If the young commander's plans aren't to be reassessed by the career professional assigned to him, then what will take the place of this traditional learning dynamic? Success in combat is less about doing as told, and more about been properly directed in the first place.

A Further Limitation

Among the other shortcomings of a Western-style bureaucracy is the continual push toward the lowest common denominator. The small-unit tactics manuals are a perfect example of this. They have been so heavily staffed as no longer to contain enough "how-to" detail on any tactical subject. In effect, any nuance the staffers couldn't agree on has been removed. Their overall intent was still good, however. It was originally thought during WWII that initiative-prone Americans could easily convert simplistic formulas into winning maneuvers. But, with too high an operational tempo and troops trained in one solution per combat scenario as if it were part of their 11 general orders, such a conversion has generally failed to occur.

In Vietnam, most infantry units didn't have any "tactical techniques" (locally tailored small-unit maneuvers) at all. That's the first thing Marine legend Wesley Fox decided to work on after taking over a rifle company in 1st Battalion, 9th Marines.

> Using football as an analogy, my players knew how to play the game, but had no team plays, much less any rehearsal of these plays. . . .
> " . . . My purpose is not to teach you anything but to pull our collective knowledge together, to get our purpose, our plays, our timing down to a razor edge."
> " . . . We will spend two hours each day here talking and walking ourselves through some offensive tactics that I feel are needed."[9]
> — 1st Lt. (and formerly enlisted) Wesley Fox

Most overly tired American grunts in Vietnam would simply mimic the moves they had been shown in Basic Infantry School despite inappropriate circumstances. In other words, at the lowest echelons, the "least common denominator" had finally resulted in mediocrity. It was not mediocrity of courage or dedication, just with regard to their predictability in combat and the evolution of small-unit tactics worldwide. To this day, most U.S. infantry manuals and schools still promulgate premachinegun tactics. No one in their right mind remains visibly upright near the front of an active enemy machinegun.

If this bureaucratic trend toward bottom-echelon ineptitude still plagues the tiny Corps with all its Carlson Raider insights, it almost certainly is continuing to cause problems within the much bigger U.S. Army.

Thankfully, the Pentagon has—of late—been trying to make warfighting more ethical. Instead of risking the lives of any more U.S. assault troops, it now tries to pinpoint every suspected enemy strongpoint or "center of gravity" with a shocking and awesome detonation. But, how ethical can that much explosive really be? And how does one decisively win a widespread conflict without a few U.S. boots on the ground to consolidate?

What "The Land of the Free" Must Do to Win Another War

Now fairly apparent to most American leaders is how battlefield morality revolves around the number of people—of any description—who get injured or killed. That includes, of course, enemy combatants.[10] If someone's mother is accidentally hit by the failing debris after a "pinpoint" U.S. bombardment, the ensuing hard feelings may add hundreds of fighters to the enemy's order of battle. Thus, more future wars might be won, if the Pentagon were to try less firepower. As in police work, not as much shooting may cost a few more American lives in the short run. But, it could save many times that number over the long haul. At some point, peace might even break out, instead of more (and possibly perpetual) warfare. If the teachings of the Church can no longer be allowed to influence the U.S. government, then this country's political leaders must come up with their own "more humanistic" approach to things.

Small, low-intensity wars can be extremely dangerous if allowed to last too long. As soon as neighbors start taking sides, a much larger conflagration—sometimes of global proportions—can ensue. Further, most limited conflicts are more easily resolved with minimal force. That's because unnecessary explosions—from whatever source—tend to foment further violence. Most U.S. citizens realize the Pentagon must maintain a fresh supply of heavy munitions for future contingencies, but they would gladly pay more in taxes to see the old ordnance just thrown away. Perpetual warfare makes them suspect a further magnification of that which President Eisenhower warned in 1961.[11]

41 SOME FORGIVENESS REQUIRED

- Does hatred for the foe in any way help the U.S. warrior?
- When might less frontline animosity actually help him?

Let the one without sin throw the first stone.

After 9/11

After the horrific events of 11 September 2001, forgiveness against Islamic militancy seemed the last thing on anyone's mind. Yet, by making *Tactics of the Crescent Moon* predeployment reading aboard many Army and Marine bases for the next 17 years,[1] many high-ranking U.S. military officers endorsed the concept. Within the preface to that book appears the following:

Vengeance is mine, I will repay, sayeth the Lord.
— Romans 12: 19-20

471

Such an Admission Was Unlikely Before

While many of God's wishes may have been more often considered by U.S. government officials prior to the dawn of the 21st Century, forgiveness was probably not one of them. That's because until the late 1980's, Attrition Warfare (2GW) remained the Pentagon's style of waging all hostilities. As painful as it may now be to admit, hatred played a big role in that way of fighting. Throughout WWI and WWII, American propaganda blatantly touted the enemy's subhuman nature. During WWII in the Pacific where Japanese troops would often pretend to give up before tossing a grenade, "killing the foe" became almost the *mantra* for U.S. Marine replacements.

But, with the lower intensity of the wars in Iraq and Afghanistan has come more of an interest in 3GW and 4GW. Body counts are no longer considered a good measure of who is winning. William S. Lind goes so far as to suggest that a few unanswered U.S. casualties may even help an occupying force.[2] That is also how a farsighted police department sees things. In effect, guardians of society must necessarily accept more danger.

The Contorted Visage of Hatred

Hatred most easily achieves a foothold where only partial knowledge of one's enemy and his beliefs are available. With regard to America's wars in Iraq and Afghanistan, that blind spot has too often been with the Islamic religion. Suffice it to say, the miniscule percentage of radicalized Islamists do not speak for the worldwide Muslim community. Most mainstream followers of the Prophet Muhammad think of the Koran as a historical document. They are no more likely to follow to its violent passages, as a Christian is to act out those in the Old Testament.

Islam, Judaism, and Christianity are all Abrahamic religions. That means they share many of the same precepts. For example, all respect the teachings of Jesus, and effectively adore Mary. A good way to defuse some of the most recent animosity between their respective followers might be to recall a story from the Crusader period. It involves the interaction between Francis of Assisi (a famous Catholic saint) and the Sultan of Egypt.

A Former Soldier Turned Priest

Before becoming a Roman Catholic Priest, Giovanni di Pietro di Bernardone had been a soldier for the Italian city state of Assisi. In a military expedition against Perugia, he was captured at the battle of Collestrada. Upon his release a year later, he attempted to join the papal forces against the Emperor Frederick II in 1205. On his journey to Apulia, he had a vision or dream that bade him return to Assisi and await the call to a new kind of knighthood.[3] After joining the priesthood as Francis, he eventually traveled to Egypt. There, he made a major contribution to the Crusades and war-making in general.

During a lull in the fighting for Damietta, Egypt, on the 5th Crusade in 1219, Francis and a fellow Catholic priest slipped across the Nile and a grisly battlefield to confer with Sultan Malik al-Kamil. Exactly what happened at that meeting is a matter of conjecture. All that is known for sure is that a humble Christian

Figure 41.1: The War Lesson of St. Francis of Assisi
(Source: Painting by Lodovico Cardi between 1597 and 1599, at the following url: https://upload.wikimedia.org/wikipedia/commons/5/57/Cigoli%2C_san_francesco.jpg.)

and prominent Muslim engaged in a reasonable public discussion of their religious differences under the worst of circumstances.[4] However, what eventually resulted from that brief interchange is almost beyond belief.

> Neither man . . . converted to the other's religion. But, the encounter deeply moved them both. One contemporary chronicler wrote that ". . . the ruler of Egypt privately asked [Francis] to pray to the Lord for him so that he might be inspired by God to adhere to the religion that most pleased God."[5]
> — *The Ligorian*, July/August 2016

The Crusader siege of Damietta subsequently succeeded. The conference had no apparent effect on its outcome, but it would have a profound influence on how Church officials viewed Islam, and possibly how Muslim leaders viewed Christianity. Francis had not only preached the gospel but also listened to the Sultan and considered his questions. By so doing he may have sensed some of the goodness and beauty within the Egyptian ruler's traditions. (Those who still doubt any existed need to experience the call to prayer at sundown in Jerusalem.[6])

> Francis' later writings show a deep respect for Islamic practices, such as prostration before God and the public call to prayer. In his last years [Francis was to die seven years later], he recommended that rulers and monks adapt these practices to a Christian context—displaying an openness to learning from other traditions that [now] stands at the heart of interfaith dialogue.[7]
> — *The Ligorian*, July/August 2016

After taking Damietta, the Christian army marched on Cairo but was cut off by the flooding of the Nile. The campaign ended in disaster with the papal legate Pelagio Galvani being forced to surrender with what was left of his army.[8]

Al-Malik al-Kamil (Naser ad-Din Abu al-Ma'ali Muhammad) was the fourth Ayyubid sultan of Egypt. During his tenure as sultan, the Ayyubids had thus defeated the Fifth Crusade,[9] and he became known to the Frankish Crusaders as Meledin. Then in 1228, the Sixth Crusade was launched by the Holy Roman Empire. Upon leaving Cyprus, its Christian forces carefully avoided any outright combat with the powerful armies of still sultan al-Kamil. That's when the former acquaintance of Francis of Assisi was unexpectedly to cede Jerusalem to them in exchange for a ten-year truce.[10]

How Those Events Pertain to Modern Warfare

The papal emissary's visit to the Muslim ruler had no apparent effect over the 5th Crusade's victory at Damietta or its later defeat due to Nile flooding. Yet, it was later to garner the primary objective of the 6th Crusade without any Christian soldiers ever having to fight the more powerful Muslim army.

Of course, warfare may have been conducted somewhat differently in the Middle Ages. While there was a lot of blood being spilled at close quarters, unit leaders seemed to take a more active role in preventing it. Some scholars think they were just following the advice of the Roman military manual *Epitome Rei Militaris*. It advised commanders only to venture directly into battle if they were confident of victory or had no other option.[11] But others believe more humanistic emotions were at work. During the wars between city states of Italy, the side that could outmaneuver the other was sometimes declared victor without any further contact. Elsewhere, the respective heads of opposing armies would occasionally fight so that their subordinates wouldn't have too. At still other places, one side would quit as soon as their leader was killed or captured.[12]

Why didn't any stories like "Francis and the Sultan" come out of the 20th Century? By the time of its worldwide conflagrations, what was later to be called "total war" had apparently been necessary. Nothing short of total surrender was ever considered, and the polarity between sides always too extreme to permit any local negotiations.

So far, the conflicts of the 21st Century are not like that. They have been lower in intensity with the loyalty of the civilian population primarily at stake. Whole tribes can sometimes shift allegiance after nothing more than a monetary payout to its chieftain. That's why the U.S. Army Special Forces village methodology at the end of Chapter 23 worked so well in Afghanistan. That very insightful Sergeant First Class drank tea with all village elders, including those who were pro-Taliban. After explaining his role as only to provide a governmental presence (as opposed to killing or arresting anyone), he dutifully preached the Kabul policies. But then, like Francis at Damietta, he listened to the other tea drinkers and carefully considered their words. Before long, he was able to see through the "double-talk" and occasionally insert a rebuttal. A local armistice of sorts was thus reached that allowed a town deep in enemy territory to be outposted for over six months. Had his tiny legation not been replaced by one from a more traditional combat outfit, the local politics might have eventually swung over to Kabul's point of view. That's how 4GW wars are successfully concluded, and among the very few ways that Afghanistan will ever be pacified.

The prime mover in this contemporary success story had been the American sergeant in charge. Among his many skills were not only mantracking, but also the ability to recite key portions of the Koran (should the need arise). As a multitour veteran of Iran and Afghanistan, he had almost certainly lost friends to enemy fire. But, as a consummate 21st Century warrior, he never allowed himself the luxury of hating his enemy counterpart.

NOTES

SOURCE NOTES:

Illustrations:

Cover art is from U.S. ARMY CENTER OF MILITARY HISTORY
ARTWORK (http://www.history.army.mil/html/artphoto/artwork.html).
It is based on a U.S. government poster entitled "AA Guns in Action:
World War II," in the Monthly Archives for November 2006, with image
designator "1106-1.jpg," and drawn by Herbert Maton Stoops. As a U.S.
government-funded project, this poster is considered in the public
domain.

Image on page 3 is from U.S. ARMY CENTER OF MILITARY HISTORY
ARTWORK (http://www.history.army.mil/html/artphoto/artwork.html).
It is from Topics image designator "4_229_46.jpg."

Images on pages 17, 64, 67, 173, and 215 are also drawn or commissioned by
the U.S. GOVERNMENT and from http://search.usa.gov. See each picture
caption for title, artist, and exact url.

Images on pages 19, 30, 190, 192, and 193 come from WIKIMEDIA.ORG.
They are in the public domain at *Wikipedia Encyclopedia,* s.v. "Battle
of Belleau Wood," "1805 Battle of Derna," "Battle of Trenton," "Battle of
San Jacinto," and "Little Round Top." They have the following image
designators: "Scott Belleau Wood.jpg," "Attack_on_Derna_by_Charles_
Waterhouse_01.jpg," "Battle_of_Trenton_by_Charles_McBarron.jpg,"
"Battle_of_San_Jacinto.jpg," and "Little_Round_Top_view_Edwin_
Forbes.jpg." See each picture caption for title, artist, and exact
url.

Images on pages 61, 95, 189, 373, and 437 are from U.S. ARMY CENTER
OF MILITARY HISTORY ARTWORK (http://www.history.army.mil/
html/artphoto/artwork.html). At Archives, their respective designators
are: "avop10-01_2.jpg," "1006-4.jpg," "Hill_609.jpg," "Image-12.jpg," and
"0507-3.jpg." See picture caption for title, artist, and exact url.

SOURCE NOTES

Picture on page 82 reprinted after asking permission by e-mail of
PINTEREST.COM. This drawing was made in 1940 and has image
designator "b0a98fccc5628b9163cedb39ff43e0cc.jpg." As an educational
nonprofit, Posterity Press considers the use of something of this age and
low resolution to be fair usage, but others must be more mindful of its
possible copyright. Copyright © Pinterest, n.d. All rights reserved.

Picture on page 90 used under provisions of GNU Free Documentation
License, from *WIKIPEDIA ENCYCLOPEDIA*, s.v. "Winter War." As
an educational nonprofit, Posterity Press considers such a reprint to be
fair usage, but others may not. Copyright © n.d. All rights reserved.

Pictures on pages 98, 267, 271, and 275 reprinted with permission of the
SWEDISH ARMED FORCES, with written assurance from Sorman
Information/Media that the artist can no longer be contacted, from *Soldf:
Soldaten I Falt,* by Forsvarsmakten, with illustrations by Wolfgang
Bartsch. Same images on pages 144, 289, 22, 23 of Swedish publication.
Copyrights © 2001 by Forsvarsmakten and Bartsch. All rights reserved.

Pictures on pages 101, 207, and 471 are public domain material from
"War on Terror Images" of the U.S. ARMY at this url: http://history.army.
mil/html/bookshelves/resmat/GWOT/art_and_photos.html. They have the
following image designators: "19b.jpg," "35a.jpg," and "36b.jpg."

Picture on page 114 was created by a U.S. GOVERNMENT AGENCY and
is thus considered within the public domain. This is an official recruiting
poster, image designator "post_usmc_168th-birthday_ww2.jpg," retrieved
from U.S. National Archives and Records Administration, by www.blue-
jacket.com.

Illustration on page 159 reprinted after asking permission of
RESEARCHGATE.NET and IWA PUBLISHING (London) for use of
the map in "Characterization of Water Pollution in Drainage Networks
Using Continuous Monitoring Data in the Citadel area of Hue City,
Vietnam," by Y. Nagano, T. Teraguchi, P. K. Lieu and H. Furumai, from
Water Science & Technology, 70(4):612-619, August 2014. This article
was retrieved in April 2017 from the following url: https://www.research-
gate.net/publication/264793281_Characterization_of_water pollution_in_
drainage_networks_using_continuous_monitoring_data_in_the_
Citadel_area_of_Hue_City_Vietnam.

Illustration on pages 198 reprinted from "CLOSING IN: MARINES IN
THE SEIZURE OF IWO JIMA," by Colonel Joseph H. Alexander,
Marines in WWII Commemorative Series, Headquarters Marine
Corps, 1994.

Picture on page 206 reprinted after written assurance from Orion
Books, London, that the copyright holders for *WORLD
ARMY UNIFORMS SINCE 1939,* text by Andrew Mollo and
Digby Smith, color plates by Malcolm McGregor and Michael
Chappell, can no longer be contacted. This illustrations is from
Part II, Plate 98, of the Orion publication. Copyright © 1975, 1980,
1981, 1983 by Blandford Books Ltd. All rights reserved.

Pictures on pages 41, 277, and 337 reproduced with permission of Dr.
Anatol Taras, Minsk, Belarus, from *PODGOTOVKA RAZVEGCHIKA:
SISTEMA SPETSNAZA GRU,* by A.E. Taras and F.D. Zaruz. The
illustrations are from pages 144-152, 173, 374/375 of Russian document.
Copyright © 1998 by A.E. Taras and F.D. Zaruz. All rights reserved.

Image on page 397 reprinted from NATIONAL GUARD IMAGE GALLERY
(http://www.nationalguard.mil/resources/photo_gallery/heritage/index.htm)
from designator: "arramadi.jpg." Only for an educational nonprofit is it fair
usage. Others must be more careful of a possible copyright. Copyright ©
n.d. All rights reserved.

Picture on page 415 reproduced with permission of RAYTHEON and the
publishers of *ARMED FORCES JOURNAL INTERNATIONAL,* from
"Revolutionary Soldier," by Glen W. Goodman, Jr., October 1999,
page 64. Copyright © 1999 Raytheon. All rights reserved.

Pictures on pages 451 and 473 are in the public domain from
WIKIMEDIA COMMONS. The files are named "Sprit of '76.2.jpeg" and
Cigoli%2C_san_francesco.jpg." They are at *Wikipedia Encyclopedia,* s.v.
"Independence Day" and "Francis of Assisi."

Picture on page 449 is from the U.S. AIR FORCE CLIPART LIBRARY
(www.usafns.com/art.shtml). It has the following image designator:
"1-07a.jpg."

Text:

Text on page xix reprinted with permission of Gene Duncan Books,
Boonville, MO, from *GREEN SIDE OUT,* by Maj. H.G. Duncan and
Capt. W.T. Moore, Jr. Copyright © 1980 by H.G. Duncan. All rights
reserved.

Text on page 179-182 reprinted with permission of a U.S. MARINE
TANK SCOUT of South African descent. Copyright © 2017 (tank scout).
All rights reserved.

ENDNOTES

Preface:

1. *Green Side Out,* by Maj. H.G. Duncan and Capt. W.T. Moore, Jr. (Booneville, MO: Gene Duncan Books, 1980).
2. "The Greatest Movies of All Time," AMC, n.d.
3. Attributed to Archilochus, ancient Greek soldier.

Chapter 1: *The Dichotomy of U.S. Intentions*

1. *History Channel* on line, s.v. "Eisenhower Warns of Military Industrial Complex," as retrieved in February 2017 from this url: http://www.history.com/this-day-in-history/eisenhower-warns-of-the-military-industrial-complex.
2. William S. Lind in Foreword to *One More Bridge to Cross: Lowering the Cost of War,* by H.J. Poole (Emerald Isle, NC: Posterity Press, 1999), p. xii.
3. Pope John Paul II, *Crossing the Threshold of Hope* (New York: Alfred A. Knopf, 1995), pp. 205, 206.
4. *Tennozan: The Battle of Okinawa and the Atomic Bomb,* by George Feifer (Boston: Houghton Miflin, 1992), p. 578; and "Okinawa: The Last Battle," by Appleman et al, p. 468, in *Military Online,* s.v. "Battle of Okinawa."
5. Thomas M. Huber, "Japan's Battle for Okinawa, April - June 1945," *Leavenworth Papers No. 18* (Ft. Leavenworth, KS: Combat Studies Inst., U.S. Army's Cmd. & Gen. Staff College, 1990).
6. Col. David H. Hackworth U.S. Army (Ret.) and Julie Sherman, *About Face* (New York: Simon & Schuster, 1989), p. 594.
7. William S. Lind in Foreword to *The Last Hundred Yards: The NCO's Contribution to Warfare,* by H.J. Poole (Emerald Isle, NC: Posterity Press, 1997), p. xiii.

Chapter 2: *2GW Fixation but No Culture of Death*

1. Constantine Menges, *China: The Gathering Threat* (Nashville, TN: Nelson Current, 2005), p. 55; R.J. Rummel, *Death by Government* (N.p., n.d.), pp. 100-101, op. cit., p. 54; Seventy-year-old Chinese man (in Shanghai airport), in conversation with author in June 2000.
2. "57,762,169 Abortions in America Since Roe vs. Wade in 1973," *LifeNews.com,* 21 January 2015.
3. "Hitler vs. Stalin: Who Killed More," by Timothy Snyder, *New York Review of Books,* 10 March 2011.

4. *Encyclopedia.com,* s.v. "Roe vs. Wade."

5. Ibid, s.v. "Dred Scott vs. Sanford."

Chapter 3: *A Further Look at America's War Record*

1. George B. Clarke, *Their Time in Hell: The 4th Marine Brigade at Belleau Wood* (Pike, NH: The Brass Hat, 1996), pp. 40-66.

2. Linda D. Kozaryn, Armed Forces Press Service, "Belleau Wood: Marines' Shrine," *Leatherneck Magazine*, 9 August 1998, p. 14.

3. Bruce I. Gudmundsson, *Stormtroop Tactics — Innovation in the German Army 1914-1918* (New York: Praeger, 1989), pp. 147-149.

4. *Wikipedia Encyclopedia,* s.v. "Battle of the Bulge," map entitled "The Sixth Panzer Army Attack."

5. Linda D. Kozaryn, "Belleau Wood," *Leatherneck,* p. 14; *History Channel* on line, s.v. "Battle of Belleau Wood Begins," at this url: http://www.history.com/this-day-in-history/battle-of-belleau-wood-begins.

6. *Britannica Encyclopedia,* s.v. "Bataan Death March"; *Wikipedia Encyclopedia,* s.v. "Philippines Campaign 1941-42."

7. Gordon Rottmann, *M3 Medium Tank vs Panzer III – Kasserine Pass 1943* (London.: Osprey Publishing, 2008), p. 74.

8. "Army Battle Casualties and Nonbattle Deaths in World War II: Final Report, 7 December 1941 - 31 December 1946," Combined Arms Research Library, Dept. of the Army, 25 June 1953, p. 92; Carlo d'Este, *Fatal Decision: Anzio and the Battle for Rome* (New York: Harper, 1991), p. 490, in *Wikipedia Encyclopedia,* s.v. "Battle of Anzio."

9. William K. Goolirck and Ogden Tanner and eds., *World War II: The Battle of the Bulge* (Alexandria, VA: Time-Life Books, 1979), pp. 30,31; Charles B. MacDonald, *The Siegfried Line Campaign,* Ctr. of Mil. Hist., U.S. Army, 1984 (previously published around 1963), in *Wikipedia Encyclopedia,* s.v. "Battle of Hürtgen Forest."

10. "Army Battle Casualties and Nonbattle Deaths in World War II: Final Report, 7 December 1941 - 31 December 1946"), Dept. of the Army, p. 92; *History Channel* on line, s.v. "Battle of the Bulgle," at this url: http://www.history.com/topics/world-war-ii/battle-of-the-bulge.

11. Richard E. Ecker, *Battles of the Korean War: A Chronology* (Jefferson, NC: McFarland & Company, 2004), p. 32.

12. Appleman, Roy (1990), *Escaping the Trap: The US Army X Corps in Northeast Korea,* 1950 (College Station, TX: Texas A&M Univ., 1950), pp. 345-348, in *Wikipedia Encyclopedia,* s.v. "Battle of Chosin Reservoir."

13. *Mao's Generals Remember Korea,* trans. and ed. Xiaobing Li, Allan R. Millett, and Bin Yu (Lawrence, KS: Univ. Press of Kansas, 2001), pp. 153-155.

14. Donna Miles, "Battle of the Bulge Remembered 60 Years Later," DoD, 14 December 2004, in *Wikipedia Encyclopedia,* s.v. "Battle of the Bulge."

15. Allan R. Millett and Peter Maslowski, *For the Common Defense* (New York: The Free Press, Macmillan, 1984), p. 460.

16. Goolirck and Tanner and eds., *World War II: The Battle of the Bulge*, p. 188.

17. Trevor N. Dupuy, David L. Bongard, and Richard C. Anderson Jr., *Hitler's Last Gamble* (New York: Harper Perennial, Harper Collins Publishers, 1994), p. 333.

18. Ibid., pp. 341, 342.

19. Ibid., pp. 463-477.

20. Ibid., pp. 498, 499.

21. Millett and Maslowski, *For the Common Defense,* p. 453.

22. Memorandum for the record by H.J. Poole.

23. *MacArthur's Jungle War: The 1944 New Guinea Campaign,* by Stephen R. Taaffe (N.p.: Modern War Studies, 1998), Amazon.com product description.

24. Memorandum for the record by H.J. Poole.

25. H. John Poole, *The Tiger's Way: A U.S. Private's Best Chance for Survival* (Emerald Isle, NC: Posterity Press, August 2003), pp. 173-176.

26. *Zfacts,* s.v. "Vietnam: Cambodia Bombing"; "Laos: Barack Obama Regrets 'Biggest Bombing in History'," *BBC News* on line, 7 September 2016, as retrieved in October 2017 from the following url: http://www.bbc.com/news/world-asia-37286520.

Chapter 4: *The Gradual Demise of Daring and Initiative*

1. "The Sand Pebbles," video cassette, 182 minutes, directed by Robert Wise, 20th Century Fox. 1966.

2. "1805—To the Shores of Tripoli," (April 27: This Day in History), *History Channel on line,* n.d.; "First Barbary War: Battle of Derna," About.com, n.d.; *Wikipedia Encyclopedia,* s.v. "Battle of Derna (1805)" and "Presley O'Bannon."

3. "Marines of the Texas Republic," by Maj.Gen. Marc A. Moore, *Marine Corps Gazette,* August 1978, p. 31.

4. "Individual Heroism Overcame Awkward Command Relationships, Confusion, and Bad Information off the Cambodian Coast," by Col. J.A. Johnson Jr., Lt.Col. R.W. Austin, and Maj. D.A. Quinlan, *Marine Corps Gazette,* October 1977, pp. 24-34.

5. Ibid.

6. *The Infantry Battalion,* FM 7-20 (Washington, D.C.: Hdqts. Dept. of the Army, 1992), chapt. 3.

7. Gudmundsson, *Stormtroop Tactics,* pp. 147-149; Poole, *The Tiger's Way,* chaps. 12 and 19.
8. Lind in Foreword to *One More Bridge to Cross,* p. xii.
9. U.S. Special Forces multi-tour operator in Afghanistan and Iraq, in a series of telephone conversations with author between 26 September 2006 and 1 February 2007.

Chapter 5: *Hidden GI Risks Within the U.S. Operating Style*

1. *Handbook on the Chinese Communist Army,* DA Pamphlet 30-51 (Washington, D.C.: Hdqts. Dept. of the Army, 1960); *Handbook on the Chinese Armed Forces,* DDI-2680-32-76 (Washington, D.C.: DIA, July 1976); *Handbook on the Chinese People's Liberation Army,* DDB-2680-32-84 (Washington, D.C.: DIA, November 1984).
2. Memorandum for the record by H.J. Poole.
3. Ibid.
4. FMFRP 12-34-I, "Pearl Harbor to Guadalcanal," by Lt.Col. Frank O. Hough, Maj. Verle E. Ludwig, and Henry I. Shaw, Jr., vol. I, *History of the U.S. Marine Corps Operations in World War II Series* (Washington, D.C.: Hist. Br., HQMC, n.d.; reprint Quantico, VA: Marine Corps Combat Develop. Cmd., 1989), p. 334.
5. "Flags of Our Fathers," DVD, 132 min., Dreamworks and Warner Bros., 2006.
6. "The Final Campaign: Marines in the Victory on Okinawa," by Joseph H. Alexander, *Marines in WWII Commemorative Series* (Washington, D.C.: Hist. and Museums Div., HQMC, 1996), p. 39.
7. Poole, *The Tiger's Way,* pp. 262-264.
8. Bob O'Bday (Marine machinegunner at Khe Sanh), in conversation with author, 30 July 2000.
9. *The 30-Year War: 1945-1975,* vol. II (Hanoi: The Gioi Publishers, 2001), p. 177.
10. Memorandum for the record by H.J. Poole.
11. Ibid.
12. Joe Normandeau (former member of 3rd Marine Raider Battalion), in conversation with author in 2015.
13. William S. Lind, "Fourth Generation Warfare's First Blow: A Quick Look," *Marine Corps Gazette,* November 2001.
14. William S. Lind, *The Maneuver Warfare Handbook* (Boulder, CO: Westview Press, 1985); *Warfighting,* FMFM 1 (Washington, D.C.: HQMC, 1989); *Tactics,* FMFM 1-3 (Washington, D.C.: HQMC, 1991).
15. H. John Poole, *Gung Ho: The Corp's Most Progressive Tradition* (Emerald Isle, NC: Posterity Press, August 2012), chaps. 1, 5, and 6.

16. H. John Poole, *Phantom Soldier: The Enemy's Answer to Firepower* (Emerald Isle, NC: Posterity Press, August 2001), chapt. 3.

17. *Handbook on the Chinese Communist Army,* DA Pamphlet 30-51.

18. Lind, *The Maneuver Warfare Handbook*; *Warfighting,* FMFM 1 (Washington, D.C.: HQMC, 1989); *Tactics,* FMFM 1-3 (Washington, D.C.: HQMC, 1991).

Chapter 6: *What Eventually Wins Most Wars*

1. Memorandum for the record by H.J. Poole.

2. *Dictionary.com.* s.v. "Asymmetric Warfare."

3. "How the Weak Win Wars: A Theory of Asymmetric Conflict," by Ivan Arreguín-Toft, *International Security,* vol. 26, no. 1 (Summer 2001), pp. 93-95.

4. Ibid.

5. Ibid.

6. *Iwo Jima: Legacy of Valor,* by Bill D. Ross (New York: Vintage, 1986), p. 135.

7. Gudmundsson, *Stormtroop Tactics,* pp. 147-149.

Chapter 7: *Safeguarding Each Combatant's Humanity*

1. "Law of War Training," by William T. Anderson, *Marine Corps Gazette,* April 1981, p. 23.

2. Ibid.; *Wikipedia Encyclopedia,* s.v. "Law of War."

3. "Law of War Training," by Anderson, p. 23.

4. John Boyd, as quoted by Lind in Foreword to *One More Bridge to Cross,* p. xii.

5. "Protocol on Prohibitions or Restrictions on the Use of Incendiary Weapons (Protocol III). Geneva, 10 October 1980," International Committee of the Red Cross, n.d.

Chapter 8: *Playing the Long Game*

1. MoH Citation for Pvt. Hector Albert Cafferata Jr., U.S. Marine Corps, as retrieved in January 2016 from the following url: http://www.history.army.mil/moh/koreanwar.html#CAFFERATA.

2. MoH Citation for Spec. Four Santiago J. Erevia U.S. Army, as retrieved in January 2016 from the following url: http://www.history.army.mil/moh/vietnam-a-l.html#EREVIA.

3. *U.S. Marines in Vietnam: Fighting the North Vietnamese 1967,* Maj. Gary Tefler, Lt.Col. Lane Rogers, and V. Keith Fleming, Jr. (Washington, D.C.: Hist. and Museums Div., HQMC, 1984), pp. 19-21.

4. *Wikipedia Encyclopedia,* s.v. "Dien Bien Phu."

5. "1/4 Afteraction Report for May 1967," as retrieved through the 1/4 Assoc. website, from the following url: http://jones-thompson.com/ onefour/AFTACTREP/1967/MAY67/aftactrep2-may67.htm.

6. John L. Coy USMC, in e-mail to author on 22 May 2016.

Chapter 9: *Never Succumbing to a Defensive Mindset*

1. *Ground Combat Operations,* MCWP3-1 (Washington, D.C.: Headquarters Marine Corps, 2002), chapt. 6.

2. "Finnish Tactics — Small Units," a U.S. Intelligence Report on Finnish Tactics in WWII, *Tactical and Technical Trends,* no. 6, 27 August 1942.

3. DA Pamphlet 20-292, *Warfare in the Far North* (Washington, D.C.: Hdqts. Dept. of the Army, n.d.), pp. 18, 19; *Wikipedia Encyclopedia,* s.v. "Salients, e-entrants and pockets"

4. *Wikipedia Encyclopedia,* s.v. "Salients, e-entrants and pockets"

5. Ibid.

6. Ibid., s.v. "Battle of Suomussalmi."

7. "U.S. Intelligence Report on Finnish Tactics in WWII."

8. *Tactics of the Crescent Moon: Militant Muslim Combat Methods,* by H. John Poole (Emerald Isle, NC: Posterity Press, 2004), chapt. 5; *Wikipedia Encyclopedia,* s.v. "Battle of Grozny (1994–95)."

9. Poole, *The Tiger's Way,* pp. 280-283.

10. Maj. Norman L. Cooling, "Russia's 1994-96 Campaign for Chechnya: A Failure in Shaping the Battlespace," *Marine Corps Gazette,* October 2001, p. 62.

11. Poole, *Phantom Soldier,* chapt. 4.

12. DA Pamphlet 20-292, *Warfare in the Far North,* pp. 18, 19.

13. Ibid.

14. *Ground Combat Operations,* MCWP3-1, p. 1-6.

15. Ibid., glossary.

16. *Warfighting,* MCWP1 (Washington, D.C.: Headquarters Marine Corps, 1997), pp. 45, 92.

17. "Finnish Tactics — Small Units."

18. Jenkki Soturi (U.S. Marine veteran of Vietnam and student of Finnish tactics), in a letter to author of 7 November 2001.

19. Motti Tactics," *Combat Forces Journal,* January 1950, pp. 12, 13.

20. Ibid., pp. 12, 13.

21. "Finnish Tactics—Small Units."

22. "Motti Tactics," pp. 12, 13.

23. "Finnish Tactics—Small Units."

24. DA Pamphlet 20-291, *Effects of Climate on Combat in Russia* (Washington, D.C.: Hdqts. Dept. of the Army, n.d.), p. 65.

25. *Global Warrior: Averting WWIII,* by H. John Poole (Emerald Isle, NC: Posterity Press, 2011), appendix A.

26. DA Pamphlet 20-292, *Warfare in the Far North,* pp. 16, 17.

27. "Motti Tactics in Finnish Military Historiography since World War II." by Pasi Tuunainen (Univ. of Eastern Finland), *International Bibliography of Military History,* issue 33. 2013, p. 135.

28. "New Approaches to Artic Warfare," by Pasi Tuunainen (Univ. of Eastern Finland), *Nordia Geographical Publications,* 43:1, p. 93.

29. *A New Era of Warfare: Finnish Thoughts on the Modern Image of War,* by J.Z. Duncker, binder with English translation (N.p.: Unknown German publisher, 1977), p. 20.

30. Ibid., p. 23.

31. DA Pamphlet 20-291, *Warfare in the Far North,* p. 65.

32. Ibid.

33. "Handbook on Japanese Forces," *TM-E 30-480* (Washington, D.C.: U.S. War Dept., 1944. Reprint, Baton Rouge, LA: LSU Press, 1991), p. 117.

34. "Finnish Tactics—Small Units."

35. *Operation Buffalo: USMC Fight for the DMZ,* by Keith William Nolan (New York: Dell, 1992).

36. *Encyclopedia Britannica,* s.v. "Russo-Finnish War."

37. "Motti Tactics," pp. 10, 11.

Chapter 10: *U.S. Grunts Now Need Policing Skills*

1. *Wikipedia Encyclopedia,* s.v. "flamethrower."

2. Ibid.; Prohibitions or Restrictions on the Use of Incendiary Weapons (Protocol III), U.S. Dept. of State, agreement signed at Geneva in 1980.

3. David Hambling, "U.S. Denies Incendiary Weapon Use in Afghanistan," *Security,* 15 May 2009.

4. "From Makin to Bougainville: Marine Raiders in the Pacific War," by Maj. Jon T. Hoffman, *Marines in WWII Commemorative Series* (Washington, D.C.: Marine Corps Hist. Ctr., 1995), pp. 1-5.

5. J. Mark Hord (long-time student of UW), review of *Terrorist Trail* in "Stratiotes' Military History Book Reviews," *Unconventional Warfare Review,* 31 January 2007, as first posted at *Defense and the National Interest* website plus www.d-n-i.net and g2-forward.

6. H. John Poole, *Dragon Days: Time for "Unconventional" Tactics* (Emerald Isle, NC: Posterity Press, August 2007), chaps. 9-12.

Chapter 11: *SWATs Can't Use All U.S. Infantry Tactics*

1. President Ronald Reagan, "Message to the Senate Transmitting a Protocol to the 1949 Geneva Conventions," as retrieved from this url: http://www.reagan.utexas.edu/archives/speeches/1987/012987b.htm; Legal Information Inst., "Geneva Conventions," as retrieved from the following url: http://www.law.cornell.edu/wex/geneva_conventions; *Wikipedia Encyclopedia,* s.v. "Protocol I" and "Protocol II."
2. "Conventional Weapon: 30/11/2011 Overview," International Committee for the Red Cross, from the following url on 28 March 2014: http://www.icrc.org/eng/war-and-law/weapons/conventional-weapons/overview-conventional-weapons.htm.
3. Memorandum for the record by H.J. Poole.

Chapter 12: *3GW Conditioning and Tactics*

1. Gudmundsson, *Stormtroop Tactics,* pp. 147-149.
2. William S. Lind and Lt.Col. Gregory A. Thiele USMC, *4th Generation Warfare Handbook* (Kouvola, Finland: Castalia House, 2015), p. 110.
3. H. John Poole, *Afrique: A Warning for America* (Emerald Isle, NC: Posterity Press, September 2015), p. 48.
4. Lind and Thiele, *4th Generation Warfare Handbook*, p. 52.
5. DA Pamphlet 550-35, "Nepal and Bhutan Country Studies," *Area Handbook Series* (Washington, D.C.: Hdqts. Dept. of the Army, 1993), pp. 1-30.
6. Gen. Van Tien Dung, *Our Great Spring Victory: An Account of the Liberation of South Vietnam,* trans. John Spragens, Jr. (Hanoi: The Gioi Publishers, 2001), p. 51.
7. Lt.Col. Robert W. Lamont, "'Urban Warrior'—A View from North Vietnam," *Marine Corps Gazette,* April 1999, p. 33.
8. Poole, *Gung Ho,* chaps. 5 and 6.
9. Maj.Gen. Robert H. Scales, U.S. Army (Ret.), "Small-Unit Dominance: The Strategic Importance of Tactical Reform," *Armed Forces Journal,* October 2010, p. 42.
10. Lind, *The Maneuver Warfare Handbook*; *Warfighting,* FMFM 1 (Washington, D.C.: HQMC, 1989); *Tactics,* FMFM 1-3 (Washington, D.C.: HQMC, 1991).
11. John Boyd, as quoted by Lind in Foreword to *One More Bridge to Cross*, p. xii.

12. Pope John Paul II, *Crossing the Threshold of Hope*, pp. 205, 206.

13. Robert Dougherty, *The Breaking Point*, in *4th Generation Warfare Handbook*, by Lind and Thiele, p. 121.

14. Martin van Creveld, *Fighting Power*, in *4th Generation Warfare Handbook*, by Lind and Thiele, p. 121.

15. Truong Chinh, *Primer for Revolt*, intro. Bernard B. Fall (New York: Praeger, 1963), pp. 114-117.

16. *McGraw-Hill Dictionary of Scientific and Technical Terms*, s.v. "Unconventional Warfare."

17. Normandeau, Joe (former member of 3rd Marine Raider Battalion), in conversations with author in October 2010.

18. "From Makin to Bougainville," by Hoffman, p. 23.

19. Poole, *Phantom Soldier*, chapt. 3.

20. *Global Warrior*, by Poole, appendix A.

Chapter 13: 4GW Conditioning and Tactics

1. Lind and Thiele, *4th Generation Warfare Handbook*, p. 110.

2. Ibid., p. 112.

3. Ibid., pp. 111, 112.

4. Ibid., p. 50.

5. Ibid., chapt. 3.

6. *The Last Hundred Yards: The NCO's Contribution to Warfare*, by H.J. Poole (Emerald Isle, NC: Posterity Press, 1997), pp. 350, 356.

7. "Motti Tactics in Finnish Military Historiography since World War II," by Tuunainen, p. 124.

8. Gudmundsson, *Stormtroop Tactics*, pp. 147-149.

9. "New Approaches to Artic Warfare," by Tuunainen, p. 95.

10. Sec. of Defense Donald H. Rumsfeld, as quoted in *Funding the Enemy: How US Taxpayers Bankroll the Taliban*, by Douglas A. Wissing (Amherst, New York: Prometheus Books, 2012), chapt. 3; and confirmed from "Poppy Fields Are Now a Front Line in Afghanistan War," by James Risen, *New York Times* on line, 16 May 2007.

11. "Poppy Fields Are Now a Front Line in Afghanistan War," by James Risen, *New York Times* on line, 16 May 2007.

12. Lind and Thiele, *4th Generation Warfare Handbook*, p. 50.

13. Ibid.

14. Ibid., pp. 66, 67.

15. Don Moser, "Their Mission Defend, Befriend," *Life Magazine*, 25 August 1967.

16. Poole, *Gung Ho*, chapt. 14.

17. Richard D. Jackson, *Yesterdays Are Forever: A Rite of Passage through the Marine Corps and Vietnam* (Galt, CA: Working Title Publishing, 2007), p. 113.

18. Assoc. of the Combined Action Program website; *U.S. Marines in Vietnam: An Expanding War, 1966,* by Jack Shulimson, HQMC, 1982, p. 239, in *Our War Was Different* by Al Hemingway (Annapolis, MD: Naval Inst. Press, 1994., p. 6; "Fact Sheet on the Combined Action Force," III MAF, 31 March 1970.

19. "List of Killed in Action: Combined Action Program, 1965-1971," as compiled and published by HQMC, and retrieved from Assoc. of the Combined Action Program website.

20. "2nd CAG Command Chronology, 1 October-30 November 1968," as retrieved from Assoc. of the Combined Action Program website.

21. Moser, "Their Mission Defend, Befriend."

22. "List of Killed in Action: Combined Action Program, 1965-1971," as compiled and published by HQMC, and retrieved from Assoc. of the Combined Action Program website.

23. Moser, "Their Mission Defend, Befriend."

24. Memorandum for the record by H.J. Poole.

25. "List of Killed in Action: Combined Action Program, 1965-1971."

26. Unofficial website for the CAP program; *Wikipedia Encyclopedia,* s.v. "Combined Action Platoon."

27. Assoc. of the Combined Action Program website; Jackson, *Yesterdays Are Forever,* p. 113; Colin Leinster, "The Two Wars of General Walt," *Life,* 26 May 1967, pp. 83, 84; "The Future Role of the Combined Action Program," by Major Michael Duane Weltsch USMC, thesis for U.S. Army's Cmd. and Gen. Staff College, 1991.

28. William C. Westmoreland, *A Soldier Reports* (New York: Da Capo Press, 1989), as quoted in *Wikipedia Encyclopedia,* s.v. "Combined Action Platoon."

29. Lewis W. Walt, *Strange War, Strange Strategy: A General's Report on the War in Vietnam* (New York: Funk and Wagnalls, 1970), p. 105, as quoted in *Wikipedia Encyclopedia,* s.v. "Combined Action Platoon."

Chapter 14: *Fewer Wars That Go On Forever*

1. Sun Tzu, *The Art of War,* trans. and with an intro. by Samuel B. Griffith, foreword by B.H. Liddell Hart (New York: Oxford Univ. Press, 1963), p. 39.

2. "Rolling Thunder (1965–8)," *American Military and Naval History Online,* 5 November 2010; *The United States Strategic Bombing Surveys,* reprinted by Air Univ. Press, Maxwell Air Force Base, October 1987; "Vietnam, Cambodia Bombing," Zfacts, as retrieved from its website on 13 January 2011.

3. *Vietnam War Almanac,* gen. ed. John S. Bowman (New York: World Almanac Publications, 1985), p. 358.

4. Bruce Cumings, in "The Battle of the Minds" segment of *Korea — The Unknown War Series* (London: Thames TV in assoc. with WGBH Boston, 1990), NC Public TV, n.d.

5. Member of U.S. Strategic Bombing Survey Team, in *Last Days of World War II,* History Channel, 28 March 1999; *The United States Strategic Bombing Surveys,* reprinted by Air Univ. Press, Maxwell Air Force Base, October 1987.

6. "The Battle of the Minds" segment of *Korea — The Unknown War Series* (London: Thames TV in assoc. with WGBH Boston, 1990), NC Public TV, n.d.

7. Cummings, in "The Battle of the Minds" segment of *Korea — The Unknown War Series.*

8. *Iwo Jima: Legacy of Valor,* by Ross, p. 163; Lt.Col. Whitman S. Bartley, *Iwo Jima: Amphibious Epic* (Washington, D.C.: Hist. Br., HQMC, 1954), p. 111.

9. Chesty Puller in *Marine,* by Burke Davis (New York: Bantam, 1964), p. 390.

10. *Global Warrior,* by Poole, appendix A.

11. Maj.Gen. Edwin Simmons USMC (Ret.), in "An Entirely New War" segment of *Korea — the Unknown War* (London: Thames TV in cooperation with WGBH Boston, 1990), NC Public TV, n.d.

12. Poole, *Gung Ho,* chaps. 3, 4, and 7.

13. *Global Warrior,* by Poole, appendix A.

Chapter 15: *Less Telegraphing of Intentions*

1. "An Entirely New War" segment of *Korea — The Unknown War Series* (London: Thames TV in assoc. with WGBH Boston, 1990), NC Public TV, n.d.

2. Ibid.

3. Max Hastings, *The Korean War* (New York: Touchstone, Simon & Schuster, 1987), p. 196.

4. *Wikipedia Encyclopedia,* s.v. "Operation Ripper."

5. Hastings, *The Korean War,* p. 196.

6. *One More Bridge to Cross: Lowering the Cost of War,* by H.J. Poole (Emerald Isle, NC: Posterity Press, 1999), p. 34.

7. Bert Hardy, photographer for the *Picture Post,* in "There is No Substitute for Victory" segment of *Korea — The Unknown War Series* (London: Thames TV in assoc. with WGBH Boston, 1990), NC Public TV, n.d.

8. Nicholas Blanford, Daniel McGrory, and Stephen Farrell, "Tactics That Have Kept the Middle East's Most Powerful Army at Bay," *The Times* (UK), 10 August 2006.

9. "Why Did Armored Corps Fail in Lebanon," by Hanan Greenberg, *Israeli News,* 30 August 2006.

10. Edward Cody and Molly Moore, "Analysts Attribute Hezbollah's Resilience to Zeal, Secrecy and Iranian Funding," *Washington Post,* 14 August 2006.

11. *The Operations Process.* FM 5-0 (Washington, D.C.: Hdqts. Dept. of the Army, 26 March 2010), p. B-16.

Chapter 16: *Captives Have Intelligence Value*

1. *The Jerusalem Bible,* Matthew 5:44 and 22:21, and Luke 6:26; "Sergeant Alvin York," by Dr. Michael Birdwell, Great War Society, as retrieved on 15 October 2009 from its website, www.worldwar1.com; "Sergeant York," DVD, 134 minutes, Warner Brothers Pictures, isbn #1-4198-3829-6.

2. Huber, "Japan's Battle for Okinawa, April - June 1945," *Leavenworth Papers No. 18.*

3. "WWII Korea Under the Rising Sun," by Allyn Vannoy, *Warfare History Network,* September 2016.

4. Ibid.

5. Ibid.

6. "Halls of Montezuma," film, 113 minutes, 20th Century Fox, 1950.

7. "Railroad Guns," History, Skylighters (225th AAA Searchlight Bn.).

8. *Modern Insurgencies and Counter-Insurgencies: Guerrillas and Their Opponents,* by Ian Frederick and William Beckett (New York: Routledge 2001), p. 198.

9. Jim Simpson, "Scouts to the Rescue," *Defense Watch,* 17 September 2003.

10. Attributed to Sun Tzu.

11. "Canticle of Zecharia," Luke 1:68-79, as reprinted on the inside front cover of *Shorter Cristian Prayer* (New York: Catholic Book Publishing Co., 1988).

Chapter 17: *Wounding More Impairs Foe Infrastructure*

1. Pope John Paul II, *Crossing the Threshold of Hope*, pp. 205, 206.

2. "Individual Heroism Overcame Awkward Command Relationships, Confusion, and Bad Information off the Cambodian Coast," by Johnson, Austin, and Quinlan, pp. 24-34.

3. Attributed to Sun Tzu.
4. Ibid.
5. "North Vietnamese Army/Viet Cong Military Medical Capabilities," Scientific and Technical Intelligence Report, from the CIA's Directorate of Science and Technology, 14 October 1968 (now declassified and approved for release 16 May 2011), preface, p. iii.
6. Ibid., summary and conclusions, p. 1.
7. Ibid., discussion, p. 9.
8. Ibid., discussion, p. 2.
9. Ibid., discussion, p. 5.
10. Ibid., discussion, p. 7.

Chapter 18: *The Quarry Need Not Be Allowed to Escape*

1. "Handbook on German Military Forces," *TM-E 30-451* (Washington, D.C.: U.S. War Dept., 1945; reprint Baton Rouge, LA: LSU Press, 1990), pp. 239-242.
2. Philip Warner, "Japanese Army of World War II," vol. 20, *Men-at-Arms Series* (London: Osprey Publications Ltd., 1972), pp. 23-25.
3. William P. Baxter, *Soviet Airland Battle Tactics* (Novato, CA: Presidio Press, 1986), pp. 132-136.
4. "North Korea Handbook," *PC-2600-6421-94* (Washington, D.C.: U.S. Dept. of Defense, 1994), p. 3-91.
5. "Handbook on the Chinese Communist Army," *DA Pamphlet 30-51*, p. 26.
6. Douglas Pike, *PAVN: People's Army of Vietnam* (Novato, CA: Presidio Press, 1986), p. 268.
7. Dupuy, Bongard, and Anderson, *Hitler's Last Gamble*, pp. 341, 342.
8. Hackworth and Sherman, *About Face.*
9. "Handbook On U.S.S.R. Military Forces," *TM 30-340* (Washington, D.C.: U.S. War Dept., 1945), republished as *Soviet Tactical Doctrine in WWII*, with foreword by Shawn Caza (West Chester, OH: G.F. Nafziger, 1997), p. V-27.
10. Warner, "Japanese Army of World War II," pp. 23-25.
11. Excerpt from *Chinese Manual on Field Fortifications*, in "A Historical Perspective on Light Infantry," U.S. Army Combat Studies Inst. Research Survey No. 6, n.d., illustration on p. 88; *Mao's Generals Remember Korea,* pp. 153-155.
12. Terrence Maitland and Peter McInerney, *Vietnam Experience: A Contagion of War* (Boston: Boston Publishing, 1968), p. 100.
13. Ho Khang, *The Tet Mau Than 1968 Event in South Vietnam* (Hanoi: The Gioi Publishers, 2001), p. 14.

493

14. Col. Huong Van Ba, as quoted in *Portrait of the Enemy,* by David Chanoff and Doan Van Toai (New York: Random House, 1986), p. 152.

15. Trinh Duc, as quoted in *Portrait of the Enemy,* by David Chanoff and Doan Van Toai (New York: Random House, 1986), p. 101.

16. Jack Shulimson, Lt.Col. Leonard A. Blaisol, Charles R. Smith, and Capt. David A. Dawson, *U.S. Marines in Vietnam: The Defining Year, 1968* (Washington, D.C.: Hist. & Museums Div., HQMC, 1997), p. 210.

17. George W. Smith, *The Siege at Hue* (New York: Ballantine Publishing, 1999), p. 203; Nicholas Warr, *Phase Line Green: The Battle for Hue, 1968* (Annapolis, MD: Naval Inst. Press, 1997); Eric Hammel, *Fire in the Streets: The Battle for Hue, Tet 1968* (Pacifica, CA: Pacifica Press, 1991), p. 296.

18. Eric Hammel, *Fire in the Streets: The Battle for Hue, Tet 1968* (Pacifica, CA: Pacifica Press, 1991), pp. 349, 350.

19. Ibid., p. 308.

20. Nicholas Warr, *Phase Line Green: The Battle for Hue, 1968* (Annapolis, MD: Naval Inst. Press, 1997), p. 217.

21. *Weatherbase,* s.v. "Hue, Vietnam," as retrieved in April 2017 from the following url: http://www.weatherbase.com/weather/weather. php3?s=25884.

22. Khang, *The Tet Mau Than 1968 Event in South Vietnam,* p. 76.

23. *History Net,* s.v. "Tet Offensive." As retrieved in April 2017 from the following url: http://www.historynet.com/tet-what-really-happened-at-hue.htm.

24. Shulimson et al, *U.S. Marines in Vietnam: The Defining Year, 1968,* p. 213.

25. "Twenty-Five Days and Nights of Continuous Fighting for the Wonderful Victory" (NVA Army, 1968), quoted in *The Siege at Hue,* by Smith, p. xv.

26. Ibid., p. 210.

27. Poole, *Phantom Soldier,* p. 194; *Wikipedia Encyclopedia,* s.v. "Viet Cong and Vietnam People's Army Logistics and Equipment."

28. Smith, *The Siege at Hue,* pp. 9, 169.

29. Hammel, *Fire in the Streets,* pp. 339, 340.

30. Shulimson et al, *U.S. Marines in Vietnam: The Defining Year, 1968,* p. 210.

31. Selectiveasia.com, s.v. "Weather for January in Central Vietnam." As retrieved in April 2017 from the following url: http://www. selectiveasia.com/vietnam-holidays/weather/january.

32. *Wikipedia Encyclopedia,* s.v. "Perfume River" and "Day Truong Son Mountains (Annamite Range)."

33. Calendar12, s.v. "Moon Phases for February 1968," as retrieved in April 2017 from the following url: https://www.calendar-12.com/moon_calendar/1968/february.

34. Khang, *The Tet Mau Than 1968 Event in South Vietnam*, pp. 49, 50.

35. Shulimson et al, *U.S. Marines in Vietnam: The Defining Year, 1968*, pp. 212, 213.

36. Ibid., p. 212.

37. *Trip Advisor,* s.v. "Thien Mu Pagoda," as retrieved in April 2017 from this url: https://www.tripadvisor.com/Attraction_Review-g293926-d451126-Reviews-Thien_Mu_Pagoda-Hue_Thua_Thien_Hue_Province.html; *Wikipedia Encyclopedia,* s.v. "Pagoda of the Celestial Lady."

38. *Encyclopedia Britannica,* s.v. "Hue."

39. *Insight Guides: Vietnam,* ed. Helen West (Singapore: APA Publications, 1991), p. 204.

40. Hammel, *Fire in the Streets,* pp. 33, 34.

41. Shulimson et al, *U.S. Marines in Vietnam: The Defining Year, 1968,* p. 352.

42. Ibid., p. 201.

43. *History Net,* s.v. "Tet Offensive."

44. Shulimson et al, *U.S. Marines in Vietnam: The Defining Year, 1968,* p. 214.

45. Ibid., p. 213.

46. Nora Levin, *The Holocaust* (New York: Thomas Y. Crowell Co., 1968), pp. 343-352.

47. "Hue City, 1968: Winning A Battle While Losing A War," by Maj. Norman L. Cooling, *Marine Corps Gazette,* July 2001.

48. *Encyclopedia Britannica,* s.v. "Hue."

49. *The Vietnam War,* DVD, 1003 minutes, documentary, by Ken Burns and Lynn Novick, *PBS,* 19 September 2017, episode six.

50. *Wikipedia Encyclopedia,* s.v. "Operation *Ke.*"

51. *Navsource Online,* s.v. "Japanese Supply Submarines," as retrieved in April 2017 from the following url: http://www.navsource.org/archives/08/08455.htm.

52. *Iwo Jima: Legacy of Valor,* by Ross, p. 135.

53. Memorandum for the record by H.J. Poole.

Chapter 19: *A Minimally Disrupted Environment*

1. "Historian Says the U.S. Is 'Losing Hearts and Minds in Afghanistan'," interview between Steve Inskeep and Lt.Col. Aaron B. O'Connell USMC, *NPR* on line, 19 April 2017.

2. Ibid.

3. Ibid.
4. Ibid.
5. Poole, *Gung Ho*, chapt. 2.
6. "Fact Sheet on the Combined Action Force," III MAF, 31 March 1970; Poole, *Gung Ho,* chapt. 14.
7. "List of Killed in Action: Combined Action Program, 1965-1971"; "The Future Role of the Combined Action Program," by Major Michael Duane Weltsch USMC, thesis for U.S. Army's Cmd. and Gen. Staff College, 1991, p. 104; Al Hemingway, *Our War Was Different* (Annapolis, MD: Naval Inst. Press, 1994, p. 11; "Fact Sheet on the Combined Action Force," III MAF, 31 March 1970.
8. Memorandum for the record by H.J. Poole.
9. "Lost Battles of the Vietnam War," as retrieved in April 2017 from the following well-respected url: http://www.g2mil.com/lost_vietnam.htm.
10. Lt.Col. R.F. Reid-Daly, *Pamwe Chete: The Legend of the Selous Scouts* (Weltevreden Park, South Africa: Covos-Day Books, 1999), pp. 182, 183.
11. Sergeant of South African descent from U.S. Marine Tank Battalion Scout Platoon, in e-mail to author on 21 May 2017.
12. Ibid.
13. "Delta Company: The Push to Baghdad," DVD, *60 Minutes,* Discovery Communications, 2008.
14. 1st. Sgt. John H. "Josh" Schmuck, in a telephone conversation with author in July 2017.
15. Sgt. Erik Rue (Marine scout/sniper and former rifleman), in telephone conversation with author on 12 May 2017.
16. "Danger Room in Afghanistan: A Close Fight, and a Couple of Miracles," by Noah Shachtman, *Security,* 27 August 2009.
17. Ibid.
18. Ibid.
19. Ibid.
20. Ibid.
21. Rue telephone conversation.

Chapter 20: *Hardly a Shot Was Fired*

1. *Wikipedia Encyclopedia,* s.v. "Battles of Lexington and Concord."
2. *American Revolutionary War Facts* website, s.v. "Battle of Trenton," as retrieved in January 2017 from the following url: http://www.american-revolutionary-war-facts.com/American-Revolutionary-War-Battle-Facts/Battle-of-Trenton-Facts.html.

3. *The American Revolutionary War* website, s.v. "Battle of Trenton, New Jersey," as retrieved in January 2016 from the following url: http://www.revolutionary-war.net/battle-of-trenton.html.

4. *U.S. Army Heritage and Information Center* website, s.v. "Yorktown Redoubt #10," as retrieved in January 2017 from this url: http://www.carlisle.army.mil/ahec/trail/Redoubt10/.

5. *Texas Military Forces Museum* website, s.v. "San Jacinto," as retrieved in December 2016 from the following url: http://www.texasmilitaryforcesmuseum.org/tnghist5.htm.

6. *Wikipedia Encyclopedia,* s.v. "Little Round Top."

7. Gregory Jaynes and the eds., *The Civil War: The Killing Ground—Wilderness to Cold Harbor* (Alexandria, VA: Time-Life Books, 1986), p. 33.

8. Ibid.

9: "Belleau Wood," by Major Stoney Bates, *Marine Corps Gazette,* November 2015.

10. *Great War Society* website, s.v. "The Battle of Belleau Wood," as retrieved in December 2016 from the following url: http://www.worldwar1.com/dbc/ct_bw.htm.

11. *Iwo Jima: Legacy of Valor,* by Ross, pp. 297-300.

12. Ibid., p. 294

13. Ibid., pp. 297-300.

14. Ibid.

15. Ibid.

16. *"Okinawa: The Last Battle,"* by Roy E. Appleman, James M. Burns, Russell A. Gugeler, and John Stevens, *U.S. Army in World War II Series* (Washington, D.C.: U.S. Army's Ctr. of Mil. Hist., 2000), pp. 322, 323.

17. *The Recapture of Guam,* by Maj. O.R. Lodge, "USMC Historical Monograph" (Washington, D.C.: Hist. Br., HQMC, 1954), pp. 89-92.

18. *Okinawa: Victory in the Pacific,* by Maj. Chas. S. Nichols, Jr., and Henry I. Shaw, Jr., "USMC Historical Monograph" (Washington, D.C.: Hist. Br., HQMC, 1955), pp. 182-184.

19. *Dan Marsh's Marine Raider Page,* created by former member of 4th Raider Battalion, s.v. "Okinawa: The Last Battle."

20. "The Final Campaign: Marines in the Victory on Okinawa," by Alexander, p. 35.

21. *Okinawa: Victory in the Pacific,* by Nichols and Shaw, p. 183.

22. "Isolation of Rabaul," by Henry I. Shaw and Maj. Douglas T. Kane USMC, part II, chapt. 4 (The Dragon's Peninsula Campaign), *History of U.S. Marine Corps Operations in World War II Series* (Washington, D.C.: Hist. Br., HQMC, 1963), pp. 130-145.

23. David Scott-Donelan (former member of Selous Scouts and SA Recce), in telephone conversation with author on June 2004; Chris Vermaak, "Rhodesia's Selous Scouts," *Armed Forces (Journal)*, May 1977.

24. Reid-Daly, *Pamwe Chete*, p. 342.

25. Ibid., pp. 182, 183.

Chapter 21: *Making Friends Out of Enemies*

1. Chris Vermaak, "Rhodesia's Selous Scouts," *Armed Forces (Journal)*, May 1977.

2. Reid-Daly, *Pamwe Chete*, p. ii.

3. Simpson, "Scouts to the Rescue."

4. Leroy Thompson, *Dirty Wars: Elite Forces vs. the Guerrillas* (Devon, England: David & Charles, 1991).

5. *Modern Insurgencies and Counter-Insurgencies,* by Frederick and Beckett, p. 198.

6. *Wikipedia Encyclopedia,* s.v. "Kit Carson Scout."

7. CORDS Historical Files, CMH, File 77, Folder 10, from *Mismanaging Mayhem,* by James Jay Carafano and Richard Weitz (Westport, CT: Greenwood Publishing Group, 2008), p. 98.

8. Ibid.

9. *Encyclopedia Britannica,* s.v. "Total War."

10. *Oxford Dictionary,* s.v. "Total War," as retrieved in January 2017 from the following url: https://en.oxforddictionaries.com/definition/total_war.

11. *Encyclopedia Britannica,* s.v. "Franco-Prussian War."

12. Ibid., s.v. "Treaty of Versailles."

Chapter 22: *Battlefield Acts of Mercy*

1. Memorandum for the record from H.J. Poole.

2. Ibid.

3. Ibid.

4. Ibid.

5. *Good Reads*, s.v. "St. Thomas Acquinas Quotes," as retrieved in January 2017 from the following url: http://www.goodreads.com/quotes/1286440-mercy-without-justice-is-the-mother-of-dissolution-justice-without.

6. *King James Bible* on line, s.v. "Micah 6:8," as retrieved in April 2017 from this url: https://www.kingjamesbibleonline.org/Micah-6-8/.

7. Lind and Thiele, *4th Generation Warfare Handbook,* p. 10.

8. Ibid., p. 14.
9. Ibid. p. 8.
10. Ibid., p. 14.

Chapter 23: *Sufficient Tiny-Element Ability on Offense*

1. Gen. John A. Lejeune, as quoted by Major Gen. O.K. Steele, in his opening address at the graduation of a Camp Lejeune Platoon Sergeants School class at the Camp Geiger Chapel around 1990.
2. "Three Levels of War," USAF College of Aerospace Doctrine, Research and Education, *Air and Space Power Mentoring Guide,* vol. 1 (Maxwell AFB, AL: Air University Press, 1997).
3. Lt Col L. D. Holder (one of the main authors of FM 100-5 in 1982), "A New Day for Operational Art," *Army Magazine,* March 1985, pp. 22–28, 32, in "Three Levels of War."
4. Allan R. Millett and Williamson Murray, "Lessons of War," *The National Interest,* Winter 1988–1989, pp. 83–95, in "Three Levels of War."
5. *The Operational Level of War* (Fort Leavenworth, KS: U.S. Army Cmd. and Gen. Staff College, December 1985), in "Three Levels of War."
6. Drew and Snow, pp. 20-21, in "Three Levels of War."
7. "Accurate information, but low-level stuff," review of *Tactics of the Crescent Moon,* by "C," on Amazon, 25 May 2010.
8. Unidentified NCOs to Chesty Puller, in FMFRP 12-110, *Fighting on Guadalcanal* (Washington, D.C.: U.S.A. War Office, 1942), pp. 35-37.
9. Col. G.C. Thomas USMC, Maj.Gen. Vandegrift's Chief of Staff, in FMFRP 12-110, *Fighting on Guadalcanal* (Washington, D.C.: U.S.A. War Office, 1942), p. 65.
10. Eric Hammel, *Guadalcanal: Starvation Island* (New York: Crown Publishers, 1987), p. 315.
11. Burke Davis, *Marine* (New York: Bantam, 1964), p. 140.
12. "Chesty' Puller's Epic Stand," by Jon T. Hoffman, *World War II Magazine*, n.d., and probably republished in *Leatherneck,* n.d.
13. Photograph caption of An Hoa Explosion, *Pinterest,* n.d.; "An Hoa Project," by Warren Stansbury, n.d., as retrieve in April 2017 from the following url: http://anhoaproject.co.uk/story-warren-stansbury.html.
14. *5th Marines Command Chronology for 23 February 1969,* in "An Hoa Project."
15. *3rd 155mm Gun Battery Command Chronology for 23 February 1969,* in "An Hoa Project."

16. Memorandum for the record by H.J. Poole.

17. Charles Soard (experienced infantry scout and frequent visitor to Vietnam), in telephone conversation with author on 28 March 2001.

18. "Biên Hòa Air Base Ammo Dump Explosion Sapper Attack," by Arnold John Houchin, originally written on 12 January 1972, then published by the Assoc. for USAF Vietnam War Veterans of Air/Security Police, through *Vietnam War Stories,* in 2005.

19. "Lost Battles of the Vietnam War."

20. "Attacks on MAG-16, Hill 22, and the Attempted Attack on the Da Nang Airfield, *3rd Marines in Vietnam* website, n.d.

21. "Lost Battles of the Vietnam War."

22. Memorandum for the record by H.J. Poole.

23. Ibid.

24. Gudmundsson, *Stormtroop Tactics,* pp. 147-149; Poole, *The Tiger's Way,* chapt. 19.

25. Memorandum for the record by H.J. Poole.

26. Gudmundsson, *Stormtroop Tactics,* pp. 147-149; Poole, *The Tiger's Way,* chapt. 19.

27. Ibid.

28. *Handbook on the Chinese Communist Army,* DA Pamphlet 30-51.

29. Poole, *Phantom Soldier,* chapt. 7.

30. U.S. *Marines in Vietnam: An Expanding War − 1966,* by Jack Shulimson (Washington, D.C.: Hist. & Museums Div., Hdqts. U.S. Marine Corps, 1982), pp. 186, 187.

31. Ibid.

32. Ibid.

33. Ibid.; "Marines Batter North Vietnamese Trying to Destroy Tanks," by Wallace Beene *(Stars & Stripes* Bureau Chief), *Tribune-Democrat* (Johnstown, PA), 28 August 1966.

34. Ibid.

35. Ibid.

36. CWO4 Charles "Tag" Guthrie USMC (Ret.) (Cam Lo defense participant and historian), in an e-mail message to author on 8 May 2017.

37. Mike Rask (A/1/4 member), as quoted in Guthrie e-mail of 8 May 20-17.

38. Don Cuncio (A/1/4 member), as quoted in Guthrie e-mail of 8 May 2017.

39. *1/4 Command Chronology,* as quoted in Guthrie e-mail of 8 May 2017.

40. Peter Mancuso (A/1/4 member), as quoted in Guthrie e-mail of 8 May 2017.

41. Larry Schorr (A/1/4 member), as quoted in Guthrie e-mail of 8 May 2017.

42. CWO4 Charles "Tag" Guthrie USMC (Ret.) (Cam Lo defense participant and historian), in an e-mail message to author on 9 May 2017.

43. Dennis Mansuour (A/1/4 member) as quoted in Guthrie e-mail of 15 My 2017.

44. U.S. *Marines in Vietnam: An Expanding War — 1966,* p. 187; Guthrie e-mail of 8 May 2017.

45. Sgt. Donald Allen Lewis (killed at Cam Lo). Note left on the Vietnam Memorial Wall.

46. SSgt. John W. Joys Navy Cross Citation, at *Home of Heroes* website.

47. "Marines Batter North Vietnamese Trying to Destroy Tanks," by Wallace Beene *(Stars & Stripes* Bureau Chief), *Tribune-Democrat* (Johnstown, PA), 28 August 1966.

48. Memorandum for the record by H.J. Poole.

49. *1st Bn., 4th Marines Command Chronology;* U.S. *Marines in Vietnam: An Expanding War — 1966,* pp. 186, 187.

50. H. John Poole, *Strategic Rifleman: Key to More Moral Warfare* (Emerald Isle, NC: Posterity Press, 2014), table 13.2.

51. Multi-tour U.S. Army Special Forces veteran of wars in Iraq and Afghanistan and expert mantracker, in e-mail and telephone conversations with author between June 2013 and May 2015.

Chapter 24: *Sufficient Tiny-Element Ability on Defense*

1. John Shaw and the editors of Time-Life Books, *Red Army Resurgent* (Chicago: Time-Life Books, 1979), p. 158.

2. Ibid., p. 167.

3. Ibid., p. 161.

4. Ibid.

5. Ibid., pp. 163-165.

6. Ibid.

7. Levin, *The Holocaust,* pp. 343-352.

8. Ibid.

9. *Wikipedia Encyclopedia,* s.v. "Warsaw Ghetto Uprising."

10. Levin, *The Holocaust,* pp. 343-352.

11. *Wikipedia Encyclopedia,* s.v. "Warsaw Ghetto Uprising."

12. Ibid.

13. Levin, *The Holocaust,* pp. 343-352.

14. *Wikipedia Encyclopedia,* s.v. "Warsaw Uprising."

15. Leon Uris, *Mila 18* (New York: Bantam, 1983), p. 363.

16. Ibid.

17. "Great Escape," *PBS's Nova,* NC Public TV, 5 June 2007.

18. Uris, *Mila 18,* p. 363.

18. Ibid.

20. Ibid., pp. 373, 374.

21. "Handbook On U.S.S.R. Military Forces," *TM 30-340,* p. V-2; *The Bear Went over the Mountain,* p. 18.

22. Khang, *The Tet Mau Than 1968 Event in South Vietnam,* p. 37.

23. Foreword to *Mao Tse-Tung On Guerrilla Warfare,* trans. Brig. Gen. Samuel B. Griffith USMC (New York: Frederick A. Praeger, Publisher, 1961), from Maj. Frank D. Pelli, "Insurgency, Counterinsurgency, and the Marines in Vietnam," *EHistory,* n.d., p. 3.

24. Khang, *The Tet Mau Than 1968 Event in South Vietnam,* p. 9.

25. Dung, *Our Great Spring Victory,* p. 11.

26. Khang, *The Tet Mau Than 1968 Event in South Vietnam,* pp. 14-16.

27. Maj. Frank D. Pelli, "Insurgency, Counterinsurgency, and the Marines in Vietnam," *EHistory,* n.d., p. 2.

28. Ibid.

29. Poole, *Phantom Soldier,* p. 143.

30. Maj.Gen. Hoang Minh Thao, *The Victorious Tay Nguyen Campaign* (Hanoi: Foreign Languages Publishing House, 1979), p. 68.

31. Khang, *The Tet Mau Than 1968 Event in South Vietnam,* p. 18.

32. Ibid., p. 34.

33. Pike, *PAVN: People's Army of Vietnam,* p. 268.

34. Khang, *The Tet Mau Than 1968 Event in South Vietnam,* pp. 15, 16.

35. *Mao Tse-tung: An Anthology of His Writings,* ed. Anne Fremantle (New York: Mentor, 1962), pp. 128, 129.

36. Khang, *The Tet Mau Than 1968 Event in South Vietnam,* p. 10.

37. James F. Dunnigan and Albert A. Nofi, *Dirty Little Secrets of the Vietnam War* (New York: Thomas Dunne Books, 1999), pp. 265, 266.

38. Khang, *The Tet Mau Than 1968 Event in South Vietnam,* p. 15.

39. Ibid.

40. Thai, *How South Vietnam Was Liberated,* p. 17.

41. Ibid., p. 75.

42. Memorandum for the record by H.J. Poole.
43. Ibid.
44. "Lost Battles of the Vietnam War."
45. Memorandum for the record by H.J. Poole.

Chapter 25: *Urban Warnings of Impending Trouble*

1. Warr, *Phase Line Green,* pp. 104-160; *Global Warrior,* by Poole. pp. 236, 237.
2. Lt.Col. Timothy L. Thomas and Lester W. Grau, "Russian Lessons Learned from the Battles for Grozny," *Marine Corps Gazette,* April 2000, pp. 45-48.
3. *The Last Hundred Yards,* by Poole, pp. 308-311.

Chapter 26: *Rural Hints of Nearby Opposition*

1. *Iwo Jima — Legacy of Valor,* by Ross, p. 135.
2. Col. Merritt A. Edson, in FMFRP 12-110, *Fighting on Guadalcanal,* from U.S.A. War Office (Washington, D.C.: U.S. Govt. Printing Office, 1942), p. 14.
3. Memorandum for the record by H.J. Poole.
4. Attributed to James Corbett, famous hunter of man-eating tigers and leopards in India from 1910 to the 1930's.
5. *All the King's Men,* by Nigel McCrery (New York: Simon & Schuster, 1999), previously titled *The Vanished Battalion* (N.p., n.d.); "All the Kings Men," *Exxon Masterpiece Theater*, London: *BBC* in conjunction with WGBH Boston, NC Public TV, 26 November 2000.

Chapter 27: *Moving More Discretely Around in a City*

1. Memorandum for the record by H.J. Poole.

Chapter 28: *Nonconfrontational Land Navigation*

1. Memorandum for the record from H.J. Poole.
2. Davis, *Marine,* p. 98.
3. Memorandum for the record from H.J. Poole.

4. Ibid.
5. Ibid.
6. FMFRP 12-110, *Fighting on Guadalcanal* (Washington, D.C. U.S.A. War Office, 1942), p. 25.
7. Sgt. Toney Price, two-hour interview by Kirk Hauser, CD, 2013.

Chapter 29: *Giving the "Slip" to a Sizeable Pursuer*

1. Memorandum for the record from H.J. Poole.
2. Chris Ronan (former Marine scout/sniper and special operator), in conversation with the author in November 2017.
3. Poole, *The Tiger's Way,* table 2.2.
4. Ibid.
5. Poole, *Dragon Days,* table 18.1.
6. Poole, *The Tiger's Way,* table 2.2.
7. Allan A. Macfarlan, *Exploring the Outdoors with Indian Secrets* (Harrisburg, PA: Stackpole Books, 1971), p. 90.
8. Poole, *Dragon Days,* table 18.1.
9. *All the King's Men,* by McCrery; "All the Kings Men," *Exxon Masterpiece Theater,* London: *BBC* in conjunction with WGBH Boston, NC Public TV, 26 November 2000.
10. David Scott-Donelan, *Tactical Tracking Operations: The Essential Guide for Military and Police Trackers* (Boulder, CO: Paladin Press, 1998), pp. 85-94.
11. Ibid., p. 3.
12. Hoang Khoi, *The Ho Chi Minh Trail* (Hanoi: The Gioi Publishers, 2001), p. 46.
13. *Combat Tracking* (Paluda, Malaysia: British Army Combat Training Center, n.d.), p. 23.
14. Scott-Donelan, *Tactical Tracking Operations,* p. 3.
15. George Robert Elford, *Devil's Guard* (New York: Dell Publishing, 1971), p. 255.
16. Scott-Donelan, *Tactical Tracking Operations,* p. 3.
17. William H. Bartsch, "Crucial Battle Ignored," *Marine Corps Gazette,* September 1997, pp. 82-84.
18. Memorandum for the record by H.J. Poole.

Chapter 30: *Foe More Constructively Considered a Criminal*

1. DA Pamphlet 550-45, "Malaysia: A Country Study," *Area Handbook Series* (Washington, D.C.: Hdqts. Dept. of the Army, 1984), pp. 50-59; Poole, *Terrorist Trail,* p. 152.
2. Pope John Paul II, *Crossing the Threshold of Hope,* pp. 205, 206.

Chapter 31: *Ruinous Urban Assault No Longer Necessary*

1. Robert R. Smith, "The War in the Pacific (Triumph in the Philippines)," *U.S. Army in World War II Series* (Washington, D.C.: U.S. Army Center of Mil. Hist., 1963 [reprint 1993]), p. 254, from "The Battle of Manila," by Thomas M. Huber, in CSI Home Publications Research MHIST [database on line] (Ft. Leavenworth, KS: Combat Studies Inst., U.S. Army Cmd. & Gen. Staff College, n.d. [updated 30 September 2002; cited 1 January 2003]), p. 4; and "37th Div. Report after Action," p. 43, from "The Battle of Manila," by Huber, p. 7.

2. Thomas M. Huber, "The Battle of Manila," in CSI Home Publications Research MHIST [database on line] (Ft. Leavenworth, KS: Combat Studies Inst., U.S. Army Cmd. & Gen. Staff College, n.d. [updated 30 September 2002; cited 1 January 2003]), p. 15.

3. Smith, "The War in the Pacific (Triumph in the Philippines)," pp. 259-260; and Richard Connaughton, John Pimlott, and Duncan Anderson, "The Battle for Manila" (Novato, CA: Presidio Press, 1995), p. 109; and "37th Div. Report after Action," p. 45; and Stanley L. Frankel, "The 37th Infantry Division in World War II" (Washington, D.C.: Infantry Journal Press, 1948), p. 272; both from "The Battle of Manila," by Huber, p. 7.

4. Huber, "The Battle of Manila," pp. 11, 12.

5. "One Minute to Zero," DVD, 105 minutes, Warner Archive, 2011.

6. "War's Hidden Chapter: Ex-GIs Tell of Killing Korean Refugees," by San-Hun Choe, Charles J. Hanley, Martha Mendoza, after investigative research by Randy Herschaft, Associated Press, 30 September 1999.

7. Article 28 of Geneva Convention IV of 1949, International Committee of the Red Cross, n.d.

8. Article 51(7), of the 1977 Additional Geneva Convention Protocol I, International Committee of the Red Cross, n.d.

9. "Blueprint on a Brilliant Raid," by Steve Macko, *ENN Daily Intel. Rpt.,* vol. 3, no. 114, 24 April 1997; *Wikipedia Encyclopedia,* s.v. "Japanese embassy hostage crisis."

10. Lamont, "Urban Warrior—A View from North Vietnam," p. 33.

11. "Blueprint on a Brilliant Raid," by Macko.

12. "Peru Hostage Crisis Comes to a Violent End," by Steve Macko, *ENN Daily Intel. Rpt.,* vol. 3, no. 113, 23 April 1997.

13. "Blueprint on a Brilliant Raid," by Macko; *Wikipedia Encyclopedia,* s.v. "Japanese embassy hostage crisis."

14. *Iwo Jima: Legacy of Valor,* by Ross, p. 333; "Closing In: Marines in the Seizure of Iwo Jima," by Col. Joseph H. Alexander, *Marines in World War II Commemorative Series* (Washington, D.C.: Hist. & Museum Div., HQMC, 1994), p. 46.

15. *Encyclopedia.com,* s.v. "Mosul," as retrieved in July 2017 from the following url: http://www.encyclopedia.com/places/asia/iraq-political-geography/mosul.

16. "The Battle for Mosul in Maps," by Paul Torpey, Pablo Gutierrez, and Paul Scruton, *The Guardian* (U.K.), 26 June 2017.

17. "Mosul Factsheet: Brief Guide to the City and the Liberation Offensive, by Hannah Lynch , *Rudaw* (Kurdish media network), 17 October 2016.

18. "What the Largest Battle of the Decade Says about the Future of War," by Ben Watson, *Defense One,* 7 July 2017; "The Battle for Mosul in Maps," by Torpey, Gutierrez, and Scruton.

19. "U.S. Confirms Coalition Strike in Mosul District Where Dozens Reported Killed," Reuters, 25 March 2017.

20. "What the Largest Battle of the Decade Says about the Future of War," by Watson.

21. Ibid.

22. Ibid.

23. "North Vietnamese Army and Viet Cong Infantry/Artillery Regiments," *Global Security,* n.d.; Hammel, *Fire in the Streets,* p. 29.

24. "What the Largest Battle of the Decade Says about the Future of War," by Watson.

25. Warr, *Phase Line Green,* pp. 104-105, 155-160; Hammel, *Fire in the Streets,* pp. 304, 305.

26. *History Net,* s.v. "Battle of Singapore"; *Wikipedia Encyclopedia,* s.v. "Battle of Singapore." 27.

27. "Special Report—How Mosul Fell," by Ned Parker, Isabel Coles, and Raheem Salman, *Reuters,* 4 October 2014.

28. Ibid.

29. Ibid.

30. Ibid.

31. Ibid.

32. "ISIS Bury 45 of Their Own Fighters ALIVE After They Fled the Battlefield," by Sam Webb, *Mirror* (U.K.), 11 May 2016, as retrieved in July 2016.

32. "Special Report—How Mosul Fell," by Parker et al.

33. Ibid.

34. Ibid.

35. Ibid.

36. Abdul Hussein Al-Obeidi, AP, "U.S. Increases Pressure on Najaf," *Jacksonville Daily News (NC),* 24 August 2004, p. 3A.

37. Ravi Nessman, AP, "U.S. Launches Airstrike in Fallujah," *Jacksonville Daily News (NC),* 6 July 2004, pp. 1A, 2A.

38. Scott Peterson, "Fallujans Flee from US, Zarqawi Fight," *Christian Science Monitor,* 19 October 2004, pp. 1, 7.

39. *ABC's Morning News,* 12 November 2004.

40. *FOX's News,* 11 November 2004.

41. *ABC's Morning News,* 12 November 2004.

42. Scott Peterson, "Marine, Insurgent Tactics Evolve," *Christian Science Monitor,* 17 November 2004, p. 6; Slobodan Lekic, AP, "Attacks Target Troops, Police," *Jacksonville Daily News (NC),* 12 December 2004, pp. 1A, 7A.

43. " 'Couple of Hundred' ISIS Fighters Left in Mosul," by Nick Paton Walsh and Mohammed Tawfeeq, *CNN* on line, 26 June 2017.

44. "What the Largest Battle of the Decade Says about the Future of War," by Watson.

45. Ibid.

Chapter 32: *Controlling the Urban Expanse*

1. Gen. David Petraeus (or an aide) in back-and-forth e-mails with the author around the late winter of 2006.

2. "Leaving Iraq," by Tom Bowman, *NPR Special Series* on line, n.d.

3. DA PAM 550-68, "Iran Country Study," *Area Handbook Series* (Washington, D.C.: Hdqts. Dept. of the Army, 1989), p. 267.

4. Sepehr Zabih, *The Iranian Military in Revolution and War* (London: Routledge, 1988), p. 14.

5. Ibid., pp. 210-212.

6. Kenneth Katzman, *Warriors of Islam: Iran's Revolutionary Guard* (Boulder, CO: Westview Press, 1993), pp. 82-84.

7. Ibid., pp. 84, 85.

8. Memo for the record by H.J. Poole.

9. Ibid.

10. H. John Poole, *Tequila Junction: 4th Generation Counterinsurgency* (Emerald Isle, NC: Posterity Press, 2008), pp. 216-219.

11. Reid-Daly, *Pamwe Chete,* pp. 71-73.

12. Peter Stiff, *The Silent War: South African Recce Operations, 1969-1994* (Alberton, South Africa: Galago Publishing, 1999), pp. 289, 290.

13. Vietnam era Marine counter-intelligence, infantry, and CAP veteran, in telephone conversations with author from 6-13 January 2012; Poole, *Gung Ho,* chapt. 14.

14. Memorandum for the record by H.J. Poole.

Chapter 33: *Countryside Cannot Be Pacified by Drone*

1. "Countries Hit By U.S. Tomahawk Cruise Missiles Since Desert Storm," *Forbes,* 17 April 2017.
2. "Charting the Data for U.S. Airstrikes in Pakistan, 2004," by Bill Roggio, *Long War Journal,* n.d.
3. "The Predator War," by Jane Mayer, *New Yorker* on line, 26 October 2009; "Al-Shabab Commander Thought to Be Killed in Somalia Airstrike," by Abdi Guled, AP, *Jacksonville Daily News (NC),* 1 August 2017, p. A9.
4. Gen. David Petraeus (or an aide), by e-mail with the author around the later winter of 2006.
5. "U.S. Should Replace Drone Strikes in Pakistan with Outreach to Tribal Areas," by Akbar Ahmed, *Christian Science Monitor* on line, 30 May 2013.
6. "Counting Civilian Casualties in the CIA's Drone War," by Meg Braun, *Foreign Policy,* 2 November 2012.
7. *Global Warrior*, Poole, table 10.1.
8. "Waziristan-Based Terror Group Takes Credit for Lahore Assault," by Bill Roggio, *Long War Journal*, 30 March 2009.
9. "U.S. Drone Strike Kills Rebels in Pakistan," from AFP, *Sydney Morning Herald* (Australia), 5 October 2010.
10. Liam Stack, "Fifth NATO Tanker Attacked in Six Days Since Pakistan Sealed Border Post," *Christian Science Monitor,* 5 October 2010.
11. Ibid.
12. "The Battle That Helped Change the Course of the 'Israeli' Occupation," *Daily Star* (Lebanon), 6 September 2000.
13. Naomi Segal, *Jewish Telegraphic Agency,* "IDF Absolved of Blame in Deaths of Naval Commandos in Lebanon," *San Francisco Jewish Community Publication,* 31 October 1997.

Chapter 34: *The Implicit Part of Every Mission*

1. "Okinawa: The Last Battle," by Appleman et al, pp. 322, 323.
2. Dictionary.com, s.v. "Mosaic Law."

Chapter 35: *What's Strategically Vital to U.S. Foes*

1. "Remarks by President Trump on the Strategy in Afghanistan and South Asia," The White House, 21 August 2017.
2. Poole, *Afrique*, table 1.2.

3. Truong Chinh, *Primer for Revolt,* intro. Bernard B. Fall (New York: Praeger, 1963), pp. 114-117.

4. *Washington Post,* 25 January 1999; and *Wall Street Journal,* 15 March 2000; in *"China's Military-Owned Businesses,"* by Shirley A. Kan, CRS Report 98-197 (Washington, D.C.: U.S. Govt. Printing Office, 17 January 2001).

5. H. John Poole, *Sinoland: The Subversion of Freedom's Bastion* (Emerald Isle, NC: Posterity Press, 2016), chapt. 19.

6. Al Santoli, "The Panama Canal in Transition: Threats to U.S. Security and China's Growing Role in Latin America," *American Foreign Policy Council Investigative Report,* 23 June 1999.

7. *CIA World Factbook,* s.v. "China: Transnational Issues."

8. "Drug Trafficking and North Korea: Issues for U.S. Policy," by Ralph F. Perl, CRS Report RL32167, last in a series of updates, 27 November 2006; Bill Powell and Adam Zagorin, "The Sopranos State," *Time,* 23 July 2007.

9. Ibid.; U.S. Dept. of State, International Narcotics Control Strategy Report [INCSR], March 2003, p. VIII-43, in "Drug Trafficking and North Korea," by Perl, p. 8.

10. Gretchen Peters, *Seeds of Terror: How Heroin Is Bankrolling the Taliban and al-Qaeda* (New York: Thomas Dunne Books, 2009), p. 31; Chanakya Sen, review of *Karachi: A Terror Capital in the Making,* by Wilson John, *Asia Times Online,* 17 January 2004; Lawrence Lifschultz, "Pakistan, the Empire of Heroin," in McCoy and Block, "War on Drugs," p. 320, and Lifschultz, *Heroin Empire,* pp. 71-72, and *The Herald* (Pakistan) during 1985, all in *Seeds of Terror,* by Peters, p. 37.

11. "A Godfather's Lethal Mix of Business and Politics," *U.S. News & World Report Online,* 5 December 2005; "How Pakistan's ISI Funds Its Proxy War," by Syed Nooruzzaman, *The Tribune* (India), 28 November 1999.

12. Peters, *Seeds of Terror,* pp. 53, 111, 155, 160; an Afghan confederate of Noorzai, in *Seeds of Terror,* by Peters, p. 74.

13. "Everyone Wants Cut in Afghan Drug Trade," from McClatchy News Service, *Jacksonville Daily News* (NC), 10 May 2009, p. A8.

14. "Hezbollah Uses Mexican Drug Routes into U.S.," *Washington Times,* 27 March 2009; Rohan Gunaratna, *Inside al-Qaeda: Global Network of Terror* (Lahore: Vanguard, 2002), pp. 164, 165; Chris Zambelis, "Radical Islam in Latin America," in *Unmasking Terror: A Global Review of Terrorist Activities,* vol. III, ed. Jonathan Hutzley (Washington, D.C: Jamestown Foundation., 2005 through 2007), p. 484.

15. Rachel Ehrenfield, *Funding Evil: How Terrorism is Financed and How to Stop It* (Chicago: Bonus Books, 2005), in *Warring on Terrorism,* by Stephen E. Hughes, part I (internet piece), 2005, pp. 24-26.

16. "Hezbollah Uses Mexican Drug Routes into U.S."

17. Joseph S. Bermudez Jr., *North Korean Special Forces* (Annapolis, MD: Naval Inst. Press, 1998), p. 147.

18. Ibid., p. 248.

19. *Mao's Generals Remember Korea,* p. 154.

20. Ibid., p. 168.

21. Ibid., p. 155.

22. Ibid., p. 154.

23. *Voina v Korea: 1950-1953,* by A.A. Kuryacheba (N.p.: Polygon Publishers, 2002), p. 582.

24. Ibid.

25. Bermudez, Jr., *North Korean Special Forces,* p. 251.

26. "North Korea's Secret Strategy in a War with America: Go Underground," by Kyle Mizokami, *The National Interest,* 6 May 2017.

27. Ibid.

28. Maj.Gen. Robert H. Scales, U.S. Army (Ret.), "Infantry and National Priorities," *Armed Forces Journal,* December 2007, pp. 14-17, 45.

29. "North Koreans Assisted Hezbollah with Tunnel Construction," Jamestown Foundation, *Terrorism Focus,* vol. III, issue 30, August 2006; *ABC's Nightly News,* 28 July 2006; Embassy World, s.v. "Embassy Listings for North Korea"; Poole, *Terrorist Trail,* pp. 35-38; Poole, *Dragon Days,* pp. 5, 6.

30. Scales, "Infantry and National Priorities," pp. 14-17, 45.

31. "North Koreans Assisted Hezbollah with Tunnel Construction," Jamestown Foundation.

Chapter 36: *Waging War with Technology Alone*

1. "60 Minutes," *CBS News,* 20 August 2017.

2. "Ground Penetrating Radar FAQ," USRadarInc., n.d.

3. Chris Ronan (former Marine scout/sniper and special operator), in conversation with the author in November 2017.

4. "U.S. Drops Largest Non-Nuclear Bomb on Islamic State," by Justin Sink, *Bloomberg News* on line, 13 April 2017.

5. Edgar O'Ballance, *Afghan Wars: Battles in a Hostile Land, 1839 to Present* (Karachi: Oxford Univ. Press, 2002), pp. 158, 253; Rohan Gunaratna, *Inside al-Qaeda: Global Network of Terror* (Lahore: Vanguard, 2002), p. 58.

6. "U.S. Drops Largest Non-Nuclear Bomb on Islamic State," by Sink; "About the Giant Bomb the U.S. Used in Afghanistan," by Anne Cronin, *Bloomberg News* on line, 13 April 2017.

7. "Afghanistan Cave Complexes 1979–2004: Mountain Strongholds of the Mujahideen," by Mir Bahmanyar (Oxford: Osprey Publishing, 2004).

8. "U.S. Drops Largest Non-Nuclear Bomb on Islamic State," by Sink.

9. Ibid.

Chapter 37: *Withdrawal and Then Rebuilding Momentum*

1. *Handbook on the Chinese People's Liberation Army,* pp. 26, 38.

2. *Tactics of the Crescent Moon,* by Poole, chapt. 1; Nigel McCrery, *All the King's Men* (New York: Simon & Schuster, 1999).

3. Timothy L. Lupfer, "The Dynamics of Doctrine: The Changes in German Tactical Doctrine during the First World War," *Leavenworth Papers No. 4* (Ft. Leavenworth, KS: Combat Studies Inst., U.S. Army Cmd. & Gen. Staff College, 1981), p. 57.

4. Ibid.

5. "Handbook on German Military Forces," *TM-E 30-451,* p. 239.

6. Ibid., p. 242.

7. *Soviet Combat Regulations of November 1942* (Moscow: [Stalin], 1942), republished as *Soviet Infantry Tactics in World War II: Red Army Infantry Tactics from Squad to Rifle Company from the Combat Regulations,* with trans., intro., and notes by Charles C. Sharp (West Chester, OH: George Nafziger, 1998), p. 55.

8. Ibid., p. 24.

9. Warner, "Japanese Army of World War II," pp. 23-25.

10. Poole, *Phantom Soldier,* chapt. 6.

11. Col. Hiromichi Yahara, *The Battle for Okinawa,* trans. Roger Pineau and Masatoshi Uehara (New York: John Wiley & Sons, 1995), p. 81.

12. Maj. Scott R. McMichael, "The Chinese Communist Forces in Korea," from "A Historical Perspective on Light Infantry," *Leavenworth Research Survey No. 6* (Ft. Leavenworth, KS: Combat Studies Inst., U.S. Army Cmd. & Gen. Staff College, 1987), p. 70.

13. Joseph C. Goulden, *Korea: The Untold Story of the War* (New York: Times Books, 1982), p. 295.

14. "North Korea Handbook," *PC-2600-6421-94,* p. 3-91.

15. Ibid., p. 3-101.

16. "Handbook on the Chinese Communist Army," *DA Pamphlet 30-51,* p. 26.

17. Michael Lee Lanning and Dan Cragg, *Inside the VC and the NVA: The Real Story of North Vietnam's Armed Forces* (New York: Ivy Books, 1992), pp. 206-208.

18. Poole, *Phantom Soldier,* chapt. 9.

19. George K. Tanham, *Communist Revolutionary Warfare* (New York: Praeger, 1967), pp. 185, 186.

20. *Operation Buffalo,* by Nolan.

21. David M. Glantz, *The Soviet Conduct of Tactical Maneuver: Spearhead of the Offensive* (London: Frank Cass, 1991), pp. 72, 73.

22. *The Bear Went over the Mountain: Soviet Combat Tactics in Afghanistan,* trans. and ed. Lester W. Grau, Foreign Mil. Studies Office, U.S. Dept. of Defense (Soviet Union: Frunze Mil. Academy, n.d.; reprint Washington, D.C.: Nat. Defense Univ. Press, 1996), p. 127.

23. Baxter, *Soviet Airland Battle Tactics,* pp. 132-136.

24. Ibid., p. 127.

25. Ibid., p. 125.

26. Ibid., pp. 125, 126.

27. Ibid., p. 136.

28. Ibid., p. 129.

29. Ibid., p. 130.

30. *The Bear Went over the Mountain,* p. 135.

31. Ibid., p. 22.

32. Ibid., p. 197.

33. Ali Jalali and Lester W. Grau, *Afghan Guerrilla Warfare: In the Words of the Mujahideen Fighters* (St. Paul, MN: MBI Publishing, 2001), first published as *The Other Side of the Mountain* (Quantico, VA: Marine Corps Combat Development Cmd., 1995), editor's commentary, p. 12.

34. Akbar, as quoted in *Afghan Guerrilla,* by Jalali and Grau, p. 5.

35. Kochay, as quoted in *Afghan Guerrilla,* by Jalali and Grau, pp. 59-61.

36. Rahim, as quoted in *Afghan Guerrilla,* by Jalali and Grau, p. 21; Poole, *Phantom Soldier,* p. 138.

37. Tayeb, as quoted in *Afghan Guerrilla,* by Jalali and Grau, p. 55.

38. Robert D. Kaplan, *Soldiers of God: With Islamic Warriors in Afghanistan and Pakistan* (New York: Vintage Books, 2001), p. 159.

39. Anthony Read and David Fischer, *The Fall of Berlin* (New York: Da Capo Press, 1995), p. 387.

40. Ibid., p. 407.

41. Ibid., pp. 393-395.

42. Ibid., p. 415.
43. *The Korean War: History and Tactics,* ed. David Rees (New York: Crescent Books, 1984), p. 45.
44. Hastings, *The Korean War,* p. 112.
45. Warner, "Japanese Army of World War II," pp. 23-25.
46. *The Korean War: History and Tactics,* p. 45.
47. Hammel, *Fire in the Streets,* p. 296.

Chapter 38: The *One-on-One Clash with Any Asian Soldier*

1. Navaho codetalker, in "Japanese Codetalkers" segment of *In Search of History,* History Channel, 30 March 1999; Marine infantryman, as quoted in *Iwo Jima: Legacy of Valor,* by Ross, p. 135.
2. Chinh, *Primer for Revolt,* pp. 114-117.
3. *The Strategic Advantage: Sun Zi & Western Approaches to War,* ed. Cao Shan (Beijing: New World Press, 1997), pp. 7, 11, 49, 50.
4. Lind and Thiele, *4th Generation Warfare Handbook,* p. 69.
5. Lind, *Maneuver Warfare Handbook,* p. 12.
6. Lind and Thiele, *4th Generation Warfare Handbook,* p. 64.
7. Ibid., pp. 73-75.
8. Lind, *Maneuver Warfare Handbook,* p. 12.
9. Poole, *Gung Ho,* chapt. 3.
10. Maitland and McInerney, *Vietnam Experience: A Contagion of War,* p. 97.
11. Gen. Vo Nguyen Giap, "Once Again We Will Win," as quoted in *The Military Art of People's War,* ed. Russel Stetler (New York: Monthly Review Press, 1970), pp. 264, 265.
12. *Handbook on the Chinese Armed Forces,* DDI-2680-32-76, pp. 5-19.
13. *Mao's Generals Remember Korea,* pp. 70, 71.
14. Dunnigan and Nofi, *Dirty Little Secrets of the Vietnam War,* p. 279.
15. Bermudez, *North Korean Special Forces,* p. 222.
16. Ibid.
17. Poole, *The Tiger's Way,* p. xxiv.
18. Poole, *Phantom Soldier,* p. 28.
19. Poole, *Phantom Soldier,* chapt.3.
20. Memorandum for the record by H.J. Poole.

21. Ibid., chapt. 15; Giap, "Once Again We Will Win," as quoted in *The Military Art of People's War,* ed. Stetler, pp. 264, 265.

22. "From Makin to Bougainville," by Hoffman, p. 5.

23. Ibid., p. 23.

24. "Gung Ho!: The Story of Carlson's Makin Island Raiders," movie, 87 minutes, Universal Studios, 1943.

25. Ibid.

Chapter 39: *Living Long Enough to Carry On the Fight*

1. Michael O'Brien, *Conscripts and Regulars: With the Seventh Battalion in Vietnam* (St. Leonards, Australia: Allen & Unwin, 1995), pp. 214, 215; Nguyen Van Mo, as quoted in *Portrait of the Enemy,* by David Chanoff and Doan Van Toai (New York: Random House, 1986), pp. 161, 162.

2. Poole, *The Tiger's Way,* part two.

3. Poole, *Gung Ho,* p. 21.

4. Memorandum for the record by H.J. Poole.

5. Poole, *Gung Ho,* chapt. 9.

6. Memorandum for the record by H.J. Poole.

7. Ibid.

Chapt 40: *An End to All Fighting Is the Goal*

1. *Merriam Webster Dictionary,* s.v. "bureaucracy."

2. *The Vietnam War,* DVD, by Burns and Novick.

3. James N. Mattis, "Memorandum for all Department of Defense Personnel," OSD012378-17/CMD016482-17, 5 October 2017.

4. Ibid.

5. Ibid.

6. Scales, "Infantry and National Priorities," pp. 14-17, 45.

7. Gy.Sgt. Rodney Walker USMC (Ret.), in telephone conversations with the author between 2007 and 2017.

8. MAROC Gunnery Sergeant from Camp Lejeune, in conversations with author around 2011.

9. Col. Wesley L. Fox, *Marine Rifleman: Forty-Three Years in the Corps* (Dulles, VA: Brassey's, 2002), pp. 237,238.

10. Pope John Paul II, *Crossing the Threshold of Hope,* pp. 205, 206.

11. *History Channel* on line, s.v. "Eisenhower Warns of Military Industrial Complex."

Chapt 41: *Some Forgiveness Required*

1. U.S. Army Combined Arms Center's "Military Deployment Reading List" from Fort Leavenworth's Combined Arms Research Library at http://www.universityofmilitaryintelligence.us/mi_library/documents/CGRecommendedReadingList.pdf as of 1 Jan. 2018; Pre-Deployment Afghanistan List (all ranks) from Joint Forces Command, COIN List for (Deploying) Marines, and Supplemental COIN List for MAJs and LTCs at http://usacac.army.mil/organizations/cace/carl/biblio and http://smallwarsjournal.com/documents/usmccoinreadinglist.pdf as of 1 January 2018.

2. Lind and Thiele, *4th Generation Warfare Handbook,* p. 9.

3. *Encylopedia Britannica,* s.v. "St. Francis of Assisi."

4. "How Three Saints Crossed Divides," by John Backman, *The Ligourian,* July/August 2016, pp. 18, 19.

5. Ibid.

6. Memorandum for the record from H.J. Poole.

7. "How Three Saints Crossed Divides," by Backman.

8. *Wikipedia Encyclopedia,* s.v. "Crusader Invasions of Egypt."

9. Adrian J. Boas, *Jerusalem in the Time of the Crusades:* Society, Landscape and Art in the Holy City Under Frankish Rule (London: Routledge, 2001), p. 1; *Saint Francis and the Sultan: The Curious History of a Christian-Muslim Encounter,* John V. Tolan (London: Oxford Univ. Press, 2009), as referenced in *Wikipedia Encyclopedia,* s.v. "Al-Kamil."

10. *Medieval Chronicals,* s.v. "Sixth Crusade," as retrieved in October 2017 from the following url: http://www.medievalchronicles.com/the-crusades/sixth-crusade/.

11. *Wikipedia Encyclopedia,* s.v. "Medieval Warfare."

12. Robert Liddiard, *Castles in Context: Power, Symbolism, and Landscape 1066 to 1500* (N.p.: Windgather Press, 2005), p. 79.

GLOSSARY

AK-47	Communist small-arms designator	Assault rifle
AP	Associated Press	American news syndicate
A-PVP	Alpha-Pyrrolidinopentiophenone	Illegal stimulant
ARVN	Army of the Republic of Vietnam	South Vietnamese ground forces
AW	Asymmetric Warfare	Conflicts between nations or groups with different military capabilities
BAR	Browning Automatic Rifle	Heavy repeating rifle used in WWII
BBC	British Broadcasting Company	UK radio/TV network
BLT	Battalion Landing Team	Amphib. task force
BLU-118/B	U.S. bomb designator	MOP Bunker Buster
C-4	U.S. detonative matter designator	Plastic explosive
C-47	U.S. aircraft designator	"Skytrain/Dakota" developed from a Douglas DC-3 transport plane and then reconfigured to drop illumination flares as "Puff the Magic Dragon"

CAG	Combined Action Group	Administrative body for many CAPs
CAP	Combined Action Platoon	Unit comprised of three PF squads, each having one U.S. Marine fire team
CIA	Central Intelligence Agency	U.S. spy organization
CNN	Cable News Network	U.S. television channel
CO	Commanding Officer	Person in command of a military unit
CP	Command Post	Place from which unit CO operates
DA	Department of the Army	Pentagon agency for extended ground warfare
DIA	Defense Intelligence Agency	U.S. information bureau on foreign foe
DMZ	Demilitarized Zone	No-mans land between countries
DoD	Department of Defense	Civilian headquarters for all U.S. military services
DPRK	Democratic People's Republic of Korea	North Korea
E-7	U.S. pay grade designator	Gunnery Sergeant or Sergeant First Class
E&E	Escape and Evasion	Eluding a pursuer, infantry part of UW
EMP	Electromagnetic Pulse	Bomb that's often disruptive/damaging to electronic devices

FARC	*Fuerzas Armadas Revolucionarias de Colombia*	Maoist rebels from Colombia (now just a political party)
FATA	Federally Administered Tribal Areas	Pakistani territories at the border with Afghanistan
FDC	Fire Direction Center	Where indirect-fire settings computed on a plotting board
4GW	4th Generation Warfare	War waged in four arenas at once— martial, religious or psychological, economic, political
GBU-43/B	U.S. bomb designator	MOAB
GI	Government Issue	Colloquial term for low-ranking member of U.S. mil. service
G-M	Grid-Magnetic	Conversion angle between map and compass
GPR	Ground-Penetrating Radar	Electromagnetic scanner
GPS	Global Positioning System	Device that resects satellite signals to determine location
GW	Guerrilla Warfare	IW normally carried out by enemy insurgents
H&I	Harassing and Interdiction	Type of artillery barrage
H&S	Headquarters and Service	Service support unit within a parent military command

HQMC	Headquarters Marine Corps	Various staff sections to help Commandant
HMMWV	High Mobility Multipurpose Wheeled Vehicle	Light truck used by U.S. forces
HW	Hybrid Warfare	Combination of conventional warfare, IW, and cyberwarfare
IED	Improvised Explosive Device	Remotely detonated landmine
IRGC	Iranian Revolutionary Guard Corps	Iranian commandos
ISI	Interservice Intelligence	Pakistani spy agency
ISIS	Islamic State of Iraq and Syria	Self-proclaimed caliphate to which other radical factions pledge allegiance
IW	Irregular Warfare	Conflict between different types of foes
KIA	Killed in Action	Those who expire in battle
KPA	Korean People's Army	NKA
LCU	Landing Craft Utility	Small boat used by amphibious forces
LP	Listening Post	Nighttime OP
LVT	Landing Vehicle Tracked	Amphibious transport
LVTH	LVT [mounting a] Howitzer	Amphibious platform with its own howitzer
M1	U.S. tank designator	Abrams main battle tank

M2	U.S. troop carrier designator	Bradley tracked fighting vehicle
M-2	U.S. machinegun designator	.50 caliber automatic weapon
M202A1	U.S. flame weapon designator	Flame assault shoulder-fired gun
M-42	U.S. anti-aircraft vehicle designator	Army self-propelled 40mm gun carrier nicknamed "Duster"
M-60	U.S. machinegun designator	7.62mm automatic weapon
MAF	Marine Amphibious Force	U.S. Marine unit
MCO	Marine Corps Order	USMC directive
MCWP	Marine Corps Warfighting Publication	USMC MW manual
MG	Machinegun	Automatic small arm
MIA	Missing in Action	Combatants who disappeared in war
MK	Israeli drone designator	Tiny remotely controlled airplane
MK-19	U.S. grenade thrower designator	Automatic thrower of grenade-like shells
MLR	Main Line of Resistance	Final defensive array across extended front
MOAB	Massive Ordnance Air Blast	Type of thermobaric bomb
MoH	Medal of Honor	Highest U.S. medal for military bravery
MOP	Massive Ordinance Penetrator	Type of conventional bomb

MOPP-4	Mission Oriented Protective Posture	Full NBC suit
MRTA	Tupac Amaru Revolutionary Movement	Guerrillas in Peru
MW	Maneuver Warfare	Way of fighting when tactical surprise can replace firepower
NATO	North Atlantic Treaty Organization	Western military alliance
NBC	Nuclear, Biological, Chemical	Weapons of mass destruction
NCO	Non-Commissioned Officer	Corporal or junior sergeant in military
9/11	11 September 2001	Day planes hit U.S. buildings in New York and Washington
NKA	North Korean Army	KPA
NPR	National Public Radio	U.S. educational radio network
NVA	North Vietnamese Army	Invader foe in Vietnam
NVGs	Night Vision Goggles	Device to enhance a soldier's nighttime viewing capability
NYPD	New York (City) Police Department	That city's principal law enforcement agency
OODA	Observe, Orient, Decide, and Act	Decision cycle of Col. John Boyd
OP	Observation Post	Battlefield viewing station

OPFOR	Opposition Forces	Aggressors for U.S. training operation
PAP	People's Armed Police	Chinese paramilitary police
PBS	Public Broadcasting Service	U.S. educational television network
PCP	Phencyclidine	Illegal hallucinogen
PF	Popular Force in Vietnam	Village militiaman
PFC	Private First Class	Lower-level U.S. military rank of E-2 pay grade
PLA	People's Liberation Army	Parent of all Chinese Armed Forces
POW	Prisoner of War	Captured combatant
PRC	People's Republic of China	Communist China.
PSTD	Post-traumatic stress disorder	Soldier malady
RCT	Regimental Combat Team	Expeditionary unit
ROK	Republic of South Korea	Korean peninsula country south of the 38th parallel
RPG	Rocket-Propelled Grenade	Ordnance launched by Communist bazooka-like weapon
S-2	Military staff designator	Headquarters section (enemy intelligence)
S-3	Military staff designator	Headquarters section (training/operations)
S/A	Small Arms	Tiny-munition weapons

SEAL	Sea, Air, and Land	U.S. Navy commando
2GW	2nd Generation Warfare	Focus on killing foe's personnel, same as traditional U.S. style (attrition warfare)
SNCO	Staff NCO	More senior enlisted leader, pay grades E-6 and above
SOCOM	Special Operations Command	America's commando headquarters
SWAT	Special-Weapon Assault Team	U.S. paramilitary police
T-55	Communist tank designator	Soviet main battle tank from WWII
T-72	Communist tank designator	Soviet main battle tank from 1972
3GW	3rd Generation Warfare	Focus on bypassing foe's strongpoints to more easily destroy his strategic assets
TNT	Trinitrotoluene	A common explosive
TOW	Tube-Launched, Optically Tracked, Wire-Guided	U.S. anti-tank missile
TTP	*Tehrik-i-Taliban Pakistan*	Pakistani Taliban
TTPs	Tactics, Techniques, and Procedures	Combat moves of squads and below
UK	United Kingdom	Great Britain and Northern Ireland
U.N.	United Nations	Alliance of worldwide countries
U.S.	United States	America

524

USAF	United States Air Force	Pentagon's aerial defense branch
USMC	United States Marine Corps	America's amphibious landing force in readiness
UW	Unconventional Warfare	For an infantrymen, E&E and fighting like a guerrilla
VBIED	Vehicle-Borne IED	Truck-mounted IED
VC	Viet Cong	NVA-advised guerrilla foe during the Vietnam conflict
WIA	Wounded in Action	Injured in combat
WWI	World War I	First global conflict
WWII	World War II	Second global conflict
ZANLA	Zimbabwe African National Liberation Army	Military wing of PRC-backed rebels in Rhodesia.
ZANU	Zimbabwe African National Union	PRC-backed rebels in Rhodesia.
ZANU P/F	Zimbabwe African National Union Patriotic Front	Modern-day political party in Zimbabwe.

BIBLIOGRAPHY

U.S. Government Publications, Databases, News Releases, Images

"Army Battle Casualties and Nonbattle Deaths in World War II: Final Report, 7 December 1941 - 31 December 1946." Combined Arms Research Library. Department of the Army, 25 June 1953. As retrieved in October 2016 from the following url: http://cgsc.cdm host.com/cdm/compoundobject/collection/p4013coll8/id/130.

Bartley, Lt.Col. Whitman S. *Iwo Jima: Amphibious Epic*. Washington, D.C.: Historical Branch, Headquarters Marine Corps, 1954.

The Bear Went over the Mountain: Soviet Combat Tactics in Afghanistan. Translated and edited by Lester W. Grau, Foreign Military Studies Office, U.S. Department of Defense, Fort Leavenworth, KS. Washington, D.C.: National Defense University Press, 1996. Originally published under its Russian title. Soviet Union: Frunze Military Academy, n.d.

"*China's Military-Owned Businesses*." By Shirley A. Kan. Congressional Research Service Report 98-197. Washington, D.C.: U.S. Government. Printing Office, 17 January 2001.

CIA World Factbook. As updated every three months. From the Central Intelligence Agency website (www.cia.gov).

"Closing In: Marines in the Seizure of Iwo Jima." By Colonel Joseph H, Alexander. *Marines in World War II Commemorative Series*. Washington, D.C.: History and Museum Division, Headquarters Marine Corps, 1994.

CORDS [Civil Operations and Revolutionary Development Support] Historical Files. CMH [U.S. Army Center of Military History]. File 77, folder 10. From *Mismanaging Mayhem: How Washington Responds to Crisis*. By James Jay Carafano and Richard Weitz. Westport, CT: Greenwood Publishing Group, 2008. As retrieved in January 2017 from the following url: https://books.google.com/books?id=XvwPiHZeyIIC&pg=PA98&dq# v=onepage&q&f=false.

DA Pamphlet 20-291. *Effects of Climate on Combat in Russia*. Washington, D.C.: Headquarters Department of the Army, n.d.

DA Pamphlet 20-292. *Warfare in the Far North*. Washington, D.C.: Headquarters Department of the Army, n.d.

DA Pamphlet 550-35. "Nepal and Bhutan Country Studies." *Area Handbook Series*. Washington, D.C.: Headquarters Department of the Army, 1993.

DA Pamphlet 550-45. "Malaysia: A Country Study." *Area Handbook Series*. Washington, D.C.: Headquarters Department of the Army, 1984.

DA Pamphlet 550-68. "Iran Country Study." *Area Handbook Series*. Washington, D.C.: Headquarters Department of the Army, 1989.

"Drug Trafficking and North Korea: Issues for U.S. Policy." By Ralph F. Perl. Congressional Research Service Report RL32167, last in a series of updates, 27 November 2006.

Excerpt from *Chinese Manual on Field Fortifications*. In "A Historical Perspective on Light Infantry," U.S. Army Combat Studies Institute Research Survey Number 6, n.d.

"Fact Sheet on the Combined Action Force." III MAF, 31 March 1970. As retrieved from the unofficial website of the CAP Program.

"The Final Campaign: Marines in the Victory on Okinawa." By Colonel Joseph H. Alexander. *Marines in WWII Commemorative Series*. Washington, D.C.: History and Museums Division, Headquarters Marine Corps, 1996.

"Finnish Tactics—Small Units." A U.S. Intelligence Report on Finnish Tactics in WWII. *Tactical and Technical Trends*, number 6, 27 August 1942. As retrieved in December 2016 from the following url: http://www.lonesentry.com/articles/ttt08/finnish-tactics.html.

FMFRP 12-34-I. "Pearl Harbor to Guadalcanal." By Lt.Col. Frank O. Hough, Maj. Verle E. Ludwig, and Henry I. Shaw, Jr. Volume I. *History of the U.S. Marine Corps Operations in World War II Series*. Washington, D.C.: Historical Branch, HQMC, n.d. Reprint Quantico, VA: Marine Corps Combat Development Command, 1989.

FMFRP 12-110. *Fighting on Guadalcanal*. Washington, D.C.: U.S.A. War Office, 1942.

"From Makin to Bougainville: Marine Raiders in the Pacific War." By Major Jon T. Hoffman. *Marines in WWII Commemorative Series*. Washington, D.C.: Marine Corps History Center, 1995.

"The Future Role of the Combined Action Program." By Major Michael Duane Weltsch USMC. Thesis for U.S. Army's Command and General Staff College, 1991.

Ground Combat Operations. MCWP-3. Washington, D.C.: Headquarters U.S. Marine Corps, 2002.

"Handbook on German Military Forces." *TM-E 30-451*. Washington, D.C.: U.S. War Department, 1945. Reprint, Baton Rouge, LA: LSU Press, 1990.

"Handbook on Japanese Military Forces." *TM-E 30-480.* Washington, D.C.: U.S. War Department, 1944. Reprint, Baton Rouge, LA: LSU Press, 1991.

Handbook on the Chinese Armed Forces. DDI-2680-32-76. Washington, D.C.: Defense Intelligence Agency, July 1976.

Handbook on the Chinese Communist Army. DA Pamphlet 30-51. Washington, D.C.: Headquarters Department of the Army, 1960.

Handbook on the Chinese People's Liberation Army. DDB-2680-32-84. Washington, D.C.: Defense Intelligence Agency, November 1984.

"Handbook On U.S.S.R. Military Forces," *TM 30-340.* Washington, D.C.: U.S. War Department, 1945. Republished as *Soviet Tactical Doctrine in WWII,* with foreword by Shawn Caza. West Chester, OH: G.F. Nafziger, 1997.

Huber, Thomas M. "The Battle of Manila." In CSI Home Publications Research MHIST [database on line]. Ft. Leavenworth, KS: Combat Studies Institute, U.S. Army Command and General Staff College, n.d. [updated 30 September 2002; cited 1 January 2003]. As retrieved in 2003 from the CSI website at the following url: www-cgsc.army.mil/csi/research/mout/mouthuber. asp.

Huber, Thomas M. "Japan's Battle for Okinawa, April - June 1945." *Leavenworth Papers No. 18.* Fort Leavenworth, KS: Combat Studies Institute. U.S. Army's Command and General Staff College, 1990.

The Operations Process. FM 5-0. Washington, D.C.: Headquarters Department of the Army, 26 March 2010. As retrieved in March 2017 from this url: https://fas.org/irp/doddir/army/fm5-0.pdf.

The Infantry Battalion. FM 7-20. Washington, D.C.: Headquarters Department of the Army, 1992.

"Isolation of Rabaul." By Henry I. Shaw and Major Douglas T. Kane. *History of U.S. Marine Corps Operations in World War II Series.* Volume II. Washington, D.C.: Historical Branch, Headquarters Marine Corps, 1963. As retrieved from the following url: www.ibiblio.org/hyperwar/USMC/II/index.html#contents.

Jalali, Ali A. and Lester W. Grau. *Afghan Guerrilla Warfare: In the Words of the Mujahideen Fighters.* St. Paul, MN: MBI Publishing, 2001. Originally published as *The Other Side of the Mountain.* Quantico, VA: Marine Corps Combat Development Command, 1995.

Joys, SSgt. John W. Navy Cross Citation. At Home of Heroes website. As retrieved in May 2017 from this url: http://www.homeofheroes. com/members/02_NX/citations/07_RVN-nc/nc_19rvn_usmcE.html.

Lupfer, Timothy L. "The Dynamics of Doctrine: The Changes in German Tactical Doctrine during the First World War." *Leavenworth Papers No. 4.* Ft. Leavenworth, KS: Combat Studies Institute, U.S. Army Command and General Staff College, 1981.

Mattis, James N. "Memorandum for all Department of Defense Personnel." OSD012378-17/CMD016482-17, 5 October 2017. As received by .pdf in October 2017 from a friend.

McMichael, Maj. Scott R. "The Chinese Communist Forces in Korea." From "A Historical Perspective on Light Infantry." *Leavenworth Research Survey No. 6.* Ft. Leavenworth, KS: Combat Studies Institute, U.S. Army Command and General Staff College, 1987.

"North Korea Handbook." *PC-2600-6421-94.* Washington, D.C.: Department of Defense, 1994.

"North Vietnamese Army/Viet Cong Military Medical Capabilities." Scientific and Technical Intelligence Report. From the CIA's Directorate of Science and Technology, 14 October 1968. Now declassified and approved for release 16 May 2011. As retrieved in June 2017 from the following url: https://www.cia.gov/library/readingroom/docs/DOC_0005647975.pdf.

"Okinawa: The Last Battle." By Roy E. Appleman, James M. Burns, Russell A. Gugeler, and John Stevens. *U.S. Army in World War II Series.* Washington, D.C.: U.S. Army's Center of Military History, 2000. As retrieved on 30 November 2011 from the following url: www.history.army.mil/books/wwii/okinawa/index.htm#contents.

Okinawa: Victory in the Pacific. By Major Chas. S. Nichols, Jr., USMC, and Henry I. Shaw, Jr. "USMC Historical Monograph." Washington, D.C.: Historical Branch, Headquarters Marine Corps, 1955. As retrieved from the following url:www.ibiblio.org/hyperwar/USMC/USMC-M-Okinawa/index.html#index.

"1/4 Afteraction Report for May 1967." As retrieved through the 1/4 Association website in 2010 from this url: http://jones-thompson.com/onefour/AFTACTREP/1967/MAY67/aftactrep2-may67.htm.

Prohibitions or Restrictions on the Use of Incendiary Weapons (Protocol III). U.S. Department of State. Agreement signed at Geneva in 1980. As retrieved in February 2017 from this url: http://www.state.gov/documents/organization/190579.pdf.

Reagan, President Ronald. "Message to the Senate Transmitting a Protocol to the 1949 Geneva Conventions." As retrieved in 2014 from the following url: http://www.reagan.utexas.edu/archives/speeches/1987/012987b.htm.

The Recapture of Guam. By Major O.R. Lodge. "USMC Historical Monograph." Washington, D.C.: Historical Branch, Headquarters Marine Corps, 1954. As retrieved from the following url: www.ibiblio.org/hyperwar/USMC/USMC-M-Guam/index.html.

"Remarks by President Trump on the Strategy in Afghanistan and
South Asia." The White House, 21 August 2017. As retrieved in
August from the following url: https://www.whitehouse.gov/the-
press-office/2017/08/21/remarks-president-trump-strategy-
afghanistan-and-south-asia.

Santoli, Al. "The Panama Canal in Transition: Threats to U.S. Security
and China's Growing Role in Latin America." *American Foreign
Policy Council Investigative Report,* 23 June 1999.

Shulimson, Jack, Lt.Col. Leonard A. Blaisol, Charles R. Smith, and
Capt. David A. Dawson. *U.S. Marines in Vietnam: The
Defining Year, 1968.* Washington, D.C.: History &
Museums   Division, Headquarters Marine Corps, 1997.

Tactics. FMFM 1-3. Washington, D.C.: Headquarters Marine Corps,
1991.

"Three Levels of War." USAF College of Aerospace Doctrine, Research
and Education. *Air and Space Power Mentoring Guide.* Volume 1.
Maxwell AFB, AL: Air University Press, 1997. As retrieved in
April 2017 from the following url: http://www.cc.gatech.edu/
~tpilsch/INTA4803TP/Articles/Three%20Levels%20of%20War=
CADRE-excerpt.pdf.

The United States Strategic Bombing Surveys. Reprinted by Air
University Press. Maxwell Air Force Base, October 1987.

U.S. Army Center of Military History. From its website,
http://www.history.army.mil.

U.S. Army Combined Arms Center's "Military Deployment Reading
List" from Fort Leavenworth's Combined Arms Research Library
at http://www.universityofmilitaryintelligence.us/mi_library/
documents/CGRecommendedReadingList.pdf as of 1 Jan. 2018;
Pre-Deployment Afghanistan List (all ranks) from Joint Forces
Command, COIN List for (Deploying) Marines, and Supplemental
COIN List for MAJs and LTCs at http://usacac.army.mil/
organizations/cace/carl/biblio and http://smallwarsjournal.com/
documents/usmccoinreadinglist.pdf as of 1 Jan. 2018.

U.S. Army Heritage and Information Center. From its website,
http://www.carlisle.army.mil.

U.S. Marines in Vietnam: An Expanding War – 1966. By Jack
Shulimson. Washington, D.C.: History and Museums Division,
Headquarters U.S. Marine Corps, 1982.

U.S. Marines in Vietnam: Fighting the North Vietnamese 1967.
By Major Gary Tefler, Lieutenant Colonel Lane Rogers, and V.
Keith Fleming, Jr. Washington, D.C.: History and Museums
Division, Headquarters Marine Corps, 1984. As retrieved in
May 2017 from the following url: US%20Marines%20in%20
Vietnam%20An%20Expanding%20War%201966%20%20PCN%
2019000308600_4.pdf.

Warfighting. FMFM 1. Washington, D.C.: Headquarters Marine Corps, 1989.

Warfighting. MCWP1. Washington, D.C.: Headquarters Marine Corps, 1997.

Civilian Publications

Analytical Studies, Databases, and Websites

"Afghanistan Cave Complexes 1979–2004: Mountain Strongholds of the Mujahideen." By Mir Bahmanyar. Oxford: Osprey Publishing, 2004. As retrieved in August 2017 from the following url: https://books.google.com/books?id=NyPDCwAAQBAJ&pg=PT28&lpg=PT28&dq=Zhawar+cave+and+tunnel+complex+in+Paktiya+province&source=bl&ots=FZHKe5UgA2&sig=ptw9vZ-Cga45cB3e Nny5sfYpDIA&hl=en&sa=X&ved=0ahUKEwiVu_2DxPDVAhVH1o MKHUkCDAAQ6AEIKTAG#v=onepage&q=Zhawar%20cave%20 and%20tunnel%20complex%20in%20Paktiya%20province&f=false.

All the King's Men. By Nigel McCrery. New York: Simon & Schuster, 1999. Previously titled *The Vanished Battalion.* N.p., n.d.

The American Revolutionary War. From its website, http://www.revolutionary-war.net.

American Revolutionary War Facts. From its website, http://www.american-revolutionary-war-facts.com.

Association of the Combined Action Program website. As retrieved from this following url: http://www.cap-assoc.org/.

Baxter, William P. *Soviet Airland Battle Tactics.* Novato, CA: Presidio Press, 1986.

Bermudez, Joseph S., Jr. *North Korean Special Forces.* Annapolis, MD: Naval Institute Press, 1998.

Boas, Adrian J. *Jerusalem in the Time of the Crusades: Society, Landscape and Art in the Holy City Under Frankish Rule* (London: Routledge, 2001.

Britannica Encyclopedia. From its website, https://www.britannica.com/.

Calender 12. From its website, calendar12.com.

Chinh, Truong. *Primer for Revolt.* Introduction by Bernard B. Fall. New York: Praeger, 1963.

Clarke, George B. *Their Time in Hell: The 4th Marine Brigade at Belleau Wood.* Pike, NH: The Brass Hat, 1996.

Connaughton, Richard and John Pimlott, and Duncan Anderson. "The Battle for Manila." Novato, CA: Presidio Press, 1995.

Dan Marsh's Marine Raider Page. Created by former member of 4th Raider Battalion. As retrieved in November 2011 from its website, www.usmcraiders.com.

Davis, Burke. *Marine.* New York: Bantam, 1964.

Dictionary.com. From its website, http://www.dictionary.com/.

Dung. General Van Tien Dung. *Our Great Spring Victory: An Account of the Liberation of South Vietnam.* Translated by John Spragens, Jr. Hanoi: The Gioi Publishers, 2001.

Dunnigan, James F. and Albert A. Nofi. *Dirty Little Secrets of the Vietnam War.* New York: Thomas Dunne Books, 1999.

Dupuy, Trevor N., and David L. Bongard, and Richard C. Anderson Jr. *Hitler's Last Gamble.* New York: Harper Perennial, Harper Collins Publishers, 1994.

Ecker, Richard E. *Battles of the Korean War: A Chronology.* Jefferson, NC: McFarland & Company, 2004.

Elford, George Robert. *Devil's Guard.* New York: Dell Publishing, 1971.

Encyclopedia Britannica. From its website, https://www.britannica.com

Encyclopedia.com. From its website, http://www.encyclopedia.com/.

Fox, Col. Wesley L. *Marine Rifleman: Forty-Three Years in the Corps* (Dulles, VA: Brassey's, 2002).

Glantz, David. M. *The Soviet Conduct of Tactical Maneuver: Spearhead of the Offensive.* London: Frank Cass, 1991.

Global Warrior: Averting WWIII. By H. John Poole. Emerald Isle, NC: Posterity Press, 2011.

Good Reads. From its website, http://www.goodreads.com.

Goolirck, William K. and Ogden Tanner and the editors of Time-Life Books. *World War II: The Battle of the Bulge.* Alexandria, VA: Time-Life Books, 1979.

Goulden, Joseph C. *Korea: The Untold Story of the War.* New York: Times Books, 1982.

Great War Society. From its website, worldwar1.com.

Green Side Out. By Maj. H.G. Duncan and Capt. W.T. Moore, Jr. Booneville, MO: Gene Duncan Books, 1980.

Gudmundsson, Bruce I. *Stormtroop Tactics—Innovation in the German Army 1914-1918.* New York: Praeger, 1989.

Gunaratna, Rohan. *Inside al-Qaeda: Global Network of Terror.* Lahore: Vanguard, 2002.

Hackworth, Col. David H. U.S. Army (Ret.) and Julie Sherman. *About Face.* New York: Simon & Schuster, 1989.

Hammel, Eric. *Fire in the Streets: The Battle for Hue, Tet 1968.* Pacifica, CA: Pacifica Press, 1991.

Hammel, Eric. *Guadalcanal: Starvation Island.* New York: Crown Publishers, 1987.

Hastings, Max. *The Korean War.* New York: Touchstone, Simon & Schuster, 1987.

Hemingway, Al. *Our War Was Different.* Annapolis, MD: Naval Institute Press, 1994.

History Channel on line. From its website, http://www.history.com.

History Net. From its website, http://www.historynet.com.

How the Weak Win Wars: A Theory of Asymmetric Conflict. By Ivan Arreguín-Toft (a postdoctoral fellow in the International Security Program at the Belfer Center for Science and International Affairs at Harvard University's John F. Kennedy School of Government). *International Security.* Volume 26, number 1 (Summer 2001), pp. 93-128. As retrieved in December 2016 from the following internet designator: http://web.stanford.edu/class/polisci211z/2.2/Arreguin-Toft%20IS%202001.pdf.

Insight Guides: Vietnam. Edited by Helen West. Singapore: APA Publications, 1991.

Iwo Jima: Legacy of Valor. By Bill D. Ross. New York: Vintage, 1986.

Jaynes, Gregory, and the editors of Time-Life Books. *The Civil War: The Killing Ground — Wilderness to Cold Harbor.* Alexandria, VA: Time-Life Books, 1986.

The Jerusalem Bible. Garden City, NY: Doubleday, 1966.

John Paul II, Pope. *Crossing the Threshold of Hope.* New York: Alfred A. Knopf, 1995.

Kaplan, Robert D. *Soldiers of God: With Islamic Warriors in Afghanistan and Pakistan.* Revised edition. New York: Vintage Books, 2001.

Katzman, Kenneth. *Warriors of Islam: Iran's Revolutionary Guard.* Boulder, CO: Westview Press, 1993.

Khang, Ho. *The Tet Mau Than 1968 Event in South Vietnam.* Hanoi: The Gioi Publishers, 2001.

Khoi, Hoang. *The Ho Chi Minh Trail.* Hanoi: The Gioi Publishers, 2001.

King James Bible on line. From its website, https://www.kingjames bibleonline.org.

The Korean War: History and Tactics. Edited by David Rees. New York: Crescent Books, 1984.

The Last Hundred Yards: The NCO's Contribution to Warfare. By H.J. Poole. Emerald Isle, NC: Posterity Press, 1997.

Lanning, Michael Lee and Dan Cragg. *Inside the VC and the NVA: The Real Story of North Vietnam's Armed Forces.* New York: Ivy Books, 1992.

Levin, Nora. *The Holocaust* (New York: Thomas Y. Crowell Co., 1968.

Lind, William S. *The Maneuver Warfare Handbook.* Boulder, CO: Westview Press, 1985.

Lind, William S. and Lt.Col. Gregory A. Thiele USMC. *4th Generation Warfare Handbook.* Kouvola, Finland: Castalia House, 2015.

Liddiard, Robert. Castles in Context: Power, Symbolism, and Landscape 1066 to 1500. N.p.: Windgather Press, 2005). As retrieved in October 2017 from this url: "https://books.google.com/books/about/Castles_in_Context.html?id=ZzhUAAAAMAAJ.

MacArthur's Jungle War: The 1944 New Guinea Campaign. By
   Stephen R. Taaffe. N.p.: Modern War Studies, 1998.
Macfarlan, Alan A. *Exploring the Outdoors with Indian Secrets.*
   Harrisburg, PA: Stackpole Books, 1971.
Maitland, Terrence and Peter McInerney. *Vietnam Experience:
   A Contagion of War.* Boston: Boston Publishing, 1968.
Mao's Generals Remember Korea. Translated and edited by Xiaobing
   Li, Allan R. Millett, and Bin Yu. Lawrence, KS: University Press
   of Kansas, 2001.
Mao Tse-tung: An Anthology of His Writings. Edited by Anne
   Fremantle. New York: Mentor, 1962.
McCrery, Nigel. *All the King's Men.* New York: Simon & Schuster,
   1999.
McGraw-Hill Dictionary of Scientific and Technical Terms. 6th Edition.
   New York: McGraw-Hills, 2003.
Menges, Constantine. *China: The Gathering Threat.* Nashville, TN:
   Nelson Current, 2005.
Medieval Chronicals. From its website, http://www.medievalchronicles.
   com.
The Military Art of People's War. Edited by Russel Stetler. New York:
   Monthly Review Press, 1970.
Military History Online. From its website, http://www.military
   historyonline.com/.
Millett, Allan R., and Peter Maslowski. *For the Common Defense.*
   New York: The Free Press, Macmillan, 1984.
*Modern Insurgencies and Counter-Insurgencies: Guerrillas and Their
   Opponents.* By Ian Frederick and William Beckett. New York:
   Routledge, 2001. As retrieved in January 2017 from this url:
   https://books.google.com/books?id=iQN4ifavThMC&pg=PA198
   &dq#v=onepage&q&f=false.
Navsource Online. From its website, http://www.navsource.org.
A New Era of Warfare: Finnish Thoughts on the Modern Image of War.
   By J.Z. Duncker. Binder with English translation. N.p.: Unknown
   German publisher 1977.
O'Ballance, Edgar. *Afghan Wars: Battles in a Hostile Land, 1839 to
   Present.* Karachi: Oxford University Press, 2002.
O'Brien, Michael. *Conscripts and Regulars: With the Seventh Battalion
   in Vietnam.* St. Leonards, Australia: Allen & Unwin,
   1995.
One More Bridge to Cross: Lowering the Cost of War. By H.J. Poole.
   Emerald Isle, NC: Posterity Press, 1999.
Operation Buffalo: USMC Fight for the DMZ. By Keith William Nolan.
   New York: Dell, 1992.
Oxford Dictionaries. From its website, https://en.oxforddictionaries.
   com.

Peters, Gretchen. *Seeds of Terror: How Heroin Is Bankrolling the Taliban and al-Qaeda.* New York: Thomas Dunne Books, 2009.

Pike, Douglas. *PAVN: People's Army of Vietnam.* Novato, CA: Presidio Press, 1986).

Poole, H. John. *Afrique: A Warning for America.* Emerald Isle, NC: Posterity Press, September 2015.

Poole, H. John. *Dragon Days: Time for "Unconventional" Tactics.* Emerald Isle, NC: Posterity Press, August 2007.

Poole, H. John. *Gung Ho: The Corp's Most Progressive Tradition.* Emerald Isle, NC: Posterity Press, August 2012.

Poole, H. John. *Phantom Soldier: The Enemy's Answer to Firepower.* Emerald Isle, NC: Posterity Press, August 2001.

Poole H. John. *Sinoland: The Subversion of Freedom's Bastion.* Emerald Isle, NC: Posterity Press, 2016.

Poole, H. John. *Strategic Rifleman: Key to More Moral Warfare.* Emerald Isle, NC: Posterity Press, 2014.

Poole, H. John. *Tequila Junction: 4th Generation Counterinsurgency.* Emerald Isle, NC: Posterity Press, 2010.

Poole, H. John. *The Tiger's Way: A U.S. Private's Best Chance for Survival.* Emerald Isle, NC: Posterity Press, August 2003.

Portrait of the Enemy. By David Chanoff and Doan Van Toai. New York: Random House, 1986.

Read, Anthony and David Fischer. *The Fall of Berlin.* New York: Da Capo Press, 1995.

Reid-Daly, Lt.Col. R.F. *Pamwe Chete: The Legend of the Selous Scouts.* Weltevreden Park, South Africa: Covos-Day Books, 1999.

Rottmann, Gordon. *M3 Medium Tank vs. Panzer III – Kasserine Pass 1943.* London.: Osprey Publishing, 2008.

Scott-Donelan, David. *Tactical Tracking Operations: The Essential Guide for Military and Police Trackers.* Boulder, CO: Paladin Press, 1998.

Selective Asia. From its website, selectiveasia.com.

Shaw, John and the editors of Time-Life Books. *Red Army Resurgent.* Chicago: Time-Life Books, 1979.

Smith, George W. *The Siege at Hue.* New York: Ballantine Publishing, 1999.

Soviet Combat Regulations of 1942. Moscow: Stalin, 1942. Republished as *Soviet Infantry Tactics in World War II: Red Army Infantry Tactics from Squad to Rifle Company from the Combat Regulations.* With translation, introduction, and notes by Charles C. Sharp. West Chester, OH: George Nafziger, 1998.

Stiff, Peter. *The Silent War: South African Recce Operations, 1969-1994.* Alberton, South Africa: Galago Publishing, 1999.

536

The Strategic Advantage: Sun Zi & Western Approaches to War. Edited by Cao Shan. Beijing: New World Press, 1997.

Sun Tzu,. *The Art of War.* Translated and with an introduction by Samuel B. Griffith. Foreword by B.H. Liddell Hart. New York: Oxford University Press, 1963.

Tactics of the Crescent Moon: Militant Muslim Combat Methods. By H. John Poole. Emerald Isle, NC: Posterity Press, 2004.

Tanham,George K. *Communist Revolutionary Warfare.* New York: Praeger, 1967.

Tennozan: The Battle of Okinawa and the Atomic Bomb. By George Feifer. Boston: Houghton Miflin, 1992.

Texas Military Forces Museum. From its website, http://www. texasmilitaryforcesmuseum.org.

The 30-Year War: 1945-1975. Volume II. Hanoi: The Gioi Publishers, 2001.

Thao, Maj.Gen. Hoang Min. *The Victorious Tay Nguyen Campaign.* Hanoi: Foreign Languages Publishing House, 1979.

Thompson, Leroy. *Dirty Wars: Elite Forces vs. the Guerrillas.* Devon, England: David & Charles, 1991.

Truong Chinh. *Primer for Revolt.* Introduction by Bernard B. Fall. New York: Praeger, 1963.

Unmasking Terror: A Global Review of Terrorist Activities. Volumes I, II, and III. The first two edited by Christopher Heffelfinger, and the third by Jonathan Hutzley. Washington, D.C: Jamestown Foundation, 2005 through 2007.

Unofficial website of the CAP Program. As retrieved from the following url: http://capmarine.com/index.htm (no longer available).

Uris, Leon. *Mila 18.* New York: Bantam, 1983.

Vietnam War Almanac. General editor, John S. Bowman. New York: World Almanac Publications, 1985.

Voina v Korea: 1950-1953. By A.A. Kuryacheba. N.p.: Polygon Publishers, 2002.

Warner, Philip. "Japanese Army of World War II." Volume 20. *Men-at-Arms Series.* London: Osprey Publications Ltd., 1972.

Warr, Nicholas. *Phase Line Green: The Battle for Hue, 1968.* Annapolis, MD: Naval Institute Press.

Wikipedia Encyclopedia. From its website, https://en.wikipedia. org/.

Yahara, Col. Hiromichi. *The Battle for Okinawa.* Translated by Roger Pineau and Masatoshi Uehara. New York: John Wiley & Sons, 1995.

Zabih, Sepehr. *The Iranian Military in Revolution and War.* London: Routledge, 1988.

Zfacts. From its website, zfacts.com.

Videotapes, Movies, DVDs, TV Programs, Slide Shows, CDs, Illustrations

"All the Kings Men." *Exxon Masterpiece Theater.* London. *BBC,* in
    conjunction with WGBH Boston. NC Public TV, 26 November 2000.
"The Battle of the Minds" segment. *Korea — The Unknown War Series.*
    London. Thames TV in association with WGBH Boston, 1990. NC
    Public TV, n.d.
"Delta Company: The Push to Baghdad." DVD. 60 minutes.
    Discovery Communications, 2008.
"1805 — To the Shores of Tripoli." (April 27: This Day in History.)
    History Channel on line, n.d. As retrieved in December 2016 from
    this url: http://www.history.com/this-day-in-history/to-the-shores-
    of-tripoli.
"An Entirely New War" segment. *Korea — The Unknown War Series.*
    London. Thames TV in association with WGBH Boston, 1990. NC
    Public TV, n.d.
"Flags of Our Fathers." DVD. 132 minutes. Dreamworks and Warner
    Brothers, 2006.
"Great Escape." PBS's *Nova.* NC Public TV, 5 June 2007.
"Gung Ho!: The Story of Carlson's Makin Island Raiders." Movie.
    87 minutes. Universal Studios, 1943.
"Halls of Montezuma." Film. 113 minutes. 20th Century Fox,
    1950.
"Japanese Codetalkers." *In Search of History.* History Channel,
    30 March 1999
Last Days of World War II. History Channel, 28 March
    1999.
"One Minute to Zero." DVD. 105 minutes. Warner Archive,
    2011.
Photograph caption of the An Hoa Explosion. *Pinterest,* n.d. As
    retrieved in April 2017 from this url: https://www.pinterest.
    com/pin/347480927472222308/.
Price, Sergeant Toney. Two-hour interview by Kirk Hauser. Audio CD,
    2013.
"The Sand Pebbles." Video cassette. 182 minutes. Directed by
    Robert Wise. 20th Century Fox. 1966.
"Sergeant York." DVD, 134 minutes. Warner Brothers Pictures,
    isbn #1-4198-3829-6.
"60 Minutes." *CBS News,* 20 August 2017. As retrieved in October 2017
    from this url: https://www.cbsnews.com/news/60-minutes-
    autonomous-drones-set-to-revolutionize-military-technology
    -2/.
The Vietnam War. DVD. 1003 minutes. Documentary. By Ken Burns
    and Lynn Novick. PBS, 19 September 2017. Ten episode
    set.

Letters, E-Mail, and Direct Verbal Conversations

Coy, John L. USMC. In e-mail to author on 22 May 2016.

Guthrie, CWO4 Charles "Tag" USMC (Ret.) (Cam Lo defense participant and historian). In e-mail messages to author on 8, 9, and 15 May 2017.

Lind, William S. In Foreword to *One More Bridge to Cross: Lowering the Cost of War*. By H.J. Poole. Emerald Isle, NC: Posterity Press, 1999.

MARSOC Gunnery Sergeant from Camp Lejeune. In conversations with author around 2011.

Multi-tour U.S. Army Special Forces veteran of wars in Iraq and Afghanistan and expert mantracker. In e-mail and telephone conversations with author between June 2013 and May 2015.

Normandeau, Joe (former member of 3rd Marine Raider Battalion). In conversations with author in October 2010 and then again in 2015.

O'Bday, Bob (Marine machinegunner at Khe Sanh). In conversation with author, 30 July 2000.

Petraeus, Gen. David (or an aide). In e-mails with the author around the late winter of 2006.

Ronan, Chris (former Marine scout/sniper and special operator). In conversation with the author in November 2017.

Rue, Sgt. Erik (Marine scout/sniper and former rifleman). In a telephone conversation with author on 12 May 2017.

Schmuck, 1st Sgt. John H. "Josh." In a telephone conversation with author in July 2017.

Scott-Donelan, David (former member of Selous Scouts and SA Recce). In telephone conversation with author on June 2004.

Sergeant of South African descent from U.S. Marine Tank Battalion Scout Platoon. In e-mail to author on 20 May 2017.

Soard, Charles (experienced infantry scout and frequent visitor to Vietnam). In telephone conversation with author on 28 March 2001.

Soturi, Jenkki (U.S. Marine veteran of Vietnam and student of Finnish tactics). In a letter to the author of 7 November 2001.

U.S. Special Forces multi-tour operator in Afghanistan and Iraq. In a series of telephone conversations with author between 26 September 2006 and 1 February 2007.

Vietnam era Marine counter-intelligence, infantry, and CAP veteran. In telephone conversations with author from 6-13 January 2012.

Walker, Gy.Sgt. Rodney USMC (Ret.). In telephone conversations with the author between 2007 and 2017.

Newspaper, Magazine, Radio, and Website Articles

"About the Giant Bomb the U.S. Used in Afghanistan." By Anne Cronin. *Bloomberg News* on line, 13 April 2017. As retrieved in August 2017 from the following url: https://www.bloomberg.com/news/ articles/2017-04-13/about-the-giant-bomb-the-u-s-used-in-afghanistan-quicktake-q-a.

"Accurate Information, but Low-Level Stuff." Customer review of *Tactics of the Crescent Moon*. By "C." At Amazon.com, 25 May 2010.

"Al-Shabab Commander Thought to Be Killed in Somalia Airstrike." By Abdi Guled. Associated Press. *Jacksonville Daily News* (NC), 1 August 2017.

"An Hoa Project." By Warren Stansbury. N.d. As retrieved in April 2017 from the following url: http://anhoaproject.co.uk/story-warren-stansbury.html.

"Article 28 of Geneva Convention IV of 1949." International Committee of the Red Cross, n.d. As retrieved in July 2017 from the following url: https://ihl-databases.icrc.org/customary-ihl/ eng/docs/v2_rul_rule97.

"Article 51(7), of the 1977 Additional Geneva Convention Protocol I." International Committee of the Red Cross, n.d. As retrieved in July 2017 from the following url: https://ihl-databases.icrc.org/ customary-ihl/eng/docs/v2_rul_rule97.

"Attacks on MAG-16, Hill 22, and the Attempted Attack on the Da Nang Airfield. *3rd Marines in Vietnam* website, n.d. As retrieved in April 2017 from the following url: http://www. 3rdmarines.net/Vietnam_Attack_on_mag_16.htm.

Bartsch, William H. "Crucial Battle Ignored." *Marine Corps Gazette,* September 1997.

"The Battle for Mosul in Maps." By Paul Torpey, Pablo Gutierrez, and Paul Scruton. *The Guardian,* 26 June 2017. As retrieved in July 2017 from the following url: https://www.theguardian.com/world/ 2016/nov/04/battle-for-mosul-maps-visual-guide-fighting-iraq-isis.

"The Battle That Helped Change the Course of the 'Israeli' Occupation." *Daily Star* (Lebanon), 6 September 2000.

"Belleau Wood." By Major Stoney Bates. *Marine Corps Gazette,* November 2015. As retrieved in December 2016 from the following url: https://www.mca-marines.org/gazette/2015/11/belleau-wood.

"Biên Hòa Air Base Ammo Dump Explosion Sapper Attack." By Arnold John Houchin. Originally written on 12 January 1972. Then published by the Association for USAF Vietnam War Veterans of Air/Security Police. Through *Vietnam War Stories,* in 2005. As retrieved in April 2017 from the following url: http://www.war -stories.com/bh-houchin-sapper-attack-ammo-dump-1972. htm.

Blanford, Nicholas and Daniel McGrory and Stephen Farrell. "Tactics That Have Kept the Middle East's Most Powerful Army at Bay." *The Times* (UK), 10 August 2006.

"Blueprint on a Brilliant Raid." By Steve Macko. *ENN Daily Intelligence Report.* Volume 3, number 114, 24 April 1997.

"Canticle of Zecharia." Luke 1:68-79. As reprinted on the inside front cover of *Shorter Cristian Prayer.* New York: Catholic Book Publishing Company, 1988.

"Charting the Data for U.S. Airstrikes in Pakistan, 2004." By Bill Roggio. *Long War Journal,* n.d. As retrieved in July 2017 from the following url: http://www.longwarjournal.org/pakistan-strikes.

"Chesty' Puller's Epic Stand." By Jon T. Hoffman. *World War II Magazine*, n.d. And probably republished in *Leatherneck,* n.d. As retrieved in April 2017 from the following url: http://www.leatherneck.com/forums/showthread.php?12034-Chesty-Puller-s-Epic-Stand.

Cody, Edward and Molly Moore. "Analysts Attribute Hezbollah's Resilience to Zeal, Secrecy and Iranian Funding." *Washington Post,* 14 August 2006.

Combat Tracking. Paluda, Malaysia: British Army Combat Training Center, n.d.

"Conventional Weapons: 30/11/2011 Overview." International Committee for the Red Cross. From the following url in March 2014: http://www.icrc.org/eng/war-and-law/weapons/conventional-weapons/overview-conventional-weapons.htm.

Cooling, Maj. Norman L. "Russia's 1994-96 Campaign for Chechnya: A Failure in Shaping the Battlespace." *Marine Corps Gazette,* October 2001.

"Counting Civilian Casualties in the CIA's Drone War." By Meg Braun. *Foreign Policy,* 2 November 2012. As retrieved in July 2017 from the following url: http://foreignpolicy.com/2012/11/02/counting-civilian-casualties-in-cias-drone-war/.

"Countries Hit By U.S. Tomahawk Cruise Missiles Since Desert Storm." Forbes, 17 April 2017. As partially retrieved in July 2017 from the following url: https://mobile.twitter.com/Forbes/status/850423003838111744.

" 'Couple of Hundred' ISIS Fighters Left in Mosul." By Nick Paton Walsh and Mohammed Tawfeeq. *CNN* on line, 26 June 2017. As retrieved in July 2017 from the following url: http://www.cnn.com/2017/06/26/middleeast/couple-hundred-isis-fighters-in-mosul/index.html#.

"Danger Room in Afghanistan: A Close Fight, and a Couple of Miracles."
By Noah Shachtman. *Wired Magazine* (Conde Nast), 27 August
2009. As retrieved in May 2017 from the following url: https://
www.wired.com/2009/08/danger-room-in-afghanistan-
a-close-range-fight-and-a-couple-of-miracles/.

"Everyone Wants Cut in Afghan Drug Trade." From McClatchy News
Service. *Jacksonville Daily News* (NC), 10 May
2009.

"57,762,169 Abortions in America Since Roe vs. Wade in 1973."
LifeNews.com, 21 January 2015.

"First Barbary War: Battle of Derna." About.com, n.d. As retrieved
in December 2016 from the following url: http://militaryhistory.
about.com/od/battleswars1800s/p/derne.htm.

"A Godfather's Lethal Mix of Business and Politics." *U.S. News &
World Report Online*, 5 December 2005.

"The Greatest Movies of All Time," AMC Networks, n.d. As retrieved
in September 2015 from the following url: http://www.amc.com/
movie-guide/tim-dirks-top-100.

"Ground Penetrating Radar FAQ." USRadarInc., n.d. As retrieved in
August 2017 from the following url: (http://www.usradar.com/about-
ground-penetrating-radar-gpr/faq/.

Hambling, David. "U.S. Denies Incendiary Weapon Use in
Afghanistan." *Security,* 15 May 2009. As retrieved in
February 2017 from the following url: https://www.wired.com/
2009/05/us-incendiary-weapon-in-afghanistan-revealed/.

"Hezbollah Uses Mexican Drug Routes into U.S." *Washington Times,*
27 March 2009

"Historian Says the U.S. Is 'Losing Hearts and Minds in Afghanistan'."
Interview between Steve Inskeep and Lt.Col. Aaron B. O'Connell
USMC. *NPR* on line, 19 April 2017. As retrieved in April 2017
from the following url: http://www.npr.org/templates/transcript/
transcript.php?storyId=524654637.

"Hitler vs. Stalin: Who Killed More." By Timothy Snyder. *New York
Review of Books,* 10 March 2011. As retrieved in September 2015
from the following url: http://www.nybooks.com/
articles/archives/2011/mar/10/hitler-vs-stalin-who-killed-more/.

Hord, J. Mark (long-time student of Unconventional Warfare). Review
of *Terrorist Trail* in "Stratiotes' Military History Book Reviews."
Unconventional Warfare Review, 31 January 2007. As first posted
at *Defense and the National Interest* website plus www.d-n-i.net
and g2-forward. Finally retrieved in March 2017 from this url:
http://archive.is/qZBj, as saved from http://uwhistory.romanhords.
com/BookReviews.html.

"How Pakistan's ISI Funds Its Proxy War." By Syed Nooruzzaman.
The Tribune (India), 28 November 1999.

"How Three Saints Crossed Divides." By John Backman. *The Ligourian,* July/August 2016.

"Hue City, 1968: Winning A Battle While Losing A War." By Maj. Norman L. Cooling. *Marine Corps Gazette,* July 2001.

Hughes, Stephen E. *Warring on Terrorism: A Comprehensive Dispatch Briefing.* Part I (internet piece), 2005.

Hussein, Abdul Al-Obeidi. Associated Press. "U.S. Increases Pressure on Najaf." *Jacksonville Daily News (NC),* 24 August 2004.

"Individual Heroism Overcame Awkward Command Relationships, Confusion, and Bad Information off the Cambodian Coast." By Col. J.A. Johnson Jr., Lt.Col. R.W. Austin, and Maj. D.A. Quinlan. *Marine Corps Gazette,* October 1977.

"ISIS Bury 45 of Their Own Fighters ALIVE After They Fled the Battlefield." By Sam Webb. *Mirror* (U.K.), 11 May 2016. As retrieved in July 2016 from the following url: http://www.mirror. co.uk/news/world-news/isis-bury-45-fighters-alive-7943328.

Jackson, Richard D. *Yesterdays Are Forever: A Rite of Passage through the Marine Corps and Vietnam.* Galt, CA: Working Title Publishing, 2007.

Kozaryn, Linda D. Armed Forces Press Service. "Belleau Wood: Marines' Shrine." *Leatherneck Magazine,* 9 August 1998.

Lamont, Lt.Col. Robert W. Lamont. " 'Urban Warrior'—A View from North Vietnam." *Marine Corps Gazette,* April 1999.

"Laos: Barack Obama Regrets 'Biggest Bombing in History'." *BBC News* on line, 7 September 2016. As retrieved in October 2017 from the following url: http://www.bbc.com/news/world-asia-37286520.

"Law of War Training," By William T. Anderson. *Marine Corps Gazette,* April 1981.

"Leaving Iraq." By Tom Bowman. *NPR Special Series* on line, n.d. As retrieved in June 2017 from the following url: http://www.npr. org/2011/12/16/143832121/as-the-iraq-war-ends-reassessing-the-u-s-surge.

Legal Information Institute. "Geneva Conventions." As retrieved in 2014 from the following url: http://www.law.cornell.edu/wex/geneva_conventions.

Leinster, Colin. "The Two Wars of General Walt." *Life,* 26 May 1967.

Lejeune, Gen. John A. As quoted by Major Gen. O.K. Steele. In his opening address to a graduating Camp Lejeune Platoon Sergeants' School class at the Camp Geiger Chapel around 1990.

Lekic, Slobodan. Associated Press. "Attacks Target Troops, Police."
    Jacksonville Daily News (NC), 12 December
    2004.

Lewis, Sgt. Donald Allen (killed at Cam Lo). Note left on the Vietam
    Memorial Wall. As retrieved in May 2017 from the following url:
    https://marines.togetherweserved.com/usmc/servlet/tws.webapp.
    WebApp?cmd=ShadowBoxProfile&type=Person&ID=
    187238.

Lind, William S. "Fourth Generation Warfare's First Blow:
    A Quick Look." *Marine Corps Gazette,* November 2001.

"Lost Battles of the Vietnam War." As retrieved in April 2017 from the
    following well-respected url: http://www.g2mil.com/lost_vietnam.
    htm.

"Marines Batter North Vietnamese Trying to Destroy Tanks." By
    Wallace Beene *(Stars & Stripes* Bureau Chief). *Tribune-Democrat*
    (Johnstown, PA), 28 August 1966.

"Marines of the Texas Republic." By Maj.Gen. Marc A. Moore.
    Marine Corps Gazette, August 1978.

Moser, Don. "Their Mission Defend, Befriend." *Life Magazine,*
    25 August 1967.

"Mosul Factsheet: Brief Guide to the City and the Liberation Offensive."
    By Hannah Lynch. *Rudaw* (Kurdish media network), 17 October
    2016. As retrieved in July 2017 from the following url:
    http://www.rudaw.net/english/middleeast/iraq/
    1610201610.

"Motti Tactics." *Combat Forces Journal,* January 1950.

"Motti Tactics in Finnish Military Historiography since World War II."
    By Pasi Tuunainen (University of Eastern Finland). *International
    Bibliography of Military History.* Issue 33. 2013. As retrieved in
    February 2017, from the following url: https://researchgate.net/
    publication/273550370.

Nessman, Ravi. Associated Press "U.S. Launches Airstrike in
    Fallujah." *Jacksonville Daily News (NC),* 6 July
    2004.

"New Approaches to Artic Warfare." By Pasi Tuunainen (University
    of Eastern Finland). *Nordia Geographical Publications,*
    43:1.

"North Koreans Assisted Hezbollah with Tunnel Construction."
    Jamestown Foundation. *Terrorism Focus.* Volume III, issue 30,
    August 2006.

"North Korea's Secret Strategy in a War with America: Go
    Underground." By Kyle Mizokami. *The National Interest,* 6 May
    2017. As retrieved in August 2017 from the following url: http://
    nationalinterest.org/blog/the-buzz/north-koreas-secret-strategy-
    war-america-go-underground-20525.

"North Vietnamese Army and Viet Cong Infantry/Artillery Regiments." *Global Security,* n.d. As retrieved in July 2017 from this url: http://www.globalsecurity.org/military/world/vietnam/nva-rgt.htm.

Pelli, Maj. Frank D. "Insurgency, Counterinsurgency, and the Marines in Vietnam." *EHistory,* n.d. As extracted on 10 November 2002 from the following url: http://www.ehistory.com/vietnam/essays/insurgency/index.cfm.

"Peru Hostage Crisis Comes to a Violent End." By Steve Macko. *ENN Daily Intelligence Report.* Volume 3, number 113, 23 April 1997.

Peterson, Scott. "Fallujans Flee from US, Zarqawi Fight." *Christian Science Monitor,* 19 October 2004.

Peterson, Scott. "Marine, Insurgent Tactics Evolve." *Christian Science Monitor,* 17 November 2004.

Powell, Bill and Adam Zagorin. "The Sopranos State." *Time,* 23 July 2007.

"The Predator War." By Jane Mayer. *New Yorker* on line, 26 October 2009. As retrieved in July 2017 from the following url: http://www.newyorker.com/magazine/2009/10/26/the-predator-war.

"Protocol on Prohibitions or Restrictions on the Use of Incendiary Weapons (Protocol III). Geneva, 10 October 1980," International Committee of the Red Cross, n.d. As retrieved in December 2016 from the following url: https://ihl-databases.icrcorg/applic/ihl/ihl.nsf/385ec082b509e76c41256739003e636d3a507447d94ad829c125641f002d2729?OpenDocument.

"Railroad Guns." Skylighters (225th AAA Searchlight Battalion). As retrieved in March 2017 from this url: http://www.skylighters.org/wwiirr/.

"Rolling Thunder (1965–8)." *American Military and Naval History Online,* 5 November 2010.

Rumsfeld, Secretary of Defense Donald H. As quoted in *Funding the Enemy: How US Taxpayers Bankroll the Taliban.* By Douglas A. Wissing. Amherst, New York: Prometheus Books, 2012. Chapter 3. As retrieved in February 2017 from this url: https://books.google.com/books?id=H8yvuUtNVSYC&pg=PT50&lpg=PT50&dq=we+don%27t+do+drugs+by+rumsfeld&source=bl&ots=fV1qWFakXz&sig=y9Qsk1EO8AY_nPJ602e3RK1Swas&hl=en&sa=X&ved=0ahUKEwjv9u_t8_7RAhVU82MKHXsmAIcQ6AEIQjAH#v=onepage&q=we%20don%27t%20do%20drugs%20by%20rumsfeld&f=false. Reconfirmed from "Poppy Fields Are Now a Front Line in Afghanistan War." By James Risen. *New York Times* on line. As retrieved on 16 May 2007 from the following url: http://www.nytimes.com/learning/students/pop/articles/16drugs.html.

Scales, Maj.Gen. Robert H., U.S. Army (Ret.). "Infantry and National Priorities." *Armed Forces Journal,* December 2007.

Scales, Maj.Gen. Robert H., U.S. Army (Ret.). "Small-Unit Dominance: The Strategic Importance of Tactical Reform." *Armed Forces Journal,* October 2010.

Segal, Naomi. *Jewish Telegraphic Agency.* "IDF Absolved of Blame in Deaths of Naval Commandos in Lebanon." *San Francisco Jewish Community Publication,* 31 October 1997.

Sen, Chanakya. Review of *Karachi: A Terror Capital in the Making,* by Wilson John. *Asia Times Online,* 17 January 2004.

"Sergeant Alvin York." By Dr. Michael Birdwell. Great War Society. As retrieved on 15 October 2009 from its website, www.worldwar1.com.

Simmons, Maj.Gen. Edwin USMC (Ret.). In "An Entirely New War" segment of *Korea – the Unknown War.* London: Thames TV in cooperation with WGBH Boston, 1990. NC Public TV, n.d.

Simpson, Jim. "Scouts to the Rescue." *Defense Watch,* 17 September 2003.

"Special Report—How Mosul Fell." By Ned Parker, Isabel Coles, and Raheem Salman. *Reuters,* 4 October 2014. As retrieved in July 2017 from this url: https://archive.org/details/SpecialReportHow MosulFellAnIraqiGeneralDisputesBaghdadsStoryReuters.

Stack, Liam. "Fifth NATO Tanker Attacked in Six Days Since Pakistan Sealed Border Post." *Christian Science Monitor,* 5 October 2010.

Thomas, Lt.Col. Timothy L. and Lester W. Grau. "Russian Lessons Learned from the Battles for Grozny." *Marine Corps Gazette,* April 2000.

"U.S. Confirms Coalition Strike in Mosul District Where Dozens Reported Killed." Reuters, 25 March 2017. As retrieved in July 2017 from the following url: https://news.cgtn. com/news/3d676a4e35457a4d/share_p.html.

"U.S. Drone Strike Kills Rebels in Pakistan." From *Agence France Presse, Sydney Morning Herald* (Australia), 5 October 2010.

"U.S. Drops Largest Non-Nuclear Bomb on Islamic State." By Justin Sink. *Bloomberg News* on line, 13 April 2017. As retrieved in August 2017 from the following url: https://www.bloomberg.com/news/articles/2017-04-13/u-s-drops-biggest-bomb-on-islamic-state-caves-in-afghanistan.

"U.S. Should Replace Drone Strikes in Pakistan with Outreach to Tribal Areas." By Akbar Ahmed. *Christian Science Monitor* on line, 30 May 2013. As retrieved in July 2017 from the following url: https://www.csmonitor.com/Commentary/Opinion/2013/0530/US-should-replace-drone-strikes-in-Pakistan-with-outreach-to-tribal-areas.

Vermaak, Chris. "Rhodesia's Selous Scouts." *Armed Forces (Journal),*
    May 1977.
"War's Hidden Chapter: Ex-GIs Tell of Killing Korean Refugees." By
    San-Hun Choe, Charles J. Hanley, Martha Mendoza. After
    investigative research by Randy Herschaft. Associated Press,
    30 September 1999. As retrieved in July 2017 from the following
    url: http://nogunri.rit.albany.edu/omeka/items/show/54.
"Waziristan-Based Terror Group Takes Credit for Lahore Assault."
    By Bill Roggio. *Long War Journal*, 30 March 2009.
"What the Largest Battle of the Decade Says about the Future of War."
    By Ben Watson. *Defense One,* 7 July 2017. As retrieved in July
    2017 from the following url: http://www.defenseone.com/feature/
    mosul-largest-battle-decade-future-of-war/.
"Why Did Armored Corps Fail in Lebanon." By Hanan Greenberg.
    Israeli News, 30 August 2006. As retrieved from the following url:
    http://www.ynetnews.com/articles/0,7340,L-3297431,00.html.
"WWII Korea Under the Rising Sun." By Allyn Vannoy. *Warfare
    History Network,* September 2016. As retrieved in March 2017
    from the following url: http://warfarehistorynetwork.com/daily/
    wwii/korea-under-the-rising-sun/.

ABOUT THE AUTHOR

After 28 years of commissioned and then noncommissioned infantry service, John Poole retired from the United States Marine Corps in April 1993. While on active duty, he studied small-unit tactics for nine years: (1) six months at the Basic School in Quantico (1966); (2) seven months as a rifle platoon commander in Vietnam (1966-67); (3) three months as a rifle company commander at Camp Pendleton (1967); (4) five months as a regimental headquarters company (and camp) commander in Vietnam (1968); (5) eight months as a rifle company commander in Vietnam (1968-69); (6) five and a half years as an instructor with the Advanced Infantry Training Company (AITC) at Camp Lejeune (1986-92); and (7) one year as the Staff Noncommissioned Officer in Charge of the 3rd Marine Division Combat Squad Leaders Course (CSLC) on Okinawa (1992-93).

While at AITC, he developed, taught, and refined courses on maneuver warfare, land navigation, fire support coordination, call for fire, adjust fire, close air support, M203 grenade launcher, movement to contact, daylight attack, night attack, infiltration, defense, offensive Military Operations in Urban Terrain (MOUT), defensive MOUT, Nuclear/Biological/Chemical (NBC) defense, and leadership. While at CSLC, he further refined the same periods of instruction and developed others on patrolling.

He has completed all of the correspondence school requirements for the Marine Corps Command and Staff College, Naval War College (1,000-hour curriculum), and Marine Corps Warfighting Skills Program. He is a graduate of the Camp Lejeune Instructional Management Course, the 2nd Marine Division Skill Leaders in Advanced Marksmanship (SLAM) Course, and the East-Coast School of Infantry Platoon Sergeants' Course.

In the 25 years since retirement, Poole has researched the small-unit tactics of other nations and written 16 other books: (1) *The Last Hundred Yards,* a squad combat study based on the consensus opinions of 1,200 NCOs and casualty statistics of AITC and CSLC field trials; (2) *One More Bridge to Cross,* a treatise on enemy proficiency at short range and how to match it; (3) *Phantom Soldier,* an in-depth look at the highly deceptive Asian style of war; (4) *The Tiger's Way,* the fighting styles of Eastern fire teams and soldiers; (5) *Tactics of the Crescent Moon,* insurgent procedures in Palestine, Chechnya, Afghanistan, and Iraq; (6) *Militant Tricks,* an honest appraisal of the so-far-undefeated *jihadist* method; (7) *Terrorist Trail,* tracing the *jihadists* in Iraq back to their home countries; (8) *Dragon Days,* an unconventional warfare technique manual; (9) *Tequila Junction,* how to fight narco-guerrillas; (10) *Homeland Siege,* confronting the 4GW assault by a foreign power's organized-crime proxies; (11) *Expeditionary Eagles,* how to outmaneuver the Taliban; (12) *Global Warrior,* forestalling WWIII with tiny contingents; (13) *Gung Ho,* how supporting arms are not needed to take strongpoint matrices; (14) *Strategic Rifleman,* how tiny semi-autonomous elements are created; (15) *Afrique,* using Africa as a model, how U.S. intelligence is being gathered incorrectly for certain adversaries; and (16) *Sinoland,* how the U.S. has been under 4GW attack from China since 9/11.

Poole has done research throughout much of the Communist and Islamist Worlds. Within the Communist World, he has been to East Germany, Russia, North Korea, China (three times), Tibet, and (North) Vietnam. Within the Islamic World, he has visited Sudan, Tanzania, Iran, Lebanon, Turkey, the Emirates, Malaysia, Bangladesh, and Pakistan (twice). Within Africa, he has traveled in Morocco, Egypt, Sudan, Tanzania, South Africa, and Zambia.

As of September 2015, he had conducted multiday training sessions (on advanced squad tactics) at 41 (mostly Marine) battalions, nine Marine schools, and seven special-operations units from all four U.S. service branches.

Between early tours in the Marine Corps (from 1969 to 1971), he served as a criminal investigator with the Illinois Bureau of Investigation (IBI). After attending the State Police Academy for several months in Springfield, he was assigned to the IBI's Chicago office. There, he worked mostly on general criminal and drug cases.

Name Index

Westmoreland, Gen. William C. 123
Winebar, Gy.Sgt. Francis E.   237, 244
Worth, Sgt. Nick   184

X

No entries.

Y

Yahara, Col. Hiromichi   424
York, Sgt. Alvin C.   141, 142

Z

Zakhilwal, Omar   418
Zeckaria   145
Zvobgo, Edison   381